Fodor's

GUATEMALA

1st Edition

by Jeffrey Van Fleet

Where to Stay and Eat
for All Budgets

Must-See Sights
and Local Secrets

Ratings You Can Trust

Fodor's Travel Publications   New York, Toronto, London, Sydney, Auckland
www.fodors.com

FODOR'S GUATEMALA
Editor: Felice Aarons

Editorial Production: Evangelos Vasilakis, Astrid deRidder
Editorial Contributors: Jeffrey Van Fleet, with help from Nicholas Gill (Adventure Learning Vacations), Lan Sluder (Maya Ruins), Victoria Patience (Essentials)
Maps & Illustrations: David Lindroth Inc.; Mark Stroud, Moon Street Cartography, cartographers; Bob Blake and Rebecca Baer, *map editors*
Design: Fabrizio LaRocca, *creative director*; Guido Caroti, Siobhan O'Hare, *art directors*; Tina Malaney, Chie Ushio, Ann McBride, *designers*; Melanie Marin, *senior picture editor*; Moon Sun Kim, *cover designer*
Cover Photo: (Hoku canoes on Lago Atitlan with San Pedro Volcano): Robert Leon/www.robertleon.com
Production/Manufacturing: Angela McLean

COPYRIGHT

1st Edition

ISBN 978-1-4000-1925-0

ISSN 1939-9901

SPECIAL SALES

This book is available at special discounts for bulk purchases for sales promotions or premiums. Special editions, including personalized covers, excerpts of existing books, and corporate imprints, can be created in large quantities for special needs. For more information, write to Special Markets/Premium Sales, 1745 Broadway, MD 6-2, New York, New York 10019, or e-mail specialmarkets@randomhouse.com.

AN IMPORTANT TIP & AN INVITATION

Although all prices, opening times, and other details in this book are based on information supplied to us at press time, changes occur all the time in the travel world, and Fodor's cannot accept responsibility for facts that become outdated or for inadvertent errors or omissions. So **always confirm information when it matters,** especially if you're making a detour to visit a specific place. Your experiences—positive and negative—matter to us. If we have missed or misstated something, **please write to us.** We follow up on all suggestions. Contact the Guatemala editor at editors@fodors.com or c/o Fodor's at 1745 Broadway, New York, NY 10019.

PRINTED IN THE UNITED STATES OF AMERICA
10 9 8 7 6 5 4 3 2 1

Be a Fodor's Correspondent

Your opinion matters. It matters to us. It matters to your fellow Fodor's travelers, too. And we'd like to hear it. In fact, we need to hear it.

When you share your experiences and opinions, you become an active member of the Fodor's community. That means we'll not only use your feedback to make our books better, but we'll publish your names and comments whenever possible. Throughout our guides, look for "Word of Mouth," excerpts of your unvarnished feedback.

Here's how you can help improve Fodor's for all of us.

Tell us when we're right. We rely on local writers to give you an insider's perspective. But our writers and staff editors—who are the best in the business—depend on you. Your positive feedback is a vote to renew our recommendations for the next edition.

Tell us when we're wrong. We're proud that we update most of our guides every year. But we're not perfect. Things change. Hotels cut services. Museums change hours. Charming cafés lose charm. If our writer didn't quite capture the essence of a place, tell us how you'd do it differently. If any of our descriptions are inaccurate or inadequate, we'll incorporate your changes in the next edition and will correct factual errors at fodors.com immediately.

Tell us what to include. You probably have had fantastic travel experiences that aren't yet in Fodor's. Why not share them with a community of like-minded travelers? Maybe you chanced upon a beach or bistro or B&B that you don't want to keep to yourself. Tell us why we should include it. And share your discoveries and experiences with everyone directly at fodors.com. Your input may lead us to add a new listing or highlight a place we cover with a "Highly Recommended" star or with our highest rating, "Fodor's Choice."

Give us your opinion instantly at our feedback center at www.fodors.com/feedback. You may also e-mail editors@fodors.com with the subject line "Guatemala Editor." Or send your nominations, comments, and complaints by mail to Guatemala Editor, Fodor's, 1745 Broadway, New York, NY 10019.

You and travelers like you are the heart of the Fodor's community. Make our community richer by sharing your experiences. Be a Fodor's correspondent.

¡Feliz viaje!

Tim Jarrell, Publisher

CONTENTS

CLOSE UPS

MAPS

ABOUT THIS BOOK

Our Ratings

Sometimes you find terrific travel experiences and sometimes they just find you. But usually it's up to you to select the right combination of experiences. That's where our ratings come in.

As travelers we've all discovered a place so wonderful that its worthiness is obvious. And sometimes that place is so experiential that superlatives don't do it justice: you just have to be there to know. These sights, properties, and experiences get our highest rating, **Fodor's Choice,** indicated by orange stars throughout this book.

Black stars highlight sights and properties we deem **Highly Recommended,** places that our writers, editors, and readers praise again and again for consistency and excellence.

By default, there's another category: any place we include in this book is by definition worth your time, unless we say otherwise. And we will.

Disagree with any of our choices? Care to nominate a place or suggest that we rate one more highly? Visit our feedback center at www.fodors.com/feedback.

Budget Well

Hotel and restaurant price categories from ¢ to $$$$ are defined in the opening pages of each chapter. For attractions, we always give standard adult admission fees; reductions are usually available for children, students, and senior citizens. Want to pay with plastic? **AE, D, DC, MC, V** following restaurant and hotel listings indicates if American Express, Discover, Diners Club, MasterCard, and Visa are accepted.

Restaurants

Unless we state otherwise, restaurants are open for lunch and dinner daily. We mention dress only when there's a specific requirement and reservations only when they're essential or not accepted—it's always best to book ahead.

Hotels

Hotels have private bath, phone, TV, and air-conditioning and operate on the European Plan (aka EP, meaning without meals), unless we specify that they use the Continental Plan (CP, with a continental breakfast), Breakfast Plan (BP, with a full breakfast), or Modified American Plan (MAP, with breakfast and dinner) or are all-inclusive (including all meals and most activities). We always

Many Listings
★	Fodor's Choice
★	Highly recommended
⊠	Physical address
⊹	Directions
⌂	Mailing address
☎	Telephone
🖷	Fax
⊕	On the Web
✍	E-mail
✑	Admission fee
☉	Open/closed times
Ⓜ	Metro stations
▭	Credit cards

Hotels & Restaurants
▯	Hotel
➷	Number of rooms
☖	Facilities
⑩	Meal plans
✕	Restaurant
▵	Reservations
↘	Smoking
⑭	BYOB
✕▯	Hotel with restaurant that warrants a visit

Outdoors
🏌	Golf
⚠	Camping

Other
⊙	Family-friendly
⇨	See also
⊠	Branch address
☞	Take note

list facilities but not whether you'll be charged an extra fee to use them, so when pricing accommodations, find out what's included.

WHAT'S WHERE

GUATEMALA CITY	Guatemala City is the political, economic, and industrial center of the country, the hub from which most roads emanate. But you shouldn't sacrifice precious days in the highlands or El Petén for time in the sprawling, congested capital. The city is divided into 21 *zonas,* but you'll likely get to know only a few of them. Zona 1, the crowded heart with a few monuments to colonialism, is budget-travel central. The newer, leafy south-side Zonas 9 and 10 have upscale hotels, restaurants, and shops.
ANTIGUA	Blessed with a near-ideal climate and a setting watched over by three looming volcanoes, this lovely old colonial city was once one of the most important centers of Spain's colonial empire. It's continuously undergoing restoration of its centuries-old churches, convents, and palaces, but is just as content to leave some structures in ruins. Antigua also has a great location; the city's proximity to Guatemala City means that travelers can fly in, exit the international airport, turn west, get to Antigua in less than an hour, and never look back until it's time to fly home. Many do.
THE HIGHLANDS	Here is the Guatemala that everyone comes to see. The vast highlands that extend west from Antigua to the Mexican border include the country's outposts on the Gringo Trail. Generations before you have shopped the twice-weekly market in Chichicastenango, studied Spanish in Quetzaltenango, and swapped travel stories with fellow visitors in Panajachel. Smoldering volcanoes, bustling markets, pine forests, and a shimmering lake all form the backdrop for vibrant indigenous cultures in a territory where you are as likely to hear one of the country's 23 Mayan languages spoken as you are to hear Spanish.
LAS VERAPACES	Sandwiched—some might say hidden—between the well-trodden indigenous highlands, colonial Antigua, the ruin-dotted Petén and the capital, Guatemala's Las Verapaces region frequently gets overlooked as merely an area to traverse to get from one more popular destination to another. A growing number of visitors, however, are giving it a closer look. The Verapaces is a two-for-one destination, with the better-known Alta Verapaz and the slightly drier Baja Verapaz encompassing the expanse. The mostly indigenous city of Cobán anchors this misty, ethereal cloud-forest region that is fast becoming Guatemala's ecotourism center. It has not become neighboring Costa Rica—at least not yet—but the area offers you whitewater sports, spelunking, swimming, and bird-watching. (Guatemala's preeminent quetzal reserve is here.)

WHAT'S WHERE

ATLANTIC LOWLANDS	Few Guatemalans have ever ventured east to their Caribbean coast, writing the region off as all rain and reggae. Mostly, yes, to both of those. It *does* rain more here than in the rest of the country, and wandering the streets of Livingston and Puerto Barrios will make you think you've taken a wrong turn to Jamaica. The European-indigenous population mix seen in the highlands gives way to a vibrant Garífuna culture along the coast, with roots in Africa and the Caribbean. The Mayan site of Quiriguá may lack fame, but it holds the same interest to visitors as some of its better-known counterpart indigenous structures. If you've come this far, consider the *de rigueur* jaunt just across the border to the Mayan ruins in Copán, Honduras.
PACIFIC LOWLANDS	Even most typical old Guatemala hands, with several trips to the country under their collective belt, have never seen the lowland region fronting the country's Pacific shore. The long coastline here doesn't translate into a string of Puerto Vallarta–type resorts. The beach and water are written off as too rocky and rough, but a beach is a beach, and what is here can be fun and funky, as evidenced by Monterrico, possibly Guatemala's only community with a true beach-town vibe. Surfers and sportfishing enthusiasts *do* know this stretch of Pacific coast however, and they, at least for now, make up the bulk of the region's foreign visitors.
EL PETÉN	The squared-off sector of northern Guatemala contains few roads and fewer towns, but what at first glance looks like the country's most inaccessible region is one of its most visited. Credit Tikal, one of Mesoamerica's most famous indigenous ruins and the ancestral homeland of the Maya, for the influx of visitors to this rain-forested lowland. Don't ignore the hundreds of other ruins that dot the region. (Archaeologists have barely scratched the surface; many of the structures remain unexcavated.) Getting here is not the arduous overland journey it once was; an airport outside the town of Santa Elena, a short distance from Tikal, makes flying a much faster option. The airport has even made day trips from Antigua and Guatemala City possible, but give the Petén a longer stay if your time permits.

WHEN TO GO

Many countries make the claim, but in Guatemala it truly applies: You'll find no bad time to visit, although some seasons are more ideal than others. For near-perfect weather in the much-visited central part of the country (Guatemala City, Antigua, and the highlands), consider a trip during the November–April dry season. These are also the months when Guatemala's most famous religious festivals (the Day of the Dead, the Burning of the Devil, the Santo Tomás celebrations in Chichicastenango, Christmas, and Lent and Holy Week in Antigua and around the country) take place. However, don't feel the need to avoid the rainy season; rains rarely impede travel here and will likely not interfere with your trip. Also, don't forget that the rest of the country (Las Verapaces, El Petén, and the Atlantic and Pacific lowlands) are apt to receive year-round showers anyway.

Guatemala isn't a "fun in the sun" kind of destination, and there's little distinction between weather-based high and low seasons. Lodging and tour rates remain fairly constant year-round. (Some hotels at popular destinations such as Antigua and Lake Atitlán raise rates on weekends.) Two big exceptions to this rule are Christmas and Holy Week, the two monster travel weeks of the year when rates skyrocket. Make reservations weeks or months in advance if you plan to travel during these times, and be willing, even then, to settle for alternate choices.

Climate

The high-elevation center of the country (Guatemala City west to the Mexican border) lives up to its self-described billing as "the land of eternal spring." Daytime temperatures reach 20 to 25°C (68 to 76°F) and may fall to 10°C (51°F) at night. The highest elevations of the Western Highlands see temperatures drop to freezing at night. This part of the country sees distinct rainy (May through October) and dry (November through April) seasons. Guatemalans confuse this situation by calling their dry season *verano* (summer) and wet season *invierno* (winter), although that conveys the opposite of the Northern Hemisphere's seasonal distinctions.

The rest of the country (the high-elevation Verapaces, low-elevation Petén, and Atlantic and Pacific coasts) sees less distinction between wet and dry seasons. Daytime temperatures in the lowlands reach 32°C (89°F), but can soar to 40°C (104°F) during March and April, the hottest months of the year around the country. Although Guatemala has suffered occasional hurricane damage through the years—Mitch in 1998 and Stan in 2005—its short Caribbean coastline offers it greater protection than neighboring countries during the June through November hurricane season.

These charts list the average daily maximum and minimum temperatures for several Guatemalan cities.

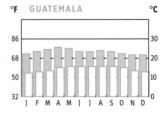

QUINTESSENTIAL GUATEMALA

Religious Celebrations

Few countries wear the past on their collective sleeves quite the way Guatemala does. Devout Catholicism, a strong indigenous tradition, and a palpitating sense of history combine to pack the calendar with religious festivals. (The introductory pages to Guatemala City's telephone directory list them all. Take a look if you're in the capital.) Antigua's Holy Week processions, Chichicastenango's Santo Tomás celebrations, and various communities' Day of the Dead observances draw visitors from around the world. Other celebrations, while no less fervent, are purely local affairs, open to outside observers willing to maintain a certain unobtrusive distance. Part Christian, part Mayan, the observances, with their clanging bells, wafting incense, and impassioned chanting, are difficult to separate into their component parts. In that regard, they perfectly mirror modern Guatemala.

Learning Spanish

Guatemalans will tell you their careful pronunciation and lack of accent make for the purest Spanish in Latin America. Although people of other nationalities would disagree, the Spanish spoken here is reasonably easy to navigate. Add to that more than 200 schools to choose from, a lower cost of living than in Spain, Mexico, or Costa Rica, and a geographic proximity (for North American visitors, at least), and you have one of the world's ideal Spanish-study locales.

Morning might begin with you and your instructor, one-on-one—that's the structure for most beginning courses here—over a cup of coffee out on the school's patio, tackling conjugations with a few props to aid you. You bid farewell and move on to a café for the afternoon, notebook in hand to review your day's lessons, also over a cup of coffee. (You'll quickly discover that coffee is also one of Guate-

mala's quintessential pleasures.) You stop by the market on your way home, and can ask for the produce by name. It's all about immersing yourself in the language. Your host family is just as grateful for the surprise accompaniment to the evening meal they've prepared for you. "*¡Magnífico!*" is their reply. "*Gracias.*"

The Lake

"I'm going to the lake." There's no need to specify *which* lake—or *lago* in Spanish—is being discussed. It's the shimmering blue Atitlán, billed as "the most beautiful lake in the world." British writer Aldous Huxley said so, and you'll likely agree. Ringed by three volcanoes—Atitlán itself formed thousands of years ago in the crater of a much larger volcano—the lake provides what is arguably Guatemala's best-known postcard view.

The friendly town of Panajachel, Guatemala's consummate, original expatri-

ate hangout, sits on Atitlán's northeast shore. Ringing the rest of the lake are a dozen other villages whose names read like a litany of the saints—Peter, John, Mark, Catherine, Anthony, James, Luke—and which you can reach via a system of cross-lake ferries and water taxis. All retain their Mayan character, some more successfully than others, and different styles of indigenous dress seen in each community. You may find yourself lingering here longer than you intended, meeting fellow travelers, swapping stories, and getting advice. The lake is just that kind of place.

IF YOU LIKE

Mayan Ruins

If you've come this far to see Mayan ruins, you're likely headed to Tikal. Good choice. But don't overlook the country's other important indigenous sites, some well known, others not. We also include a nod to a famous Mayan site just across the border in Honduras, an easy day trip for travelers to Guatemala.

Tikal, El Petén. Nothing surpasses the sight of Tikal's towering temples rising out of virgin rain forest. Adding to the mystique of the place is the fact that the site was virtually unknown to the outside world until the mid-1800s.

Quiriguá, Atlantic Lowlands. The lowlands' most important Mayan city dwarfed the nearby site of Copán in size and importance, even if few people remember that today. Ease of access from many points around the country makes Quiriguá worth a visit.

Copán, Honduras, Atlantic Lowlands. The intricate art and detailed carvings on the structures here have earned Copán the moniker of "the Paris of the Maya world." The ruins sit just across the border into Honduras, and have a tourist-friendly town right next door to boot.

Churches

Guatemalan churches cover the spectrum from strictly interpreted Catholic dogma to ancient Mayan rituals. The more isolated the area and the stronger the indigenous tradition, the more difficult to tell where one ends and the other begins. However, no matter what goes on inside them, many of Guatemala's churches count as among the most beautiful in Central America.

La Merced, Antigua. The old colonial capital's brightly painted church with the wedding-cake exterior is a favorite. La Merced is so important to the history of Antigua that it's the usual starting point for the city's famous Holy Week processions.

Santo Tomás, Chichicastenango, Highlands. Everyone heads to the famous Sunday market in Chichicastenango, but make time for a far less touristed detour to the town's principal church. Inside you'll get a primer on the blending of devout Catholicism with equally devout, and even older, Mayan tradition.

Basilica of Esquipulas, Atlantic Lowlands. Numerous miracles have been attributed to the *Cristo Negro* (Black Christ) inside this 18th century church, making it Guatemala's—some would argue Central America's—most important pilgrimage site, and the precious object it houses its most important object of veneration.

The Great Outdoors

It's not quite Chile or Costa Rica—not yet, at least—but Guatemala's outdoor offerings are gaining it a place on the Latin American–ecotourism circuit. You can go bird-watching, turtle-watching, biking, hiking, caving, climbing, rafting, fishing, and boating with a growing number of outfitters. The newest addition to the activities mix is the canopy tour, a zip line that lets you glide through the treetops courtesy of a helmet and a very secure harness.

Scaling Volcanoes, Antigua and Guatemala City. The proximity of the Pacaya, Agua, Fuego, and Acatenango volcanoes to two of the country's most visited cities means you can hike (or sometimes bike) to their summits and be back in time to regale your dinner companions with tales of oozing lava.

Spelunking, Las Verapaces. Limestone caverns are said to perforate the entire underground of the Verapaces region. Lanquín and Candelaria are two of the most accessible caves, and remain sites of pilgrimage and observance of Mayan rituals.

Sportfishing, Pacific Lowlands. Guatemala's Pacific coast is the new kid on the block in sportfishing circles, and can satisfy dreams of reeling in a marlin or sailfish. Get in there before the rest of the world finds out.

Boating the Río Dulce, Atlantic Lowlands. Navigate the river passing through a narrow, forested canyon between the port town of Livingston and inland Lake Izabal. Pass by Afro-Caribbean Garífuna villages, hot springs, and a colonial-era fortress in the process.

Markets

No shortage of upscale tourist shops proffer their wares, but there's nothing like the sights, smells, and sounds of a real Guatemalan market. Every town holds one, usually one or two days a week. Some began life as local markets but have morphed into largely tourist affairs. Others maintain their locals-only feel, although all are welcome. Sharpen your bargaining skills, but not too ruthlessly. Prices are already reasonable, and that difference of few quetzals means more to the vendor than to you.

Chichicastenango, Highlands. Thursday and Sunday market days in this highland town are Guatemala's most famous. We know travelers who dismiss the whole affair as "too touristy," but legions of visitors can't be *that* wrong. The Chichi outing is a fun way to spend a day.

Sololá, Highlands. This town near Lake Atitlán holds a large market each Tuesday and Friday, and provides you with an opportunity to see local-to-local sales in action. Browsing will turn up a few good buys in textiles, too.

Mercado Municipal, Antigua. Beyond the snazzy, gentrified face of Antigua, its municipal market, a few blocks west of the city center, buzzes with all the activity of a highland indigenous bazaar. This is the place where residents come to shop for daily supplies.

Mercado Central, Guatemala City. Smack-dab in the center of the city, behind the cathedral, sits the multistoried central market. It's primarily a local affair, but it's brimming with handicrafts for those with the patience to look. Just beware of pickpockets.

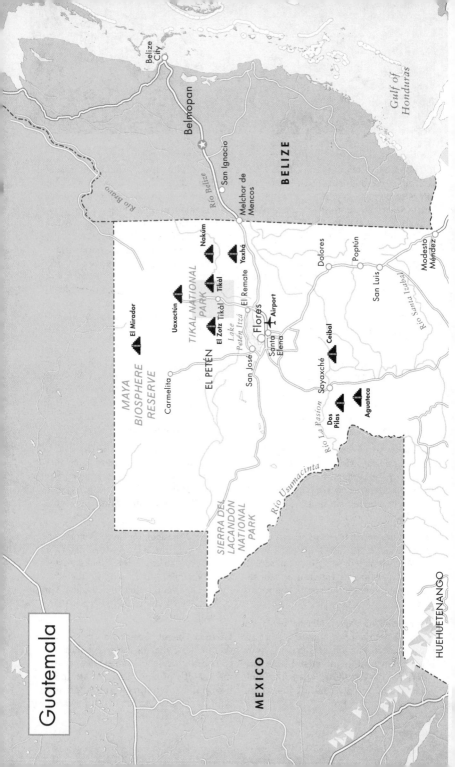

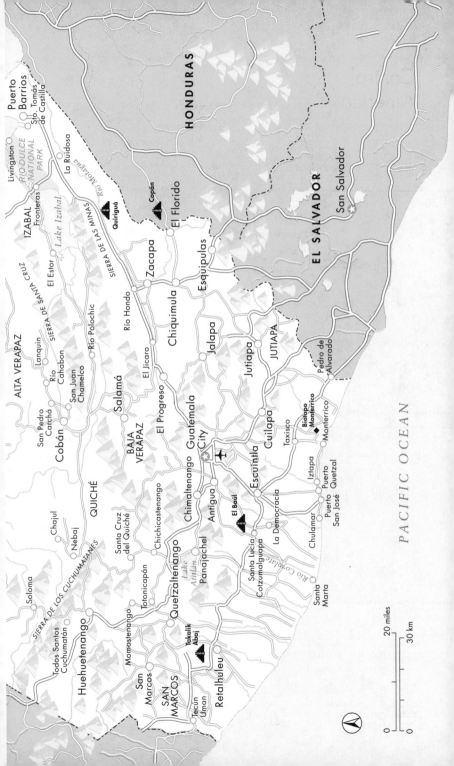

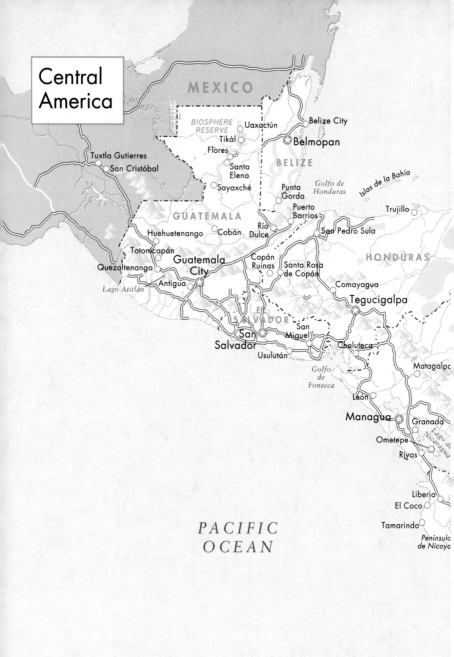

Central America

MEXICO

Tuxtla Gutierres
San Cristóbal

BIOSPHERE
RESERVE   Uaxactún
Tikàl
Flores
Santa
Elena
Sayaxché

Belize City
Belmopan
BELIZE

Golfo de
Honduras

Islas de la Bahía

Trujillo

Punta
Gorda
Puerto
Barrios
San Pedro Sula

HONDURAS

GUATEMALA

Huehuetenango   Cobán
Río
Dulce
Totonicapán
Quezaltenango
Guatemala
City
Copán
Ruinas
Santa Rosa
de Copán
Comayagua
Tegucigalpa
Lago Atitlán   Antigua

EL
SALVADOR   San
Miguel
San
Salvador
Usulután
Choluteca
Matagalpo

Golfo
de
Fonseca

León

Managua
Granada

Ometepe
Rivas

Lago de Nicaragua

Liberia
El Coco

Tamarindo   Península
de Nicoya

PACIFIC
OCEAN

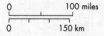

0   100 miles

0   150 km

JAMAICA

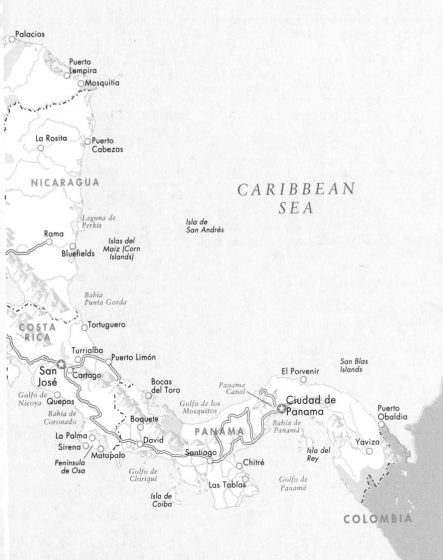

Palacios

Puerto
Lempira
Mosquitia

La Rosita   Puerto
Cabezas

NICARAGUA

*CARIBBEAN
SEA*

*Laguna de
Perlas*

*Isla de
San Andrés*

Rama
Bluefields

*Islas del
Maíz (Corn
Islands)*

*Bahía
Punta Gorda*

COSTA
RICA

Tortuguero

Turrialba

San   Cartago
José   Puerto Limón

Bocas
del Toro

*Panama
Canal*

El Porvenir

*San Blas
Islands*

*Golfo de
Nicoya* Quepos

*Golfo de los
Mosquitos*

Ciudad de
Panama

*Bahía de
Coronado*

Boquete

*Bahía de
Panamá*

Puerto
Obaldía

La Palma
Sirena

David

PANAMA

Matapalo

Santiago

*Isla del
Rey*

Yaviza

*Península
de Osa*

Chitré

*Golfo de
Chiriquí*

Las Tablas

*Golfo de
Panamá*

*Isla de
Coiba*

COLOMBIA

GREAT ITINERARIES

Guatemala's small size—about the same as England or Louisiana—leads to the temptation to try to see it all during a short visit. This ignores the fact that it still takes time to get from one place to another. The country has a good primary highway system, but secondary and tertiary roads can be slower going. A rushed trip also overlooks the huge number of wonderful cultural and natural attractions in Guatemala.

In that vein, we present a first-timer's itinerary that takes in Guatemala's best-known highlights and can be fit into a week. Most of it is confined to a small geographical area; the one far-flung sight can be squeezed in only via a round-trip flight. We follow that with add-ons of one to three days each, which take in some lesser known areas, useful to mix and match if you have a few more days, or to squeeze into a weeklong visit if you want a faster-paced trip.

THE GRINGO TRAIL
7 days
Days 1 & 2: Antigua
If you're a typical visitor, you'll fly into Guatemala City. Make a beeline out the airport door for the numerous minivan shuttles that meet each flight to take you to the old colonial capital of Antigua, less than an hour west. You can't throw a rock without hitting an old church, convent, monastery, or palace (or the ruins of one). The city is compact and doable on your own, but if you like your sightseeing done efficiently, you can sign on to a walking tour. Any non-sightseeing time can be filled with shopping for handicrafts and jade, Antigua's signature souvenir, and dining at the best selection of restaurants outside the capital.

⇨ *Antigua in Chapter 2.*

Days 3 & 4: Lake Atitlán
A couple of hours west of Antigua takes you to the Lake Atitlán, one of the Guatemala's and the hemisphere's natural wonders. Look up "tourist friendly" in the dictionary, and you just might see a picture of the gleaming lake and its trademark trifecta of volcanoes. The area presents you with a choice of towns to see and in which to stay. Traditionally, visitors have opted for sociable Panajachel, Guatemala's consummate expat hangout, but hot, hip San Pedro La Laguna is giving Pana a run for its money these days. And nothing says you can't see a good portion of the dozen towns ringing Atitlán. A system of ferries and water taxis makes it a breeze.

⇨ *Panajachel & Lake Atitlán in Chapter 3.*

Day 5: Chichicastenango
Guatemala's most famous market takes place each Thursday and Sunday in the highland town whose name everyone shortens to "Chichi." Things get underway by midmorning, and by 3 PM the market starts to wind down and the vendors pack up, anxious to be back home before dark. Though the Thursday market will not disappoint, come on Sunday if your schedule permits. This allows you also to take in mass in Chichi's Santo Tomás church and observe the ultimate blending of Maya and Catholic rituals.

⇨ *Chichicastenango in Chapter 3.*

Day 6 & 7: Tikal
It's back to Guatemala City for an early-morning flight to the country's most famous Mayan ruins. (The journey overland to the remote Petén region takes about 10 hours, so flying is vastly efficient.) The hour-long flight deposits you

outside the small town of Santa Elena, where you'll find lodging as well as in Flores, Santa Elena's pleasant twin "city." The ruins themselves lie about 64 km (40 mi) north, and if you go on an organized tour, that transportation is taken care of. There are one-day tours to Tikal for those short on time, but an overnight trip gives you extra time to explore.

⇨ *Tikal in Chapter 7.*

Tips & Transportation

This itinerary may require some juggling to schedule your market trip to Chichicastenango on a Thursday or Sunday. Flights to Tikal leave early in the morning, so getting to La Aurora International Airport from Antigua is a far easier task. You may wish to insert your two days there between Antigua and Lake Atitlán. Unless you insist on absolute flexibility, your own vehicle is not necessary and is actually a bother for this itinerary. As two of the country's most popular travel destinations, Antigua and Panajachel have no shortage of shuttle services to take you anywhere in greater comfort than on a public bus, and at Atitlán itself, water travel is the norm.

GUATEMALA CITY
1 day
Day 1: The Capital Circuit

Guatemala City suffers from bad public relations, and bad location: Antigua is so close, why not just go there? But the capital has at least a day's worth of sights in the Old City, its historic center, and several museums near the airport. Cap off your day with a scrumptious restaurant meal and a stay in one of the upscale hotels in the city's *Zona Viva.*

⇨ *Guatemala City in Chapter 1.*

Tips & Transportation

The capital's La Aurora International Airport lies within the city limits, some suggest too close for comfort, but you're just a few minutes' drive from the New City once you land. After you've checked in at your hotel, taxis are the easiest and safest way to get around.

THE VERAPACES VOYAGE
3 days
Day 1: Cobán

The hub of the Verapaces region lies a five-hour drive north of Guatemala City. An early-morning start still gives you an afternoon to explore the town. In particular, hike up to the El Calvario shrine for the best views around, or grab a taxi for a short ride just out of town to the gardens at the Vivero Verapaz.

⇨ *Cobán in Chapter 4.*

Day 2: Biotopo Quetzal

To paraphrase Benjamin Franklin, early to bed and early to rise gives a man (and woman) the best chance of seeing the resplendent quetzal. Get an early-morning start to head about an hour south of Cobán to the nature reserve specifically dedicated to preserving Guatemala's national bird. Stop for lunch on the way back at any of the family-owned restaurants that line the highway.

⇨ *Biotopo Quetzal in Chapter 4.*

Day 3: Semuc Champey & Lanquín

The pools and water caverns of Semuc Champey, about a two-hour drive from Cobán, make a splendid place to cool off with a swim in the midday heat. (The site sits at a lower elevation than cool Cobán, so you will notice the warmth here.) Cap off the afternoon (and cool off some more) with a hike through the nearby caves of Lanquín.

⇨ *Semuc Champey & Lanquín in Chapter 4.*

Tips & Transportation

Having your own car is ideal for this region, but public bus service from Guatemala City is comfortable and convenient. Numerous minivan shuttles also connect Antigua with Cobán. Any of the Cobán–Guatemala City buses can drop you at the entrance to the Biotopo Quetzal. You'll need to wait for a return bus at the end of your visit. It's nearly impossible to do Semuc Champey and Lanquín via public transportation, but numerous Cobán outfitters include both as part of a daylong tour. Lanquín, in particular, is best done with a guide who knows the way through the caves; portions of the hike can be a bit tricky.

THE CARIBBEAN CORRIDOR

2 days

Day 1: Livingston & Siete Altares

Livingston, on the Caribbean coast, is the quintessential port city, more reminiscent of faraway Jamaica than of the rest of Guatemala. Here's the catch: no roads lead here. You'll need to take land transportation to nearby Puerto Barrios and connect with a ferry or water taxi across Amatique Bay. Near Livingston lie the beautiful waterfalls of Siete Altares.

⇨ *Livingston & Siete Altares in Chapter 5.*

Day 2: Río Dulce

The canyoned, forested river connecting Livingston with inland Lake Izabal is one of Guatemala's spectacular nature excur-

sions, including a stop at the San Felipe fortress, constructed by the Spanish to thwart upriver attacks by pirates.

⇨ *Río Dulce in Chapter 5.*

Tips & Transportation

You can reach Puerto Barrios on the Atlantic coast easily by public transportation from Guatemala City or from Cobán, making the Caribbean a reasonable add-on following a visit to Las Verapaces. Only two public ferries per day connect Puerto Barrios with Livingston, but frequent water-taxi service fills in the gaps. You can also rearrange these days by starting your Río Dulce trip inland at the town of Fronteras, where the river meets Lake Izabal, then heading out to Livingston. The logistics of a Río Dulce make a tour worth your time. Enough robberies have happened to people going to Siete Altares on their own, that we recommend the security of a group tour, many of which also include a walking tour of Livingston.

Guatemala City

WORD OF MOUTH

"Guatemala City doesn't have a good reputation. However, I did spend time there and found it interesting. I think that if you stay in the Zona Viva, stay "low key," and be careful, you'll be OK."

—raquel z

"If you feel you must see Guatemala City, a day is plenty there. Charming Antigua is about a 45 minute drive from Guatemala City. Many folks go directly from the airport to Antigua."

—yestravel

THE TOURIST BUZZ IS THAT there's little reason to visit Guatemala City. Ancient ruins, colonial cities, flamboyant markets and spectacular mountains beckon just a short distance away, after all, and convenient transportation links make it a breeze to get in and out of town quickly without spending any time here. It is true that the one-time "jewel of Central America" has lost much of its luster.

The fact remains that the isthmus' largest metropolis has exactly what you'd expect from an urban area of 2.5 million people—the best selection of restaurants, hotels, nightlife, shopping, and museums in the country. The country's only true city does grow on you, although it probably takes longer than the typical short visit that most travelers give the place.

To its credit, the municipal government is trying to improve life here by sprucing up the historic center, beefing up security, moving electric wiring underground, and adding lots of greenery. It's still a struggle, and the sprawling capital will never rival the refinement of nearby Antigua, but if you stay here long enough, you just might start using the same affectionate name residents give to their city: "Guate."

ORIENTATION & PLANNING

ORIENTATION

Most Guatemalan cities are divided into numbered sectors. Guatemala City has 21 such *zonas*, although you will likely spend time in only five of them. Zona 1, the Old City, encompasses the heart of the capital and contains most of its historic sights and budget lodgings. On the south side of the capital, the New City takes in Zonas 9, 10, and more, and is home to most of Guatemala City's upscale lodgings, restaurants, shopping, and nightlife. Between the Old and New Cities lies the somewhat seedy Zona 4, notable because it contains many bus terminals. La Aurora International Airport and several fine museums lie in Zona 13, south of Zonas 9 and 10. Numbered *avenidas* (avenues) run north–south, whereas *calles* (streets) run west–east. Addresses are given as a numbered avenida or calle followed by two numbers separated by a dash: the first number is the previous cross street or avenue and the second is a specific building. Building numbers increase as they approach the higher-numbered cross streets and then start over at the next block, so 9 Avenida 5–22 is on 9 Avenida near 5 Calle, and 9 Avenida 5–74 is on the same block, only closer to 6 Calle. There *is* logic, however complex, to the system. Hit the pavement and you'll get the hang of it. A word of warning: make sure you're in the right zone. Each zone replicates the same grid system. In theory, the same address could appear 21 times throughout the city. Street signs always specify which zone you're in.

The city's major arteries are 6 and 10 avenidas: 6 Avenida runs from Zona 1 to Zona 4 to Zona 9, passing three series of identically numbered calles; 10 Avenida runs through Zonas 1 and 4 before becoming

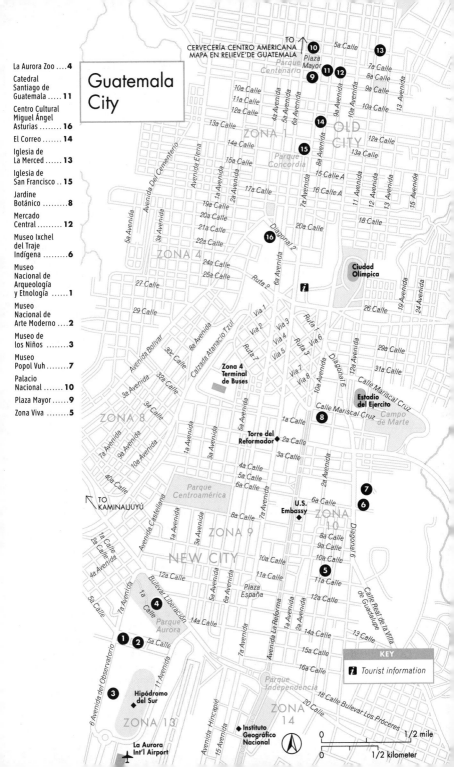

Guatemala City

La Aurora Zoo **4**

Catedral
Santiago de
Guatemala **11**

Centro Cultural
Miguel Ángel
Asturias **16**

El Correo **14**

Iglesia de
La Merced **13**

Iglesia de
San Francisco .. **15**

Jardine
Botánico **8**

Mercado
Central **12**

Museo Ixchel
del Traje
Indígena **6**

Museo
Nacional de
Arqueología
y Etnología **1**

Museo
Nacional de
Arte Moderno **2**

Museo de
los Niños **3**

Museo
Popol Vuh **7**

Palacio
Nacional **10**

Plaza Mayor **9**

Zona Viva **5**

TO
CERVECERÍA CENTRO AMERICANA
MAPA EN RELIEVE DE GUATEMALA

TO
Plaza
Mayor

Parque
Centenario

ZONA 1

OLD
CITY

Parque
Concordia

ZONA 4

Avenida Del Cementerio

Avenida Elena

Calzada Atanacio Tzul

Avenida Bolívar

ZONA 8

Zona 4
Terminal
de Buses

Torre del
Reformador

Parque
Centroamérica

ZONA 9

NEW CITY

Ciudad
Olímpica

Estadio
del Ejército

Campo
de Marte

Calle Mariscal Cruz

Calle Mariscal Cruz

U.S.
Embassy

ZONA
10

TO
KAMINALJUYÚ

Avenida Castellana

Bulevar Liberación

Parque
Aurora

Hipódromo
del Sur

ZONA 13

La Aurora
Int'l Airport

Plaza
España

Avenida La Reforma

Parque
Independencia

ZONA
14

Calle Real de la Villa de Guadalupe

18 Calle Bulevar Los Próceres

Instituto
Geográfico
Nacional

Avenida Hincapié

KEY

🛈 *Tourist information*

0   1/2 mile

0   1/2 kilometer

the 10-lane Avenida La Reforma in Zona 10. Comfort seekers tend to stick to the New City, whereas those interested in bargain shopping and budget lodging head for the Old City.

PLANNING

WHEN TO GO

The capital has distinct rainy (May to October) and dry seasons (November to April). Being the center of business and politics, Guatemala City hosts more visitors during the week than on weekends. It's the obvious choice for the beginning or end of your Guatemala visit since the country's major airport sits inside the city limits.

WHAT TO DO

"Eat, drink, and be merry" sums it up for Guatemala's burgeoning capital. Toss in visits to a couple of Guatemala City's world-class museums, too. There's no question that parts of the sprawling city are chaotic and congested, and yet the quiet, polished streets of the New City, with their fine restaurants and comfy hotels, can be a much-needed dose of civilization after hitting the country's more remote sights. Guatemala City's problem will always be that equally polished, equally fine, equally comfy Antigua sits nearby and offers those same advantages with a stunning colonial city as backdrop to boot.

RESTAURANTS & CUISINE

As befits the capital city, restaurants represent the country's various regional cuisines as well as a sampling of fare from around the world. Together, they make up Guatemala's best dining scene. You'll find upscale eateries (as well as all the U.S. chains) in the New City, but a few fine old institutions still hold court in the Old City.

ABOUT THE HOTELS

The Old City remains the province of budget lodgings. Some of its hostelries were at one time the grandest hotels in Central America; today, a bit of that elegance has faded, but these places still retain much character. International high-rise hotels have set up shop in the New City's Zonas 9 and 10. There are also a few smart and fashionable boutique hotels. The New City's proximity to the airport means that you hear the planes come and go when you stay there. Given the preponderance of business travelers who come to the capital, reservations are always a good idea during the week.

GETTING AROUND

Traffic can be bad here, but a good system of cross-city boulevards and highways makes getting around Guatemala City not too horrendous. However, we suggest leaving your vehicle in your hotel's parking lot and taking taxis. They're reasonably priced, ubiquitous, and easy to flag down. After dark, have your hotel or restaurant call one for you. If you do drive, try to avoid weekday rush hours, 7 to 8:30 AM and 4 to 6 PM. The public bus system is not safe to use here, and should be avoided.

EXPLORING

1

THE NEW CITY

Whereas the Old City is the real Guatemala, the modern look and fast pace of the New City's Zonas 9 and 10 are reminiscent of upscale districts in other Latin American cities. This is especially the case in Zona Viva, the posh center of Zona 10, where dozens of smart restaurants, bars, and clubs stay open long after the rest of the city goes to bed. During the day the New City's museums and cultural sites draw an equally affluent and savvy crowd. While the glitz and glamour of the Zona Viva are a welcome relief for travel-weary visitors, it is a far cry from the authentic, rustic enchantment to be found in the pueblos and backstreets of the rest of the country.

GUATEMALA CITY TIPS

■ All outlying distances in Guatemala are marked from the capital's Plaza Mayor.

■ *Ciudad de Guatemala* is the Spanish translation of "Guatemala City," but it is hardly used. As you make your way to the capital, signs direct you simply to GUATEMALA.

■ Guatemala City sits smack-dab in the center of the country, and Guatemalans refer to everywhere else outside the capital as "the interior."

■ We strongly recommend against using the public urinals scattered around the Old City.

Avenida La Reforma splits the New City down the middle, with Zona 9 to the west, and Zona 10 to the east. ■TIP→ **To save confusion, always check which zone your destination is in before heading there.**

WHAT TO SEE

❹ La Aurora Zoo. It's small, but the capital's zoo is well-arranged and well-maintained. The facility contains four exhibit areas: the African savanna, the Asian subcontinent, the Mesoamerican tropics, and the down-home farm. You'll see everything from giraffes and elephants to cows and ducks. ■TIP→ **The zoo's proximity to the nearby Children's Museum makes the combined two a convenient outing for families with kids.** ⊠ *La Aurora Park, Zona 13* ☎*2475-0894* ⊕*www.aurorazoo.org.gt* 🎟*Q18;* ⏱*Tues.–Sun. 9–5.*

❽ Jardín Botánico. The small but lovely Botanical Garden at the northern end of Zona 10 contains an impressive collection of plants managed by the Univesidad de San Carlos. Your ticket price also includes admission to a small, adjoining natural-history museum, which, frankly, has seen better days, but is currently undergoing a renovation. ⊠*Av. La Reforma 0–63, Zona 10* ☎*Gardens, 2331–0904; museum 2334–6065* 🎟*Q10* ⏱*Weekdays 8:30–3, Sat. 8:30–12:30.*

❻ Museo Ixchel del Traje Indígena. The city's best museum, the Ixchel Museum of Indigenous Dress, focuses on textiles of Guatemala's indigenous community, with an impressive array of handwoven fabrics from 120 highland communities, some of which date from the 19th century. It

Fodor'sChoice ★

will provide you with a good background in the regional differences among textiles before you head out to the highlands. You'll also find sculptures, photographs, and paintings, including works by Andres Curruchich, an influential Guatemalan folk painter. Multimedia and interactive weaving displays make the museum engaging for all ages—watch one of the short introductory videos describing the museum's holdings to get your grounded—and there's a café, a bookstore, and a terrific gift shop. The only drawback is its location—at the bottom of a long hill at the Universidad Francisco Marroquín. ⊠*End of 6 C. at 6 Av., Zona 10* ☎*2331–3662* ⊕*www.museoixchel.org* 🎫*Q35* ☉*Weekdays 9–5, Sat. 9–1.*

> **VIVE . . . GUATEMALA**
>
> At the intersection of 7 Avenida and 2 Calle, stands the **Torre del Reformador** ("Tower of the Reformer"), a smaller version of the Eiffel Tower, topping out at 75 meters (245 feet). The tower came from the United States and was constructed in 1935 to mark the centennial of the birth of President Justo Rufino Barrios, known for implementing liberal reforms during his late-19th-century tenure. (Barrios's portrait adorns the five-quetzal bill.) The tower is not equipped for climbing.

① ★ **Museo Nacional de Arqueología y Etnología.** Dedicated to the history of the Maya, the National Museum of Archaeology and Ethnology has a large and excellent collection of Mayan pottery, jewelry, masks, and costumes, as well as models of the ancient cities. The jade exhibit, in particular, is stunning. The museum is a must in understanding the link between ancient and modern Mayan cultures, but the exhibits are labeled in Spanish only. ⊠*Edificio 5, La Aurora Park, 6 C. and 7 Av., Zona 13* ☎*2475–4399* ⊕*www.munae.gob.gt* 🎫*Q30* ☉*Tues.–Fri. 9–4, weekends 9–noon and 1:30–4.*

② **Museo Nacional de Arte Moderno.** Surrealism and multimedia work are among the wide range of styles represented at the National Museum of Modern Art. Some of the collection does go back to the early-19th-century independence period. Many of Guatemala's most distinguished artists are represented here, including Efraín Recinos and Zipacna de León. Exhibits include works by other Latin American artists from similar periods. ⊠*Edificio 6, La Aurora Park, Zona 13* ☎*2472–0467* 🎫*Q10* ☉*Tues.–Fri. 9–4, weekends 9–noon and 1:30–4.*

③ ⟳ **Museo de los Niños.** Via interactive exhibits, the capital's splendid Children's Museum takes the young and young-at-heart on a journey through space, the human body, a coffee plantation, or a giant Lego exhibit. Take your pick. Multiple tickets are available at a slight discount Friday afternoon and weekends. We recommend making a kids' day out by combining this museum with a visit to the nearby zoo. ⊠*La Aurora Park, 5 Calle 10–00, Zona 13* ☎*2475–5076* ⊕*www.museode-losninos.com.gt* 🎫*Q35* ☉*Tues.–Thurs. 8–noon and 1–5, Fri. 8–noon and 2–6, weekends 10–1:30 and 2:30–6.*

A BIT OF HISTORY

Guatemala City exists only because of the 1773 earthquake that leveled nearby Antigua. Authorities decided once and for all to move their capital to supposedly safer ground after several such seismic events during colonial times. The new city broke ground three years later with the stately name *La Nueva Guatemala de la Asunción.* ("The New Guatemala of the Assumption"),presiding over Spain's colony of Central America for nearly a half-century more before becoming the capital of an independent Guatemala.

The land wasn't empty pre-1776, however. The Maya had lived here for 2,500 years before the relocation of the colonial capital, as evidenced by the ruins of Kaminaljuyú, today nearly swallowed up by modern development in Zona 7. True to historical patterns in developing countries, waves of migration from poor rural areas have caused the capital to balloon in size, including those who fled to the capital during Guatemala's long civil war, looking for safety when violence shook the highlands. Many shantytowns ring the city as a result.

That much-vaunted safety from seismic activity that led colonial authorities to set up shop here proved an illusion: three major earthquakes rocked Guatemala City in the 20th century, the most devastating taking place in February 1976 killing 23,000 people. Small tremors remain a fact of life in the capital. With the government struggling to upgrade building codes, it is hoped that the next "big one" will cause less damage.

NEED A BREAK?

Satisfy your sweet tooth on the porch of Café Zurich (✉ *6 Av. 12–58, Zona 10* ☎ *2334–2781*), a former colonial home. The menu has specialty coffees as well as chocolate, chocolate, and more chocolate.

7 ★ **Museo Popol Vuh.** Religious figures, animals, and mythological half-animal–half-man creatures with stolid eyes, hawkish noses, and fierce poses inhabit this museum. Though much smaller than the city's other museums, Popol Vuh has an interesting display of well-preserved stone carvings from the Preclassic period, with the earliest pieces dating from 1500 BC. Some statues are quite large, all the more impressive given that they were each cut from a single stone. Also look for the "painted books," which were historical records kept by the Maya. The most famous is the museum's namesake, the *Popol Vuh,* otherwise known as the Mayan Bible, which was lost (and later recovered) after it was translated into Spanish. An ample collection of colonial artifacts and rotating special exhibitions round out the museum's offerings. Monthly evening public lectures, in Spanish only, deal with topics related to the institution's holdings. ✉ *Universidad Francisco Marroquín, End of 6 C., Zona 10* ☎ *2338–7896* ⊕ *www.popolvuh.ufm.edu.gt* 🚌 *Q35,* ⊙ *Weekdays 9–5, Sat. 9–1.*

5 **Zona Viva.** The so-called "lively zone" is undoubtedly the most cosmopolitan area of town. The daytime crowd is mostly business executives, but at night a more vivacious bunch takes over. The precise definition of the neighborhood differs depending on whom you talk

Kaminaljuyú

Who says you can't find Mayan ruins in the metropolitan area? From 300 BC to AD 900, an early Mayan city of some 50,000 people flourished in what is now the heart of Zona 7 in one of Guatemala City's many gorges. What you can see today, about 100 mounds and platforms, is but a fraction of the original city, most of which is buried beneath today's urban sprawl. Excavation of this impressive site, which includes the bases of several pyramids, began in 1925, triggered by the simple act of a local soccer team digging into the ground to expand its practice field. Many of the figurines and artifacts originally unearthed were thought to be associated with burial, leading authorities to dub the site with its present name, a Quiché term meaning "hills of the dead." No one knows for sure what the city was originally called. Many of the objects found here are now on display at the Museo Popol Vuh.

to, but it roughly centers on the area from Avenidas La Reforma and 4, and Calles 12 and 14, fanning out from there. Streets accommodate pedestrians overflowing from the narrow sidewalks on which restaurants have introduced outdoor seating, and lines extend from bars. You won't find the boutiques that characterize most upscale neighborhoods; those that do exist are mostly inside the large, international-chain hotels. ⊠*Zona 10.*

THE OLD CITY

Older and grittier than the New City, the Old City has the hustle and bustle of many Central American capitals. But walking around the area, especially around the Plaza Mayor, is quite pleasant. The frenetic colors and sounds of the metropolis can be daunting at first, but with a little patience—and, of course, a well hidden money pouch—the downtown experience can be both memorable and exhilarating.

WHAT TO SEE

⑪ Catedral Santiago de Guatemala. Built between 1778 and 1867, Guatemala City's cathedral replaced the old Catedral de Santiago Apóstol in Antigua, destroyed in that city's 1773 earthquake. The structure is a rare example of colonial architecture in the Old City. Standing steadfast on the eastern end of Plaza Mayor, it is one of the city's most enduring landmarks, having survived the capital's numerous 20th century earthquakes. The ornate altars hold outstanding examples of colonial religious art, including an image of the Virgen de la Asunción, the city's patron saint. Off a courtyard on the cathedral's south side—enter through the church—stands the Museo de la Arquidiócesis de Santiago Guatemala, the archdiocesan museum with a small collection of colonial religious art. ⊠*8 C. and 7 Av., Zona 1* ☎*2232–7621; museum, 2232–2527* ⊕*www.catedraldeguatemala.org* ☑*Free, Q20 for museum* ☉*Cathedral: Mon.–Wed. and Fri.–Sat. 7–1 and 2–6, Thurs. and Sun. 7–6; museum: Tues.–Sat. 9–1 and 2–5, Sun. 9–2.*

16 **Centro Cultural Miguel Ángel Asturias.** The city's fine-arts complex consists of the imposing Teatro Nacional and the open-air Teatro del Aire Libre. Named for Guatemala's Nobel Prize–winning novelist who spent much of his life in exile for opposing Guatemala's dictatorship, the hilltop cluster of buildings overlooks the Old City. Check out the performance schedule while you're here and pick up a ticket if something strikes your fancy. Prices are far less than you'd pay at a comparable venue in Europe or North America. ✉*24 C. 3–81, Centro Cívico* ☎*2232–4041* ⊕*www.teatro-nacional.com* ✆*Free* ⊗*Weekdays 10–4.*

14 **El Correo.** You can mail packages from your hotel, but it's far more fun to come to the main post office, housed in a cantaloupe-color structure dating from the colonial era. At press time, it was undergoing a renovation, paid for by a grant from the Spanish government. ✉*7 Av. 12–11, Zona 1* ☎*2232–6101* ⊗*Weekdays 8:30–5:30, Sat. 9–1.*

13 **Iglesia de La Merced.** If religious iconography is one of the reasons you're in Guatemala, step inside this lovely church dating from 1813 to see its baroque interior. Many of the elaborate paintings and sculptures originally adorned La Merced in Antigua but were moved here after earthquakes devastated that city. ✉*5 C. 11–67, Zona 1* ☎*2232–0631* ⊗*Daily 6–7.*

15 **Iglesia de San Francisco.** The Church of St. Francis, built by its namesake Franciscan order between 1800 and 1851, is known for its ornate wooden altar. A small museum explains the church's history. ✉*13 C. 6–34, Zona 1* ☎*2232–3625* ⊗*Daily 10–4.*

12 **Mercado Central.** A seemingly endless maze of underground passages is home to the Mercado Central, where handicrafts from the highlands are hawked from overstocked stalls. It's not as appealing as the open-air markets in Antigua or Chichicastenango, but the leather goods, wooden masks, and woolen blankets found here are often cheaper. There are skilled pickpockets in the market, so keep an eye on your belongings. ✉*8 C. and 8 Av., Zona 1* ☎*No phone* ⊗*Mon.–Sat. 9–6, Sun. 9–noon.*

10 **Palacio Nacional.** The grandiose National Palace was built between 1937 and 1943 to satisfy the monumental ego of President Jorge Ubico Castañeda. It once held the offices of the president and his ministers, but now many of its 320 rooms house a collection of paintings and sculptures by well-known Guatemalan artists from the colonial period to the present. Look for Alfredo Gálvez Suárez's murals illustrating the history of the city above the entry. The palace's ornate stairways and stained-glass windows are a pleasant contrast to the gritty city outside its walls. ■TIP→ **Admission is free, but you must visit with a guide who will take you on a 45-minute highlights tour, which leaves at fixed times throughout the day.** Your visit includes a stop at the presidential balcony off the banquet room. If the palace is a must on your itinerary, call ahead to confirm that it is open; the building occasionally closes for presidential functions. ✉*6 C. and 7 Av., Zona 1* ☎*2232–8550* ✆*Free* ⊗*Weekdays 9–5:30. Tours depart every 15 mins, 9:15–noon and 2–5* PM; *every 30 mins, noon–2.*

❾ **Plaza Mayor.** Some people refer to this expanse as the Parque Central, but, despite a few trees, it's more vast concrete plaza than park. Clustered around this historic square are landmarks that survived the 19th and 20th centuries' earthquakes. One original building did not get through the 1917 earthquake: the colonial-era Palacio del Gobierno, which once stood on the plaza's west side, was leveled and later cleared, adding a second city block to the expanse of the square. In the center of the plaza is a fountain where children sometimes splash, while their parents relax on the nearby benches. Photographers set up shop here on weekends, putting up small backdrops of rural scenes—you can have your picture taken in front of them. ⊠ *Between 6 and 8 Cs. and 6 and 7 Av., Zona 1.*

WHERE TO EAT

THE NEW CITY

Guatemala City has the varied cuisine you'd expect in a major city. Finer restaurants are clustered in the New City. Virtually every street in the Zona Viva has a selection of tempting restaurants, making it almost impossible to choose. Some tried-and-true favorites are listed below. Fortunately, the Zona Viva is small enough that you can stroll around until you find that perfect place.

WHAT IT COSTS IN GUATEMALAN QUETZALES					
	¢	$	$$	$$$	$$$$
RESTAURANTS	under Q40	Q40–Q70	Q70–Q100	Q100–Q130	over Q130

Restaurant prices are per person for a main course at dinner.

ECLECTIC

$$$–$$$$ ✕ **Zumo.** Longtime favorite Siriacos was reborn as Zumo in 2007, and
Fodor'sChoice takes the often overused term "fusion cuisine" seriously. The chef here
★ mixes in-season Guatemalan ingredients with an around-the-world menu. We like the shrimp in mango sauce with avocado butter, and the wonton ravioli stuffed with sweet potato and salmon drenched in an almond cream sauce. Top it off with a mango mousse and a selection from a reasonably priced wine list (one of the best in the capital), and impeccable service. The new owner has added lots of whimsical fountains to this century-old brick-and-stucco former carriage house. ⊠ *1 Av. 12–12, Zona 10* ☎ *2334–6316* ▤ *AE, D, DC, MC, V* ⊙ *Closed Sun. No lunch Sat.*

$$–$$$$ ✕ **Jake's.** If you only have one meal in Guatemala City, head to Jake
Fodor'sChoice Denburg's place. A painter-turned-restaurateur, Jake uses his creative
★ talents on food, producing dishes ranging from handmade smoked-chicken tortellini to *robalo* (snook) in a green-pepper sauce. The crowning achievement is the *vaquero chino* (Chinese cowboy), a tenderloin steak served with a sweet soy, espresso, and star anise sauce. The restaurant is a beautiful converted farmhouse with hardwood ceilings, tile floors, an outdoor patio, and new lounge. The wine list is quite possibly

CLOSE UP

Mapa en Relieve

If you want to get the lay of the land before you head out to the country, this unusual relief map depicts Guatemala's precipitous topography. The layout is so immense—1,800 square meters, or 19,500 square feet—that your best view is from an observation tower. What makes it even more amazing is that it was completed in 1905, before satellite and aerial topography, and long before Google Earth. The flashy Spanish-language Web site focuses on the late-19th- and early-20th-century development and construction of the map, a labor of love of engineer (and amateur geographer) Francisco Vela (1859–1909). Altitudes are greatly exaggerated: horizontally, the map uses a 1:10,000 scale, but vertically, it's 1:2,000. The map lies several blocks north of the Old City, not far from the Cervecería Centro Americana and its brewery tour; a taxi is your best bet for getting here.

⊠ *Parque Minerva, 6 Av. Norte final, Zona 2* ☎ *2254-1114* ⊕ *www.mapaenrelieve.org* 🚌 *Q15* ⊙ *Daily 9–5.*

the best in Central America. ⊠ *17 C. 10–40, Zona 10* ☎ *2368-0351* ⊟ *AE, D, DC, MC, V* ⊙ *No dinner Sun.*

GUATEMALAN

$$$–$$$$ ✕ **Los Ranchos.** A pretty blue colonial facade with picture windows welcomes you to Guatemala's best steak house. Most meats, including the rib eye and chateaubriand, come from the United States, but the specialty of the house, a skirt steak called the *churrasco los ranchos,* is a hearty cut that hails from Argentina. Ask your server to recommend one of the excellent wines from Chile or France. Save room for dessert, which ranges from tiramisu to *tres leches,* a type of cake injected with sweetened condensed milk, evaporated milk, and cream. ⊠ *2 Av. 14–06, Zona 10* ☎ *2363-5028* ⊟ *AE, DC, MC, V.*

$$–$$$ ✕ **Hacienda Real.** Small stone pedestals containing hot coals warm the
★ dining room, so even on a chilly day you needn't pass up this charming restaurant serving authentic Guatemalan fare. Choose from platters of robalo, steak, or pork, all served with a variety of savory condiments like fresh salsa, pickled carrots, and jalapeños. The attentive, exuberant servers bring endless baskets of warm tortillas, but try not to fill up—the truly incomparable caramel flan shouldn't be missed. To top off the experience, mariachi bands stroll through the place on most evenings. ⊠ *13 C. 1–10, Zona 10* ☎ *2333-5408* ⊟ *AE, MC, V.*

$$–$$$ ✕ **Hacienda de los Sánchez.** This Zona Viva steak house is known for its quality cuts of beef, yet the atmosphere has won over more than one vegetarian. The brick-floor dining room calls to mind the American West, with such touches as sturdy wooden tables and old saddles. Eat inside or on the plant-filled patio under the big tent overhang. Grilled and barbecued meats dominate the menu, but you can also order chicken and seafood. There's a decent wine list. ⊠ *12 C. 2–25, Zona 10* ☎ *2360-5428* ⊟ *AE, D, DC, MC, V.*

$–$$$$ ✕ **Casa Chapina.** For an around-Guatemala tour of the country's cuisine, we like this colorful New City restaurant with its bright lime-wash

A TOUR AND A BREW

The capital's **Cervecería Centro Americana** has brewed the majority of the beer sold in Guatemala since 1886. If you've been traveling around the country, you've seen (and likely sampled) Gallo, its ubiquitous flagship beer, pronounced *GAH-yo*. The *cervecería* manufactures a complete line of beverages, including Gallo Light, Victoria lager, dark bock beer Moza, and Malta Gallo malt liquor. Gallo, incidentally, is marketed in the United States, but under the name "Famosa." (A certain famous California winery already holds the rights to the "Gallo" name there.)

The brewery offers fun, informative hour-long tours in Spanish and English of its installations several blocks north of the Old City each Monday to Thursday at 9 and 11 AM and 3 PM. (A taxi is the best way to get here.) Reservations aren't necessary, but the brewery recommends calling ahead to make sure your desired time doesn't conflict with that of a large group, and also to be sure an English-speaking guide is available. Best of all, the whole thing is free, and the tour concludes with samples (also free) in the brewery café.

⊠ *3 Av. Norte final, Zona 2* ☎ *2289-1555* ⊕ *www.cerveceriacentro-americana.com.*

stucco walls and lots of flowers. The emphasis is on typical national dishes such as *pollo loroco* (chicken-and-vegetables), *pepián* (chicken fricassee in pumpkin and sesame sauce), *kaq'ik* (a hearty turkey stew from the Verapaces), and *frijoles blancos* (white beans). Be sure to accompany whatever you order with the restaurant's warm homemade tortillas. ⊠ *1 Av. 13–42, Zona 10* ☎ *2367–6688* ⊟ *AE, D, DC, MC, V.*

ITALIAN

$$–$$$$

Fodor'sChoice

★

✕ **Tamarindos.** Italian and Asian dominate at one of Guatemala City's best restaurants, Tamarindos serves up innovative, decidedly eclectic fare ranging from duck in tamarind sauce to Thai-style curries. Curlicue lamps and whimsical sofas that seem straight out of *Alice in Wonderland* bring a bit of postmodernism to an old city. It's an exhilarating destination for dinner, but the reasonably priced menu also makes this an excellent choice for lunch. The excellent wine list includes choices from around the globe. ⊠ *11 C. 2–19A, Zona 10* ☎ *2360–5630* ⊟ *AE, D, DC, MC, V* ☉ *Closed Sun.*

$$

✕ **Tre Fratelli.** Run by three hip Guatemalans, this bustling restaurant caters to the city's young professionals. The food is definitely Italian, but there are plenty of local touches. Favorites include *fettuccine frutti di mare* (with seafood), ravioli *alla Bolognese* (with a variety of meats), and the *quattro stagione* (four-season) pizza. Top your meal off with chocolate mousse, homemade ice cream, or a cappuccino or espresso brewed in real Italian coffee urns. The place is fun, active, a little noisy, and has an ample nonsmoking section. ■TIP➔ **It's a good place to bring kids if you're looking for familiar cuisine and surroundings.** ⊠ *2 Av. 13–25, Zona 10* ☎ *2366–2678* ⊟ *AE, MC, V.*

SPANISH

$$–$$$$ ✕**De Mario.** The menu here is one of the country's most original, combining flavors from both sides of the Atlantic: you can enjoy such Spanish traditions as paella and roast suckling pig or more local offerings like robalo with a mushroom sauce. The restaurant has a much-deserved reputation for impeccable service. ⊠ *1 Av. 12–98, Zona 10* ☎ *2339–2331* ⊟ *AE, D, DC, MC, V* ⊘ *No dinner Sun.*

> **COFFEE IN AN INSTANT**
>
> Historians credit one George Washington (not *that* George Washington), an Englishman living in Guatemala in the early 20th century, with the invention of instant coffee. A chemist by trade, Washington fiddled with the residue in his coffee pot to come up with an idea for a dried product to which hot water could be added for a quick cup. He patented his invention and marketed it here as "Red E Coffee."

THE OLD CITY

AMERICAN

¢–$ ✕**Europa Bar & Restaurante.** Plan on hearing as much English spoken as Spanish at this long-standing hangout for American expats opened by an Oregon native. Expect comfort food like hamburgers, mashed potatoes, and chili, as well as diner-style breakfasts of eggs, bacon, and hash browns. In the 2nd-floor bar you can play a game of backgammon or watch soccer on cable TV. ⊠ *11 C. 5–16, Zona 1* ☎ *2253–4929* ⊟ *AE, D, DC, MC, V* ⊘ *Closed Sun.*

GUATEMALAN

$–$$ ✕**Arrin Cuan.** Ask locals to recommend a place to eat in the Old City, and chances are they'll send you to this spirited Guatemalan favorite. The decor couldn't be simpler—wooden masks adorn the walls and soda-bottle flower vases add a touch of color to each table. The flavorful cuisine, typical of the Cobán region, includes *kaq'ik* (a spicy turkey stew), *gallo en chicha* (chicken in a slightly sweet sauce), and *sopa de tortuga* (turtle soup). More adventurous types will want to sample the roasted tepezcuintle. ■TIP➔ **On Friday and Saturday night live marimba music fills the restaurant.** A branch in the New City opened in 2006, and dishes up the same regional cuisine from Las Verapaces. The business has even opened up food-court stands in several shopping centers around town, but we suggest you partake in one of the sit-down outlets. ⊠ *5 Av. 3–27, Zona 1* ☎ *2238–0242* ⊠ *16 C. 4–32, Zona 10* ☎ *2366–2660* ⊟ *AE, DC, MC, V.*

MEXICAN

¢–$ ✕**El Gran Pavo.** You can't miss this restaurant—it's in a pink building with a gaudy neon sign on top. The interior is just as flashy; bright colors dazzle you as you walk past sombreros, blankets, and other Mexican kitsch and a mariachi band holds court most nights. The standard tacos and enchiladas are on the menu, but you'll also run across items like *aujas norteñas* (grilled beef strips covered with a red sauce and surrounded by avocado slices) and *camarones siempre joven* (shrimp in a spicy black-chili sauce). The restaurant is open past midnight, one of the few places in the city center to keep such late hours. ⊠ *13 C. 4–41, Zona 1* ☎ *2230–0049* ⊟ *AE, DC, MC, V.*

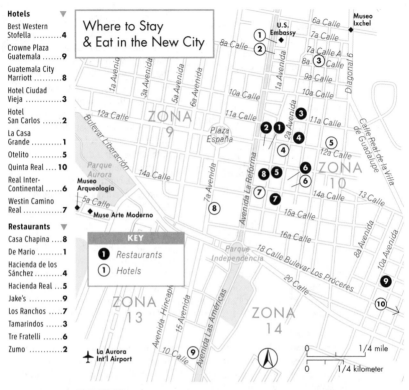

SPANISH

$$–$$$ **✕Altuna.** Waiters in white jackets and ties move briskly around the covered courtyard that serves as the main dining room. If you want a bit more privacy, ask to be seated in one of several adjacent rooms decorated with Iberian paintings, photographs, and posters. The Spanish and Basque menu is fairly limited; consider the calamari, paella, or filet mignon with mushroom sauce. A branch in the New City, while newly constructed, maintains the old style and impeccable service of the original city-center restaurant. ⊠*5 Av. 12–31, Zona 1* ☎*2253-6743* ⊠*10 C. 0–45, Zona 10* ☎*2332-6576* ▭*AE, D, DC, MC, V* ⊗*Closed Mon., no dinner Sun.*

Fodor'sChoice ★

$ **✕El Mesón de Don Quijote.** In the heart of the Old City, this colorful restaurant serves respectable cuisine from northern Spain (Asturias, to be exact). Though popular with old-timers, it's also a favorite late-night spot (it's open until 1 AM). The long bar adjoining several dining rooms hosts live musicians who play under a flashy painting of a flamenco dancer. The extensive menu has such palate pleasers as seafood casserole, sliced Spanish ham, lentils with sausage, and paella big enough for four people. On weekdays people head here for the four-course prix-fixe lunch. ⊠*11 C. 5–27, Zona 1* ☎*2232-1741* ▭*AE, DC, MC, V* ⊗*Closed Sun.*

WHERE TO STAY

Guatemala City has the country's widest range of accommodations. Upscale hotels are found in the New City, while more moderately priced lodgings are clustered in the Old City.

WHAT IT COSTS IN GUATEMALAN QUETZALES				
¢	$	$$	$$$	$$$$
HOTELS	under Q160	Q160–Q360	Q360–Q560	Q560–Q3760	over Q760

Hotel prices are for two people in a standard double room, including tax and service.

THE NEW CITY

$$$$ **Otelito.** This colonial house has character that most other hotels can't match. Ivy-covered walls give way to a cozy reception area. Some rooms surround a breezy courtyard overflowing with potted plants, whereas others share a balcony reached by a spiral staircase. The softly lighted rooms have wooden paneling and tile floors, as well as elegant touches like dried flowers. The Middle Eastern restaurant is an ideal lunch spot. Take a table on the tranquil patio where hummingbirds surround a melodic fountain. Pros: close to action, lively restaurant. Cons: occasional noise from courtyard. ⊠*12 C. 4–51, Zona 10* ☎*2339–1811* ⊕*www.otelito.com* ⤶*11 rooms, 1 suite* ⌂*In-room: no a/c, Wi-Fi. In-hotel: restaurant, room service, bar, no elevator, public Internet, airport shuttle, parking (no fee)* ☰*AE, D, DC, MC, V* ⦿|*BP.*

$$$$ **Quinta Real.** The colossal Quinta Real has a neocolonial style—with vaulted ceilings and arabesque arches—and excellent views of the city and the neighboring volcanoes from its hilltop perch. A series of ponds and cascades play out below a covered bridge, which leads to you to the main building. Suites are elegantly appointed with colonial art and sumptuously soft bedding. The only drawback is its location slightly outside the city. **Pros:** colonial decor, great views. **Cons:** out-of-town location. ⊠*Prolongación Blvd. Los Próceres, Km 9, Zona 15* ☎*2427–0000, 800/457–4000 in U.S.* 🖷*2427–0001* ⊕*www.quintareal.com.gt* ⤶*123 suites* ⌂*In-room: safe, refrigerator, DVD, Wi-Fi. In-hotel: restaurant, room service, bar, gym, pool, laundry service, airport shuttle, parking (no fee), no-smoking rooms* ☰*AE, D, DC, MC, V* ⦿|*BP.*

$$$$ **Westin Camino Real.** With every imaginable amenity and a staff that
★ aims to please, it isn't surprising that the immense Camino Real has hosted everyone from rock stars to heads of state. The spacious reception area lies just beyond a long foyer lined with overstuffed leather chairs. Stately rooms are furnished with carved French provincial–style pieces. Executive floors hold spacious suites with room for business travelers to spread out. French doors in the rooms on the executive floors provide views of the nearby volcanoes. Pros: close to action, chain amenities, good shopping arcade. Cons: no Wi-Fi. ⊠*14 C. and Av. La Reforma, Zona 10* ☎*2333–3000, 800/228–3000 in U.S.* 🖷*2337–4313* ⊕*www.westin.com* ⤶*271 rooms* ⌂*In-room: safe,*

refrigerator, Ethernet. In-hotel: 2 restaurants, room service, 3 bars, tennis courts, pools, gym, concierge, laundry service, airport shuttle, parking (no fee) ⊟AE, DC, MC, V.

$$$–$$$$ **Guatemala City Marriott.** Although its facade won't win any awards, this hotel does earn points for its excellent location not far from the Zona Viva. The lovely lounge offers rest to the weary; relax with a cocktail in one of the comfortable armchairs as you listen to jazz. You can always head to the Cabaña Club, a spacious spa and sports facility. Rooms are nicely furnished and each has a small balcony with a view of the city. Pros: chain amenities. Cons: several blocks to Zona Viva. ⊠*7 Av. 15–45, Zona 9* ☎*2410–1777, 800/228–9290 in North America* 📠*2332–1877* ⊕*www.marriott.com* ➦*385 rooms* ♿*In-room: safe, refrigerator. In-hotel: 3 restaurants, room service, bar, tennis court, pool, gym, spa, laundry service, airport shuttle, parking (no fee)* ⊟*AE, D, DC, MC, V* ⦿*BP.*

$$$–$$$$ **Real InterContinental.** A giant statue of bartering Maya greets you at the entrance of the towering InterContinental in the center of the Zona Viva; on either side are sweeping staircases. Despite this nod to the ancient world, the hotel is decidedly modern throughout; comfortable rooms have modern art on the walls. The very good French restaurant imported its chef from Paris. Other restaurants, as well as shops and boutiques, are within walking distance. Pros: chain amenities, close to action. Cons: ⊠*14 C. 2–51, Zona 10* ☎*2379–4444* 📠*2379–4445* ⊕*www.ichotelsgroup.com* ➦*239 rooms* ♿*In-room: no a/c (some), safe, refrigerator, Ethernet. In-hotel: 3 restaurants, room service, bar, pool, gym, spa, laundry service, concierge, public Wi-Fi, parking (no fee)* ⊟*AE, DC, MC, V* ⦿*BP.*

$$$ **Crowne Plaza Guatemala.** Giant glass elevators in the atrium-style lobby ascend to a dizzying view of the city. With 22 meeting rooms and 16 ballrooms, the hotel is designed to accommodate large conventions. Rooms on the south side have the most impressive views of the surrounding volcanoes—even the health club overlooks their peaks. The hotel is convenient to the airport, but it's quite a distance from the Zona Viva. Pros: chain amenities, close to airport, splendid views. Cons: airport noise. ⊠*Av. Las Américas 9–08, Zona 13* ☎*2422–5000* 📠*2422–5001* ⊕*www.ichotelsgroup.com* ➦*184 rooms, 17 suites* ♿*In-room: safe, refrigerator (some), Ethernet, Wi-Fi. In-hotel: 2 restaurants, room service, bar, pool, gym, spa, laundry service, airport shuttle, parking (no fee)* ⊟*AE, D, DC, MC, V* ⦿*EP, BP.*

$$$ **Hotel San Carlos.** Formerly the owner's own home, this modest colonial structure puts a little space between you and the bustling Zona Viva. Floor-to-ceiling windows in the reception area look out onto a sunny courtyard dotted with statues. Sloping stairs lead up to the individually decorated rooms. Other rooms in an annex are newer, but they lack the charm of those in the main house. Pros: small hotel with big amenities, lovely rooms in main house. Cons: plain rooms in annex. ⊠*Av. La Reforma 7–89, Zona 10* ☎*2362–9076* 📠*2331–6411* ⊕*www.hsancarlos.com* ➦*20 rooms, 3 suites* ♿*In-room: no a/c, safe, kitchen (some), Wi-Fi. In-hotel: restaurant, bar, pool, no elevator, laun-*

dry service, public Internet, airport shuttle, parking (no fee) ⊟*AE, MC, V* ⏉*CB.*

$$ ⬚**Best Western Stofella.** For those who feel more at home in smaller hotels, Stofella is a real find. A short staircase leads to a flower-filled reception area. Charming rooms have small sitting areas. Ask for one of the original rooms, as those added during a recent renovation lack character. If you're feeling social, join the other guests in the cozy bar. **Pros:** close to action, chain amenities, no high-rise feel. **Cons:** no Wi-Fi. ⊠*2 Av. 12–28, Zona 10* ☎*2410–8600* 🖷*2410–8606* ⊕*www.best-western.com* ⤶*70 rooms* ⬧*In-room: safe, Ethernet. In-hotel: restaurant, room service, bar, gym, laundry service, public Internet, parking (no fee)* ⊟*AE, D, DC, MC, V* ⏉*CB.*

$$ ⬚**La Casa Grande.** This stately hotel is one of the best options in the New City. You enter through iron gates then step into a small reception area that leads to a comfortable lounge with a fireplace to keep out the chill. The restaurant spills out into the courtyard; its cast-iron chairs are surrounded by arches covered with dangling philodendrons. Traditional tile floors grace the rooms, which are furnished with antiques. Rooms in the front open onto a balcony, but those in the back are quieter. Pros: big amenities, intimate. Cons: no Wi-Fi. ⊠*Av. La Reforma 7–67, Zona 10* ☎*2332–0914* ⊕*www.casagrande-gua.com* ⤶*28 rooms* ⬧*In-room: no a/c (some). In-hotel: restaurant, bar, no elevator, laundry service, public Internet, parking (no fee)* ⊟*AE, D, DC, MC, V.*

$$ ⬚**Hotel Ciudad Vieja.** In a sector of the city with few budget lodgings, the Ciudad Vieja, a few blocks north of the Zona Viva, counts as a real find. Two floors of rooms are arranged around a lovely, elongated garden, with small restaurant situated at one end of the courtyard. Rooms are spacious and pleasantly furnished with two queen-size beds each. Pros: good value, friendly staff. Cons: several blocks from Zona Viva. ⊠*8 C. 3–67, Zona 10* ☎*2331–9104* ⊕*www.hotelciudadvieja.com* ⤶*26 rooms* ⬧*In-room: no a/c, Wi-Fi. In-hotel: restaurant, room service, bar, no elevator, laundry service, public Internet, parking (no fee)* ⊟*AE, D, DC, MC, V* ⏉*BP.*

THE OLD CITY

$$ ⬚**Pan American.** The grande dame of downtown hotels, the Pan Ameri-
★ can was for many years the most luxurious lodging in town. To step into the dark-wood lobby of this former mansion is to leave the confusion of the city behind. A covered courtyard with attractive wrought-iron chandeliers spills out from the restaurant, whose servers wear traditional highland dress. The rooms are small but attractive, with tile floors, handmade rugs and bedspreads, and walls adorned with traditional paintings. Pros: lively restaurant, good value. Cons: small rooms, slight mustiness. ⊠*9 C. 5–63, Zona 1* ☎*2232–6807* 🖷*2232–6402* ⊕*www.hotelpanamerican.com.gt* ⤶*51 rooms* ⬧*In-room: no a/c, Wi-Fi. In-hotel: restaurant, concierge, laundry service, public Internet, airport shuttle, parking (no fee)* ⊟*AE, DC, MC, V.*

$ ⬚**Fortuna Royal.** This hotel has succeeded where few others have by offering stylish accommodations for a reasonable rate, making it a

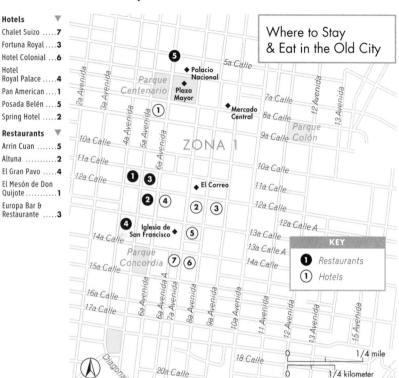

favorite of Central American business travelers who don't have big expense accounts. The marble-floor lobby gives way to rooms with plush carpeting and cheery floral wallpaper. To top it off, everything is immaculately clean. Pros: good value. Cons: small rooms. ⊠*12 C. 8–42, Zona 1* ☎*2238–2484* 🖷*2220–5998* ⊕*www.hotelfortunaroyal. com* ↰*21 rooms* ⌂*In-room: no a/c. In-hotel: restaurant, room service, bar, public Internet, parking (no fee)* ☰*AE, D, DC, MC, V.*

$ 🖫**Hotel Colonial.** It occupies a lovely 19th-century house, but this hotel isn't quite as charming inside. However, the reception area overlooks an enclosed patio overflowing with potted plants, and the lounge is furnished with reproductions of antiques. The rooms all have colonial-style furnishings; some of the larger ones have very nice views. Pros: lovely garden, quiet street. Cons: plainly decorated rooms. ⊠*7 Av. 14–19, Zona 1* ☎*2232–6722* 🖷*2232–8671* ⊕*www.hotelcolonial. net* ↰*42 rooms* ⌂*In-room: no a/c. In-hotel: parking (no fee)* ☰*AE, DC, MC, V.*

$ 🖫**Hotel Royal Palace.** This diamond-in-the-rough hotel is a welcome retreat from the frantic pace of the streets outside. A tile fountain reminiscent of Andalusia is the centerpiece of the courtyard. The rooms are slightly musty but are nevertheless comfortable and quiet. Ask for one with a view of 6 Avenida—it's a great way to view the action without having to fight the crowds. Pros: comfortable, good value, yesteryear

SAFE AND SECURE IN THE OLD CITY

The congested streets of Zona 1 have a reputation, not completely undeserved, for being unsafe—many visitors avoid downtown Guatemala City entirely—but with a few precautions and a lot of common sense, you can visit or stay in the historic center with minimal worry. A few hours should suffice to see the Old City sights, depending on the time spent in the Mercado Central labyrinth. Here are some tips:

■ **Ask hotel personnel for the lay of the land.** If you're staying in the city center, get that valuable where-to-go and where-not-to-go advice from those who work at your hotel. They know the neighborhood better than anybody.

■ **Carry as little as possible.** The standard no-flashy-jewelry, minimal-cash, well-hidden money-belt advice

applies. Carry a photocopy of the pertinent pages of your passport, and leave the original in your hotel safe if possible.

■ **Walk purposefully.** Look like you know where you're going, even if you're hopelessly lost. Standing on a street corner with a puzzled look and your open Fodor's guide brands you as a tourist. Pop into a store or other public interior to get your bearings and ask for directions if you need to. Your best bet is to duck into the cathedral, sit in a pew and map out your route (and perhaps get a bit of divine guidance).

■ **Take taxis, especially at night.** Whether you're staying or just visiting here, at night, travel by cab, even for very short distances. Your hotel or restaurant will be happy to call one for you.

ambience. Cons: some street noise, rooms could use paint job. ⊠*6 Av. 12–66, Zona 1* ☎*2220–8970* ☐*2220–8975* ⊕*www.hotelroyalpalace. com* ⤳*76 rooms* ☖*In-hotel: restaurant, bar, gym, concierge, public Internet, airport shuttle, parking (no fee)* ☐*MC, V.*

$ ▦**Posada Belén.** This little bed-and-breakfast on a quiet side street is

Fodor'sChoice   exceptional thanks to the couple that runs it. Built in 1873, the family's
★   former home has been renovated just enough to combine old-world charm with modern comfort. Rooms have tile floors, handwoven bedspreads, and walls decorated with Guatemalan paintings and weavings. A small but impressive collection of Mayan artifacts graces the dining room. Family-style meals are made to order by the owners, who are also a great source of information about the city. ■TIP→**You get a slight discount on the already reasonable rates if you pay in cash.** Pros: knowledgeable staff, pretty garden, quiet street. Cons: some noise from courtyard. ⊠*13 C. A 10–30, Zona 1* ☎*2253–4530* ☐*2251–3478* ⊕*www. posadabelen.com* ⤳*10 rooms* ☖*In-room: no a/c, no phone, safe, no TV. In-hotel: airport shuttle, parking (no fee)* ☐*AE, DC, MC, V.*

¢–$ ▦**Chalet Suizo.** This quiet hotel has been popular with budget travelers for more than 40 years. An attractive central courtyard behind the reception area is a great place to relax. Facing a series of smaller courtyards, the rooms are all fairly plain. The staff is friendly and will happily store your extra luggage while you travel around the country. Pros: knowledgeable staff, good value, great place to meet fellow travelers. Cons: small rooms, lack of decor. ⊠*7 Av. 14–34, Zona 1* ☎*2251–3786*

🖷2232–0429 ✎*chaletsuizo@tur-bonett.com* ⮒*25 rooms, 15 with bath* ⟁*In-room: no a/c, no phone, no TV. In-hotel: restaurant, laundry facilities, parking (no fee)* ▤*AE, D, DC, MC, V.*

¢–$ 🖵**Spring Hotel.** Most rooms here face a pleasant courtyard with cast-iron tables and chairs and lots of greenery. Several on the 2nd floor share a balcony that overlooks the avenue. A small café behind the courtyard is a great place to relax after a day of exploring the city. Next door is a refuge for street children, so keep your eyes open for those tempted to pickpocket a less-than-alert tourist. Pros: lovely courtyard, friendly café. Cons: street noise. ✉*8 Av. 12–65, Zona 1* 🖷*2230–2858* 🖷*2232–0107* ✎*hotelspring@hotmail.com* ⮒*39 rooms, 32 with bath* ⟁*In-room: no a/c, no phone, safe. In-hotel: parking (no fee)* ▤*MC, V.*

NIGHTLIFE & THE ARTS

The Zona Viva is the city's nightlife center, offering everything from bars (sedate or lively) to noisy discos. Strolling the streets is especially entertaining, as people come here to see and be seen. Dress codes have been implemented by some of the nicer places, which generally means men must wear dress shoes to be admitted. Expect lines at the most popular places.

Old City nightspots have more character than those in the New City, so they shouldn't be passed up just because the area isn't the greatest. Never walk alone at night, especially south of 15 Calle. Pick a place you want to visit, take a taxi there, and have your hotel or restaurant call one to take you back.

THE ARTS

As Spain is Guatemala's mother country, its **Centro Cultural de España** (✉*24 C. 3–81, Zona 1* 🖷*2232–4041* ⊕*www.centroculturalespana.com.gt*) keeps up an active Spanish-language calendar of music, art, theater, and lectures, with something going on several nights a week.

The city's cultural venue par excellence, the **Centro Cultural Miguel Ángel Asturias** (✉*24 C. 3–81, Zona 1* 🖷*2232–4041*) has an active program of music, dance, and theater presentations by national and international groups. Most large shows are held at its Teatro Nacional; smaller presentations take place at the complex's smaller theaters. Loosely affiliated with the U.S. embassy, the **Instituto Guatemalteco Americano** (✉*1 Ruta 4–05, Zona 4* 🖷*2422–5555* ⊕*www.iga.edu*) presents an active calendar of cultural offerings by Guatemalan and international groups.

NIGHTLIFE

BARS

THE NEW CITY Like its namesake 1980s television show, friendly **Cheers** (⊠ *13 C. 0–40, Zona 10* ☎*2368–2089*) draws a friendly crowd, mostly for the sporting events being show on the big-screen TVs. The **Brass Beer Company** (⊠ *3 Av. 12–48, Zona 10* ☎*2332–3329*) serves a variety of excellent microbrews to a mellow crowd. Despite its name, **William Shakespeare Pub** (⊠ *13 C. and 1 Av., Zona 10* ☎*2331–2641*) doesn't exactly evoke an English pub, but is a convivial place to stop for a drink.

A branch of the outlet by the same name in Antigua, **Frida's** (⊠ *3 Av. 14–60, Zona 10* ☎*2367–1611*) is a place to knock back a margarita with a few friends with prints by Mexican artists Frida Kahlo and Diego Rivera as backdrop. **Giuseppe Verdi** (⊠ *Westin Camino Real, 14 C. at Av. La Reforma, Zona 10* ☎*2333–3000*) is an upscale bar that caters mostly to tourists.

We like **Kloster** (⊠ *13 C. 2–75, Zona 10* ☎*2334–3882*), a German *oom-pah-pah* kind of place with a variety of fondues as well as tasty microbrews. Throw a few (and throw down a few) at **Boliche's Fun Plaza** (⊠ *Blvd. Los Próceres 26–55, Zona 10* ☎*2366–3956*), which is, as far as we know, Guatemala City's only bar-slash-bowling alley.

THE OLD CITY A sporting event, local or U.S., is always on the big-screen TV at low-key expat hangout **Europa Bar & Restaurante** (⊠ *11 C. 5–16, Zona 1* ☎*2253–4929*).

CLUBS

THE NEW CITY A fun crowd heads to **Salambo** (⊠ *1 Av. 13–70, Zona 10* ☎*2366–5096*), where the ambience—Thursday through Sunday—is decadently campy.

THE OLD CITY If you feel like dancing, go to **El Gazevo** (⊠ *6 C. 3–07, Zona 1* ☎*2230–2660*).

GAY & LESBIAN

Guatemala City's same-sex scene is hidden, discreet, and changes frequently. Nearly all the venues are in the Old City. They're all frequented by an under-30 crowd.

THE OLD CITY A lively, young gay crowd frequents **Black & White** (⊠ *11 C. 2–54, Zona 1* ☎*5904–1758*) Wednesday through Sunday night, and there always seem to be drink specials on tap.

The mellow **Café del Arco** (⊠ *12 C. 8–52, Zona 1* ☎*2232–5527*) serves light, café-style food to a mixed clientele, nightly except Sunday. A mixed gay-lesbian group frequents **El Encuentro** (⊠ *5 Av. 10–52, Zona 1* ☎*2232–9235*) every night of the week, save Sunday.

A mostly male crowd dances Wednesday through Sunday nights away quite wildly at **Ephebus** (⊠ *4 C. 5–30, Zona 1* ☎*2253–4119*). A mixed gay-lesbian-straight clientele hits the dance floor at **Karma** (⊠ *11 C. 5–27, Zona 1* ☎*No phone*), Wednesday through Sunday night.

LIVE MUSIC

THE NEW CITY Attracting an international crowd, **Sesto Senso** (⊠*2 Av. 12–81, Zona 10* ☎*2361–6987*) offers live music ranging from Guatemalan folk to American pop.

THE OLD CITY If you're looking for something a little different, **La Bodeguita del Centro** (⊠*12 C. 3–55, Zona 1* ☎*2230–2976*) draws an intellectual crowd with its live music and poetry readings.

> **GIMME A KISS**
>
> If you're here on an extended language-study trip, you might get a bit homesick. Tune in to Guatemala City's KISS-FM, which broadcasts in English and plays a steady diet of U.S. and British pop hits, present and past, at 97.7 FM.

SHOPPING

With the exception of the big market in the Old City, shop hours are weekdays 9 to 1 and 3 to 7, Saturday 9 to 1. The midday break is gradually disappearing in the capital.

ART

THE NEW CITY Works by contemporary Guatemalan painters are on display at **El Ático** (⊠*4 Av. 15–45, Zona 14* ☎*2368–0853*). **Galería Ríos** (⊠*C. Montúfar 0–85, Zona 9* ☎*2331–7071*), in the Centro Commercial Plaza, has a good selection of works by local artists. **Sol de Río** (⊠*5 Av. 10–22, Zona 9* ☎*2334–1377*) is a small, but well worth a visit.

BOOKS

THE NEW CITY The gift shop at **Museo Popol Vuh** (⊠*End of 6 C., Zona 10* ☎*2338–7896*) has an interesting collection of books on art, archaeology, and history.

English In the Zona Viva, **Sophos** (⊠*Av. La Reforma 13–89, Zona 10* ☎*2334–6797* ⊕*www.sophosenlinea.com*) is one of the best places in the city to find books in English (as well as German and French), and comes closest to capturing that Borders- or Barnes & Noble–bookstore aura, although on a smaller scale. Grab a cup of coffee while you peruse the shelves, or enjoy it in the front courtyard. For those here on a longer sojourn, the **Instituto Guatemalteco Americano** (⊠*1 Ruta 4–05, Zona 4* ☎*2422–5555*) has an extensive lending library of English-language titles. **Boomarks/Etc. Ediciones** (⊠*6 Av. 12–35, Zona 10* ☎*2332–4935*) has a decent selection of English-language books, with an emphasis on politics and history. There are many children's books on the shelves, too. **Geminis** (⊠*3 Av. 17–05, Zona 14* ☎*2366–1031*) sells recent English-language titles.

Spanish Although the selection at **Artemis Edinter** (⊠*12 C. 1–25, Zona 10* ☎*2335–2649*) is entirely in Spanish, you'll find many beautiful coffee-table books on Guatemala here, as well as a nice selection of kids' books for that child on your list who is learning Spanish.

HANDICRAFTS

■ TIP→ **A number of stores east of Avenida La Reforma sell handmade goods.**

THE NEW CITY **In-Nola** (✉*18 C. 21–31, Zona 10* ☎*2367–2424* ⊕*www.in-nola.com*)
★ specializes in textiles, but you'll also find wool and leather items. It's your best bet if you only have time to pop into one shop. **Topis Cerámica** (✉ *Blvd. Los Próceres and 8 Av., Zona 10* ☎*2337–3838*) has a fine selection of pottery by artists from Antigua. **Típicos Reforma Utatlán** (✉*14 C. 7–77, Zona 13* ☎*2232–7008*) has an excellent selection of textiles made in highland villages.

Goods from highland artisans can be found at the **Mercado de Artesanías** (✉*Blvd. Juan Pablo II, Zona 13* ☎*2472–0208*). The spacious **San Remo** (✉*14 C. 7–61, Zona 9* ☎*2334–1388*) has a wide variety of handcrafted items.

The elegant **Casa Solares** (✉*Av. La Reforma 11–07, Zona 10*) is pricey, but you can be certain that you are buying the best-quality goods. In addition to *artesanía,***Colección 21** (✉*12 C. 4–65, Zona 14* ☎*2368–1659*) has an art gallery featuring works by local painters. **Cerámicas Decorativas Artesanales** (✉*1 Av. 12–41, Zona 10* ☎*2334–1160*) sells hand-crafted tiles in colonial or contemporary style.

THE OLD CITY If you're in the market for *típica,* roughly translated as "typical goods," head to **Mercado Central** (✉*8 C. and 8 Av., Zona 1* ☎*No phone*). **Lin-Canola** (✉*5 C. 9–60, Zona 1* ☎*2253–0138*) has an excellent selection of típica and other wares. The prices are often inexpensive.

JEWELRY

THE NEW CITY **Esmeralda** (✉ *Westin Camino Real, 14 C. and Av. La Reforma, Zona 10* ☎*2333–3000*) specializes in settings of the precious green stone. **Jades** (✉ *Westin Camino Real, 14 C. and Av. La Reforma, Zona 10* ☎*2368–3689* ✉ *Marriott, 7 Av. 15–45, Zona 9* ☎*2339–7777*), the well-known jewelry shop in Antigua, has two branches in the Zona Viva.

L'Elegance (✉ *Westin, Camino Real, 14 C. and Av. La Reforma, Zona 10* ☎*2333–3000*) sells exquisitely crafted silver trays, vases, jewelry boxes, and place settings by the Italian Camusso family. In addition to jewelry, **Albuhi** (✉*20 C. 25–96, Zona 10* ☎*2368–3842*) has a terrific selection of picture frames, plates, candlesticks, and religious articles crafted from Guatemalan pewter.

LEATHER

THE NEW CITY **Arpiel** (✉*Av. La Reforma 15–54, Zona 9* ☎*2331–5097* ✉*Av. Las Américas 7–20, Zona 13*) has reasonably priced leather goods. **Príncipe de Gales** (✉*2 C. 16–28, Zona 15* ☎*2369–6802*) sells clothing, including hand-tailored leather items.

THE OLD CITY **Piel Kabal** (✉*10 Av. 16–24, Zona 1* ☎*2238–3600*) sells custom-made leather jackets.

LANGUAGE SCHOOLS IN GUATEMALA CITY

Guatemala City doesn't immediately leap to mind when contemplating Spanish instruction, but the city offers a number of fine language institutes. Reflecting the large number of business travelers who come to the capital, you'll see a higher percentage of such enrollees among the student population at schools here.

■ **Academia Easy** (✉ *14 Av. 13–68, Zona 10* ☎ *2337–3970* ⊕ *www. easyfacil.com)..*

■ **Academia Europa** (✉ *15 C. 2–64, Zona 10* ☎ *2363–5025* ⊕ *www.aca-demia-europa.com)..*

■ **Berlitz** (✉ *Av. La Reforma 7–62, Zona 10* ☎ *2362–4444* ⊕ *www. berlitz-ca.net)..*

■ **Centro de Idiomas Oxford** (✉ *20 C. 23–59, Zona 10* ☎ *2368–1332* ⊕ *www.olcenglish.com)..*

■ **Instituto Guatemalteco Americano** (✉ *Ruta 1 4–05, Zona 4* ☎ *2422–5555* ⊕ *www.iga.edu)..*

■ **Universidad de San Carlos** (✉ *Av. La Reforma 0–63, Zona 10* ☎ *2331–0904* ⊕ *www.usac.edu.gt)..*

DAY TRIP FROM GUATEMALA CITY

The lovely colonial city of Antigua remains the most popular day excursion from Guatemala City for tourists and residents alike—the latter head out especially on weekends, many to attend weddings in Guatemala's most popular wedding locale. (We admit that the majority of international visitors stay in Antigua and make the capital their day trip instead.) The Mayan ruins of Mixco Viejo lie 60 km (36 mi) north of the capital and make an easy, do-it-yourself trip if you have a vehicle. Many operators lead ascents to the Volcán Pacaya south of the city. Although many people do this excursion on their own, we recommend going with an organized tour for safety reasons, both criminal and volcanic. *(See Antigua's Volcanoes box, in Chapter 2.)*

Tourist attractions around the country can be your excursions, thanks to numerous tour operators who offer organized trips. Antigua and Mixco Viejo are among the offerings, as are day trips to Lake Atitlán. Chichicastenango appears on the tour lists on Thursday and Sunday market days. (Most Chichi trips include a stop at the lake.) Operators organize day excursions from the capital farther afield to the Mayan ruins at Copán, Honduras, or to Guatemala's very own Tikal in El Petén. Flying is the only way to do Tikal in one day (although it's preferable to overnight at the ruins). The flight takes less than one hour, as compared to 10 hours overland.

MIXCO VIEJO

North of Guatemala City lie the 12th-century Mayan ruins of Mixco Viejo. The mountaintop site, thought to be largely ceremonial, was one of the last Mayan sites to fall to Pedro de Alvarado and the conquistadors in 1525. Excavation began on the site's 120 structures in 1954.

Temples and palaces make up Mixco Viejo, but most notably, it contains several ball courts used in the Mayan ballgame of *pitziil*, a game with many variations seen throughout pre-Columbian indigenous civilizations. (Historians today group the games under the general heading *ulama*, a Nahuatl word meaning simply "ballgame.") Objectively, it resembled a mix of soccer and volleyball, but for the Maya, pitziil transcended mere sport, providing a cosmic link between mortals and gods, between past and future.

Mixco Viejo is no Tikal or Quiriguá, but it's a favored destination for weekend visitors from the capital who come for the splendid views of the surrounding countryside. A small museum documents the history of the site. ⊠*60 km (36 mi) north of Guatemala City* 🕾*No phone* 🎫*Q20* 🕙*Daily 7–4:30.*

GUATEMALA CITY ESSENTIALS

TRANSPORTATION

BY AIR
Most international flights into Guatemala head to the newly renovated Aeropuerto Internacional La Aurora (GUA). International airlines serving the airport are American, Continental, Copa, Cubana, Delta, Iberia, Mexicana, Spirit Air, Taca, United, and US Airways.

Domestic airlines Inter Regional (a division of Taca) and TAG fly between the capital and Aeropuerto Internacional Mundo Maya outside the twin towns of Flores and Santa Elena in El Petén.

TO & FROM THE AIRPORT   Less than a mile from the New City, Aeropuerto Internacional La Aurora is convenient if a bit too close. A taxi from the airport to Zonas 9 or 10 runs Q60 to Q80—drivers gladly accept dollars if you haven't had a chance to change money. Minivan shuttles to Antigua, less than one hour away, meet most flights, too. You pay a Q30 airport tax upon departure.

Domestic Carriers **Inter Regional** (🕾*2332-6034* ⊕*www.taca.com*). **TAG** (🕾*2360-3038* ⊕*www.tag.com.gt*).

International Carriers **American** (🕾*2422-0000* ⊕*www.aa.com*). **Continental** (🕾*2385-9610* ⊕*www.continental.com*). **Copa** (🕾*2385-5555* ⊕*www.copaair.com*). **Cubana** (🕾*2361-0857*). **Delta** (🕾*2360-7954* ⊕*www.delta.com*). **Iberia** (🕾*2332-0911* ⊕*www.iberia.com*). **Mexicana** (🕾*2333-6001* ⊕*www.mexicana.com*). **Taca** (🕾*2470-8222* ⊕*www.taca.com*). **United** (🕾*2336-9900* ⊕*www.ual.com*). **US Airways** (🕾*2970-0880*).

Contacts **Aeropuerto Internacional La Aurora** (🕾*2331-8392*).

BY BUS
TO & FROM GUATEMALA CITY   The *terminal de buses,* or main bus station, is in Zona 4. From here you can catch a bus to almost anywhere in the country. Autobuses de Oriente has service to the Atlantic Lowlands, Las Verapaces, and El Petén. Transgalgos travels to the highlands.

Some companies run small mini-vans, which are a much more comfortable way to travel. Atitrans, Autobuses de Oriente, Transportes Express, and Turansa, offer shuttle service to most cities.

Information Atitrans (☎ 7832–3371 ⊕ www.atitrans.com). **Autobuses de Oriente** (☎ 2238–3894). **Transgalgos** (☎ 232–3661 or 220–6018). **Transportes Express** (☎ 2431–5500). **Turansa** (☎ 7832–2928).

WITHIN GUATEMALA CITY Guatemala's network of red public buses logs dozens of thefts (and a few armed robberies) each day. Your chances as an outsider of escaping unscathed are slim, so we advise against using the system. Taxis are plentiful and reasonably priced; take them instead. The exception to the "no bus" rule is the TransMetro, a system of green public buses that travel on special lanes and stop at fixed stations with ample security. The first line opened in 2007; however, it runs a route through Zonas 1, 3, 8, 11, and 12, where visitors are not likely to find themselves. More routes are in the works at this writing.

THE NEW GUA

Visitors to Guatemala during recent years have endured utter chaos at the capital's La Aurora International Airport (airport code = GUA) as they weaved through mazes of tarp-covered construction. The payoff came at the end of 2007 as one of Central America's tiniest airports was reborn thanks to a $30 million makeover—spacious check-in areas, more and larger boarding gates, new shops and restaurants, and a capacity to handle triple the number of flights are the happy result.

BY CAR

Driving in Guatemala City is a headache. You can expect narrow streets jammed with traffic at just about any time of day. Things get better once you move out of the center of the city, and the narrow streets give way to broad boulevards. Drives to nearby destinations like Antigua, for example, can be quite pleasant.

■ TIP→ Vehicle break-ins are common in the capital, so park in a guarded lot. All expensive and most moderate hotels have protected parking areas. Avoid leaving anything of value in the car.

CAR RENTAL If you're not intimidated by Guatemala City's winding mountain roads, renting a car is a great way to see the countryside. There are several international agencies at Aeropuerto Internacional La Aurora and in the New City. Reputable local companies include Ahorrent, Tabarini, and Tikal.

Local Agencies Ahorrent (✉ 13 C. 2–02, Zona 9 ☎ 2383–2800 ⊕ www.ahorrent. com). **Avis** (✉ 6 C. 7–64, Zona 9 ☎ 2339–3249 ⊕ www.avis.com). **Budget** (✉ 6 Av. 11–24, Zona 9 ☎ 2332–7744 ⊕ www.budgetguatemala.com.gt). **Hertz** (✉ Av. Hincupié 11–01, Zona 13 ☎ 2470–3710 ⊕ www.hertz.com). **National** (✉ 12 C. Montúfar 7–69, Zona 9 ☎ 2360–2030 ✐ national@intelnet.net.gt). **Tabarini** (✉ 2 C. A 7–30, Zona 10 ☎ 2331–2643 ⊕ www.tabarini.com). **Tikal** (✉ 2 C. 6–56, Zona 10 ☎ 2332–4721 ⊕ www.tikalrentacar.com).

TAXIS Taxis can be found waiting at hotels and intersections or can be flagged down on the street. Most do not have meters, so negotiate a price before getting in. We recommend having your hotel or restaurant call a taxi for you at night—establishments are happy to do it—and that you use the services of a cab even if you're only going a short distance. Within a single zone, a ride should cost Q20 to Q25; between zones expect to pay Q30 to Q50.

CONTACTS **Amarillo Express** (☎ 2470–1515). **Las Américas** (☎ 2362–0583). **Verde Express** (☎ 2475–9595). **Yellow-Car** (☎ 2437–4824).

CONTACTS & RESOURCES

EMERGENCY

Emergency Services The ever-present Meykos chain has reputable pharmacies all over the city. Both Centro Médico and Hospital Herrera Llerandi have English-speaking staff and are accustomed to dealing with foreigners. The Red Cross (*Cruz Roja* in Spanish) serves as an ambulance and rescue service.

Cruz Roja (☎ 125). **Fire** (☎ 122). **Police** (☎ 120).

Hospitals **Centro Médico** (✉ 6 Av. 3–47, Zona 10 ☎ 2279–4949 ⊕ www.centro-medico.com.gt). **Hospital Herrera Llerandi** (✉ 6 Av. 8–71, Zona 10 ☎ 2384–5959 ⊕ www.herrerallerandi.com).

Pharmacies **Meykos** (✉ 18 C. 25–76, Zona 10 ☎ 2363–5903 ✉ 6 Av. 5–01, Zona 9 ☎ 2385–1504 ⊕ www.meykos.com).

MAIL & SHIPPING

El Correo, the country's postal service, is improving all the time, and is fine for postcards and letters. To ship important packages, use DHL, FedEx, or UPS. All have offices in the New City.

Overnight Services **UPS** (✉ 12 C. 5–53, Zona 10 ☎ 2421–6000). **DHL** (✉ 12 C. 5–12, Zona 10 ☎ 2339–8400). **FedEx** (✉ 14 Av. 7–12, Bodega 20, Zona 14 ☎ 2366–8536).

Post Offices **El Correo** (✉ 7 Av. 12–11, Zona 1 ☎ 2232–6101).

MONEY MATTERS

You can exchange currency or traveler's checks at almost any bank in Guatemala City. Banquetzal is one of many banks with numerous branches around town, including one at the airport. Baco Agromercantil has a large office on Avenida La Reforma between Zonas 9 and 10. Bancared is Guatemala City's largest network of ATMs with 150 outlets around the city, as well as about 80 around the rest of Guatemala. Several upscale hotels have ATMs on the premises.

Information **Banco Agro Mercantil** (✉ Av. La Reforma, Zona 9 ☎ 2331–1501). **Banquetzal** (✉ Aeropuerto Internacional La Aurora, Zona 13 ☎ 2362–9741).

SAFETY

Guatemala City has a bad reputation, and you do need to be on your guard, but it is really no more dangerous than any other large city in a developing country. To avoid being preyed upon by pickpockets and other unsavory characters, leave expensive jewelry and watches at home, carry purses and camera bags close to your body—or better yet, consider not carrying them at all—take along only as much cash as you need. Carry a photocopy of your passport, leaving the original in your hotel safe. At night stick to well-lighted areas and take taxis, even for very short distances.

TOURS

These reputable major tour operators offer half- and full-day tours of the capital as well as day trips outside the city.

Contacts **Clark Tours** (⊠ 7 Av. 14–76, Zona 9 ☎ 2412–4700 ⊕ www.clarktours. com.gt). **Gray Line Tours** (⊠ 1 Av. 13–22, Zona 10 ☎ 2383–8600 or 2470–3850 ⊕ www.graylineguatemala.com). **Jaguar Tours** (⊠ 13 C. 3–40, Edificio Atlantis, 3rd fl., Zona 10 ☎ 2363–2640). **Maya Expeditions** (⊠ 15 C. A 14–07, Zona 10 ☎ 2363–4955 ⊕ www.mayaexpeditions.com). **Mayabalam** (⊠ 33 Av. A 6–41, Zona 7 ☎ 2439–0343 ⊕ www.mayabalam.com). **Tropical Tours** (⊠ 3 C. A 3–22, Zona 10 ☎ 2339–3662 ⊕ www.tropicaltoursoperador.com). **Turansa** (⊠ Km 15, Carretera Roosevelt, local 69, Zona 11 ☎ 2437–8182 ⊕ www.turansa.com). **Unitours** (⊠ 7 Av. 7–91, Zona 4 ☎ 2230–0696 ✎ unitours@infovia.com.gt).

VISITOR INFORMATION

Inguat, Guatemala's ever-helpful government tourism office, is open weekdays 8 to 4 and has an information desk in the lobby of its building in Zona 4. The airport office stays open daily 6 AM to midnight.

Information **Inguat** (⊠ 7 Av. 1–17, Zona 4 ☎ 2421–2800 or 801/494–8281 ✉ Aeropuerto Internacional La Aurora, Zona 13 ☎ 2331–4256 ⊕ www.visit-guatemala.com).

Antigua

WORD OF MOUTH

"The colonial architecture, the volcanos, the church ruins, the hidden courtyard gardens, the hip international restaurants and bar scene—Antigua was hopping. We had dinner at Casa Santa Domingo; it was pretty good. The hotel is beautiful; almost too beautiful in a Disney-esque way. My tipple of choice was Zacapa rum. Incredible."

—Carta_Pisana

"On the central park in Antigua there's a little row of shops. In the middle there's a bookstore. If you go in . . . and . . . wander out through the back door you will have a surprise: a darling garden/fountain area with . . . a great little café. Antigua is full of these beautiful little hidden gardens."

—Suzie2

www.fodors.com/forums

FILLED WITH VESTIGES OF ITS colonial past—cobblestone streets, enchanting squares, and deserted convents—Antigua, one of Latin America's loveliest cities, instantly transports you back hundreds of years to when the Spanish ruled this land. The city lost out on its role as colonial capital in the late 18th century, and yet with the reverence shown here to the past, you may think *Antigüeños* don't realize that era is over. No matter—Antigua likely relishes its role as the capital of Guatemalan tourism far more.

Today you'll find a mountainside enclave that is vastly more pleasant than Guatemala City. At a1,530-meter (5,019-foot) altitude, its pleasant climate lives up to that oft-repeated boast that Guatemala is the land of eternal spring. Antigua is also a favored escape for wealthy Guatemalans and its higher prices mean that many others cannot afford to live here, so they travel to the city each day to sell their wares. An ever-increasing influx of visitors has brought in some of the country's finest hotels and restaurants, a collection of boutiques and galleries, and several dozen Spanish-language schools that attract students from all over the world.

ORIENTATION & PLANNING

ORIENTATION

Street naming in Antigua's city center, where you'll spend much time, differs slightly from that of other Guatemalan cities. *Avenidas* (avenues) run north–south, beginning with 1 Avenida in the east and increasing in number as you go west. *Calles* (streets) run east and west, beginning with 1 Calle in the north and increasing in number as you go south. Like New York City, avenidas split into *norte* (north) and *sur* (south) at 5 Calle, the Palacio de Capitanes Generales side of the Parque Central. Calles split into *oriente* (east) and *poniente* (west) at 4 Avenida, the cathedral side of Parque Central. Building numbering begins for both at these dividing points and continues sequentially until the street's end without regard to blocks. Numbers on one side of the street increase independently of those on the opposite side, meaning that the 40s sequence might be across the street from the 20s. Take heart: the complex system does make some sense once you see it yourself.

PLANNING

WHEN TO GO

A distinct division between rainy (November to April) and dry (May to October) seasons makes winter and spring months the ideal time to be in Antigua. This is also prime time for Antigua's many religious observances, the most famous of which is Semana Santa (March or April). Holy Week brings a series of daylong vigils, processions, and reenactments of Christ's last days in Jerusalem. You'll see Roman centurions charging through the streets on horseback, boulevards carpeted with colored sawdust and flowers, and immense hand-carried floats wend-

A BIT OF HISTORY

Founded in 1543, the city was christened *La Muy Noble y Muy Leal Ciudad de Santiago de los Caballeros de Goathemala* ("The Very Noble and Very Loyal City of St. James of the Knights of Guatemala"), named for the apostle St. James, the patron saint of the conquistadors. For more than 200 years it administered a region that stretched from Mexico's Yucatán peninsula south to Costa Rica. Along with Lima and Mexico City, Antigua was one of the grandest cities of the Americas.

By the late 18th century the city had been decimated by earthquakes several times. Because it was a major political, religious, and intellectual center—it had 32 churches, 18 convents and monasteries, 7 colleges, 5 hospitals, and a university—it was always rebuilt. Powerful tremors struck again in late 1773, reducing much of the city's painstakingly restored elegance to rubble. The government reluctantly relocated to a supposedly safer site 45 km (28 mi) east, where Guatemala City now stands. The now-former capital became *La Antigua Guatemala* ("the old Guatemala"), still its official name.

Ironically, it is because Antigua was abandoned that it retains so much of its colonial character. Only the poorest inhabitants stayed put after the capital was moved, and being of limited means, they could only repair the old structures, not tear them down or build new ones. In the 1960s laws took effect that limited commercial development and required what development did occur to keep within the city's colonial character. The National Council for the Protection of Antigua Guatemala was formed in 1972 to restore the ruins, maintain the monuments, and rid the city of such modern intrusions as billboards and neon signs. Restoration projects, both private and public, have transformed Antigua into Guatemala's most popular tourist destination.

ing their way through throngs of onlookers. ■ TIP→ **Make reservations months in advance if you plan to be here for Semana Santa.**

Antigua's tourist population increases dramatically on weekends as Guatemala City residents head out from the capital to their favorite destination. The city fits nicely into the beginning or end of your trip. Its proximity to Guatemala City's La Aurora International Airport makes it a good first or last place to visit.

WHAT TO DO

Few places in the Americas hold such a repository of colonial architecture. Some still serve their original purpose, whereas others have morphed into hotels, restaurants, and shops. Still others stand magnificently in ruins. If ever there were a place you could overdose on history, Antigua is it. Avoid the temptation to rush from church to convent to monastery to palace and off to another church, all in one morning. (You'll see dazed tour groups doing exactly that.) Build in some downtime and delight in the small things (ice cream, music, or shoe shines) that make this one of the hemisphere's most special places. (*See Antigua, Antigüeño Style box, below.*)

RESTAURANTS & CUISINE

Like Guatemala City, but on a smaller scale, Antigua assembles a mix of regional and international cuisines into its restaurant scene. Few other cities pack such a variety into a 10-block-by-10-block area. Here's good rule of thumb: expensive restaurants line the streets east of the city's Parque Central. Less pricey options line those west of the park.

ABOUT THE HOTELS

The old parlor game of guessing what lies behind Antigua's walls—buildings directly front sidewalks with nary a hint of what lies behind the gate—could apply to the city's hotels, too. (One of our favorite Antigua lodgings has a wooden gate in serious need of a coat of paint, but unimagined elegance lurks behind.) Inside all, you'll find rooms arranged around a central garden in the old colonial style. Most newly constructed hotels are also arranged thus. As with restaurants, more expensive hotels line the streets east of Parque Central. ■ TIP→ **Few lodgings offer air-conditioning, but you'll rarely miss it here.** Most hotels raise rates Friday and Saturday night, since Antigua is a popular weekend tourist destination for Guatemalans. Expect lodging rates to go up by 50% during Christmas and Holy Week.

GETTING AROUND

With limited parking and a majority of hotels, restaurants, and sights in a small area, Antigua is a quintessential walking city. If you have a vehicle, leave it in your hotel's parking lot (most upscale lodgings offer parking). We recommend taking a taxi after 9 PM. Have your hotel or restaurant call one for you at night.

EXPLORING

WHAT TO SEE

🔟 **Arco de Santa Catalina.** The only remnant of the once-enormous Con-
★ vent of St. Catherine is this beautiful yellow arch that spans 5 Avenida Norte, a street locals call Calle de Santa Catalina. The convent was founded in 1613 with only four nuns, but by 1693 its growing numbers forced it to expand across the street. The arch was built to allow the sisters to pass from one side to the other unseen. ⊠ *5 Av. Norte and 2 C. Poniente* ☎ *7832–0184* 💲 *Q30.*

⑥ **Casa Popenoe.** A short loop through this beautifully restored colonial mansion takes you through courtyards and several rooms containing decorative items, including original oil paintings, fine ceramic dishes, and other items that have been in the house since its original construction in 1636. An English-speaking guide is usually available. Since this is a private home, hours are limited. ⊠ *1 Av. Sur 2* ☎ *7832–1767* 💲 *Q10, under 10 free* ☉ *Mon.–Sat. 2–4.*

🔞 **Casa del Tejido Antigüo.** This is the place to come for background information on the rainbow of textiles you'll see when you head out to the highlands. Exhibits present the utilitarian "how it's made" facts, delve into the cultural meaning of the patterns, and show how designs dif-

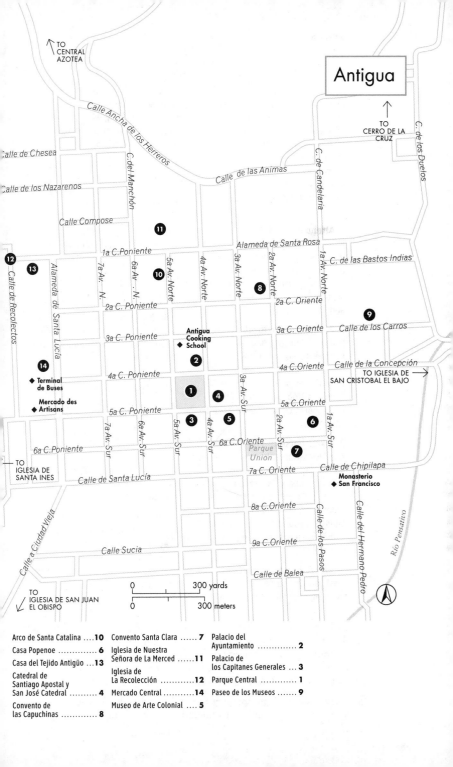

Antigua

↑ TO
CENTRAL
AZOTEA

↑ TO
CERRO DE LA
CRUZ

Calle Ancha de los Herreros

Calle de Chesea

Calle de los Nazarenos

Calle Compose

C. de las Bastos Indias

Calle de las Animas

C. de Candelaria

C. del Manchón

1a C.Poniente

Alameda de Santa Rosa

7a Av. N.

6a Av. - N.

5a Av. Norte

4a Av. Norte

3a Av. Norte

2a Av. Norte

1a Av. Norte

2a C. Poniente

2a C. Oriente

11

12

13

10

8

9

Calle de los Carros

3a C. Poniente

3a C. Oriente

Antigua
Cooking
School

2

4a C.Oriente

Calle de la Concepción
TO IGLESIA DE →
SAN CRISTOBAL EL BAJO

4a C. Poniente

14

◆ Terminal
de Buses

1

4

3a Av. Sur

5a C.Oriente

Mercado des
◆ Artisans

3

5

2a Av. Sur

6

5a C. Poniente

5a Av. Sur

4a Av. Sur

6a C.Oriente

1a Av. Sur

TO
IGLESIA DE
SANTA INES

6a C.Poniente

7a Av. Sur

6a Av. Sur

Parque
Union

7

Calle de Chipilapa

Calle de Santa Lucía

7a C. Oriente

Monasterio
◆ San Francisco

8a C.Oriente

Calle de los Pasos

Calle del Hermano Pedro

Río Pensativo

Calle Sucia

9a C.Oriente

Calle a Ciudad Vieja

Calle de Balea

TO
IGLESIA DE SAN JUAN
EL OBISPO

Alameda de Santa Lucía

Calle de Recolectos

C. de los Duelos

| 0 | | 300 yards |
| 0 | | 300 meters |

Arco de Santa Catalina **10**

Casa Popenoe **6**

Casa del Tejido Antigüo ...**13**

Catedral de
Santiago Apostal y
San José Catedral **4**

Convento de
las Capuchinas **8**

Convento Santa Clara **7**

Iglesia de Nuestra
Señora de La Merced **11**

Iglesia de
La Recolección **12**

Mercado Central **14**

Museo de Arte Colonial **5**

Palacio del
Ayuntamiento **2**

Palacio de
los Capitanes Generales ...**3**

Parque Central **1**

Paseo de los Museos **9**

ANTIGUA, ANTIGÜENO STYLE

The city packs a plethora of monuments into a compact area, but we recommend savoring the city leisurely, the way locals do. (Don't take our suggestions below as a list of items you have to check off.) Remember that most sights close promptly at 5 PM and that some ruins are closed on Sunday and Monday.

1. **Attend mass.** History and religion interlock in Antigua like nowhere else. The city's numerous churches hold mass several times a day, all week long. Even if you aren't Catholic, this is Antigua at its most devout, and well worth a look.

2. **Pay homage to Brother Pedro.** Pedro de San José Betancur, Guatemala's very own saint, is said to intercede on behalf of the faithful who pray at his tomb in the San Francisco Monastery, although we can't guarantee your request will be answered.

3. **Take a horse-drawn carriage ride.** It's a wonderful way to see the city by day. Wagons congregate on the central park. Expect to pay Q200 per hour. Drivers are happy to give running commentary, but speak little English. If you want a tour in your own language, bring along your own guide.

4. **Jockey for the perfect photo position.** The Santa Catalina arch is the symbol of the city; and standing in front of it is the *de rigueur* photo. Your best chance of getting a clear shot is on Sunday, when Avenida 5 Norte, the street running under the arch, is closed to traffic.

5. **Listen to the marimbas.** Music from the buzzing, xylophone-like marimba wafts from restaurants and hotel gardens, or out on the street as small ensembles spontaneously set up shop. Don't forget to leave a coin in their collection bowls for the entertainment.

6. **Scope out a bench in the Parque Central.** Antigua's tree-shaded central park is *the* people-watching venue in the city. You may have to circle benches like a vulture on Sunday when everybody else has the same idea.

7. **Get a shoe shine.** Locals pay Q5 to have their shoes polished to a brilliant shine. You'll likely be asked double that, but don't quibble over price with the kids who approach you in the central park. (They speak little English, but they do know the words "Shoe shine?") It's still a bargain and your shoes will look like new again.

■TIP→ **On the topic of shoes, flimsy soles mean you'll feel every cobblestone press through the bottoms of your feet. Wear something sturdy and comfortable.**

fer from region to region. Prices tend to be higher in the museum gift shop than other places around the country. It's near the central Market, several blocks from the city center; call if you need transportation. ✉*1 C. Poniente 51* ☎*Tourist police: 7832–3169* ⊕*www.casadeltejido.org* 🎫*Q5; under 12, free* ☉ *Weekdays 9–5:30, weekends 9–5.*

❹ **Catedral de Santiago Apóstol y San José Catedral.** Upon your first peek inside, you may wonder why the cathedral of Central America's preeminent colonial city seems so small. That's because what you see is one of only two remaining chapels in what was once the city's main house of worship. The lovely white cathedral was completed in 1680 but destroyed in an earthquake less than 100 years later. Out back are the stark but magnificent ruins of the original cathedral—well worth a look for the nominal admission price. Although restoration is underway, no plans exist to reopen the old cathedral as a house of worship. ⊠ *4 Av. Sur, east side of Parque Ctl.* ☎ *7832–0909* 🔄 *Ruins Q3* ⊙ *Daily 9–5.*

❾ **Convento de las Capuchinas.** Anti★ gua's largest convent was built by the Capuchin nuns, whose number had swelled because they, unlike other sisterhoods, did not require young women to pay dowries to undertake the religious life. They constructed the mammoth structure in 1736, just a decade after the first of their order arrived from Madrid. The convent was abandoned after the earthquake of 1773, even though damage to the structure was relatively light. In the 1940s the convent was restored and opened to the public. The ruins, which are quite well preserved, include several lovely courtyards and gardens, the former bathing halls, and a round tower lined with the nuns' cells—two of which illustrate cloistered life with rather eerie mannequins. Climb to the roof for a memorable view of the surrounding landscape. The building now houses the offices of the Consejo Nacional para la Protección de La Antigua Guatemala, the national council charged with preservation and restoration of the city. ⊠ *2 Av. Norte at 2 C. Oriente* ☎ *7832–0184* 🔄 *Q30* ⊙ *Daily 9–5.*

❼ **Convento Santa Clara.** Shortly after it was founded in 1699, the Convent of St. Clara grew to be a rather elaborate complex housing nearly 50 nuns. When it was destroyed by an earthquake in 1717, the sisters quickly rebuilt it. It was struck by violent tremors again in 1773, and the site was finally abandoned. The remaining arches and courtyards make a pleasant place to roam. Keep an eye out for hidden passages and underground rooms. ⊠ *2 Av. Sur at 6 C. Oriente* ☎ *7832–0743* 🔄 *Q30* ⊙ *Daily 9–5.*

⓫ **Iglesia de Nuestra Señora de La Merced.** The Church of Our Lady of ★ Mercy is one of Antigua's most eye-catching attractions, known for its fanciful yellow stucco façade that incorporates Mayan deities. The attached monastery, which has an immense stone fountain in the central courtyard, has excellent views of nearby volcanoes. The church was built in 1548, only to be destroyed by an earthquake in 1717. It

---

COOKING CLASSES

The **Antigua Cooking School** (⊠ *5 Av. Norte 25B* ☎ *5944–8568* ⊕ *www.antiguacookingschool. com*), will teach you Guatemalan cooking skills that let you eat for a lifetime. Each four-hour class includes instruction in preparing three local dishes, plus tortillas and black beans (the requisite accompaniments to any Guatemalan meal). You get your hands dirty and help in the preparation and, of course, in the sampling at the conclusion of class. Classes are Tuesday and Thursday at 1 PM, and Wednesday, Friday, and Saturday at 10 AM. The per-person fee is Q375. Reserve a spot at least two days in advance.

was finally rebuilt in 1765, six years before a second massive earthquake forced the city to be abandoned. Architect Juan Luis de Dios Estrada wisely designed the church to be earthquake resistant. The squat shape, thick walls, and small, high windows are responsible for La Merced surviving the 1773 quake with barely a crack. The church did suffer significant damage in the 1976 earthquake, but a massive restoration project reinforced the stone floor. ⊠ *1 C. Poniente and 6 Av. Norte* ☎ *7832–0559* 🚌 *Q5* ⊙ *Daily 8:30–6.*

🄬 **Iglesia de La Recolección.** Despite opposition from the city council, which felt the town already had plenty of monasteries, La Recolección was inaugurated in 1717, the same year it was destroyed by an earthquake. Like many others, it was quickly rebuilt but shaken to the ground again in 1773. A stone arch still graces the church stairway, but the ceiling did not fare so well—it lies in huge jumbled blocks within the nave's crumbling walls. The 1976 earthquake inflicted further damage. The monastery is in better shape though, with spacious courtyards lined with low arches. Enter by a small path to the left of the church. ⊠ *1 C. Poniente at C. de Recolectos* ☎ *7832–0743* 🚌 *Q30* ⊙ *Daily 9–5.*

🄮 **Mercado Central.** The smell of fresh fruits and vegetables will lead you to this unassuming market, the place where local residents come to shop for all manner of day-to-day goods. Women in colorful skirts sell huge piles of produce culled from their own gardens. Their husbands are nearby, chatting with friends or watching a soccer match. ⊠ *Between Alameda de Santa Lucía and C. de Recolectos.*

🄯 **Museo de Arte Colonial.** On the former site of the University of San Carlos, the Museum of Colonial Art, its cloisters left largely intact through the shakier centuries, holds a collection of mostly 17th-century religious paintings and statues commissioned by the Castilians. There's also a display of photographs of Semana Santa celebrations. ⊠ *C. de La Universidad and 4 Av. Sur* ☎ *7832–0429* 🚌 *Q25* ⊙ *Tues.–Fri. 9–4, weekends 9–noon and 2–4.*

NEED A BREAK? Wander over to Cookies, Etc. (⊠ *4 C. Oriente and 3 Av. Norte*), a 7-table café and pastry shop serving 15 kinds of homemade cookies filled with nuts, chocolate, coconut, oatmeal, and spices.

🄰 **Palacio del Ayuntamiento.** As in colonial times, the City Hall continues to serve as the seat of government. Today it also houses two museums, the Museo de Santiago (Museum of St. James) and Museo del Libro Antiguo (Museum of Antique Books). The former, which is housed in what was once the city jail, displays colonial art and artifacts; Central America's first printing press, dating from the late 17th century, is displayed in the latter, along with a collection of ancient manuscripts. Given the delicate nature of the collection in both museums, photography is forbidden. ⊠ *4 C. Poniente, north side of Parque Ctl.* ☎ *7832–5511* 🚌 *Q10* ⊙ *Tues.–Fri. 9–4, weekends 9–noon and 2–4.*

🄱 **Palacio de los Capitanes Generales.** Restoration is underway at this writing of the Palace of the Captains General, easily recognized by its stately archways, and once the font of Spanish colonial power in the

CLOSE UP

A Bell-Ringing Saint

Guatemala points with pride and reverence to its very own saint, Pedro de San José Betancur (1626–1667), a native of the Canary Islands who came to Central America at age 31. Hermano Pedro (Brother Pedro), as he was known, became a familiar sight on the streets of Antigua, ringing a bell, and collecting alms for the poor and homeless long before the Salvation Army came up with the idea. He wasn't actually a priest—try as he might, he couldn't master the studies necessary for ordination—but Rome conferred the title of a new religious order, the Bethlehemites, on Pedro and his associates in recognition of their charity. His good works led many to dub him the "St. Francis of the Americas."

Pedro is often credited with originating the custom of the *posada,* the pre-Christmas procession seen throughout Latin America, in which townspeople reenact Mary and Joseph's search for a room at the inn.

Pope John Paul II canonized Pedro in 2002, and his tomb at the **Monasterio San Francisco** has become an even more important local landmark than it was. Many miracles are ascribed to Hermano Pedro; according to tradition, a prayer and a gentle tap on his casket will send you help. His remains have since been moved to a more finely rendered receptacle to the left of the main altar. The remainder of the ruins, dating from 1579, house a small museum dedicated to Pedro's legacy. You can see his simple clothes and the knotted ropes he used for flagellation. The upper floor is worth a visit for the incredible views of the surrounding hinterland and volcanoes. Enter the ruins through a small path near the rear corner of the church.

✉ *7 C. Oriente and 1 Av. Sur* 🕿 *No phone* 🎫 *Ruins and museum Q3, church free* 🕑 *Church, daily 6:30–6:30; ruins and museum, daily 9–4:30.*

region. It now houses the friendly, helpful Inguat tourism office in addition to some other governmental agencies. ✉ *5 C. Poniente, south side of Parque Ctl..*

❶ Parque Central. Surrounded by old colonial buildings, this tree-lined square is the center of Antigua, and one of Latin America's most pleasant central parks. Residents and travelers alike pass quiet afternoons on shady benches listening to the trickling Fuente de las Sirenas, conversing with neighbors, and getting their shoes shined under the jacaranda trees. Flowering *esquisúchil* (borage) trees accent the park; locals refer to them as *árboles de Hermano Pedro,* the tree of Pedro de San José Betancur, Guatemala's own saint. Legend holds that the flowers have curative powers for all manner of ailments. ✉ *Bounded by 4 and 5 Cs. and 4 and 5 Avs..*

❾ Paseo de los Museos. The Casa Santo Domingo hotel complex contains several small museums that deal with art, pharmacology, and archaeology from pre-Columbian, colonial, and contemporary eras. There are also workshops where you can watch wax and ceramics being crafted. All are open to the public. ✉ *3 C. Oriente 28* 🕿 *7820–1220* ⊕ *www.casasantodomingo.com* 🎫 *Q30* 🕑 *Daily 9–6.*

OUTSIDE
TOWN

Centro Azotea. Three modest museums make up this cultural center in the village of Jocotenango just outside Antigua. *K'ojom* means "music" in various Mayan languages, and **Casa K'ojom** highlights the musical traditions of Guatemala's vastly diverse indigenous population. An interesting 15-minute documentary film is a good introduction for the newcomer touring the collection of musical instruments and other artifacts. A gift shop sells locally made crafts, simple instruments, and recordings of Guatemalan music. While you're here, learn about harvesting and roasting coffee beans at the **Museo del Café**, on the adjacent coffee plantation, which has a working mill dating from 1883. The **Rincón de Sacatepéquez** contains dioramas exhibiting the dress of indigenous peoples in this part of Guatemala. The center also offers horseback riding around the farm on Tuesday and Thursday. The fee is Q50. The museum is in the village of Jocotenango, 2 km (1 mi) from Antigua. Free minivan shuttles leave from the south side of the Parque Central in front of the Inguat office. Taxis from Antigua run Q20 to 25. ⊠ *C. del Cementerio Final, Jocotenango* ☎7832–0907 ⊕*www. centroazotea.com, www.kojom.org, www.cafeazotea.com* ☜*Q30* ⊗ *Weekdays 8:30–4, Sat. 8:30–2 (last tour at 2).*

Cerro de la Cruz. If the Santa Catalina arch is Antigua's iconic symbol, the view from this hillside perch north of the city, with its cross in the foreground, city rooftops and Volcán Agua in the background, is its best-known postcard vista. In person, the view is even better, but ⚠**under no circumstances should you make the walk up the hill on your own**. Tales of robbery along the way are legion. Antigua's Tourist Police offer a free, armed, guided escort for walkers up the hill every day at 10 AM and 3 PM. Walks depart from the police offices at 4 Avenida Norte on the east side of the Palacio de Ayuntamiento, one-half block north of the cathedral. ⊠ *1½ km (1 mi) north of Antigua on 1 Av. Norte* ☎*Tourist police: 7832–0535* ☜*Free* ⊗*Daily walks at 10* AM *and 3* PM.

WHAT IT COSTS IN GUATEMALAN QUETZALES				
¢	$	$$	$$$	$$$$
RESTAURANTS under Q40	Q40–Q70	Q70–Q100	Q100–Q130	over Q130

Restaurant prices are per person for a main course at dinner.

WHERE TO EAT

CAFÉS

¢–$ ✕**L'Espresso Café.** Black-T-shirted waiters scurry around, serving up a delicious selection of light café fare, the foundation of which is various pastas and crepes. Accompany your meal with gourmet coffees or smoothies topped off with a vanilla, mango, chocolate, or pistachio gelato–form dessert. The decor is minimalist chic; there are brick walls and an exposed high-beam ceiling, and you're seated at a glass table on a stool covered with a burlap coffee sack. The view out the front door is the stark Compañía de Jesús, the colonial ruins of the Jesuit church, bathed in a soft, mysterious light each evening. If you come here for

CLOSE UP

Earthquake!

Quakes large and small have ravaged the history of Guatemala, a nation that forms part of the seismically active "Ring of Fire" encircling the Pacific Rim. Two major earthquakes rocked Antigua in colonial times, first in 1717, then again in 1773. (Several lesser ones also hit the city.) The latter event leveled many structures in the city—contrary to popular belief, it did not completely destroy Antigua—and precipitated the transfer of the capital to supposedly safer ground in the nearby Ermita Valley, the site of present-day Guatemala City.

Folk wisdom held that the new capital's numerous ravines and gorges would absorb seismic shocks. Unfortunately, this was not so. Earthquakes caused significant damage and loss of life in Guatemala City in 1902, 1917, and 1918, but no one could begin to imagine the tragedy that would strike

in February 1976 when a 7.5-magnitude quake hit the capital, killing 23,000 people and causing $1 billion in damage to the entire region.

Seismologists attribute the activity to the east–west Motagua fault, which separates the North American and Caribbean tectonic plates and slices through the center of Guatemala. The smaller Mixco fault runs perpendicular to the Motagua and passes between Antigua and Guatemala City.

In a perverse way, the earth's rumblings and grumblings have benefited Antigua. The ash spewed from nearby volcanoes fertilizes the soil, and has turned the countryside around the city into a lush, abundant agricultural region. Experts say that Guatemala Antigua, some of the world's finest coffee, owes its high quality to that fertile volcanic soil.

dinner, make it an early one; the place closes at 8 PM. ⊠ *6 Av. Norte 4* ☎ *7832–0539* ⊟ *AE, D, DC, MC, V*

¢–$ ✕**Rainbow Café.** We could picture Che plotting the revolution here at this café, a hangout of young expats in the heart of Antigua's language-school district. You'll find some meat on the menu, but vegetarian fare dominates. (We love the falafel and hummus dishes.) The place is immensely popular. Don't be afraid to ask if you can squeeze in if you see no available tables indoors or in the courtyard. There are lectures, in English, on some topic of political interest each Tuesday evening, and live music many other nights. ⊠ *7 Av. Sur 8* ☎ *7832–4205* ⊟ *No credit cards.*

¢   ✕**The Bagel Barn.** The name is apt. Anything and everything in the bagel realm makes up the bulk of the menu in the this place just around the corner from the Parque Central. You'll find an equally wide variety of smoothie flavors here as well as decaf coffee (a real rarity in this country). Stop by at 4:15 or 7:15 PM for the nightly screenings of late-run Hollywood films on DVD; there's a huge selection of those, too. ⊠ *5 C. Poniente 2* ☎ *7832–1224* ⊟ *AE, D, DC, MC, V.*

¢   ✕**Café Condesa.** Breakfast starts at 6:45 AM and specials such as toast topped with strawberries, papaya, or mango, and omelets made with fresh vegetables will give you plenty of sightseeing fuel. After such a big breakfast, don't count on eating much for the rest of the day. For lunch, try the quiche or the Brie plate; the homemade pies and pastries

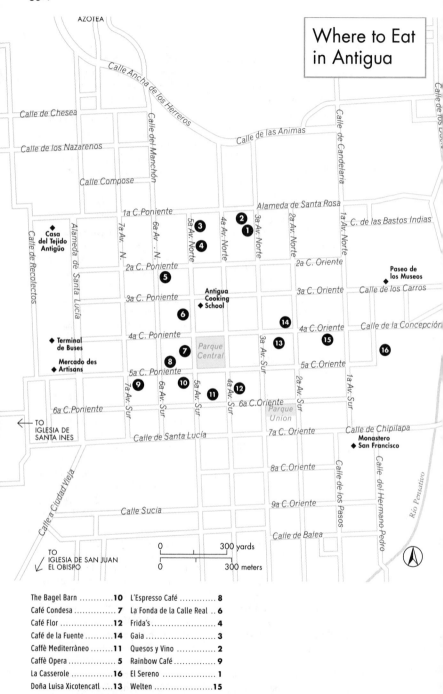

Where to Eat
in Antigua

are also notable. You can eat in the café's airy dining room or grab a cappuccino and a sweet roll at Café Condesa Express next door. Either way, the location right on the Parque Central can't be beat. ⊠*5 Av. Norte, west side of Parque Ctl.* ☎*7832–0038* ▭*MC, V.*

¢ ✕**Café de la Fuente.** This popular eatery takes over the courtyard of La Fuente, a classy collection of shops in a renovated colonial estate. Classical music creates a peaceful atmosphere. The international breakfasts, served until 11 AM, are excellent and the Mexican-style eggs *ranchero* are not to be missed. There are several vegetarian options. La Fuente also makes one of the best desserts in town—a decadently rich chocolate brownie topped with coffee ice cream and chocolate syrup. The Q20 daily lunch special is a good bet. ⊠*4 C. Oriente 14, at 2 Av. Norte* ☎*7832–4520* ▭*AE, D, DC, MC, V.*

ECLECTIC

¢ ✕**Doña Luisa Xicotencatl.** This restaurant—named after the mistress of
★ Spanish conquistador Pedro de Alvarado—is something of a local institution; tables are scattered throughout a dozen rooms, but it's still not easy to get a seat. Early-morning specialties include fruit salad, pancakes, and very fresh bread (the bakery is right downstairs). Sandwiches and other light fare make for ample lunch and dinner options. The service can be slow, but the eclectic decor makes the wait pleasant. The bulletin board downstairs is an excellent source of information for travelers. ⊠*4 C. Oriente 12 at 3 Av. Norte* ☎*7832–2578* ▭*AE, D, DC, MC, V.*

FRENCH

$$–$$$ ✕**La Casserole.** Classic French dishes incorporate subtle Guatemalan influences at La Casserole. Although the menu changes every week or so, there are a few constants—seafood bouillabaisse cooked in a slightly spicy tomato sauce and steak tenderloin with a salsa made from spicy *chiltepin* peppers are two standouts. The peach-and-gold walls of this restored colonial mansion are lined with rotating painting and photography exhibits. ⊠*Calle jón de la Concepción 7* ☎*7832–0219* ▭*AE, D, DC, MC, V* ⊘*Closed Mon. No dinner Sun.*

ITALIAN

$$–$$$$ ✕**Welten.** You'll feel like a guest in a private home when you arrive at
Fodor'sChoice this restaurant. Take your pick of tables, which are on a patio with
★ cascading orchid plants, by a small pool, festooned with candles and flower petals, in the rear garden, or in one of the elegantly appointed dining rooms. The menu includes homemade pasta dishes, such as *anolini* served with a creamy pepper-and-cognac sauce, as well as fish and meat dishes served with a variety of sauces. All the vegetables are organic, and the bread is baked right on the premises. ⊠*4 C. Oriente 21* ☎*7832–0630* ▭*AE, D, DC, MC, V* ⊘*Closed Tues.*

$$–$$$ ✕**Café Opera.** You half expect Enrico Caruso to emerge from the shadows when you walk into this trattoria a couple of blocks from the La Merced church. It's generally a bit cluttered and crowded, and it fills up quickly. You'll find overflow seating on the back patio, but sitting out there isn't nearly as atmospheric. For an Italian restaurant, the selection of pastas is small, but the café's signature plates are its various tender-

loin dishes—we like the beef prepared with gorgonzola cheese, nuts, and rosemary. Accompany your meal with a wide selection of panini and a gelato for dessert. ⊠*6 Av. Norte 17* ☎*7832–0727* ⊟*AE, D, DC, MC, V.*

$ ×**Café Mediterráneo.** For Italian food in the city, this tiny restaurant
★ can't be beat. Northern Italian specialties, delicious antipasti, and delicate homemade pastas are among the favorites. Wash it all down with a selection from the affordable wine list. The atmosphere and decor are low-key. Instead of giving out individual menus, waiters lug the menu board to your table to explain what's available. Hours can be a bit capricious; evening dining may begin at 6 or 7 PM, or whenever the restaurant opens, but the service is first rate. Reservations are recommended. ⊠*6 C. Poniente 6A* ☎*7832–7180* ⊟*AE, D, DC, MC, V* ⊗*Closed Tues.*

¢–$ ×**Quesos y Vino.** One of Antigua's best small Italian restaurants moved around the corner to more spacious digs in 2007, and still serves up homemade pastas, pizzas from a wood-burning oven, and a variety of home-baked breads. Choose from an impressive selection of cheeses and wines sold by the bottle or glass. This is mostly a place to stop for a light bite, rather than a full meal. Most of the seating in the new place is outside, but you'll find plenty of covering to duck under on a rainy day. ⊠*1 C. Poniente 1, near Arco de Santa Catalina* ☎*7832–7785* ⊟*V* ⊗*Closed Tues.*

LATIN AMERICAN

$$$–$$$$ ×**El Sereno.** One of Antigua's original elegant restaurants is in a 16th-century house near La Merced church a few blocks north of the Parque Central. The place is huge and does a brisk event business, but offers plenty of secluded tables for intimate, candlelight dinners. Lunch is served in the downstairs courtyard; dinner expands to the upstairs terrace with stupendous mountain and city views, and gorgeous end-of-day sunsets. The menu changes every few months, but always consists of a mix of Guatemalan and international fare—perhaps a three-meat *pepián*, or a tarragon leg of lamb with a mango shrimp salad on the side. ⊠*4 Av. Norte 16* ☎*7832–0501* ⊟*AE, D, DC, MC, V.*

$–$$ ×**La Fonda de la Calle Real.** An old Antigua favorite, this place has three locations serving the same Guatemalan and Mexican fare. The original restaurant, on 5 Avenida Norte near Parque Central, has pleasant views from the 2nd floor. It tends to be a bit cramped, however. Newer spaces, across the street and around the corner on 3 Calle, are in colonial homes spacious enough to offer indoor and outdoor seating. Musicians stroll about on weekends. The menu includes *queso fundido* and the restaurant's famous *caldo real* (a hearty chicken soup). ⊠*3 C. Poniente 7 at 5 Av. Norte* ☎*7832–0507* ⊠*5 Av. Norte 5 at 4 C. Poniente* ⊟*AE, D, DC, MC, V.*

$ ×**Frida's.** Looking for a place where you and your friends can knock back a few margaritas? At this festive cantina the whole group can fill up on Mexican fare, including taquitos, enchiladas, and burros, the diminutive siblings of the American-style burrito. Things really get going when the mariachi band shows up. Fans of Frida Kahlo and Diego Rivera will find a great selection of prints from these veritable

CLOSE UP

Burning the Devil

The night of each December 7, Guatemalan communities engage in the traditional *Quema del Diablo* ritual, a symbolic burning of the devil. The date marks the eve of the Feast of the Immaculate Conception of the Virgin Mary, and is chosen to symbolize the eternal struggle between good and evil. Just as Thanksgiving customarily ushers in the holiday season in the United States, the Quema kicks off Christmastime in Guatemala.

Townspeople traditionally would spend the day cleaning unwanted items from their homes, because of a legend holding that the devil inhabits household objects that had remained idle. Residents piled their discarded goods in the street and set them on fire as a way of burning the devil from the house and the evil from the family's life.

Safety, health, and environmental concerns now temper the observances, at least in urban areas, and most communities no longer permit the free-for-all of hundreds of unsupervised fires on their streets. Most towns and cities now hold one controlled bonfire in which a wooden figure of the devil is burned, and firefighters are present to keep things from getting out of hand.

masters—the menu even bears Frida's signature portrait. ⊠*5 Av. Norte 29* ☎*7832–1296* ▭*AE, D, DC, MC, V.*

MIDDLE EASTERN

$–$$$ ✕**Gaia.** Lebanon comes to Guatemala at this old favorite on busy Avenida 5 Norte. The fare is standard Middle Eastern: lamb or beef kabobs, couscous, tabouli, or *patush,* a Syrian salad. You have several seating choices here: you can sit on throw pillows at low tables in the front room, or at one of the private booths out in the back courtyard. If you're so inclined, partake of an after-dinner flavored hookah in the front lounge. Come early to get a seat for the Thursday-evening belly-dancing show. It gets underway at 8:30 PM. ⊠*5 Av. Norte 35A* ☎*7832–3670* ▭*AE, D, DC, MC, V.*

THAI

¢–$ ✕**Café Flor.** Once this homey restaurant switched from Mexican to Asian cuisine, it never looked back. The friendly proprietors serve a menu that includes Thai curries, Chinese noodles, and Indian vegetable dishes. Be careful—some of the dishes, especially the curries, are quite spicy. Asian food aficionados will find the food not at all like the real thing, but Antigua is, after all, about as far from the source as you can get. On weekends the restaurant is open until midnight. There's live piano music nightly. The restaurant is popular with the many students studying Spanish in Antigua. ⊠*4 Av. Sur 1* ☎*7832–5274* ▭*AE, D, DC, MC, V.*

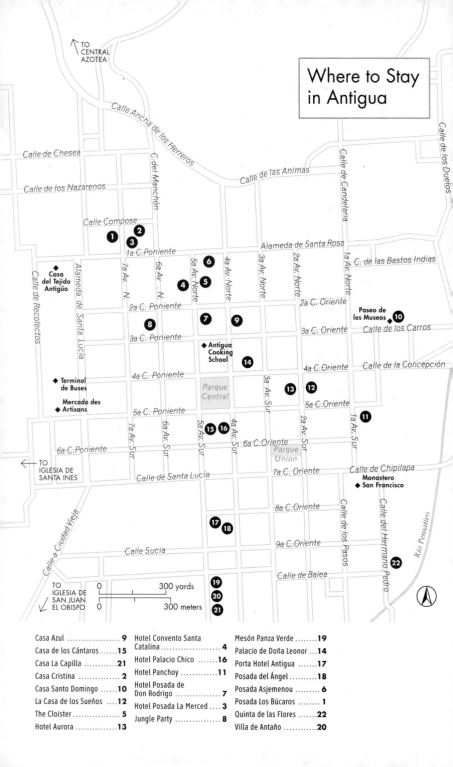

Where to Stay in Antigua

TO CENTRAL AZOTEA

Calle Ancha de los Herreros

Calle de los Duelos

Calle de Chesea

Calle de los Nazarenos

Calle de las Ánimas

Calle de Candelaria

C. del Manchón

Calle Compose

Alameda de Santa Rosa

7a Av. Norte

C. de las Bastos Indias

Casa del Tejido Antigüo

1a C. Poniente

7a Av. N.

6a Av. N.

5a Av. Norte

4a Av. Norte

3a Av. Norte

2a Av. Norte

Alameda de Santa Lucía

Calle de Recolectos

2a C. Poniente

2a C. Oriente

Paseo de los Museos

3a C. Poniente

3a C. Oriente

Calle de los Carros

Antigua Cooking School

4a C. Oriente

Calle de la Concepción

Terminal de Buses

4a C. Poniente

Parque Central

3a Av. Sur

2a Av. Sur

5a C.Oriente

Mercado des Artisans

5a C. Poniente

7a Av. Sur

6a Av. Sur

5a Av. Sur

4a Av. Sur

6a C. Oriente

1a Av. Sur

6a C.Poniente

Parque Union

TO IGLESIA DE SANTA INES

7a C. Oriente

Calle de Chipilapa

Calle de Santa Lucía

Monastero San Francisco

8a C.Oriente

Calle a Ciudad Vieja

Calle de los Pasos

Calle del Hermano Pedro

Río Pensativo

9a C.Oriente

Calle Sucia

Calle de Balea

TO IGLESIA DE SAN JUAN EL OBISPO

0   300 yards

0   300 meters

Casa Azul **9**	Hotel Convento Santa Catalina **4**	Mesón Panza Verde **19**
Casa de los Cántaros **15**	Hotel Palacio Chico **16**	Palacio de Doña Leonor ...**14**
Casa La Capilla **21**	Hotel Panchoy **11**	Porta Hotel Antigua **17**
Casa Cristina **2**	Hotel Posada de Don Rodrigo **7**	Posada del Ángel **18**
Casa Santo Domingo **10**		Posada Asjemenou **6**
La Casa de los Sueños **12**	Hotel Posada La Merced ... **3**	Posada Los Búcaros **1**
The Cloister **5**	Jungle Party **8**	Quinta de las Flores **22**
Hotel Aurora **13**		Villa de Antaño **20**

WHERE TO STAY

	WHAT IT COSTS IN GUATEMALAN QUETZALES				
	¢	$	$$	$$$	$$$$
HOTELS	under –Q160	Q160–Q360	Q360–Q560	Q560–Q760	over Q760

Hotel prices are for two people in a standard double room, including tax and service.

$$$$ ⊞ **Casa Santo Domingo.** This elegant hotel was built around the ruins of the ancient Monasterio Santo Domingo, taking advantage of its long passageways and snug little courtyards. Dark carved-wood furniture, yellow stucco walls, and iron sconces preserve the monastic atmosphere, but luxurious amenities abound. Unfortunately, the food at the restaurant is considerably less inspiring than the rest of the package. ■TIP→ **This is one of those hotels that serves as a tourist attraction in its own right—do visit its museums and grounds—but for guests here, the outside visitors occasionally translate into a lack of intimacy.** Pros: historic setting, lovely gardens. Cons: several blocks from city center, many outside visitors to hotel. ⊠ *3 C. Oriente 28* ☎ *7832–1222* 📠 *7832–4155* ⊕ *www.casasantodomingo.com.gt* 🛏 *126 rooms* ♂ *In-room: no a/c, safe, refrigerator. In-hotel: restaurant, room service, bar, pool, spa, concierge, laundry service, airport shuttle, parking (no fee)* ⊟ *AE, D, DC, MC, V* ¶○¶ *EP.*

$$$$ ⊞ **Palacio Doña Leonor.** The one-time palace of Leonor de Alvarado de Cueva, the daughter of Spanish conquistador Pedro de Alvarado, now serves as a lovely hotel, and when completed, is expected to give Casa Santo Domingo a run for its money in Antigua's top-notch sweepstakes. Just half a block off the Parque Central, it's the most centrally located hotel in the city. The large, flat-screen televisions in each room are a nice touch—one almost never seen in Guatemala—but look a bit out of place among the colonial elegance of canopied beds, period art, fireplaces, stone-tile floors, and garden. Descending the beautiful grand staircase will make you will look just as grand as we assume Doña Leonor did. Pros: central location, historic setting, many amenities. Con: some street noise in front rooms. ⊠ *4 C. Oriente 8* ☎📠 *7832–2281* ⊕ *www.palaciodeleonor.com* 🛏 *22 rooms* ♂ *In-room: no a/c, no phone, safe, Wi-Fi. In-hotel: restaurant, bar, pool, spa, no elevator, public Internet, parking (no fee)* ⊟ *AE, D, DC, MC, V* ¶○¶ *BP.*

$$$$ ⊞ **Porta Hotel Antigua.** As a tasteful combination of colonial elegance and modern comfort, Porta Hotel Antigua, part of a small Guatemalan chain, is one of the city's most popular lodgings. The sparkling pool, set amid lush gardens, is a treat after a day exploring the dusty city streets. Standard rooms have plenty of space for two, whereas one- and two-level suites can house a whole family quite comfortably. The oldest part of the hotel is a colonial-style building with a restaurant, bar, and a beautiful sitting room. A new building opened down the street in 2007 and, although constructed in the old colonial style, contains more modern rooms. Although this is now the city's largest lodging, nothing is overpowering about the place. Weddings are sometimes held in a sunny esplanade overlooking the ruins of Iglesia de San José. Pro: chain

amenities with individualized décor. **Con:** several blocks from city center. ⊠*8 C. Poniente 1* ☎*7832–2801, 888/790–5264 in North America* ☎*7832–0807* ⊕*www.portahotels.com* ➘*8 suites, 105 rooms* ⚙*In-room: no a/c, safe. In-hotel: 2 restaurants, room service, bar, pool, laundry service, parking (no fee)* ⊟*AE, D, DC, MC, V* ⦿*BP.*

$$$$
Fodor'sChoice
★
★ **Posada del Ángel.** You'd never know from the unassuming, borderline-rickety wooden gate that you're at the threshold of Antigua's most beautiful lodging. It's all part of the ruse at this truly angelic inn. Large corner fireplaces warm the rooms, each of which is decorated with well-chosen antiques. Those on the main floor look out onto a plant-filled courtyard, and the large suite on the 2nd floor has a private rooftop terrace. The staff has catered to presidents and prime ministers—former U.S. president Bill Clinton, who stayed in the upstairs suite, is the most famous guest on the register—but you'll receive the same fine service. **Pros:** attentive service, lovely courtyard. **Con:** several blocks from city center. ⊠*4 Av. Sur 24A* ☎*7832–5244* ☎*7832–0260* ⊕*www.posadadelangel.com* ➘*1 suite, 4 rooms* ⚙*In-room: no a/c. In-hotel: room service, bar, concierge, airport shuttle, parking (no fee), no elevator* ⊟*AE, D, DC, MC, V.*

$$$–$$$$
▥ **Casa de los Cántaros.** Of Antigua's upscale lodging offerings, this one feels most like a small home, although two "newer" rooms recently incorporated into the hotel are in the building next door. "New" is relative here, in that both buildings date from the 17th century. Grapefruit and orange trees festoon the garden; their fruits supply the juice for breakfast. Rooms vary in size here—one is huge—but all contain cedar furniture, ample colonial art, fireplaces, and dressing rooms. The owner is very nice, but she can be a little intense at times. **Pros:** historic setting, lovely garden. **Con:** somewhat overbearing owner. ⊠*5 Av. Sur 5* ☎*7832–0674* ☎*7832–0609* ➘*3 rooms, 2 suites* ⚙*In-room: no a/c, no phone, no TV (some). In-hotel: restaurant, laundry service, parking (no fee)* ⊟*No credit cards* ⦿*BP.*

$$$–$$$$
▥ **Casa La Capilla.** *Capilla* means "chapel" in Spanish and, indeed, you'll find one here in the middle of this lodging's requisite fine colonial garden, the site of occasional weddings and church services. But sacred the place is not. The chapel also hosts weekly poker games, yoga classes, or corporate dinners. Next to the chapel is a log-fire sauna, perfect to warm away aches from walking up and down Antigua's cobblestone streets. There's a fun vibe here among the colonial elegance. Rooms are arranged around the garden, and have high-beam ceilings, lime-wash walls, plenty of colonial-era art decorating the walls, and guests get personal mobile phones. Huge breakfasts consist of freshly squeezed juices and pastries. **Pros:** many activities, friendly atmosphere. **Con:** occasional noise from courtyard. ⊠*5 Av. Sur 21* ☎*7832–0182* ⊕*www.lacapillahotel.com* ➘*6 rooms, 1 apartment* ⚙*In-room: no a/c, no phone, DVD, Wi-Fi. In-hotel: restaurant, bar, pool, laundry service, parking (no fee)* ⊟*AE, D, DC, MC, V* ⦿*CP.*

$$$–$$$$
▥ **The Cloister.** This aptly named hotel began life as a cloistered convent near the Santa Catalina arch that dates from about 1700. We imagine its original inhabitants never experienced such luxury. Rooms are arranged around a beautiful garden that has a bubbling fountain and

2

wrought-iron patio furniture for enjoying a lovely Antigua afternoon. Each room comes with fireplace, library, terra-cotta floors, oak furnishings, and exposed high-beam ceilings. You enter some of the rooms via Dutch-style half-doors. Two of the rooms have a sleeping loft. Many comparable lodgings in the city charge much more, so you're looking at good value. **Pros:** historic setting, lovely garden, good value. **Con:** some street noise in front rooms. ⊠ *5 Av. Norte 12* ☎ *7832–0712* ⊕ *www.thecloister.com* ↻ *7 rooms* ♿ *In-room: no a/c, no phone, no TV. In-hotel: restaurant, public Wi-Fi, parking (no fee)* ⊟ *No credit cards* ⏱ *BP.*

$$$–$$$$
Fodor'sChoice
★

Mesón Panza Verde. A beautiful courtyard with a fountain and colorful gardens welcome you to this retreat. The elegant rooms downstairs open onto small gardens, whereas the romantic suites upstairs have four-poster beds piled high with down comforters and terraces where hammocks swing in the breeze. ■TIP→ **The rooftop patio is wonderful in late afternoon or early morning, and the restaurant ($–$$$$) is one of the best in town.** The meat dishes are particularly good, such as the *lomito* (pork) bourguignonne with escargot. ■TIP→ **The hotel and restaurant maintain an active evening cultural-events program open to the public.** **Pros:** good views, great restaurant, active cultural program. **Con:** small rooms downstairs. ⊠ *5 Av. Sur 19* ☎ *7832–1745* 🖷 *7832–2925* ⊕ *www.panzaverde.com* ↻ *3 rooms, 9 suites* ♿ *In-room: no a/c, safe. In-hotel: restaurant, bar, laundry service, parking (no fee), public Internet, no elevator* ⊟ *AE, D, DC, MC, V* ⏱ *BP.*

$$$–$$$$
Fodor'sChoice
★

Villa de Antaño. Your first just-inside-the-gate glance here is the parking lot. Keep your disappointment in check, however. Loveliness lurks behind this rambling, ochre-colored building's front door. The six room offerings are a mix-and-match affair, and each is decorated differently. The largest contains a fireplace, whirlpool tub, glassed-in shower and huge walk-in closet. The two smaller suites have their own patio, and the sole 2nd-floor room comes equipped with kitchen and private dining balcony; the volcano views are stupendous. Common to all are colonial paintings, cedar beds, tables, and marble or stone-and-bronze floors, all set among elegant common areas such as the three sitting rooms (each with fireplace) and a rushing fountain in a beautiful garden. **Pros:** great views, many amenities. **Con:** several blocks from city center. ⊠ *5 Av. Sur 31* ☎ *7832–9539* ⊕ *www.villadeantano.com* ↻ *1 room, 4 suites, 1 villa* ♿ *In-room: no a/c, kitchen (some), refrigerator (some), Wi-Fi. In-hotel: restaurant, bar, laundry service, parking (no fee)* ⊟ *AE, D, DC, MC, V* ⏱ *BP.*

$$$

Casa Azul. Not many hotels have guest books filled with recommendations for specific rooms, but the ones on the 2nd floor are so good that people want to be sure to share them with others. The upstairs rooms are more expensive, but they're larger and brighter and have views of the volcanoes; all rooms are painted in washes of red and, of course, blue (*azul* means "blue" in Spanish). Communal-sitting rooms open onto a pleasant courtyard; breakfast is served beside the small pool. **Pros:** central location, nice courtyard. **Con:** dimly lit rooms. ⊠ *4 Av. Norte 5* ☎ *7832–0961* 🖷 *7832–0944* ⊕ *www.casazul.guate.com*

Something Old, Something New

Antigua's colonial magnificence disappeared in one day in 1773 following a massive earthquake. With the move of the capital to nearby Guatemala City, there was no need (and no money) to restore Antigua's treasures. Urban legend holds that the city was totally leveled and completely abandoned following the earthquake; neither is true, but nearly two centuries of stagnation did follow.

Things changed in the 1960s with a newfound interest among residents in preserving and restoring that former glory once again. The Guatemalan government had declared Antigua a national monument in 1944, a title largely ceremonial, but the Protective Law for the City of La Antigua Guatemala, enacted by the national government in 1969, would change the fortunes of the city forever.

Key to those newfound fortunes was the formation of an active Consejo Nacional para la Protección de La Antigua Guatemala (National Council for the Protection of Antigua Guatemala), whose efforts have focused on the rescue and restoration of some 50 monuments. That work comes at a price—money is scarce in Guatemala—but the governments of Spain, Japan, and Taiwan have chipped in to fund several projects. Guatemalan corporate sponsors—including cement manufacturer Cementos Progreso, Pepsi, chicken restaurant chain Pollo Campero, and national telephone company Telgua—have made generous donations, as well.

In a more general sense, beyond specific projects, the council actively spearheaded the elimination of street advertising from businesses. Walk down any Antigua street and you'll notice that signs are conspicuously and pleasantly discreet. Next on the council's wish list—it's a long shot to be sure—is the elimination of vehicular traffic from select downtown streets. You can get a taste of this on Sunday, when Avenida 5 Norte, the street passing under the Santa Catalina arch, is closed to traffic.

An influx of visitors from around the world has nevertheless been an end result, but the restoration projects have always been undertaken as a matter of civic pride and not to create a vast outdoor museum.

Current and recent council projects include:

- **Iglesia de Nuestra Señora de La Merced:** reinforcement of arcades in cloister and restoration of *Jesús Nazareno* figure.

- **Iglesia de San Cristóbal El Bajo:** structural reinforcement of damage from 1976 earthquake.

- **Iglesia de San Juan El Obispo:** restoration of church bell.

- **Iglesia de Santa Inés:** restoration of façade, remodeling of atrium, and exterior illumination.

- **Palacio de los Capitanes Generales:** reinforcement of roof tiles and rotted wood.

- **Rescate del Color Antigüeño ("rescue of Antigua color"):** ongoing campaign to repaint buildings in their original colors; most activity on 1 Avenida Norte, 2 Avenida Sur, 7 Avenida Norte, and 3 Calle Oriente.

- **San José Catedral:** restoration of figures on cathedral facade damaged in 1976 earthquake.

2

⮒ *14 rooms* ⟐ *In-room: no a/c, safe, refrigerator. In-hotel: pool, no elevator, parking (no fee)* ⊟*AE, D, DC, MC, V* ⊘*BP.*

$$$ ⊞ **La Casa de Los Sueños.** This stunning colonial mansion, converted into an elegant bed-and-breakfast, may truly be the house of your dreams, as the name implies. A lovely patio is covered on all sides by hanging plants. A joyful antique hobbyhorse and a square grand piano reside in the sitting room. Tastefully decorated with antiques, the rooms are painted the washed-out hues that typify Antigua. **Pro:** historic setting. **Con:** several blocks from city center. ⊠*1 Av. Norte 1* ☎☎*7832–9897* ⊕*www.lacasadelossuenos.com* ⮒*8 rooms* ⟐*In-room: no a/c. In-hotel: restaurant, pool, parking (no fee)* ⊟*AE, D, DC, MC, V* ⊘*BP.*

$$$ ⊞**Hotel Posada de Don Rodrigo.** A night in this restored colonial mansion is a journey back in time. All the rooms have soaring ceilings and gorgeous tile floors and are set around two large courtyards and several smaller gardens. A tile fountain trickles in the dining room, which is on a garden terrace; to the side a woman prepares tortillas on a piping-hot grill. Indulge in a serving on Antigua flan, a dessert layered with figs and sweet potatoes. Light sleepers, beware: the lively marimba band can sometimes play long into the night. The lodging is part of a two-hotel chain, with another branch in Panajachel. **Pros:** historic setting, lively evening entertainment. **Con:** some noise from garden. ⊠*5 Av. Norte 17* ☎☎*7832–0291* ⊕*www.posadadedonrodrigo.com* ⮒*55 rooms* ⟐*In-room: no a/c. In-hotel: restaurant, bar, laundry service, parking (no fee)* ⊟*AE, D, DC, MC, V* ⊘*CP.*

$$ ⊞**Hotel Aurora.** This genteel inn, still run by the same family that opened it in 1923, has an unbeatable location in the heart of the city. The dimly lighted colonial-style rooms face a beautifully tended garden. You can relax on a tiled portico strewn with plenty of comfortable rattan chairs. Rooms have wooden furniture and old-fashioned armoires. **Pro:** lovely garden. **Con:** dimly lit rooms. ⊠*4 C. Oriente 16* ☎☎*7832–0217* ⊕*www.hotelauroraantigua.com* ⮒*19 rooms* ⟐*In-room: no a/c, no phone. In-hotel: parking (no fee)* ⊟*AE, D, DC, MC, V* ⊘*CP.*

$$ ⊞**Hotel Convento Santa Catalina.** This hotel was built among the ruins of an old convent of which only the often-photographed Arco de Santa Catalina remains. The spacious rooms, all a bit dimly lighted, are tastefully decorated with handicrafts and handwoven bedspreads. Most face a verdant courtyard where a smattering of tables and chairs encourages you to settle in with a good book. The modern rooms in the annex are brighter and have kitchenettes. **Pros:** central location, historic setting. **Cons:** dimly lit rooms, occasional street noise in front rooms. SI ⊠*5 Av. Norte 28* ☎*7832–3080* ☎*7832–3610* ⊕*www.conventohotel.com* ⮒*16 rooms* ⟐*In-room: no a/c (some), kitchen (some). In-hotel: restaurant, parking (fee), public Wi-Fi* ⊟*AE, D, DC, MC, V.*

$$ ⊞**Hotel Palacio Chico.** The so-named "Little Palace" formed part of the original Palacio de los Capitanes Generales complex, and so sits at a prime location just around the corner from the Parque Central. Rooms vary in size, so look at a few before you decide. All contain terra-cotta floors and colonial-style furnishings. The hotel serves a full breakfast on Sunday, but goes continental the other six days of the week. **Pro:**

central location. **Con:** small rooms. ⊠*4 Av. Sur 4* ☎*7832–0406* ⊕*palaciochico.enantigua.com* ↩*7 rooms* ♨*In-room: no a/c, no phone. In-hotel: laundry service, parking (no fee)* ▤*V* ⊤⊙*|BP, CP.*

$$ ☷ **Hotel Panchoy.** The Panchoy sits behind a gate in an odd complex of three separate hotels. It's the bright yellow one, and the only one of the three we recommend. Carpeted rooms are simply furnished with beds, tables, tile floors, and a private patio or balcony. The hotel is entirely nonsmoking. **Pro:** good budget value. **Cons:** Spartan furnishings, several blocks from city center. ⊠*1 Av. Norte 5A* ☎*7832–1020* ☷*7832–1030* ⊕*www.hotelpanchoy.com* ↩*21 rooms* ♨*In-room: no a/c, no phone, refrigerator. In-hotel: no elevator, laundry facilities, parking (no fee), no-smoking rooms* ▤*AE, D, DC, MC, V* ⊤⊙*|EP.*

$$ ☷ **Posada Los Búcaros.** The pretty fountain that gives this hotel its name—*búcaro* refers to a water jar—set against a wall in the courtyard, is just one of the little touches that make this hotel special. The rooms have red-tile floors and wrought-iron furnishings. The owner and staff are extremely friendly. **Pros:** friendly owners, good value. **Con:** several blocks from city center. ⊠*7 Av. Norte 94* ☷☷*7832–2346* ↩*15 rooms* ♨*In-room: no a/c. In-hotel: parking (no fee)* ▤*No credit cards.*

$$ ☷ **Quinta de las Flores.** Located several blocks southeast of the city center, Quinta de las Flores has plenty of peace and quiet along with views of three volcanoes from the well-tended gardens and the open-air dining room. This 19th-century hacienda combines colonial comfort with a sense of whimsy—the decor includes modern takes on traditional crafts. All rooms have fireplaces to keep you cozy on chilly evenings. The quaint bungalows, which sleep as many as five, even have small kitchenettes. **Pros:** quiet atmosphere, lovely gardens. **Cons:** several blocks from city center. ⊠*C. del Hermano Pedro 6* ☎*7832–3721* ☷*7832–3726* ⊕*www.quintadelasflores.com* ↩*14 rooms, 5 bungalows* ♨*In-room: no a/c, no phone, kitchen (some), refrigerator. In-hotel: restaurant, bar, pool, no elevator, laundry service* ▤*AE, D, DC, MC, V* ⊤⊙*|EP.*

$ ☷ **Casa Cristina.** Rooms acquire progressively more amenities as you go up the stairs in this friendly hotel on a small street near the La Merced church. First-floor rooms are a tad spartan, with only beds and tables. By the time you get to 2nd floor, there are televisions and nicer furnishings, and the two 3rd-floor rooms offer art on the stone-wash walls and nice views of the Volcán Agua. The hot-water supply is limited here (5:30 to 10 AM and 6 to 10 PM, but, all in all, this is a nice budget find. **Pros:** good value, friendly owner. **Con:** limited hot water. ⊠*Callejón Camposeco 3A* ☷☷*7832–0623* ⊕*www.casa-cristina.com* ↩*10 rooms* ♨*In-room: no a/c, no phone, refrigerator (some), no TV (some). In-hotel: no elevator, public Internet, public Wi-Fi* ▤*No credit cards* ⊤⊙*|CP.*

$ ☷ **Hotel Posada La Merced.** A pair of conjoined colonial homes—leading to a pair of two colonial garden courtyards—make up this friendly lodging a block from its namesake church. Rooms are simply furnished with wood furniture and colonial-style art. A few of the larger rooms have their own kitchen, and are large enough to accommodate a family. (All rooms are nonsmoking, which is another family-friendly feature.) Elsewhere in the hotel, you'll have access to shared kitchen facilities. The hotel offers discounts for long-term stays, as well as baggage storage if you plan to travel elsewhere around Guatemala. **Pros:** friendly owners, family friendly. **Con:** small rooms. ✉ *7 Av. Norte 43 A* ☎ *7832–3197* ☎ *7832–3301* ⊕ *www.merced-landivar.com* ⤳ *23 rooms, 21 with bath, 1 apartment* ♿ *In-room: no phone, kitchen (some), no TV, Wi-Fi. In-hotel: no elevator, laundry service, no-smoking rooms* ☰ *V* ❍ *EP.*

$ ⊞ **Posada Asjemenou.** There are plenty of charming hotels in colonial mansions, but you won't pay through the nose at this one. The rooms are clean and comfortable, although a bit dark—door panels serve as their only windows—and the staff is friendly and eager. The small café serves breakfast and snacks. Lots of good bagels are on the menu. If you're hankering for more substantial fare, head to the nearby pizzeria run by the same family. **Pros:** good value, lively restaurant. **Cons:** no outside windows, occasional noise from courtyard. ✉ *5 Av. Norte 31, at 1 C. Del Arco* ☎ *7832–2670* ✉ *asjemenou1@yahoo.com* ⤳ *14 rooms, 11 with bath, 3 with shared bath* ♿ *In-room: no a/c, no phone, no TV. In-hotel: restaurant, bar* ☰ *AE, MC, V* ❍ *CP.*

¢ ⊞ **Jungle Party.** The cleanest, cheapest, and friendliest budget hostel in Antigua, Jungle Party is the place for backpackers and bargain hunters who enjoy its little touches like nightly happy hours and Saturday-evening barbecues. The simple, shared rooms with bunk beds are spotless and the showers have plenty of hot water. The pleasant courtyard restaurant has funky orange and yellow mushroom-shape chairs and swinging hammocks for lounging. Salvadoran owner Monica is happy to help with travel arrangements. They also serve some of the best smoothies Antigua has to offer. **Pros:** friendly atmosphere, many activities. **Con:** occasional noise from countyard. ✉ *6 Av. Norte 20* ☎ *7832–0463* ⊕ *www.junglepartyhostal.com* ⤳ *35 beds in 6 dormitories* ♿ *In-room: no a/c, no phone, no TV. In-hotel: restaurant, bar, laundry service, public Internet* ☰ *AE, DC, MC, V* ❍ *BP.*

NIGHTLIFE & THE ARTS

Nightlife, Antigua style, offers you the chance to flex your cultural knowledge, or to flex your arm hoisting a few with friends. The city is filled with watering holes. Many of those within a few blocks of the Parque Central are favored by people studying Spanish at one of the many language schools.

Your best source for upcoming events is the monthly English-language *Revue* magazine (⊕ *www.revuemag.com*). The same company publishes the monthly Spanish-language magazine, *Recrearte* (⊕ *www. revistarecrearte.com*) with a similar focus. Pick up a free copy of either in hotels and restaurants around town, or check out their respective Web sites.

THE ARTS

Numerous cultural events sprinkle Antigua's evening calendar, including two regularly scheduled weekly lecture series in English, both of which, unfortunately, take place on Tuesday evenings.

Antigua Tours' Elizabeth Bell presents a slide show entitled **Antigua: Behind the Walls** each Tuesday evening at 6 PM at the CSA language school (⌂6 Av. Norte 15 ☎7832–5821). She has assembled her vast collection of images during her almost four decades in Antigua. Admission is Q40, and proceeds go to buy textbooks for area elementary schools. Bell supplements her weekly offerings on Wednesday during the six weeks of Lent with a slide presentation devoted to Antigua's Semana Santa processions, also 6 PM, at the same place.

Weekly lectures in English with a political or social bent on some topic related to Guatemala get underway on the patio at the **Rainbow Café** (⌂7 Av. Sur 8 ☎7832–4205) each Tuesday evening at 5:30 PM. Come early. Seats fill up quickly, but don't be afraid to grab a chair at a partially occupied table. Admission is Q25.

The city's most active cultural venue is the **Centro Cultural El Sitio** (⌂5 C. Poniente 1 ☎7832–3037 ⊕www.elsitiocultural.org), which presents concerts, films, and lectures (always in Spanish) several nights a week.

The **Mesón Panza Verde** (⌂5 Av. Sur 19 ☎7832–1745 ⊕www.panza-verde.com) hotel and restaurant is known for its weekly Art Flicks and Dharma Flicks film series—most films are in English—as well as the occasional concert.

The Spanish government funds the **Centro Cultural de España** (⌂6 Av. Norte between 3 and 4 C. Poniente ☎7832–1276), as it does with similar institutions all over Latin America. Something is going on, whether a film, lecture, or concert, a couple nights a week. Nearly all presentations are in Spanish.

NIGHTLIFE

BARS

Down a beer with proudly Bohemian friends at **Café No Sé** (⌂1 Av. Sur 11C ☎5242–3574). Unpretentious **El Muro Pub** (⌂3 C. Oriente 19D ☎7832–8849) variously has classic-rock nights, darts nights, and just all-around good times and good conversation. If you're homesick for a pub head to **Reilly's** (⌂5 Av. Norte 31), where pub grub and Guinness are served in a relaxed atmosphere. Jan, the friendly expat owner, serves up a variety of concoctions to help you forget the travails of the day. Its Sunday-night pub quiz is an Antigua institution. Upstairs from Frida's is **El Ático** (⌂5 Av. Norte 29 ☎7832–1296), a popular local hangout. The pool table is free as long as you're drinking.

Guatemalans and foreigners alike enjoy the contemporary elegance of **La Sala** (⌂6 C. Poniente 9 ☎7832–9524). Tuesday is movie night, live music is on tap Thursday to Saturday nights, and Sunday is salsa night. They close their doors around midnight, but the party continues on inside until the wee hours of the morning. Chow down on pub grub with a friendly expat crowd at **Micho's Pub** (⊠4 C. Oriente 10 ☎7832–5680). If the interior bar gets too smoky, move to the back patio.

Root for your favorite team at **Monoloco** (⊠5 Av. Sur 6 ☎7832–4235), where soccer matches are always on the television. Wash down one of the giant burritos with a pint of one of the microbrews. **Sabor Cubano** (⊠4 C. Oriente 3A ☎7832–4137) dishes up music and food, Cuban-style evenings, Thursday through Sunday. **Sangre** (⊠5 Av. Norte 33A ☎5656–7618) serves wine and *bocas* (appetizers) for your noshing pleasure each evening.

LIVE MUSIC
The conversation is convivial and the cocktails are inexpensive at **Riki's** (⊠4 Av. Norte 4 ☎No phone). Live music is yours seven nights a week, with jazz on Wednesday, Saturday, and Sunday. **La Peña de Sol Latino** (⊠5 C. Poniente 15C ☎7832–1668) has Latin music nightly beginning at 7 PM.

DANCE CLUBS
You can dance Wednesday through Sunday night away at **La Casbah** (⊠5 Av. Norte 45 ☎7832–2640). Latin rhythms make the place popular. A packed salsa club with a gin-and-tonic, 1920s speakeasy feel, **La Sin Ventura** (⊠5 Av. Sur 8 ☎7832–4884) frequently has live bands on the weekends. A 20-something crowd heads to **Torero's** (⊠Av. Los Recolectos 6 ☎7832–5141) Thursday to Saturday nights out near the Central Market.

OUTDOOR ACTIVITIES

BIKING
The rolling hills that surround Antigua make for great mountain biking. Local agencies rent bikes as well as equipment like helmets and water bottles. **Mayan Bike Tours** (⊠1 Av. Sur 15 ☎7832–3383) offers trips ranging from easy rides in a morning or afternoon to more challenging treks lasting several days. **Old Town Outfitters** (⊠5 Av. Sur 12 ☎7832–4171 ⊕www.bikeguatemala.com) caters to a backpack crowd, but its trips are suitable for people of all ages. It also offers volcano hikes and rock-climbing excursions.

HIKING
Antigua's best volcano expeditions are offered by **Eco-Tours Chejos** (⊠3 C. Poniente 24 ☎7832–2657), whose friendly owner has climbed Volcán Pacaya more than 1,800 times. The prices are higher than most, but there are usually fewer people in each group. **Sin Fronteras** (⊠5 Av. Norte 15A ☎7832–1017 ⊕www.sinfront.com) will take you on a one-day trip to Pacayá or a two-day trip to Fuego or Acatenango. **Voyageur** (⊠4 C. Oriente 14 ☎7832–4237) is a reputable outfitter with excursions to Pacaya. **Adrenalina** (⊠5 Av. Norte 31 ☎7832–1108 ⊕www.adrenalinatours.com) also leads daily guided hikes to all four volcanoes.

CLOSE UP

Antigua's Volcanoes

Four volcanoes make up this region's sector of a seismic spine that runs the width of Guatemala from the Mexican to Salvadoran borders, forming a ridge between the highlands and the Pacific Lowlands. Three of these masses are directly visible from Antigua. Two of the volcanoes make for popular ascents if you are in reasonable shape; the others require considerable climbing experience. Don't wear sandals to climb any of these monoliths; the volcanic rock can be razor sharp.

The volcanoes' popularity and proximity to the metropolitan area have translated into safety issues, criminal in addition to volcanic. The worst of the problems took place a decade ago, and since then, security has been beefed up, and crime on the volcanoes' slopes is at its lowest in years. The risk still exists however, and we suggest only making the ascent as part of an organized excursion. Many operators in Antigua and Guatemala City lead trips to the volcanoes. Ask about security precautions they take.

Volcán Agua: Agua is the nearly perfectly conical mass that looms 10 km (6 mi) directly south of Antigua and forms its postcard backdrop. The 3,760-meter (12,335-foot) mountain was named "water" by Spanish colonists who saw the volcano spew rivers of water and rock over their original capital at nearby Ciudad Vieja in 1541. That is the last time Agua erupted, although volcanologists say that the volcano will always pose some risk to Antigua. Agua offers the easiest ascent of the four regional volcanoes, but its lack of activity means you go for the views and little else. Excursions depart from the nearby village of Santa María de Jesús.

Volcán Acatenango and **Volcán Fuego**: It's impossible not to discuss these two volcanoes together, joined at the hip as they are by a high ridge. Area residents refer to the massif, 19 km (11½ mi) southwest of Antigua, as the *camellón* ("the big camel"). Acatenango itself is two summits, the 3,976-meter (13,044-foot) Pico Mayor and the 3,880-meter (12,729-foot) Yepocapa. Acatenango blew its top in 1924 and 1927, but has been dormant for more than three decades. However, sulfur gases fizz up through its fumaroles. The same is not true for the continuously active 3,763-meter (12,345-foot) Fuego, whose name means "fire" in Spanish. The name is apt, low-level though its activity may be. Climbing Fuego and Acatenango is for experts only.

Volcán Pacaya: The area's most popular volcano ascent is to Pacaya, not visible from Antigua itself and most associated with Guatemala City. The 2,252-meter (7,388-foot) peak sits 25 km (15½ mi) southeast of Antigua, and the same distance south of the capital's La Aurora International Airport. Pacaya's popularity stems from its activity. It has logged 23 major eruptions since the 16th century—the last in 2005—and near constant displays of smoke and lava since 1965. Eruptions in 1998 and 2000 blanketed much of the region with ash and closed the airport for several days each. Excursions to Pacaya leave from either Antigua or Guatemala City. Most depart in the early afternoon to get you to the summit in time for the early-evening spectacle. The vapors smell terrible, so bring a handkerchief to cover your nose. You'll also want a sweater as the sun begins to set.

SHOPPING

The single largest concentration of shops can be found in the **Mercado de Artesanías** (⊠*4 C. Poniente and Alameda de Santa Lucía*), but stroll down any street and you'll find boutiques selling everything from finely embroidered blouses to beautiful ceramics.

BOOKS

Thanks to its sizable expatriate population, Antigua has Guatemala's best selection of English-language reading material. Facing Parque Central, **La Casa del Conde**

> ### SPAAAAH
>
> **Antigua Spa Resort.** Massages, facials, and a variety of other treatments are available at this spa (aka Jardines del Spa), roughly 3 km (2 mi) from Antigua in the village of San Pedro El Panorama. Free transportation to and from Antigua is provided when you book an appointment. ⊠ *3 Av. 8-66, Zona 14* ☎*7832-3960 or 2333-4620* ☎*7832-3968.*

(⊠*5 Av. Norte 4* ☎*7832-3322*) has a good selection of books. Along with new and used books, **Hamlin & White** (⊠*4 C. Oriente 12A* ☎*7832–7075*) sells newspapers and magazines. Hamlin & White's sister store, **Tiempo Libre** (⊠*5 Av. Norte 25B* ☎*7832–1816*), stocks an equally good selection of books. **Librería del Pensativo** (⊠*5 Av. Norte 29* ☎*7832–0729*) has a huge selection of used books and **Un Poco de Todo** (⊠*5 Av. Norte 10* ☎*7832–4676*) is a good fallback for a decent selection of English titles.

CLOTHING

The **Central American Art Gallery** (⊠*1 Av. Norte 10* ☎*7832–0618*) offers a contemporary-patterned twist on the standard Mayan textile fare. **Colibrí** (⊠*4 C. Oriente 3B* ☎*7832–6404*) sells traditional back-strap-loom textiles prepared by a local women's cooperative. **Katún** (⊠*5 C. Poniente 2* ☎*7832–6601*) crafts a nice selection of cotton T-shirts with exclusive designs that make a nice change from the ubiquitous Gallo beer wear. **Nativo's** (⊠*5 Av. Norte 25B* ☎*7832–6556*) carries a great selection of shawls, sashes, and blouses in traditional design. **Nim Po't** (⊠*5 Av. Norte 29* ☎*7832–2681*) is a self-proclaimed *centro de textiles tradicionales*. Here you'll find a large selection of fabrics from a few dozen neighboring villages. **Pues Si Tú** (⊠*4 C. Poniente 30* ☎*7832–7837*) is a little shop that carries a variety of clothing in traditional patterns.

A 10-minute drive southwest of Antigua brings you to San Antonio Aguas Calientes, a dusty little village built around a hot springs. It's worth a special trip here to visit **Artesanías Unidas** (⊠*San Antonio Aguas Calientes* ☎*7831–5950*) known for its incomparable selection of handwoven fabrics.

GALLERIES

Centro de Arte Popular Galería (⊠*3 Av. Norte 10* ☎*7832–6634*) is a small gallery that features works by contemporary Guatemalan artists. An excellent selection of primitivist paintings is on display at **Wer Art Gallery** (⊠*4 C. Oriente 27* ☎*7832–7161*).

All That Glitters

Several jade shops and factories populate the streets east of Antigua's Parque Central. Although Guatemala's best-known gem is extracted in the eastern part of the country near Zacapa, jade is inexorably linked with Antigua, where the processing and polishing goes on. Much of the work is done by hand, and most shops have an affiliated factory, sometimes at another location, sometimes out in back, open to guided tours.

The umbrella term "jade" technically encompasses two types of silicate stone: nephrite and jadeite. Nephrite is mined in East Asia, giving rise to its sometimes name "Chinese jade." It's less durable, and less valuable than the rarer jadeite, which is found only in Guatemala, Russia, and Myanmar. High content of sodium, aluminum, iron, cobalt, and nickel give jadeite its distinctive durability and brilliance. Though green is the color usually associated with jadeite—experts recognize 25 tones of green—black, white, and lavender also make up its spectrum.

Olmec, Mayan, and Aztec peoples in pre-Columbian Mesoamerica highly prized the stone. In fact, the Olmec established lucrative jade trade routes throughout the region. The Spanish observed the Maya using the mineral to cure various loin and kidney ailments, and so gave it the name *piedra de ijada* (stone of loin), from which the English word jade was taken. The jade became so integral a part of Mayan funeral masks that it was deemed to be a passport to the afterlife. Indeed, one of the requisite items for sale in most shops here, among the standard jewelry offerings, is an entirely jade reproduction of the famous sixth-century Tikal funeral mask unearthed in 1963.

TIPS:
Two bits of advice regarding jade shopping: First, a lot of the "jade" floating around Antigua (and even the market in Chichicastenango) isn't jade at all. Don't buy from the vendors who sidle up to you on the street here and say, "Jade, mister?" Their wares *are* dirt cheap, but who knows what you're actually getting? It's possibly quartz. Make your purchases from a reputable shop in Antigua or Guatemala City, one that can certify that you have purchased true jadeite. Such an establishment is not going to gamble its reputation on a knock-off stone.

The pronunciation of the word in Spanish, where *J* is always rendered with an *H*-sound, is *HAH-day*.

La Antigua Galería de Arte (⊠4 *C. Oriente 15* ☎7832–2124 ⊕*www.artintheamericas.com*) features works from the 19th and 20th centuries. The **Mesón Panza Verde** (⊠5 *Av. Sur 19* ☎7832–1745) hotel and restaurant has a small collection of rotating exhibits.

Centro Cultural El Sitio (⊠5 *C. Poniente 15* ☎7832–3037) screens many films and hosts concerts in addition to maintaining a small gallery.

HANDICRAFTS

With a wide selection of wood figures and carvings and jewelry, **Casa de Artes** (⊠4 *Av. Sur 11* ☎7832–0792 ⊕*www.casadeartes.com.gt*) is a nice place to browse. **Casa de los Gigantes** (⊠7 *C. Oriente 18* ☎7832–

4656) has a good selection of quality items, including genuine antique festival masks. **El Mercadito** is a warren of vendors' stalls (⊠*5 Av. Norte 4A* ☎*No phone*) that offers standard souvenir fare. **La Casa de Angelina** (⊠*4 C. Oriente 22* ☎*7832–0203*) sells surreal items made of carved wood. For hand-painted pottery by local artisans, try **Topis Diseños** (⊠*5 Av. Norte 20B* ☎*7832–2429*).

JEWELRY

Jade is mined in the eastern part of the country, but it is fashioned into jewelry almost exclusively in Antigua. Most of the jade shops offer free tours of their facilities, so you can see how the stones are selected, cut, and polished. The craftsmanship is beautiful, and many pieces are quite affordable by U.S. standards. **La Casa del Jade** (⊠*4 C. Oriente 10* ☎*7832–3974* ⊕*www.lacasadeljade.com*) is small but nice. Perhaps the best place to watch artisans carving the green stone is at **Jades** (⊠*4 C. Oriente 34* ☎*7832–3841* ⊕*www.jademaya.com*). Former U.S. president Bill Clinton bought a necklace here for daughter Chelsea; his photo greets you as you walk in. With a small in-house workshop, **Jades Imperio Maya** (⊠*5 C. Oriente 2* ☎*7832–0927* ⊠*4 C. Poniente 16B* ☎*7832–0699* ⊕*www.jadesimperiomaya.com*) has an extremely friendly staff.

Tired of green stones? **Joyería del Angel** (⊠*4 C. Oriente 5A* ☎*7832–5334*) has a fine selection of 100% jade-free jewelry. **Platería Típica Maya** (⊠*7 C. Oriente 9* ☎*7832–2883*) is a top-notch silver retailer.

SIDE TRIPS

As in Guatemala City, Antigua's numerous tour operators can take you out to much of the country on a day trip. Guatemala City lies less than one hour away, as do several volcanoes in the immediate region (*see Antigua's Volcanoes box, above*). Panajachel and Lake Atitlán are about two hours west of town. The famous Thursday and Sunday markets in Chichicastenango are a must. The famous Maya ruins at Copán, Honduras, lie a few hours away (*see Chapter 5*), as does Guatemala's own claim to fame in the Mayan world, Tikal in El Petén. That last one, if done as a day trip, entails a flight from Guatemala City.

ANTIGUA ESSENTIALS

TRANSPORTATION

BY AIR

The nearest airport is Guatemala City's Aeropuerto Internacional La Aurora, a little less than an hour's drive away. If your hotel does not offer a transfer from the airport, there are plenty of shuttle buses that run this route.

BY BUS

Several companies run frequent shuttle buses between Guatemala City and Antigua. Adrenalina, Atitrans, and Turansa are all reputable companies. Buses leave every 15 minutes from 18 Calle and 4 Avenida in Zona 1 in Guatemala City. They depart on a similar schedule from the bus station in Antigua. It's best to call ahead for reservations, but you can also purchase tickets on board.

Adrenalina, Atitrans, and Turansa also offer service to the Western Highlands, with the cost ranging from Q100 for Chichicastenango and Panajachel to Q200 for Quetzaltenango. You can also catch a public bus at the terminal, which is cheaper but much less comfortable. There are one or two direct buses to Panajachel and Quetzaltenango each day, as well as five or six bound for Chichicastenango. Tickets cost about Q16.

Shuttle Companies **Adrenalina** (✉ *5 Av. Norte 31* ☎ *7832-1108* ⊕ *www. adrenalinatours.com*). **Atitrans** (✉ *6 Av. Sur 8* ☎ *7832-3371* ⊕ *www.atitrans.com*). **Turansa** (✉ *9 C. y Salida a Ciudad Vieja* ☎ *7832-2928* ⊕ *www.turansa.com*).

Bus Stations **Terminal de Buses** (✉ *Alameda Santa Lucía at 4 C. Poniente*).

BY CAR

The roads around Antigua are mostly well paved, so drives through the countryside can be quite pleasant. Keep on your guard, though, as other vehicles may ignore traffic laws and common sense. As one jovial man behind the wheel of a bus recently said, "All drivers in Guatemala are crazy."

To reach Antigua, drive west out of Guatemala City via the Calzada Roosevelt, which becomes the Pan-American Highway. Signs direct you either to ANTIGUA or ANTIGUA GUATEMALA. At San Lucas Sacatepéquez turn right off the highway and drive south to Antigua. The last several kilometers before Antigua have a steep descent. Note the FRENE CON MOTOR warnings ("engine brake")—use your lowest gear—and the RAMPA DE EMERGENCIA signs for the emergency off-ramps for vehicles whose brakes give out. If you're coming from the highlands, head south near Chimaltenango.

If you want to rent a car to explore Antigua, it's a good idea to do so in Guatemala City's Aeropuerto Internacional La Aurora. In Antigua, reputable local agencies are Ahorrent and Tabarini.

Local Car Rental Agencies **Ahorrent** (✉ *6 C. Poniente 29 A* ☎ *2332-7744* ⊕ *www.ahorrent.com*). **Tabarini** (✉ *6 Av. Sur 22* ☎ *7832-8107* ⊕ *www.tabarini. com*).

TAXIS

A taxi between Guatemala City and Antigua should cost about Q200. Many run between Aeropuerto Internacional La Aurora and Antigua. Taxis Antigua has a good reputation. Your hotel or restaurant can call a taxi for you after dark. Most Antigua taxis are three-wheeled Bajaj vehicles made in India. People here refer to them as "tuk-tuks."

Contacts **Taxis Antigua** (☎ *7832-0479*).

CLOSE UP

Coffee? Macadamia Nuts?

The northern Las Verapaces is the country's area most culturally and historically tied to coffee (see *The Magic Bean box, in Chapter 4*), but Guatemala Antigua gets rave reviews as the country's best-known java ambassador to the world. Several *fincas* (plantations) lie near Antigua and offer tours. If your interests run more to macadamia nuts, one farm raises those, too. Make reservations at least one day in advance for any of the following options.

Finca Filadelfia (⊠*150 meters [492 feet] north of Iglesia de San Felipe de Jesús* ☎*7831–1191* ⊕*www.rdaltoncoffee.com*) offers coffee tours weekdays 9 AM and 2 PM, Sat. 9 AM. **Finca Los Nietos** (⊠*6 km [4 mi] from Antigua, San Lorenzo El Cubo* ☎*7831–5438* ⊕*www.fincalosnietos.com*) also offers coffee tours weekdays 8 to 11 AM. **Finca Valhalla** (⊠*7 km [4 mi] southwest of Antigua, ½ km [¼ mi] before San Miguel Dueñas* ☎*7831–5799 or 7888–6308*) has daily macadamia tours, from 7 AM to 5 PM.

CONTACTS & RESOURCES

EMERGENCIES

For all emergencies call the municipal police department. Officers patrol most blocks downtown in male–female pairs. Look for them in white pullover shirts, dark trousers, and baseball caps. Contact the tourist police for free, regularly scheduled escorts to the Cerro de la Cruz, information, and minor matters. The office is just around the corner from the Parque Central, and is open 24 hours.

Emergencies Police (⊠*5 C. Poniente, west end of Palacio del Capitánes* ☎*7832–0251*). **Tourist police** (⊠*4 Av. Norte, Palacio del Ayuntamiento* ☎*7832–0535*).

Hospitals Hospital Privado Hermano Pedro (⊠*C. de Los Peregrinos and 4 Av. Sur* ☎*7832–1190*).

Pharmacies Farmacia Fénix (⊠*5 C. Poniente 11C* ☎*7832–0503*).

INTERNET

With its sizable population of expatriates, Antigua has a good supply of Internet cafés. The competition is fierce, so expect very low prices. Enlaces and Enlínea have conveniently located offices. Antigua Post also has a scanner.

Contacts Antigua Post (⊠*6 Av. Sur 12*). **Enlaces** (⊠*6 Av. Norte 1*). **Enlínea** (⊠*1 C. Poniente 9* ⊠*1 Av. Sur 17* ⊠*5 Av. Sur 12*).

MAIL & SHIPPING

El Correo, Antigua's main post office, is across from the bus station. You can drop off your letters here, or ask the staff at your hotel to mail them for you. For packages try Envíos Etc.

Overnight Services Envíos Etc. (⊠*3 Av. Norte 26*).

Post Offices El Correo (⊠*4 C. Poniente and Calzada Santa Lucía* ☎*7832–0485*).

MONEY MATTERS

Banquetzal has an office where you can exchange U.S. dollars and traveler's checks, on the north side of Parque Central. It stays open weeknights until 7 PM and weekends until 1 PM. You won't have a problem finding ATMs in Antigua. The Bancared system, with a machine near Parque Central, has one that accepts Cirrus- and Plus-affiliated cards.

Contacts **Bancared** (⊠4 C. Poniente 22). **Banquetzal** (⊠4 C. Poniente 12 ☎7832–1111).

SAFETY

Antigua is one of Guatemala's safest cities, and the streets around Parque Central are patrolled by the municipal and tourist police. Farther from the square you should walk in groups or take taxis after the sun goes down. Be careful in the countryside, where there have been some robberies. If you plan to tackle one of the nearby volcanoes, hire a reputable guide and ask what safety precautions the company takes.

TOURS

There are a number of travel agencies that can book you on trips around the region and throughout the country. Among the better known are Chiltepe Tours, Rainbow Travel Center, Vision Travel, and Turansa. One of the best is Antigua Tours, run by independent guide and long-time resident Elizabeth Bell. It offers all sorts of personalized trips, from walking tours of Antigua, daily except Sunday, to excursions to Lake Atitlán, Chichicastenango, and Tikal.

A number of *fincas* (farms) in the hills around Antigua offer tours. Finca Los Nietos, and Finca Filadelfia, both coffee plantations, and Finca Valhalla, a macadamia farm, are both southwest of the city.

Tour companies **Adrenalina** (⊠5 Av. Norte 31 ☎7832–1108 ⊕www.adrenalina-tours.com). **Antigua Tours** (⊠3 C. Oriente 28 ☎7832–5821 ⊕www.antiguatours. net). **Chiltepe Tours** (⊠7 C. Poniente 15 ☎5709–0913 ⊕www.chiltepetours. com). **Rainbow Travel Center** (⊠7 Av. Sur 8 ☎7832–4202). **Turansa** (⊠9 C. Poniente at Salida a la Ciudad Vieja ☎7832–4691). **Vision Travel** (⊠3 Av. Norte 3 ☎7832–3293 ⊕www.guatemalainfo.com).

VISITOR INFORMATION

Inguat, the national tourism office, has an office in the Palacio de los Capitanes Generales, on the south side of Parque Central. It is open weekdays 8 to 1 and 2 to 5 and opens at 9 on weekends.

Information **Inguat** (⊠5 C. Poniente, Palacio de los Capitanes Generales ☎7832–0763).

LANGUAGE SCHOOLS

Antigua ranks second to Quetzaltenango in sheer number of Spanish schools within its city limits. Its desirability as a place to live means that tuition and living costs skew slightly higher here than elsewhere around the country. The city's huge international population (resident, student, and tourist) leads to an oft-stated disadvantage to studying here: it becomes distressingly easy to spend all your out-of-class time with other English speakers. This is only a problem if you make it one. Don't succumb, and you can learn as much Spanish here as you can anywhere. Speaking of not succumbing, sign up with reputable schools such as the ones below and not with the touts who greet you at the public bus terminal.

Academia de Español Intercontinental (✉7 Av. Norte 56 ☎7832-5147 ⊕www.spanishantigua.com).

Academia de Español Probigua (✉6 Av. Norte 41B ☎7832-2998 ⊕www.probigua.org).

Alameda Spanish Academy (✉6 Av. Sur 7 ☎7832-1525 ⊕www.alamedaacademy.com).

APPE (✉1 C. Oriente 15 ☎7832-2552 ⊕www.appeschool.com).

Casa de Lenguas (✉6 Av. Norte 40 ☎7832-4846 ⊕www.casadelenguas.com).

Centro América Spanish Academy (✉Callejón Santa Ana ☎7832-5147 ⊕www.guacalling.com/ca).

Centro de Aprendizaje de Español Universal (✉2 Av. Sur 34 ☎5508-5999 ⊕www.universalspanishschool.com).

Centro Lingüístico La Unión (✉1 Av. Sur 21 ☎7832-7337 ⊕www.launion.edu.gt).

Centro Lingüístico Maya (✉5 C. Poniente 20 ☎7832-0656 ⊕www.clmmaya.com).

Cima del Mundo Spanish School (✉4 C. Oriente 35 ☎7832-0064 ⊕www.nurimaruschool.com).

CSA (✉6 Av. Norte 15 ☎7832-3923 ⊕www.learncsa.com).

Don Pedro de Alvarado Escuela de Español (✉1A C. Poniente No. 39 ☎7832-6645 ⊕www.donpedrospanishschool.com).

Guate-Linda Language Center (✉6 C. Poniente 40 ☎7832-0720 ⊕www.guatelindacenter.com).

Happy Spanish House (✉C. de los Pasos 7A ☎7832-1940 ⊕www.happyspanishhouse.com).

Ixchel Spanish School (✉3 Av. Sur 6 ☎7832-7137 ⊕www.ixchelschool.com).

Los Capitanes Generales Spanish Academy (✉4 Av. Sur 2 ☎7832-8769 ⊕www.loscapitanes.com).

San José El Viejo Spanish School (✉5 Av. Sur 34 ☎7832-3028 ⊕www.sanjoseelviejo.com).

Spanish Academy Antigüeña (✉7 C. Oriente 15 ☎7832-5057 ⊕www.acad.conexion.com).

Spanish Academy Sevilla (✉1 Av. Sur 8 ☎7832-5101 ⊕www.sevill-antigua.com).

Zamora Academia (✉9 C. Poniente 7 ☎7832-7670 ⊕www.learnspanish-guatemala.com).

The Highlands

WORD OF MOUTH

"We took the boat from Panajachel to Santiago Atitlán, across Lake Atitlán. It's a noteworthy trip: the beautiful blue lake is surrounded with volcanic mountains, often puffing."

—shadowcatcher

"We've been to Chichicastenango three times, but the last time, we were so unhappy with the market that we left early. The market has grown, and they've made the aisles so narrow that you can hardly get up/down them to look at anything. And we found the prices were better and the quality the same or better in Panajachel."

—sandy_b

THE REGION THAT LOCALS CALL the *Occidente* (west) or the *Altiplano* (high plain) is the Guatemala that everyone comes to see. The highlands begin near the colonial capital of Antigua and run all the way to the border of Mexico, in a spectacular stretch of territory where grumbling volcanoes rise above broad alpine lakes, narrow river ravines, subtropical valleys, misty cloud forests, and pastoral plains. All this makes the highlands an ideal place for outdoor activities.

The highlands equal nature, but for most visitors, they offer Guatemala's ultimate cultural experience. The region is home to the majority of Guatemala's indigenous people, most of whom live in small villages nestled in the valleys and perched on the hillsides. Village life consists of backbreaking work in the fields. Most survive on subsistence farming, selling what little is left over. Entire families pack fruits, vegetables, and whatever else they have onto their backs and head to market. Highland markets were once a local affair, but in the past decade or so they have begun to attract the attention of the rest of the world. Market day, held at least once a week in most communities, is as much a social gathering as anything else. Activity starts in the wee hours, when there is still a chill in the air. Bargaining and selling are carried out in hushed, amicable tones. The momentum wanes around late afternoon as the crowds depart, eager to head home before the sun sinks behind the mountains.

This combination of natural and cultural beauty leads us to use an oft-overused term to describe the highlands: the region is Guatemala at its most fabulous. We wager you'll agree.

ORIENTATION & PLANNING

ORIENTATION

This immense region seems a bit more manageable if you envision it as four clusters. Panajachel and Lake Atitlán lie at the southeastern corner of the region, and are most visitors' first encounter with the highlands. Chichicastenango and the El Quiche heartland to the north form a second group of attractions, although most visitors don't make it past Chichi to Santa Cruz del Quiché and Nebaj farther north. Quetzaltenango, the country's second largest city, and its orbit of mountain-market towns form a third bunch of places to visit. Off toward the Mexican border, Huehuetenango and Todos Santos Cuchumatán are the final, less-visited cluster and the heart of the country's Mam culture.

PLANNING

WHEN TO GO

The highlands have distinct rainy (May to October) and dry (November to April) seasons, the latter of which offers the best weather conditions for outdoor-market shopping, lake boating, and volcano hiking. Travel during the rainy season is rarely a hardship; it usually rains

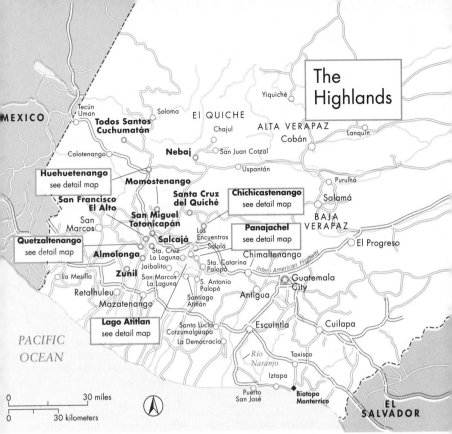

just for a couple of hours in the afternoon. Evenings get chilly enough for a jacket, and can get downright cold the farther west you travel. In December and January temperatures dropping to near freezing at higher elevations. That said, the highlands have no weather-based high and low seasons per se. The region does see a greater number of visitors in July and August, and during Christmas and Holy Week.

Time spent here combines nicely with a visit to Antigua or Guatemala City (two or three hours from Lake Atitlán, respectively) or the Pacific Lowlands. Crisp Quetzaltenango sits a scant hour from balmy Retalhuleu.

GETTING AROUND

Your own vehicle is ideal (but far from essential) for exploring this vast region. Although mountainous, Guatemala's highlands are not the Andes, so driving isn't too treacherous, and primary and most secondary roads are in decent shape. The Pan-American Highway forms the transportation spine of this region, although most of what you'll want to see lies off the highway. (The northern hub city of Huehuetenango and the market town of Salcajá are the only two sights we list that actually sit on the highway.) North of Huehuetenango and Nebaj, roads deteriorate to dirt or gravel.

A BIT OF HISTORY

Following the decline of lowland Mayan society in Guatemala's northern Petén region, beginning around AD 500, subsequent generations began to seek refuge in the adjoining highlands, carving out livelihoods of agriculture and commerce for themselves. Although we tend to think of "Maya" as a monolithic concept, these were several distinct peoples, speaking different languages, who saw little in common with their compatriots in the next valley. Alone, each group proved no match for Pedro de Alvarado and the Spanish conquistadors, who were able to employ a divide-and-conquer strategy to subjugate most of them.

Much of the country's 1960 to 1996 civil war was fought in the highlands. During the "scorched earth" campaigns of the early 1980s, entire towns were burned to the ground and tens of thousands of people were tortured and killed by paramilitary forces. The violence was designed to terrify the indigenous people into refusing to assist the rebel guerrillas. Thousands fled into the mountains or across the border into Mexico or Belize.

Although many issues remain unresolved, the people of the highlands are now weary of fighting, and most, regardless of their wartime sympathies, say that they simply want peace. The army is gone, thankfully stripped of its internal-security role, and has been replaced by civilian police, whose members come from their local communities. Problems remain, and grievances are numerous, but everyone seems interested in moving on and putting the past behind them.

Large, Greyhound-style buses connect Guatemala City with Quetzaltenango and Huehuetenango. Beyond that, the infamous cramped "chicken buses" form the backbone of the transportation network here. Most visitors opt for the comfort of scheduled minivan tourist shuttles to get to most other points.

WHAT TO DO

The Guatemala of the postcards and tourist brochures doesn't disappoint. The highlands' what-to-do list grows out of its position as the bridge between pre- and post-Columbian Mesoamerica. This region blends the best of Mayan and European cultures. Although Christianity has been practiced here for 500 years, it still has seemingly only a tentative hold. Experience the cacophony of weekly markets, the drifting incense, the exploding fireworks, the rumbling volcanoes, and a morning boat ride zipping across Lake Atitlanán.

RESTAURANTS & CUISINE

You'll find a few international restaurants in Quetzaltenango (by virtue of its being a large city) and in Panajachel (due to its concentration of tourists), but local cuisine in the highlands echoes the land itself: hearty, filling, and substantial. A few signature highland dishes appear on the menus of most local restaurants. Chicken *pepián* (a fricassee in pumpkin and sesame sauce), chile relleno (a stuffed bell pepper), and *arroz con pollo* (chicken with rice) all make use of abundant regional ingre-

VOLCANO VIEWS

From left to right, the three volcanoes you see that make that oh-so-perfect backdrop across Lake Atitlán from Panajachel are: **Volcán Atitlán** (3,523 meters/11,560 feet), **Volcán Tolimán** (3,151 meters/10,340 feet), and **Volcán San Pedro** (3,023 meters/9,920 feet). All are dormant. San Pedro is logistically the easiest of the three to climb—access is via San Pedro La Laguna—but "easy" is relative here. The ascent is steep, and that makes for a steep descent, too. (Think about it.) The trail gets slippery in sections, even during the dry season, and rarely levels off to allow you to catch your breath. Your reward for the grueling hike? The views from the top of San Pedro of the entire lake region are stunning. Atitlán and Tolimán have been ascended, but their remoteness relative to San Pedro has meant occasional robberies of climbers. No matter which one of the three lake volcanoes you attempt, we recommend you climb with an organized excursion.

The 3,772-meter (12,375-foot) **Volcán Santa María** keeps watch over Quetzaltenango. Santa María last erupted in 1902. It and accompanying earthquakes caused widespread damage to the city and to the slopes heading down to the Pacific coast, and killed an estimated 1,500 people. The eruption was said to spew ash as far away as San Francisco, California, and decimated the region's coffee industry, but paradoxically, Santa María's volcanic ash provided a much-needed and fertilizing boost to the countryside near Antigua, allowing that city to take the lead in coffee production. If you can handle the altitude, the dormant volcano is a reasonable day-trip ascent, with stupendous views east as far as Volcán Pacaya south of Guatemala City, and as far west as far as Mexico. The real treat is the view of the nearby 3,500-meter (11,482-foot) **Volcán Santiaguito,** which hatched through the earth during the 1902 eruption of Santa María. Santiaguito, continuously active since then, is too dangerous to climb in its own right. Clouds move in and obscure the views by late morning, making a very early morning start essential. Although safety is far less a concern here than for the volcanoes close to the capital or Atitlán, a few robberies of solo hikers have occurred. We recommend you undertake the trip with an organized tour.

Guatemala's highest peak, the 4,220-meter (13,845-foot) **Volcán Tajumulco,** sits outside the small city of San Marcos, 48 km (29 mi) northeast of Quetzaltenango, and a scant 15 km (9 mi) from the Mexican border. As with Santa María, if you can handle the altitude—gauge your abilities carefully—the ascent itself is reasonable. Numerous Quetzaltenango outfitters organize two-day, one-night Tajumulco trips.

Adrenalina Tours (⊠ *12 Av. 4–25, Zona 1, Quetzaltenango* ☎ *7761–4509* ⊕ *www.adrenalinatours.com*). leads excursions up the Santa María and Tajumulco volcanoes.

Atitrans (⊠ *3 Av. 3–47, Zona 2, Panajachel* ☎ *7762–2246*). leads ascents up the San Pedro volcano.

Quetzaltrekkers (⊠ *Casa Argentina, Diagonal 12 8–67, Zona 1, Quetzaltenango* ☎ *7765–5895* ⊕ *www.quetzaltrekkers.com*). leads trips up the Santa María volcano.

dients. Accompanying them might be frijoles (black beans, usually mashed up with a bit of onion and tomato sauce), corn tortillas, and a caramel-custard flan for dessert. Lunch is the big meal of the day in small-town eateries. Lighter fare is served for dinner in this early-to-bed, early-to-rise region.

ABOUT THE HOTELS

International hotel chains are nowhere to be found in this region,

> **PACKING TIP**
>
> Guatemala has been dubbed the "land of eternal spring," and this region's warm afternoons and cool evenings fit the bill. But Quetzaltenango and other high-altitude towns can get downright cold at night, especially in the winter. There's no need to overpack, but a sweater or jacket is essential.

and aside from a couple of resort-type accommodations on Lake Atitlán, the highlands remain the province of smaller lodgings, most less than 30 rooms each. That makes reservations a good idea any time of year, but especially on weekends. Air-conditioning is unheard of in this part of the country, but you won't miss it at these altitudes. Heat may seem a far more pressing concern, especially the farther west you travel, where the nighttime temperatures get colder. Many lodgings contain *chimineas,* or fireplaces, in their rooms. If not, don't be afraid to ask for an extra blanket.

WHAT IT COSTS IN GUATEMALAN QUETZALES					
	¢	$	$$	$$$	$$$$
RESTAURANTS	under Q40	Q40–Q70	Q70–Q100	Q100–Q130	over Q130
HOTELS	under Q160	Q160–Q360	Q360–Q560	Q560–Q760	over Q760

Restaurant prices are per person for a main course at dinner. Hotel prices are for two people in a standard double room, including tax and service.

LAGO ATITLÁN

Postcard-perfect Lago Atitlán lies at the foot of three massive dormant volcanoes—San Pedro (3,023 meters/9,920 feet), Tolimán (3,152 meters/10,340 feet), and Atitlán (3,523 meters/11,560 feet). Early in the morning and on calm nights the lake's water is as smooth as glass, capturing the huge volcanic cones in its reflection. You'll see why this is arguably the loveliest spot in Guatemala, and why British writer Aldous Huxley dubbed Atitlán "the most beautiful lake in the world."

Most visitors find a place to stay, park for the duration, and make cross-lake day trips (*see Lake Savvy box, below*). More than a dozen communities ring Atitlán. Each has its own personality, and you should be able to find one that matches yours. Panajachel anchors the lake at its one o'clock position, and offers the most polished infrastructure for visitors. Continuing clockwise, intensely traditional Santa Catarina Palopó, and even more traditional San Antonio Palopó lie on Atitlán's eastern shore. Across the lake from Panajachel, Santiago Atitlán welcomes visitors to enjoy its rich culture, tradition, and history—but on its terms. Just east lies party-hearty San Pedro La Laguna, the hot new

Weaving Culture, Weaving History

It is said that the Mayan goddess Ixchel gave the art of weaving to her people. Today's Mayan descendents still make fervent use of that gift in generating the riot of bold, cultural color that punctuates the muted green and brown natural tones of the highlands.

Key to the taut weave of Guatemalan textiles is the back-strap loom, a technique peculiar to this part of the world. Characteristics always identify the wearer with a specific town, a salient feature of indigenous Guatemalan clothing. Although today's Mayan-descended peoples proudly wear their attire as a badge of where they live, the structure actually began as a dress code implemented by Spanish colonial officials. They wanted to be able to identify their subjects by community of origin for tax-collection purposes. The system took on a far darker side during Guatemala's civil war when the government used clothing to identify and target specific indigenous communities.

A brief visit to the highlands will let you scratch the surface in identifying community differences: you'll begin to recognize the bright turquoises and bold geometric patterns of Santa Catarina Palopó; the tight embroidery of Nebaj, the showy, embroidered flowers and birds of Santiago Atitlán, or the knot tie-dyes of Salcajá.

A bit of vocabulary: a *huipil,* sometimes spelled *guipil,* refers to a woman's blouse. Structurally, it is little more than two pieces of cloth sewn together, but what a huipil lacks in tailoring, it more than makes up for in elaborate design. Equally simple

in fit is her *corte,* a wraparound skirt, also woven with complex patterns. In some communities, women wear a *tocoyal,* a piece of cloth wrapped tightly and worn as a circular headdress. (Alternately, this headgear is called a *cinta,* but foreigners often refer to it simply as a "halo.") What about traditional menswear? You won't see much of that, period—you'll come to that realization after a short time in the highlands—except in a few isolated communities such as Todos Santos Cuchumatán, where men still don a traditional woven shirt (*camisa*) and knee-length trousers (*calzoncillos*). Those trousers may be convered by an apron-like *sobrepantalón,* and a belt or sash (*faja*) might accent the ensemble.

The market for Guatemalan textiles has grown by leaps and bounds, and many villages have benefited, but, alas, many of the finer points of the weaving tradition are being left by the wayside to accommodate the frenzied shoppers. The traditional back-strap looms are speedily being replaced with gleaming sewing machines so garments can be churned out faster. The patterns that once relayed information about the wearer's town are now abandoned for those favored by visitors. Even those garments not destined for the tourist market have undergone change. The explosion of vendors selling *ropa americana*—literally "American clothing," but a generic term referring to secondhand clothes—means that a pair of jeans or a sweater can be had for a fraction of the cost (and time) it takes to produce a huipil and corte.

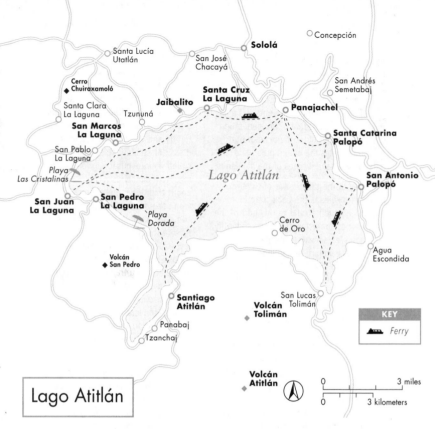

Lago Atitlán

destination on the budget-travel circuit. Next door is indigenous, environmentally minded San Juan La Laguna followed by tiny Jaibalito, so small that it doesn't appear on some maps. New Age devotees dock at San Marcos La Laguna, and, almost completing the loop around the lake, Santa Cruz La Laguna captures that middle ground if you want to kick back and relax without too much fuss.

PANAJACHEL

110 km (68 mi) northwest of Antigua.

The classic route to Panajachel takes you from Guatemala City past Chimaltenango. Just beyond the Los Encuentros crossroads that leads north to Chichicastenango, follow the signs that direct you south to Panajachel through Sololá. An alternate route turns southwest beyond Chimaltenango to Patzún, then to Panajachel. This isolated route fell into disuse for many years because of numerous robberies. The problem seems to have abated. Most transport uses the Sololá route, which is smoother and more convenient.

The quiet Cakchiquel village of Panajachel on the northern shore of Lago Atitlán began welcoming international visitors during the heady,

LAKE SAVVY

Regularly scheduled passenger ferries ply the route between Panajachel and Santiago Atitlán during daylight hours. Boats depart the dock at the foot of Calle Rancho Grande in Panajachel at 6:30, 9, 9:30, and 10:30 AM, and 1, 3, 4:30, and 5 PM, with return trips from Santiago at 6, 7, 11:45 AM, and 12:30, 1:30, and 4:30 PM. You'll pay Q20, and the journey takes just under an hour. Private boat taxis supplement service on this route—they slice the Pana–Santiago ferry time in half. Other boat taxis fill in the gaps to and between other lake towns, departing from the foot of Panajachel's Calle del Embarcadero, two blocks from the ferry dock. Taxi service is collective: the driver departs after the boat fills up—the wait is never more than 30 minutes—and makes stops at towns along the shore. If you wish to hire a boat for yourself, expect to pay Q200 for the ride. You can negotiate the price of the entire boat for very short distances, say Panajachel to Santa Cruz La Laguna.

■TIP→ **If you are prone to motion-sickness, make your cross-lake jaunt in the morning when the water surface is usually as smooth as glass.** By early afternoon, a wind that locals call the *xocomil* picks up, making for a choppy ride. In any case, try to be on your final boat of the day heading back to Panajachel by 4 PM, after which selection thins out as drivers make plans to be back home before dark.

hippie 1960s, and never looked back. This is still Guatemala's consummate hangout, a place where many end up staying longer than planned. And who can blame them? Bordered by three volcanoes that drop off into the crystalline waters of Lago Atitlán, Panajachel's setting could hardly be more dramatic. For better or for worse, the '60s are over and the "Pana" of old has been tamed. Once exclusively the province of bare-bones lodging for those with bare-bones resources, the town has matured in its middle age and today welcomes visitors of all stripes and budgets. It remains as fun as ever and counts an ever-increasing number of activities to keep you occupied. There may still be a few Dead Heads floating around, but today's Panajachel is a place you would be proud to take your parents.

Panajachel centers on seven-block Calle Santander, which connects the lakefront with the fringes of the original village, and typifies the main drag of a resort town; open-air restaurants, bars, and vendors' stalls line the street, giving you a front-row seat to observe the passing parade of pedestrians, dogs, and tuk-tuks. Three-wheel motorized Bajaj RE taxis made in India, common here and elsewhere in Guatemala. The inland end of Calle Santander hooks up with Calle Principal, the highway leading north and east out of town. Avenida de los Árboles climbs the hill to the old part of town. You'd never know you were in a tourist mecca when you stand on the small plaza in front of the town's lovely church. Especially on its Thursday market day, Panajachel looks pretty much like any other highland village.

THE LAKE, LONG-TERM

It's not all about staying in a hotel at the lake. This is a part of Guatemala where people can rent a house or flat for a few days and chill out. What's available reflects each community's demographics. Panajachel's mostly year-round population rarely leaves long enough to rent places out. If they do, it's through an informal process that short-term visitors can rarely take advantage of. The same holds true in Santiago Atitlán and San Pedro La Laguna.

Smaller lake communities with substantial numbers of seasonal residents are a good bet. Property-management firms rent out homes during owners' absences. Santa Catarina Palopó and, to a lesser extent, San Antonio Palopó contain many exclusive homes whose owners live in Guatemala City much of the year. Housing is a tad more modest, though still quite comfy, in San Marcos La Laguna, Santa Cruz La Laguna, and Jaibalito, all of which have numerous seasonal residents.

The longer you stay, the lower your cost per day turns out to be. Most management firms won't handle stays of less than a week. Although $1,000 per week for a two-bedroom house sounds expensive, split among four people, the price compares to that of an upscale hotel here. It's impossible to find rental properties on the lake around Christmastime. A rental for Holy Week should be arranged far in advance, but is not as difficult. Some properties come with options for cook and cleaning staff. Don't expect Internet access or potable water—stock up on bottled water from local stores.

Your other long-term option here is a homestay in conjunction with Spanish study. Both Panajachel and San Pedro La Laguna have language schools that can arrange boarding with local families. Expect housing to be modest.

In Panajachel, both **Atitlán Solutions** (✉ *C. Santander* ☎ *7756–2111* ⊕ *www.realestateatitlan.com*) and **Terra-X** (✉ *C. Santander* ☎ *7756–2111* ⊕ *www.terraxatitlan.com*) handle real estate and property management in this part of the country.

For a brief history of the lake and its people head to the **Museo Lacustre de Atitlán.** Here you'll find a handful of informative displays tracing the history of the region back to precolonial times. ✉ *End of C. Santander, in the Hotel Posada de Don Rodrigo* ☎ *7762–2326* 💳 *Q35* ⊙ *Daily 8–6.*

The **Reserva Natural Atitlán** (✉ *2 km [1 mi] west of Panajachel* ☎ *7762–2565* ⊕ *www.atitlanreserva.com* ⊙ *Daily 8–4* 💳 *Q50*) has a walking trail that loops through a small river canyon, crossing suspension bridges, and passing a butterfly atrium and enclosures of spider monkeys and coatimundis. If you feel like playing Tarzan, the complex contains a zip-line tour (Q125), where you glide through the forest canopy courtesy of a series of cables, a helmet, and a very secure harness. There's also a private beach for a bit of posteducational relaxation. Campsites are available in the park, or if you'd like a bit more luxury, cabins ($$), albeit spartan ones, are also available.

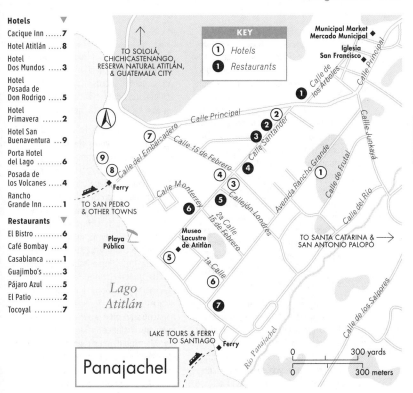

Panajachel

WHERE TO EAT

■ TIP➔ If you stay on Calle Santander, ask for rooms that don't face the street, and consequently don't get the street noise.

$$–$$$$ ✕ **Casablanca.** Panajachel's most elegant restaurant, Casablanca has a white-walled dining room with windows overlooking the main street. The handful of tables on the upper level is much more intimate. The menu is ample, if a bit overpriced, and includes a few seafood and fish standouts such as lobster and black lake bass, as well as tenderloin in a green-pepper sauce. Musicians occasionally entertain. ⊠ *C. Principal 0–93, at C. Santander* ☎ *7762–1390* ▭ *AE, D, DC, MC, V.*

$–$$ ✕ **Tocoyal.** Our favorite in-town lakefront restaurant, with great views
★ from its picture window, takes its name from the tightly wrapped cloth worn as a headdress by Tzutuhil women in the area. This is about as elegant as Panajachel gets: waiters in white shirts and bow ties scurry around and serve pepián or chile relleno on the local side of the menu, or a good steak if you're looking for something international. This is still Pana, though, so you don't need to dress up. ⊠ *C. del Lago* ☎ *7762–1555* ▭ *AE, D, DC, MC, V.*

¢–$ ✕ **El Bistro.** Hummingbirds dart among flowering vines at this romantic
Fodor'sChoice eatery on the shores of Lago Atitlán. Enter through an iron gate that
★ leads into a garden hidden behind a low wall. There are outside tables

I, Rigoberta Menchú . . . Mostly

In 1992 the Nobel Peace Prize was awarded to Guatemalan writer Rigoberta Menchú, raised in the tiny highland village of San Miguel Uspantán. Menchú was born in 1959, just before a string of military dictators usurped control of Guatemala for 36 war-filled years. She grew up as dozens of opposition and guerrilla groups rose to resist them. Along with many of her family members, Menchú opposed the dictatorship with peaceful demonstrations that included peasants from various regions. When she was eventually forced into exile, she continued her opposition to Guatemala's military rule by drawing international attention to the repressive regime.

In 1983 she published her testimonial, *I, Rigoberta Menchú: An Indian Woman in Guatemala*, and the plight of Guatemala's indigenous people—and the brutality of the military regime—was revealed in wrenching detail. In her book Menchú described losing two brothers to malnutrition on a coffee plantation and the razing of her village by wealthy land prospectors. Most disturbingly, Menchú related the story of a third brother, who was kidnapped by the army, tortured, and then burned alive.

In 1999 American anthropologist David Stoll challenged Menchú's account with the publication of *Rigoberta Menchú and the Story of All Poor Guatemalans*. His research suggested that the conflict over the lands of Menchú's village was actually a long-running dispute between her father and his in-laws and that although Menchú's brother was unquestionably kidnapped, tortured, and murdered by the military, it was probably not carried out in the manner that Menchú had suggested. Although still a potent symbol of indigenous rights, Menchú is now viewed by some with incredulity.

Whether or not Menchú personally witnessed the events she describes, it is indisputable that hundreds of indigenous workers, particularly children, died of disease, malnutrition, or outright abuse on the plantations. It is also clear that the military committed innumerable acts of brutality, including public executions, in villages all across the country. In 1998 the Guatemalan Truth Commission sponsored by the United Nations denounced the military's actions during the civil war as genocide. Some argue that if Menchú's account wasn't wholly her own, but included incidents suffered by other indigenous men and women, it doesn't detract from the horror of what occurred. If she included the experiences of others to draw attention to a conflict the international community had ignored for more than 20 years, they argue, can anyone really blame her?

Stoll himself admits Menchú is fundamentally right about the army's brutality, though he downplays it considerably, no doubt to bolster his own book's more dubious claim: that it was the guerrillas, not the ruling generals, who were responsible for igniting political violence in the highlands. But it is the debunking of Rigoberta Menchú that he will be remembered for and that will forever endear him to Guatemala's war criminals, many of whom remain in public life.

—Gary Chandler

and a pair of intimate dining rooms. All the delicious Italian food, from the tasty bread to the fresh pasta, is homemade. Two standout specialties are the fettuccine *arrabiata* (with a slightly spicy tomato sauce), and the steak au poivre (cooked in a wine sauce and black pepper) served with fresh vegetables. ⊠*End of C. Santander* ☎7762–0508 ⊟*AE, D, DC, MC, V.*

¢–$ ✕**Café Bombay.** Despite the name, you'll find very little Indian about the cuisine here. The menu is a real catch-all and "vegetarian" is a better description to describe the falafel, pita, pad thai, burritos, lasagna, and key lime pie. Dine inside, or grab one of the umbrella-covered tables on the front deck and survey the action on Calle Santander. ⊠*C. Santander* ☎7762–0611 ⊟*No credit cards.*

> **HURRICANE STAN**
>
> In October 2005 Hurricane Stan, the 18th named tropical storm of a record season, made landfall on Mexico's Yucatán peninsula on October 4. It brought torrential rains that drenched the entire region. Lake Atitlán was hit especially hard by landslides as a direct result of the rains Stan spawned. An estimated 1,500 people died, many in Santiago Atitlán. Damage repair has come slowly. The main bridge connecting Panajachel with communities on the lake's eastern shore reopened in May 2007, thanks to construction aid from the government of Korea.

¢–$ ✕**Guajimbo's.** The Uruguayan and American business owners provide the live acoustic music many evenings here at one of Calle Santander's liveliest restaurants. Grab a seat in this semi-open-air place, enjoy the entertainment and survey all that transpires on the main drag. Uruguayan-style beef tenderloin rules, as do *churtos* (beef cutlets prepared variously with mozzarella cheese, ham, bacon, peppers, or olives). ⊠*C. Santander* ☎7762–0063 ⊟*AE, D, DC, MC, V* ☉*Closed Thurs.*

¢–$ ✕**Pájaro Azul.** Tired of frijoles? There isn't a single bean to be found
★ at this café, which serves up outstanding crepes. Choose from a small but creative menu of savory dinner crepes—fill them with vegetables, tofu, chicken, or pork—and sweet dessert crepes—we like the banana–brown sugar–yogurt Jamaica one—or pick and choose among your favorite ingredients. While you wait you can thumb through a pile of back-issue magazines (including, oddly enough, the *New Yorker*). ⊠*C. Santander, next to the post office* ☎7762–2596 ⊟*No credit cards* ☉*Closed Thurs.*

¢–$ ✕**El Patio.** Although it's known by the outdoor patio with umbrella-covered tables that gives the place its name, most of the restaurant's tables are inside a large dining room decorated with lots of palms and ferns, and a few indigenous drawings on the wall. Nevertheless, the lunch and dinner menus offer great variety, including such items as pepper steak, roast pork, and chicken à la king. It's also a popular spot for breakfast. You'll find a couple of Internet computers to log on after you eat. ⊠*C. Santander* ☎7762–2041 ⊟*AE, D, DC, MC, V.*

WHERE TO STAY

$$$$ ✕⊞**Hotel Atitlán.** Keep any disappointment in check until you arrive.
FodorśChoice You turn into a quiet cove northwest of Panajachel, and will spot an
★ ugly high-rise building. That isn't this hotel. This Spanish-style inn

consists of a main building flanked by two-story wings that surround a pool. The extensive grounds border on a long stretch of shoreline and the Reserva Natural Atitlán, a wooded reserve crossed by footpaths and hanging bridges. The rooms, each with tile floors, carved wooden furniture, and handwoven bedspreads, have balconies overlooking the gardens or the lake. Even if you don't stay here, stop by for views of the lake at sunset. The restaurant ($–$$$) is reliable, if a bit overpriced. Weekly rates, which include all meals, are available. ⊠ *2 km (1 mi) northwest of Panajachel* ☎ *7762–1441, 2334–0641 in Guatemala City* 🖷 *7762–0048, 2334–0640 in Guatemala City* ⊕ *www.hotelatitlan.com* 🛏 *62 rooms, 6 suites* ⚇ *In-room: no a/c, Wi-Fi. In-hotel: restaurant, bar, tennis court, pool, beachfront, no elevator, laundry service, public Internet, parking (no fee)* ═ *AE, D, DC, MC, V* ⊙ *EP, all meals included.*

$$$$ 🏨 **Hotel Posada de Don Rodrigo.** At the end of Calle Santander, this excellent hotel—there's a branch by the same name in Antigua—possesses some of the best views of the lake (they would be even better if not for the giant waterslide in the way). The rooms make use of handwoven fabrics from the local communities. Ask for one of the newer rooms, which have better views. Relax by the pool or in one of the hammocks hung along a breezy corridor. There's a small on-site museum that gives insight into the history of the Maya. ⊠ *End of C. Santander* ☎ *7762–2326* 🖷 *7762–2329* ⊕ *www.posadadonrodrigo.com* 🛏 *39 rooms* ⚇ *In-room: no a/c (some). In-hotel: restaurant, room service, pool, laundry service, public Internet, parking (no fee)* ═ *AE, D, DC, MC, V* ⊙ *EP.*

$$$–$$$$ 🏨 **Hotel San Buenaventura.** The well-manicured gardens of this small complex lead down past a shallow pool, bricked Mayan sauna, and Jacuzzi to a private beach. Although many of the condos lack good views of the lake, their barrel-roof brick ceilings and understated Moorish influence more than make up for it. This is a great place for groups or families—each bungalow has a separate living area, fully outfitted kitchen, and private terrace. The San Buenaventura sits in the same cove as the Hotel Atitlán above. ⊠ *2 km (1 mi) west of Panajachel* ☎ *7762–2559, 2337–0461 in Guatemala City* 🖷 *7762–2059, 2337–1961 in Guatemala City* ⊕ *www.hotelsanbuenaventura.net* 🛏 *10 bungalows* ⚇ *In-room: no a/c, kitchen. In-hotel: restaurant, bar, pool, beachfront, bicycles, public Wi-Fi, parking (no fee)* ═ *AE, D, DC, MC, V* ⊙ *BP.*

$$$ 🏨 **Porta Hotel del Lago.** At six stories high, Panajachel's biggest in-town hotel is a veritable skyscraper at six stories high, and also has the most amenities. Although it lacks the character of smaller hotels, it's comfortable and convenient and has top-notch service. Rooms have balconies overlooking the public beach on Lago Atitlán. The huge restaurant next door looks out onto the pool. ⊠ *End of C. Rancho Grande at C. Buenas Nuevas* ☎ *7762–1555, 2361–9683 in Guatemala City* 🖷 *7762–1562, 2361–9667 in Guatemala City* ⊕ *www.portahotels.com* 🛏 *90 rooms, 10 suites* ⚇ *In-room: no a/c, safe (some). In-hotel: 2 restaurants, room service, bar, pool, gym, laundry service, parking (no fee)* ═ *AE, D, DC, MC, V.*

$$-$$$ **Rancho Grande Inn.** A German immigrant by the name of Milly Schleisier opened this string of bungalows back in the 1940s. In so doing, she created what is still one of the most charming of Panajachel's accommodations, melding the designs of country houses in her home-land with the colorful culture of her adopted country. Each of the bun-galows is unique; the largest bungalow, which can sleep up to five, has a fireplace. Breakfast is served family-style every morning. ✉*C. Ran-cho Grande* ☎*7762–2255* 🖷*7762–2247* ⊕*www.ranchograndeinn. com* 🛏*17 bungalows, 1 bungalow suite* ⚒*In-room: no a/c. In-hotel: restaurant, pool, parking (no fee)* ▭*AE, MC, V* ⦿*BP.*

$$ **Cacique Inn.** This inn is a collection of little buildings about a block from the main street. Spacious, if sparsely furnished, rooms have slid-ing-glass doors that open onto the lovely garden. The rooms may seem a bit cool because of the tile floors, but they have fireplaces that warm you up in a snap. The grounds are surrounded by a wall, which makes the terraces by the pool a private place to sunbathe. The restaurant (¢–$$) is one of the best in town, serving a wide selection of Guatemalan dishes. The agreeable chefs will sometimes even prepare dishes to order. ✉*C. del Embarcadero, near C. Principal* ☎*7762–1205* 🖷*7762–2053* 🛏*33 rooms* ⚒*In-room: no a/c. In-hotel: restaurant, room service, bar, pool, parking (no fee)* ▭*AE, DC, MC, V* ⦿*EP.*

$$ **Hotel Dos Mundos.** Set amid colorful gardens, this hotel gives you com-fortable accommodations without the hefty price tag of more deluxe digs. The medium-size rooms are simply and tastefully furnished. Most open onto the pool area—these are set way back from the street, giving you no sense of being smack-dab in the center of town—where you can spend your afternoon on a lounge chair with a cocktail. The restaurant has a certain elegance, with tables set beneath a soaring thatch roof. The menu includes well-made pasta dishes and lots of wine. ✉*C. Santander 4–72* ☎*7762–2078* 🖷*7762–0127* ⊕*www.hoteldosmundos.com* 🛏*22 rooms* ⚒*In-room: no a/c, no phone, safe. In-hotel: restaurant, room service, bar, pool, no elevator, parking (no fee)* ▭*AE, D, DC, MC, V* ⦿*BP.*

$ **Hotel Primavera.** Friendly owners are a nice plus at this budget find with mostly 2nd-floor rooms in the center of town. Of the hotels we recommend in Panajachel, this one is closest to the bar action on Calle Santander. The noise is really only a problem on weekends, but rooms 1, 8, and 9 do not face the street and make for quieter evenings. Their bay windows face a center courtyard occupied by the sedate restau-rant downstairs. Those three rooms are larger than the others and have fireplaces, too. We like Room 9 in particular; it has its own inte-rior balcony. ✉*C. Santander* ☎*7762–2052* 🖷*7762–0171* ⊕*www. primaveraatitlan.com* 🛏*10 rooms* ⚒*In-room: no a/c, no phone. In-hotel: restaurant, no elevator, laundry service, public Internet* ▭*No credit cards* ⦿*EP.*

$ **Posada de los Volcanes.** The friendly owners here operate their own small tour company, and are likely to be your guide or driver if you use their services. The layout isn't complicated: four levels, three rooms, and a communal veranda on each level. Those at the top have great views of the lake. Rooms themselves are bright, colorful, and simply furnished.

Although it's on Calle Santander, the place is far enough removed from the string of bars and restaurants to feel quiet and secluded, but still within walking distance of the action. ⊠*Across from post office, C. Santander* ☎*7762–0244* 📠*7762–2367* ⊕*www.posadadelosvolcanes. com* 🔌*12 rooms* ⚫*In-room: no a/c, no phone. In-hotel: no elevator, parking (no fee)* ═*AE, D, DC, MC, V* ⬤*EP.*

NIGHTLIFE

As a resort town, Panajachel has some of the liveliest nightlife in the highlands. Calle Santander is the place to see and be seen. Stroll the street, look for a bar, café, or restaurant to park yourself, and watch the parade go by. Many other bars cluster near the intersection of Avenida de los Arboles and Calle Principal on the fringes of the old town.

The **Circus Bar** (⊠*Av. de los Arboles* ☎*7762–2056*) is a popular spot for locals and travelers alike, and often has live music. The **Pana Rock Café** (⊠*C. Santander* ☎*7762–2194*) has live music many nights, and wins Panajachel's loudest-bar award.

The dimly lighted **Chapiteau Disco** (⊠*Av. de los Arboles* ☎*7762–374*) plays mostly rock, Wednesday through Saturday.

Up above the fray of Calle Santander, **La Terraza** (⊠*C. Santander, near Av. de Los Arboles* ☎*7762–0041*) has an open-air, casual elegance perfect for early-evening cocktails. They also have a good menu focusing on continental favorites like rabbit and fondue Bourguignonne. **Solomon's Porchá** (⊠*C. Principal* ☎*7723–0751*) screens films several nights a week.

You can enjoy good Mexican food at the aptly named **Sunset Café** (⊠*C. Santander*). There's live music almost every night.

OUTDOOR ACTIVITIES

WATER SPORTS   Water sports are becoming more popular at Lago Atitlán, giving the lake a Club Med feel. You can rent a canoe from **Diversiones Acuáticas Balom** (⊠*On the public beach near ferry terminals* ☎*7762–2242*). It's best to get out early and be back by noon, as the afternoon winds can be fierce. The company also offers tours of the lake.

BIKING   For exploring the countryside you can rent a mountain bike at **Moto Servicio Quiché** (⊠*Av. de los Arboles at C. Principal*) and pedal over to nearby villages.

SHOPPING

Panajachel's weekly Thursday market (mostly fruits, vegetables, and animals) takes place in the old town near the church. Calle Santander is one long open-air souvenir market, lined on both sides with vendors who hang their wares from fences and makeshift stalls. Examine the items carefully, as goods purchased here are often not the best quality.

An outdoor market called **Tinamit Maya** (⊠*C. Santander*) is easily the best place for reasonably priced artesanía.

El Guipil (⊠*C. Santander*) is a large boutique with a varied selection of handmade items from highland villages.

Ojalá Antiques (⊠*Av. de los Arboles*) has a small but excellent selection of antiques.

SANTA CATARINA PALOPÓ

4 km (2½ mi) southeast of Panajachel.

Santa Catarina Palopó provides an odd mix of deep-seated Cakchiquel tradition and sumptuous luxury in the vacation homes outsiders have built on the fringes of this small town. You'll be surrounded by the brilliant blues and greens of huipils worn by local women as you walk down the cobblestone streets of this picturesque town. (Interestingly enough, the women used to wear predominantly red huipils, but an influx of tourists in the 1960s requesting turquoise blouses caused the local women to change their traditional dress and adopt the gringafied turquoise color scheme.) This is one of the few places in the highlands where men retain traditional dress; their clothing echoes the geometric designs seen in women's huipils here. From here you'll be treated to magical views of the trio of volcanoes that loom over the lake. In Santa Catarina you'll see ramshackle homes standing within sight of luxury chalets whose owners arrive as often by helicopter as they do by car.

WHERE TO STAY & EAT

$$ ✕▦ **Villa Santa Catarina.** Villa Santa Catarina has outstanding views. The long yellow building with an adobe-tile roof has small rooms, each with a private balcony overlooking the lake. The restaurant ($–$$) serves international fare including pastas, sandwiches, and chicken. You can relax in the pool or head to a series of natural hot springs that are only a few hundred feet away. ⊠*C. de la Playa* ☎*7762–1291, 2334–8136 in Guatemala City* ☎*7762–2013* ⊕*www.villasdeguatemala.com* ⇲*36 rooms* ☒*In-room: no a/c. In-hotel: restaurant, bar, pool, no elevator, laundry service, public Internet, public Wi-Fi, parking (no fee)* ☰*AE, D, DC, MC, V* Ⓞ*EP.*

$$$$ ▦ **Casa Palopó.** By far the best B&B on the lake, luxurious Casa Palopó

Fodor'sChoice has an almost mystical atmosphere. Each of the seven rooms in the

★ main house, decorated with religious-theme artworks from around the world, offer incredible views of the volcanoes. Muted blues run throughout this former villa, mirroring the colors of the lake. Most baths have giant tubs perfect for prolonged soaks. Just down the road, an annex offers two equally sumptuous suites, each with its own pool and hot tub. ⊠*Km 6.8, Santa Catarina Palopó* ☎*7762–2270* ☎*7762–2721* ⊕*www.casapalopo.com* ⇲*7 rooms, 2 suites* ☒*In-room: no a/c, no phone, refrigerator, no TV. In-hotel: restaurant, room service, bar, pool, gym, beachfront, no elevator, public Internet, public Wi-Fi, parking (no fee), no kids under 15* ☰*AE, D, DC, MC, V.*

SAN ANTONIO PALOPÓ

6½ km (4 mi) southeast of Santa Catarina Palopó, 11 km (6½ mi southeast of Panajachel.

San Antonio Palopó is a quiet farming town, larger, but much less known, than neighboring Santa Catarina Palopó. Most people have plots of land on terraced gardens where they grow green onions, which you may see them cleaning down by the lake. This is one of only a handful of regions in Latin America where men still dress in traditional costumes on a daily basis. Their pants have geometric motifs and calf-length woolen wrap-arounds fastened by leather belts or red sashes. Women go about their business wearing white blouses with red stripes.

The beautiful adobe **Iglesia de San Antonio Palopó** stands in a stone plaza that marks the center of town. The interior is particularly peaceful. During the day the steps are a meeting place where all passersby are sure to stop for a while.

WHERE TO STAY

$ 🖭 **Terrazas del Lago.** This charming hotel overlooking the lake is notable for its floral-pattern stone tiles. Simply decorated rooms have wooden tables and iron candlesticks. Those in front have patios with great vistas. A small restaurant serves simple meals, while several terraces are perfect for a quiet cup of afternoon tea. ⊠ *C. de la Playa* ☎ *7762–0157* 📠 *7762–0037* ⊕ *www.hotelterrazasdellago.com* 🛏 *12 rooms* ⚒ *In-room: no a/c, no phone, no TV. In-hotel: restaurant, parking (no fee)* ⊟ *No credit cards.*

SHOPPING

On the main street, not far from the church, is an excellent women's textile cooperative, where you see master weavers in action. The process is fascinating to watch, and the finished fabrics are stunning. There's a small shop on-site where the proceeds help sustain the cooperative.

SANTIAGO ATITLÁN

21 km (13 mi) west of San Antonio Palopó

Santiago Atitlán is 30 to 60 minutes by boat from Panajachel.

★   Across the lake from Panajachel, lies its rival in size, Santiago Atitlán, a small city with a fascinating history. With a population of about 48,000, this capital of the proud and independent Tzutuhil people is one of the largest indigenous communities in Guatemala. They resisted political domination during the country's civil war, which meant that many residents were murdered by the military. After a 1990 massacre in which 11 unarmed people were killed, the villagers protested the presence of the army in their town. To everyone's surprise, the army actually left, and Santiago Atitlán became a model for other highland towns fighting governmental oppression.

A road that leads up from the dock is lined on both sides with shops selling artesanía—take a good look at the huipils embroidered with

CLOSE UP

The Heroes of Santiago Atitlán

Oklahoma native Father Stanley Rother (1935–1981) arrived as a missionary in Santiago Atitlán in 1968. During his 13 years here, he translated the New Testament into and celebrated mass in the local Tzutuhil language. As time went on, he began to decry the treatment of Guatemala's indigenous peoples at the hands of the army and paramilitary forces. In January 1981, Rother returned to the United States after being warned that paramilitary groups had targeted him, but he hankered to return to Guatemala where he felt he belonged. He did so, but on July 28, 1981, the priest was murdered, presumably by paramilitaries, in the rectory adjoining the parish church. Although Rother is buried in Oklahoma, his heart is interred in the church here. A nascent movement to have Rother beatified and eventually canonized has been undertaken by officials of the Archdiocese of Oklahoma City (⊕www.catharchdioceseokc.org). Click on the site's OUR HISTORY link for information. Rother's writings were compiled post-humously and published in a book, *The Shepherd Cannot Run: The Letters of Stanley Rother.*

Turn the clock ahead to December 1, 1990, when, by all accounts, a night of drunken revelry on the part of soldiers posted near Santiago turned tragic. Townspeople assembled just outside of town after midnight December 2 to discuss what could be done about harassment from army forces. They had witnessed the deaths of hundreds of their fellow citizens throughout the war. When soldiers appeared to break up the meeting, members of the assemblage began to hurl stones. Soldiers fired into the crowd, killing 11, many of them children, and injuring 40. The massacre drew national outrage, and townspeople petitioned to have the military forces removed from the town. President Serrano Elías himself apologized and complied. To this day, the Guatemalan army, whose internal security role has been virtually eliminated since the 1996 peace accords, does not set foot in Santiago Atitlán.

elaborate depictions of fruits, birds, and spirits, Santiago's signature designs. Many local women wear a *tocoyal*, which is a 12-yard-long band wrapped around their forehead. Older men also wear traditional dress, sporting black-and-white-stripe calf-length pants with detailed embroidery below the knee.

The main road leads to the squat white 1547 **Iglesia de Santiago Apóstol,** the church dedicated to town patron St. James the Apostle, but where Tzutuhil deities can be seen in the woodwork around the pulpit. Fondly remembered one-time American parish priest Father Stanley Rother was assassinated in the church rectory by right-wing death squads in 1981 for his outspoken support of the Tzutuhil cause.

On the road west to San Pedro, **Parque de la Paz** commemorates a dozen Tzutuhil people, including several children, who were killed when the army open fired on a peaceful demonstration that protested the military presence here. The memorial is a sober reminder of Guatemala's tortured past.

WHERE TO STAY & EAT

$$–$$$ ╳▣ **Posada de Santiago.** This longtime favorite has deluxe accommoda-
Fodor'sChoice tions in private stone-wall bungalows with volcano views, as well as
★   a few rooms and suites in the main building. Pass through the carved-
wood doors of your bungalow and you'll find a fireplace and thick
wool blankets piled high on the bed. The restaurant (¢–$) serves exqui-
site food, such as smoked chicken píbil in a tangy red sauce and Thai
coconut shrimp. The wine list is surprisingly extensive. On the premises
is a small store where you can rent canoes and mountain bikes. ⊠*1 km
(½ mi) south of town* ☎*7721–7366* 🖳*7721–7365* ⊕*www.posadade-
santiago.com* ↘*9 rooms, 3 suites, 7 bungalows* ⌂*In-room: no a/c,
no TV (some). In-hotel: restaurant, bar, pool, bicycles, public Internet*
🖃*AE, D, DC, MC, V.*

$$ ╳▣ **Bambú.** Run by a Spanish expatriate, Bambú is known for its excel-
lent restaurant (¢–$$), an A-frame dining room warmed by a crackling
stone fireplace. On the beautifully tended grounds are a string of thatch-
roof bungalows with private patios overlooking the lake. Stone path-
ways loop through a series of taxonomically arranged gardens (cacti
in one, flowers in the next, and so on)—most of the restaurant's fruits,
vegetables, and herbs are cultivated out back. Canoes are available for
paddling around the lake. ⊠*1 km (½ mi) east of town* ☎*7721–7332*
🖳*7721–7333* ⊕*www.ecobambu.com* ↘*11 bungalows* ⌂*In-room:
no a/c, no TV. In-hotel: restaurant, bar, pool, parking (no fee)* 🖃*AE,
DC, MC, V.*

SAN JUAN LA LAGUNA

3 km (1.5 mi) north of San Pedro La Laguna.

To get here, take a water taxi from Santiago Atitlán and ask the driver
to drop you at the Muelle Uxlabil, the Ecohotel Uxlabil's own dock.
The boat ride from San Pedro La Laguna takes five minutes.

The tiny, one-hotel village of San Juan La Laguna bills itself as "the
cleanest town in Guatemala," and it lives up to its claim. San Juan is a
great place to get away from the crowds and get a more authentic look
at indigenous life on the lake.

There are several artisan collectives in the town's center. **Lema** (⊠*San
Juan La Laguna* ☎*5967–7747*) is an association of local weavers who
use environmentally friendly dyes in their work. Atitlán is known for its
fair-trade coffee, and a local 140-member cooperative, **La Voz que Clama
en el Desierto** (⊠*San Juan La Laguna* ☎*7723–2301*)—that translates
as "The voice that cries in the desert"—offers tours of its coffee-pro-
cessing facilities and artisan shop. Call to arrange a visit.

WHERE TO STAY

$ ▣ **Ecohotel Uxlabil.** San Juan La Laguna's best (and only) lodging option,
the Uxlabil has its own thatched dock and extensive grounds with a
medicinal herb garden, Mayan sauna, and Jacuzzi. The simple rooms
have textured walls reminiscent of beach sand, rather hard beds, and
traditional textile bedclothes. ⊠*San Juan La Laguna, Muelle Uxlabil*

☎5990–6016, 2366–9555 *in Guatemala City* ⊕*www.uxlabil.com* ⟿*10 rooms, 2 bungalows* ⌂*In-room: no a/c, kitchen (some), no TV. In-hotel: restaurant, bar* ⊟*AE, D, DC, MC, V* ⦿*BP.*

SAN PEDRO LA LAGUNA

"It's the new Pana," proclaim its growing number of fans. Indeed, as Panajachel and its international population have matured—a few wags would say "gentrified"—the young and the restless have crossed the lake and set up shop in burgeoning San Pedro La Laguna. This traditional Tzutuhil fishing village knows it is on the cusp of something, but what that "something" will be can only be revealed in someone's crystal ball. This is still proudly budget-travel territory. For now, lodgings and facilities fall into the "as long as you're not too fussy" category, but all offer good value for very little money. That will no doubt change as the world begins to discover San Pedro.

WHERE TO STAY

¢ 🏨**Casa Elena.** There's no phone, no fax, and no e-mail. Just show up and ask for a room. Either they have one or they don't. Expect very basic, but very cheap and acceptable accommodation, with two beds and a table in each concrete-block room. ⊠*7 Av. and 8 C.* ☎*No phone* ⟿*20 rooms, 7 with bath* ⌂*In-room: no a/c, no phone, no TV.* ⊟*No credit cards* ⦿*EP.*

¢ 🏨**Hotel Mansión del Lago.** Rooms are simple here—expect tiled floors and two beds each—but the hillside location above the dock gives you the best views in town, especially if you lodge on the top floor. All guests have access to the rooftop terrace. ⊠*4 Av. and 8 C.* ☎*7721– 8041* 🖷*7721–8195* ⊕*www.hotelmansiondellago.com* ⟿*18 rooms, 16 with bath* ⌂*In-room: no a/c, no phone no TV (some). In hotel: no elevator, public Internet, laundry service, parking (no fee)* ⊟*V* ⦿*EP.*

¢ 🏨**Hotel Nahual Maya.** Make this your first choice in San Pedro. It costs no more than the other budget options, and provides you with a big step up in quality. Rooms situate on 2 floors—those on the top floor have good views—and are bright and cheery, with either double or a pair of twin beds. ☎*7721–8158* ⟿*16 rooms* ⌂*In-room: no a/c, no phone, no TV (some). In-hotel: no elevator, parking (no fee)* ⊟*No credit cards* ⦿*EP.*

SAN MARCOS LA LAGUNA

15-min by boat from Panajachel.

San Marcos has acquired fame as a center of New Age devotion, thanks to the presence of the Las Pirámides del Ka meditation center/lodge. The tiny village does cater mostly to tourists of all stripes, however, and even those whose vacation schedule is not "Yoga at 9, meditation at 10" will find their own bliss here. (San Marcos is home to a couple of our favorite Guatemalan hotels.) From the dock you can reach the center of the village by walking uphill along a narrow cobblestone path. The village itself has one or two stores and a restaurant around

CLOSE UP Drinking & Smoking with the Saints

Arguably Guatemala's most curious object of veneration is the cigar-smoking, rum-swilling deity Maximón. He is still actively idolized a few places in the highlands, most notably here in Santiago Atitlán, and in the small town of Zunil, near Quetzaltenango, where he is known by his alternate name, San Simón.

Scholars debate just what Maximón (whose name is pronounced *Mah-shee-MOHN*) is supposed to represent. His cult likely descended from worship of the Mayan god Mam, but the Catholic church holds that he is the apostle Peter. (Peter's original name was Simon, of course.) Some suggest that Maximón is really Judas Iscariot, the betrayer of Jesus. Others liken him to Spanish conquistador Pedro de Alvarado. In any case, according to tradition, he is more a malevolent than benevolent being, and it's best to stay on his good side with offerings.

As you get off the boat here in Santiago, small children may offer to lead you to the **Casa de Maximón**, the local home housing his figure, in exchange for a few quetzals. (Five suffices.) You will need their guidance, for Maximón's guardianship changes each year during an elaborate Holy Week observance, a different member of the local *cofrade* (religious society) taking charge of the wooden idol and accommodating his many faithful followers. When the children bring you to the house, you'll be ushered inside to see the shrine. Maximón's stern figure is dressed much like a 19th-century Spanish nobleman, and is said to like cigars and rum. If you haven't brought such items to leave in the collection plate, another Q5 bill will do just fine. (Make it Q10 if you plan to take a photo.) Maximón is reputed to have proffered myriad favors, from curing illnesses to helping the faithful get a bigger house. We can't vouch for your success.

the central square. ■TIP➔ **If you plan on staying in San Marcos you should remember to bring a flashlight, as much of the town lacks electricity.**

WHERE TO STAY & EAT

¢ ✕**Il Giardino.** An open-air restaurant centered around a bamboo hut and a fire pit, this little Italian eatery offers continental favorites like fondue and spaghetti, and also has a good selection of vegetarian entrées. There's live music from time to time, making this one of San Marcos' social hubs. Be sure to leave room for the delicious tiramisu. ⊠*San Marcos La Laguna* ☎*5891–0482* ⊟*No credit cards.*

$–$$ 🏠**Posada Schumann.** Full of old-fashioned charm, this little inn has bungalows set along a narrow swath of garden stretching down to the lake. Exposed stonework and unfinished wood paneling lend the place a slightly rustic feel, but the rooms are enlivened by the festive colors from local textiles. The hot water can be unreliable. You'll get a 10% discount if you pay in cash rather than with a credit card. ⊠*San Marcos La Laguna* ☎*5202–2216* ⊕*www.posadaschumann.com* ⟋*6 rooms, 2 rooms without bath, 4 bungalows* ⌂*In-room: no a/c, no phone, safe, kitchen (some), refrigerator (some), no TV. In-hotel: restaurant, laundry service* ⊟*AE, D, DC, MC, V.*

$ ⊞**Hotel Jinava.** This small hotel is in a secluded cove and each of its
Fodor'sChoice stone-floor, stucco bungalows is shaded by avocado and papaya trees.
★ Ask the friendly German owner to make you a tropical drink, one of
his favorite pastimes. If piña coladas aren't your thing, request a mas-
sage—he is rumored to be the best masseur on the lake. The restaurant
serves up great curries and other international dishes. ⊠*San Marcos La
Laguna* ☎*5406–5986* ⊕*www.hoteljinava.com* ⇆*5 bungalows* ⬦*In-
room: no a/c, no phone, no TV. In-hotel: restaurant, bar, no elevator*
⊟*No credit cards.*

$ ⊞**Las Pirámides del Ka.** Here is the place that gives San Marcos its New
Age-y reputation. The tranquillity of the lake provides the perfect setting for this yoga retreat, which offers day-, week-, and monthlong
courses. Pyramid-shape cabins concentrate energies for spiritual-
ists seeking that elusive "Om." The price includes accommodations,
classes, and use of the sauna and other facilities. You stay here, you're
expected to participate. As they are fond of saying here: This isn't really
a hotel. ⊠*San Marcos La Laguna* ☎*205–7151 or 205–7302* ⊕*www.
laspiramidesdelka.com* ⇆*5 rooms* ⬦*In-room: no a/c, no TV. In-hotel:
restaurant* ⊟*No credit cards.*

JAIBALITO

10-min boat trip west of Panajachel.

So small that it rarely appears on maps of the region, Jaibalito is the
most undisturbed of the villages surrounding Lago Atitlán. Santa Cruz
La Laguna is a short walk away, but otherwise Jaibalito is quite isolated. There is no boat service after 6 PM, so this village is only for those
seeking peace and quiet.

WHERE TO STAY & EAT

$$ ✕⊞**La Casa del Mundo.** Built atop a cliff overlooking the azure waters,
this gorgeous inn has unquestionably the best vantage point for gazing
at Lago Atitlán. All the rooms have views, but those from Number 1
and Number 3 are the most breathtaking. If you can tear yourself away
from the windows, you'll notice the beautifully decorated rooms have
wood-beam ceilings, red-tile floors, and stucco-and-stone walls hung
with local handicrafts. If you want to get a closer look at the lake, kay-
aks are available. Meals are served family style in the cozy restaurant
(¢–$). ⊠*Jaibalito dock* ☎*5218–5332* ⊕*www.lacasadelmundo.com*
⇆*12 rooms, 8 with bath* ⬦*In-room: no a/c, no phone, no TV. In-
hotel: restaurant, no elevator* ⊟*No credit cards.*

$ ✕⊞**Vulcano Lodge.** This lodge amidst a coffee plantation has well-
tended gardens strung with hammocks for afternoon naps. The taste-
fully decorated rooms are on the small side, but they all have private
terraces. Alas, there are no views of the lake. The restaurant (¢–$)
serves up international favorites. ⊠*Jaibalito* ☎*5410–2237* ⊕*www.
atitlan.com/vulcano.htm* ⇆*8 rooms, 1 suite* ⬦*In-room: no a/c, no
phone, no TV. In-hotel: restaurant, no elevator* ⊟*AE, DC, MC, V.*

SANTA CRUZ LA LAGUNA

10-min boat ride west of Panajachel.

DECEMBER 29, 1996

Guatemala has just over a decade of peace under its belt, a fact you'll be reminded of each time you pick up a one-quetzal coin. paz firme y duradera (FIRM AND LASTING PEACE) reads the inscription, along with the date the peace accords were signed ending the 36-year civil war. On the center of the coin, the word *paz* (peace) flows into a stylized illustration of a dove.

Yours truly, first view of Santa Cruz La Laguna is the hubbub of a couple of hotels and a few vendors who hang around the dock. (A boat is realistically the only way to get here.) It's a steep walk up to the hillside village itself, but the hale and hearty are rewarded with a stroll through a Tzutuhil community that most travelers overlook. The square adobe houses are positioned precariously on the slopes, looking as if they might be washed away by the next heavy rain. A highlight of this little village is a squat adobe church, the **Iglesia de Santa Cruz,** in the main plaza. Make sure to look inside at where the walls are lined with carved wooden saints.

WHERE TO STAY & EAT

¢–$ ✕⌂ **Arca de Noé.** Magnificent views are the big draw at this rustic retreat. Rooms, in several wood-and-stone bungalows, are small but neat. The delicious home cooking is served family style in the main building, which resembles a New England farmhouse. The menu changes constantly, but each meal comes with fresh vegetables, and bread hot out of the oven. Electricity is solar-generated, with gas used to fuel the supply of hot water. ⊠ *Santa Cruz La Laguna* ☎ *5515–3712* ✎ *arcasantacruz@yahoo.com* ➘ *10 rooms, 5 with bath, 5 bungalows* ⚡ *In-room: no a/c, no phone, no TV. In-hotel: restaurant* ⊟ *No credit cards.*

¢–$ ✕⌂ **La Iguana Perdida.** The traditionally backpacker-oriented "Lost Iguana" is part hotel and part summer camp. It hasn't forgotten its roots, but it's upgrading some of its offerings. The restaurant serves up good family-style meals, and the dormitory rooms can hold up to eight of your traveling companions. For a bit more privacy choose one of the stone-floor, thatch-roof bungalows lit with kerosene lamps. Guests tend to be fairly young—most come for scuba-diving courses. You can also choose from Spanish, art, or weaving classes, too. ■ TIP➔ **Stop by for the Saturday-night barbecue, even if you aren't staying here.** ⊠ *Santa Cruz La Laguna* ☎ *5706–4117, 7762–2621 in Panajachel* ⊕ *www. laiguanaperdida.com* ➘ *14 rooms, 3 cabins, 2 dormitory rooms* ⚡ *In-room: no a/c, no phone, no TV. In-hotel: restaurant, bar, diving, no elevator, public Internet* ⊟ *No credit cards.*

OUTDOOR ACTIVITIES

There are plenty of opportunities for hiking in the hills around Santa Cruz. It is the starting point of a scenic four-hour walk to San Marcos La Laguna. The trail passes through several tiny villages and over gusty bluffs overlooking the lake.

Lago Atitlán's wealth of underwater wonders draws divers from around the world. **ATI Divers** (⊠*Iguana Perdida* ☎*5706–4117* ⊠*C. Santander, Panajachel* ☎*7762–2621*) is a certified diving school that offers courses for all levels, from basic certification to dive master.

SOLOLÁ

5 km (3 mi) north of Panajachel.

The Atitlán area's "metropolis" of Sololá is the region's administrative capital. Sololá lies a steep, 20-minute climb up from Panajachel and offers stunning mountainside views of the lake. You'll find one of Guatemala's largest markets here. Something goes on a smaller scale every weekday, but Friday is the principal market day, with produce and a decent selection of souvenirs for sale. Sololá remains one of the few places in the highlands where men wear traditional dress, in particular, gold-embroidered jackets distinctive to the town. Sololá's symbol of pride is its 1914 clock tower, still ticking despite damage in Guatemala's 1976 earthquake.

EN
ROUTE
A crossroads called Los Encuentros marks the turnoff on the Pan-American Highway for Chichicastenango. Just north of the junction, you'll pass through a mandatory vehicle inspection. El Quiché, the region Chichicastenango is in, is a protected agricultural zone. Officials need to determine that you aren't bringing in any outside produce with attendant pests who have hitched a ride.

CHICHICASTENANGO

Fodor'sChoice ★ *37 km (23 mi) north of Panajachel, 108 km (67 mi) northwest of Antigua.*

Perched on a hillside, Chichicastenango ("the place of the nettles") is in many ways a typical highland town. The narrow cobblestone streets converge on a wide plaza where most days you'll find a few old men passing the time. You'd hardly recognize the place Thursday and Sunday, the two days a week on which one of the world's most famous markets takes place, when row after row of colorful stalls fill the square and overflow into the adjoining alleys. There's a dizzying array of handmade items, from wooden masks to woolen blankets to woven baskets. Much of the artesanía is produced for tourists, but walk a few blocks in any direction and you'll find where the locals do their shopping. South of the square is a narrow street where women sell chickens. To the east you might run across a family trying to coax a just-purchased pig up a rather steep hill.

Believe it or not, Chichicastenango does exist the other five days a week; if come here on, say, a Tuesday, you'll have the place to yourself. Few tourists actually do that. At just an hour from Panajachel, two hours from Antigua or Quetzaltenango, or three hours from the capital, Chichicastenango will always be Guatemala's consummate day trip for most. But a visit here on a *non*-market day gives you a chance to see "Chichi"—few people ever bother to wrap their tongues around the entire six-syllable name—one of the spiritual centers of Quiché Mayan culture, at its most serene.

EXPLORING

Chichicastenango does offer more than its market, and a shopping break to see the town's sights is essential if you want some insight into Quiché culture. On market days, a small cadre of guides certified by Inguat, the national tourist office, meets the tour buses. (Look for them in their red vests and Inguat badges.) They speak Spanish and English, and can rustle up colleagues who speaks French, German, or Italian if need be. On many levels, we recommend their services. They can provide insight into the sights that you'll never get on your own. They are also protection insurance: there have been a few robberies of tourists visiting the cemetery and the Pascual Abaj shrine. Guides charge Q200 for a half-day tour, or Q60 for an hour-long abbreviated circuit.

WHAT TO SEE

❸ Capilla de Calvario. Across from the Iglesia de Santo Tomás is this squat little chapel. It doesn't attract the attention that its much larger neighbor does, but from its steep steps you'll have a nice view of the market. As with the Santo Tomás church below, ■**TIP→ photography is prohibited inside this church.** ⊠ *West end of Parque Ctl..*

❺ Cementerio. Filled with mausoleums painted brilliant shades of teal, yellow, and orange, the town's cemetery is one of the most colorful in the highlands. You'll be treated to wonderful views of the city's red rooftops. In the midst of headstones topped with crosses you'll doubtless find candles and incense—evidence of Mayan rituals. ⊠ *West end of 8 C.*

❷ Iglesia de Santo Tomás. Standing watch over the square is this gleaming white Dominican church, busy with worshippers all day and late into the night. The structure dates from 1540 on the site of an ancient temple, and locals say a block of stone near the massive front doors is all that remains of the altar. The Quiché people still consider Chichicastenango their spiritual city. Church officials look the other way as Mayan ceremonies are still practiced here today. Some worshippers wave around pungent incense during the day, and at night others toss rose petals and pine needles into a raging fire right on the steps of the church. The age-old ritual has darkened the once-white steps leading to the church entrance. On the topic of entering, ■**TIP→ outsiders should not pass through the front doors. Instead, enter through the door via the courtyard on the building's right side. Also, under no circumstances should you take photos inside the church.** ⊠ *East end of Parque Ctl.*

❹ Museo Regional. If you want to learn more about the history of Chichicastenango, check out this little colonial-era building, which displays pre-Columbian artifacts that came from the private collection of a local priest. ⊠ *Next to Iglesia de Santo Tomás* 🖼 *Donation suggested.*

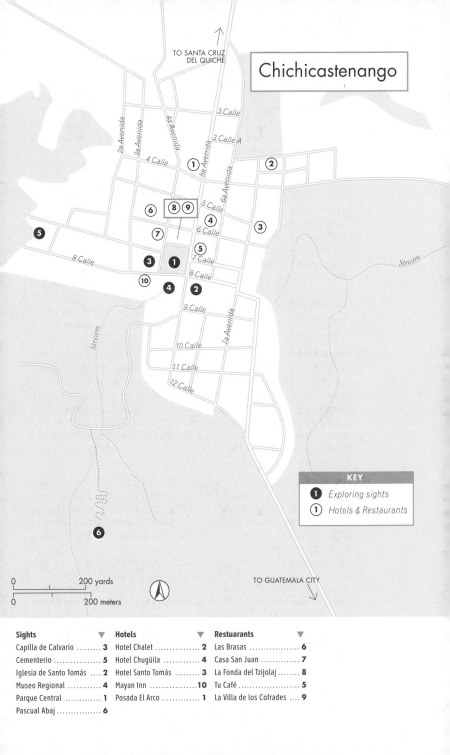

TO SANTA CRUZ
DEL QUICHÉ

Chichicastenango

2a Avenida
3a Avenida
4a Avenida
5a Avenida
6a Avenida
7a Avenida

3 Calle
3 Calle A
4 Calle
5 Calle
6 Calle
7 Calle
8 Calle
8 Calle
9 Calle
10 Calle
11 Calle
12 Calle

Stream
Stream

KEY

| 1 | *Exploring sights* |
| 1 | *Hotels & Restaurants* |

TO GUATEMALA CITY

| 0 | 200 yards |
| 0 | 200 meters |

Sights ▼	**Hotels** ▼	**Restuarants** ▼
Capilla de Calvario **3**	Hotel Chalet **2**	Las Brasas **6**
Cementerio **5**	Hotel Chugüila **4**	Casa San Juan **7**
Iglesia de Santo Tomás **2**	Hotel Santo Tomás **3**	La Fonda del Tzijolaj **8**
Museo Regional **4**	Mayan Inn **10**	Tu Café **5**
Parque Central **1**	Posada El Arco **1**	La Villa de los Cofrades **9**
Pascual Abaj **6**		

SPINNING AROUND THE MAYPOLE

Take Chichicastenango's market and ratchet up the color and excitement several notches. Sound impossible? Just come here between December 13 to 21, and you'll see how possible it is as the city pays homage to St. Tomás, its patron saint, in its annual Día de Santo Tomás celebrations.

Chichi explodes with parades and dances over the entire week. During the festivities, the *cofrades* (city leaders) parade in elegant silver costumes and carry staffs topped by magnificent sun medallions. In the *Baile de la Conquista* ("Dance of the Conquest") and masked dancers reenact the meeting of Old and New Worlds.

The highlight of Santo Tomás is a variation on a maypole dance, called the *palo volador* ("flyer's pole"). Anyone can dance on the ground, but these participants—four of them dress as birds and represent the four directions—start at the top, wrapped in their own individual strands of rope and unravel a bit with each spin through the air until they arrive, completely unwrapped, safely on the ground. The dance requires elaborate choreography, with dancers making 13 rotations around the pole during their descent. As with all in Mayan culture, there's method to the math (and in this case, to the madness): 13 x 4 = 52, the number of years in one cycle of the Mayan calendar.

1 Parque Central. As in most colonial villages, the heart of Chichicastenango is its central square, and any tour begins here. It's pretty tranquil here when the market isn't going on, but on Thursday and Sunday when hundreds of vendors (and buyers) arrive from near and far. The market long ago outgrew this square and spills onto adjoining streets. All the major sights are either here or nearby. Three blocks north is Arco Gucumatz, an arch over 5 Avenida where you watch vendors heading to the square the night before or very early the morning of market day. ⊠ *5 Av. and 7 C..*

6 Pascual Abaj. This ancient Mayan shrine, perched on a hilltop south of town, is often vandalized by overzealous Christians. The elongated stone face of the waist-high idol is always restored so that believers can return to their daily prayers. Local shamans lead villagers in special rites that occasionally include slaughtered chickens. Because it's one of the most accessible of the highland shrines, Pascual Abaj often attracts travelers eager to see these rituals firsthand. Try to be as unobtrusive as possible and always ask permission before taking photos. To see the shrine, follow 9 Calle until you see the signs for the narrow footpath up the hill. Boys hanging around the Parque Central will offer to guide you to the shrine for a small fee and can tell you when the rituals will take place. We recommend using the services of the official red-vested Inguat guides instead. There is a mask factory on-site. ⊠ *South of Chichicastenango.*

WHERE TO EAT

Chichicastenango's eateries do a brisk business on market day. No matter where you eat lunch on Thursday and Sunday, expect a few vendors to stroll in and show you their wares, even if you dine on the 2nd floor. Proprietors don't seem too anxious to shoo them away, but a simple "*No, gracias*" from you is all it takes for them to leave.

> **WATCH YOUR CAMERA**
>
> Photography is a touchy subject here. It is prohibited outright inside the Santo Tomás and Calvario churches on the main plaza. Snapping away outdoors at people observing rituals in the cemetery or at the Pascual Abaj shrine is also considered intrusive.

¢–$ ✕**Las Brasas.** An eclectic collection of local handicrafts brightens the walls of this excellent 2nd-floor steak house. The chef, formerly of the Hotel Santo Tomás, grills up a great steak, but there are plenty of other options, including a delicious *longaniza* (a spicy sausage similar to chorizo). Music and a full bar keep things lively, but not intrusively so. ⊠6 C. 4–52, 2nd level ☎7756–2226 ▭AE, D, DC, MC, V ☻BP.

¢–$ ✕**Casa San Juan.** Though right smack-dab in the middle of the market hubbub, this peaceful 2nd-floor restaurant, with its wrought-iron chairs and wood tables, offers a reasonably quiet respite from the activity below. These folks dish up their signature *pollo estilo San Juan* (a chicken breast in tomato sauce), with guacamole salad and rice on the side. The menu makes a big deal of specifying that the chile relleno is "not spicy." It's actually a beef and vegetable-filled bell pepper, a signature highland dish. Be sure to accompany your main dish, whatever it is, with the warm homemade tortillas. Sunday lunch gives way to a sumptuous buffet. ⊠4 Av. 6–58 ☎7756–2086 ▭AE, D, DC, MC, V ☻Closed Mon. Breakfast served Thurs. and Sun.

¢–$ ✕**La Fonda del Tzijolaj.** This restaurant's 2nd-story balcony overlooking Plaza Mayor is a great place to watch the vendors set up on the eve of the market. The *pollo chimichurri* (chicken in an herb sauce) is one of the best choices from the mostly traditional menu. There are also a few surprises, such as pizza and pasta. ⊠7 C. and 4 Av., Centro Comercial Santo Tomás 30 ☎7756–1013 ▭AE, D, DC, MC, V.

¢–$ ✕**La Villa de los Cofrades.** With two locations within a block of each other, it's hard to miss this longtime favorite. The smaller of the two has patio seating right on the Parque Central, where you can watch the vendors setting up their stalls while you feast on Belgian waffles or sip one of the finest cappuccinos in the country. If you're in a hurry to get to the market, remember that the service here can be miserably slow. The other location, called simply Los Cofrades, a block away on 5 Calle, has a less hectic atmosphere on a 2nd floor that lets you survey the fringes of the market. ⊠6 C. and 5 Av. ⊠Centro Comercial Santo Tomás 11 ☎7756–1643 ▭AE, D, DC, MC, V ☻Closed Mon. and Tues.

¢ ✕**Tu Café.** Take a break from shopping at this tiny eatery—you'll find just 10 tables here—with spartan decor on the corner of the Parque Central. This place offers a huge selection of sandwiches—choose from chicken, various cheeses, ham, roast beef, or club—or opt for the daily

CLOSE UP

Market Days in the Highlands

Believe it or not, highland markets mean more than Thursday and Sunday in Chichicastenango. Most towns hold a market one or two days a week, drawing buyers and sellers from miles around. None are as famous to the outside world as Chichi's, but you'll feel like a real insider, for example, knowing that the twice-weekly market in Momostenango is the place to go for good buys on blankets. Others have nothing you'd be interested in buying; colorful though Nebaj's Thursday affair is, you'll likely not want to cart a hen home, even if she is a prolific egg layer. Vendors at lesser-known markets rarely see outsiders; all will be amused to welcome an obvious visitor. Show an interest, strike up a conversation, make a new friend or two, and always ask permission before you take photos of individuals.

Almolonga: produce. *Wednesday, Saturday*

Chajul: produce, some textiles. *Tuesday, Friday*

Chichicastenango: souvenirs, textiles, produce, livestock. *Thursday, Sunday*

Chimaltenango: souvenirs, textiles, produce. *Monday, Friday*

Compalapa: textiles, produce, livestock. *Tuesday*

Huehuetenango: textiles, produce, livestock. *Wednesday*

Momostenango: woolens, blankets, produce, livestock. *Wednesday, Sunday*

Nebaj: produce, livestock. *Thursday, Sunday*

Olintepeque: livestock. *Tuesday*

Panajachel: produce, livestock. *Thursday*

Quetzaltenango: produce, livestock, some textiles. *First Sunday of month*

Sacapulas: produce, livestock, some textiles. *Thursday*

Salcajá: textiles, produce, livestock. *Tuesday*

San Andrés Xecul: produce, livestock. *Thursday*

San Francisco El Alto: produce, livestock, some textiles. *Friday*

San Lucas Tolimán: textiles, baskets. *Tuesday, Friday*

Santa Cruz del Quiché: produce, livestock. *Thursday*

Santiago Atitlán: textiles. *Friday*

Sololá: produce, some textiles. *Friday*

Todos Santos Cuchumatán: produce. *Thursday, Saturday*

Totonicapán: toys, ceramics, produce, livestock. *Tuesday, Thursday, Saturday*

Zacualpa: produce. *Thursday, Sunday*

Zunil: textiles. *Monday*

lunch special, with a main course, usually chicken-based—perhaps a *pepián*, with a side of rice and vegetables—for Q25. You can fortify yourself early in the day, too, with a breakfast of omelets or pancakes. ⊠ *5 Av. 6–44* ☎ *7756–1448* ⊟ *No credit cards* ☽ *BP.*

WHERE TO STAY

Lodgings in town raise their rates the nights before and of market day. There aren't that many hotels in Chichi, so make reservations if you plan to be in town on any of those nights. Stay here on a Monday, Tuesday, or Friday night and you'll pay a lot less.

$$$ ✕⌂ **Hotel Santo Tomás.** Built in the Spanish style around a central court-
Fodor's Choice yard, Hotel Santo Tomás is one of the town's best lodgings. Breezy
★ passageways in which hundreds of plants spring from rustic clay pots lead past two trickling fountains. Spacious rooms are decorated with traditional textiles and antique reproductions. Each has a fireplace to warm you when the sun goes down. The back of the hotel is quieter and has views of the surrounding countryside. The large restaurant (¢–$$) serves an excellent lunch buffet on market days. ⊠7 Av. 5–32 ☎7756–1316 or 7756–1061 ⧠7756–1306 ⊕*www.paginasamarillas. com/hotelsantotomas.htm* ⌫70 rooms ⌂In-room: no a/c, no phone, no TV. In-hotel: restaurant, bar, pool, gym, no elevator, parking (no fee) ⊟AE, D, DC, MC, V.

$$$ ⌂ **Mayan Inn.** Long regarded as Chichcastenango's "second hotel" (after the Santo Tomás), the Mayan Inn is certainly acceptable but is showing its age. A good coat of paint and a much-needed face-lift would restore this hostelry's one-time status as one of the country's top hotels. Rooms with corner fireplaces surround a series of beautifully maintained garden courtyards. Most have wide windows overlooking the pine-covered hills. The service is as impeccable as always—an attendant in traditional costume is assigned to each room. ⊠3 Av. at 8 C., behind El Calvario church ☎7756–1176, 2470–4700 in Guatemala City ⧠7756–1212, 2470–4701 in Guatemala City ⊕*www.mayaninn. com.gt* ⌫30 rooms ⌂In-room: no a/c, no phone, no TV. In-hotel: restaurant, bar, laundry service, parking (no fee) ⊟AE, D, DC, MC, V.

$ ⌂ **Hotel Chugüila.** This hotel, in an older building a few blocks north of the plaza, has a variety of rooms facing a cobblestone courtyard. The plant-filled portico leading to most rooms is scattered with inviting chairs and tables. Rooms are simply furnished, and a few have fireplaces. The hotel even offers its own rooftop market with 45 vendors on Thursday and Sunday market days. ⊠5 Av. 5–24 ☎7756–1134 ⧠7759–9412 ✉*hotelchuguila@yahoo.com* ⌫15 rooms ⌂In-room: no a/c, no phone. In-hotel: restaurant, no elevator, public Internet, parking ⊟No credit cards.

$ ⌂ **Posada El Arco.** This small hotel has a distinctly homey feel. The spacious rooms are clean, if a tad musty, and tastefully decorated with *típica*. All rooms have fireplaces for the chilly evenings. To get here, climb up the stairs to the top of the arch that crosses 5 Avenida and turn left. ⊠4 C. 4–36 ☎7756–1255 ⌫8 rooms ⌂In-room: no a/c, no phone, no TV. In-hotel: no elevator, laundry facilities, parking (no fee) ⊟No credit cards.

¢ ⌂ **Hotel Chalet.** The Alps are nowhere to be seen, but at the very least, the sun-splashed breakfast room at this cozy little hotel does the name justice. The rooms are smallish but not cramped. Wooden masks and other handicrafts adorn the walls. A pleasant terrace is a great place for relaxing after a taxing day of roaming the markets. The hotel is down a small unpaved road near 7 Avenida, and removed from the cacophony of market central. ⊠3 C. C 7–44 ☎7756–2286 📠7756–1793 🛏9 rooms ♿In-room: no a/c, no phone, no TV. In-hotel: no elevator ▭AE, D, DC, MC, V.

SHOPPING

Although the market is paramount, Chichicastenango has a decent selection of fixed shops selling high-quality souvenirs and artisan work. Many are on 6 Calle, the street you're likely to walk between your tour van and the market and back. Here's the kicker: Most of them open only on Thursday and Sunday market days.

Casa Maya (⊠6 C. ☎7756–1349) has a distinctive array of quality T-shirts. **Típica Maya** (⊠6 C. 6–35 ☎5910–1424) offers a good selection of women's clothing—in particular, woven huipils and cortes.

Galeri'a de Artes Pintores de Chichicastenango (⊠6 C. ☎5443–0074) exhibits primitivist paintings created by a cooperative of 12 local artisits. We especially like the hand-painted Nativity scenes at **Tashe Artesanía** (⊠6 C. 6–13 ☎7756–1622) among all the other ceramics for sale.

Bucking the trend and staying open every day of the week, **De Colores** (⊠6 C. 6–21 ☎7756–1027) deals in woven and embroidered textiles, sweaters and blouses. Check out the selection of cute oven mitts and pot holders.

NIGHTLIFE & THE ARTS

Nightlife is limited in hard-working Chichicastenango, although there are many tiny bars along the streets surrounding the plaza where you can join the locals for a beer. Do not stray from the city center at night as there have been numerous attacks by *maras* (gangs).

Las Brasas (⊠6 C. 4–52 ☎7756–2226) occasionally has live music.

Café San Juan (⊠4 Av. San Juan 6–58 ☎7756–2086) has a refreshing neocolonial feel and live music on the weekends. The light fare is also quite good.

EL QUICHÉ

It doesn't get much traffic, but adventurous travelers may want to continue north from Chichicastenango for further glimpses of the region called El Quiché, where you'll find traditional villages on pine-covered hills.

SANTA CRUZ DEL QUICHÉ

19 km (12 mi) north of Chichicastenango.

A half-hour north of Chichicastenango lies the provincial capital of Santa Cruz del Quiché, which serves as a base for exploring the area. Quiché, as the town is commonly called, is known for its pretty white

MARKET DAY IN CHICHICASTENANGO

Chichicastenango's famous Thursday and Sunday market is also one of Guatemala's top-notch fun things to do. Although a Thursday visit won't disappoint, come here for the Sunday market if your schedule permits. During your shopping breaks, you can observe the fascinating rituals on the steps of the Santo Tomás church; they mix Mayan and Catholic, and the boundary is never clear.

At dawn, mist swirls around the vendors as they set up shop. Firecrackers go off and smoky incense wafts from the steps of the church in anticipation and celebration of the ritual of market day.

Haggling is expected here. First ask around and do some comparison-shopping before zeroing in on that huipil you have your eye on. Brush up on your Spanish numbers. Vendors speak little English, and for many of them, Spanish is a second language, too. Offer something slightly above one-half the first price asked by the vendor. From there you both can compromise. Don't bargain *too* hard though; goods are already reasonably priced here, and those few extra quetzals mean far more to the salesperson than to you.

Unlike the fixed shops in town, market sellers aren't set up to handle credit cards. Some, but not all, will accept U.S. dollars, and even if they do, you'll likely get quetzals in change. Try to bring small denominations, no matter which currency you pay with.

Tours depart on market days from many places around the country. (Cruise ships that dock at Puerto Quetzal on the Pacific coast on Thursday or Sunday also offer their passengers optional shore excursions to Chichi.) Some include only transport and "Be back at the van at 2 PM and we'll head back" instructions from your driver. Others may include a lunch voucher, often at the Hotel Santo Tomás. Some of the Guatemala City and Antigua departures make a stop at Lake Atitlán on the way to or from. As far as we know, not even "fully escorted tours" include shopping guides.

Things begin to wind down by midafternoon as the shoppers head out, and vendors, anxious to get home before dark, start to pack up. Here's another advantage to lodging in Chichicastenango: Savvy market shoppers know that this is the hour for the best bargains, with sellers frequently willing to give discounts on items they won't have to lug home.

We hear complaints about the market: "There are too many tourists." "The walkways between vendors' stalls are too narrow." "I see too many things I don't want to buy." Yes. Yes. And, yes. It gets crowded, but that's part of the fun. (On that note of crowding, do watch your things. The market is generally safe, but a few wallet-snatchers prey on unsuspecting shoppers.) Despite all appearances to the contrary, this age-old spectacle does not exist for visitors. Chichicastenango has been a center of trade since pre-Columbian times. Many vendors' stalls burst at the seams with souvenirs these days, but the real focus of Chichi's market are fruits, vegetables, and poultry—all the day-to-day goods that sustain the families who come here twice a week. Always has been. Always will be.

church on the east side of the Parque Central. It was built from the stones taken from a Mayan temple destroyed by the Spanish.

North of town is **K'umarcaaj,** the ancient capital of the Quiché kingdom. This once-magnificent site was destroyed by Spanish conquistadors in 1524. The ruins haven't been restored, but they are frequently used for Mayan rituals. A taxi to and from the ruins should cost less than Q60. You can also walk the pleasant 3-km (2-mi) route without much difficulty. Follow 10 Calle out of town, where it becomes a dirt road. A tight S curve is the halfway point. The road forks at the bottom of a hill; take the road to the right.

WHERE TO STAY & EAT

¢ ✕ **Comedor Flipper.** A cage of lively birds lends a cheerful atmosphere to this small eatery, which serves good Guatemalan fare. The *avena* (a warm wheat beverage) is delicious, especially on a cold morning. There is no sign of the restaurant's trusty namesake, though a ceramic sailfish atop the refrigerator comes close. ⊠ *1 Av. 7–31, around the corner from Hotel San Pasqual* ☎ *No phone* ⊟ *No credit cards.*

$ ▥ **Hotel San Pasqual.** This little hotel has a definite charm, most of it emanating from the engaging couple that runs it. The simple rooms, with handwoven bedspreads, surround a sunny courtyard. Clotheslines full of the day's laundry stretch to the roof next door. The shared baths are clean, but hot water is available only in the morning. ⊠ *7 C. 0–43, Zona 1* ☎ *7755–1107* ⚡ *40 rooms, 11 with bath* ⚐ *In-room: no a/c, no phone, no TV. In-hotel: parking (no fee)* ⊟ *No credit cards.*

NEBAJ

95 km (59 mi) north of Santa Cruz del Quiché.

A fascinating part of the highlands, although one of Guatemala's most inaccessible regions, is the so-called Ixil Triangle. It's home to the indigenous Ixiles, who speak a unique Mam-based language, different than the Quiché spoken in the surrounding area. Isolation has meant that the people here have been able to preserve a rich culture; you'll have some trouble finding fluent Spanish speakers here. Women wear bright-red cortes with green or yellow huipils; men have mostly abandoned traditional wear, but retain colorful sashes, which may decorate an otherwise Western outfit of jeans and sweater. For many years, traditional Ixil wear meant doom for the people here; the war hit this region hard, with the Ixiles specifically targeted for elimination. Out of fear for their own safety, many people here abandoned their traditional costume, and only began to don it again since the signing of the peace accords.

The main town in this region is Nebaj, where cobblestone streets lead to a central plaza with a large colonial church. On Thursday and Sunday the town swells with people who come from the surrounding villages to sell their distinctive weavings. Besides shopping, hiking in the surrounding mountains is the main draw for tourists.

CLOSE UP

Dancing with the Dead

Colorful cemeteries, with their turquoises and pinks, mauves and sky blues, play an integral part in the living fabric of contemporary Guatemalan society. It's not uncommon to see entire families visiting their deceased relatives on Sundays. But a visit to the cemetery need not be mournful, and they often bring a bottle of alcohol to share amongst themselves, occasionally tipping the bottle to the earth, so that their dead relatives also get their share. Incense is burned and shamans perform ancient rites alongside Catholic and evangelical priests. The November 2 observance of the Day of the Dead gives family members their greatest chance to celebrate and honor their deceased relatives with music, dance, song, festivals and, yes, much drinking and merriment.

Celebrating the dead rather than mourning their passing is a Mayan tradition that reaches back to pre-Columbian times. The *Popol Vuh* or Mayan Bible as it's sometimes referred to looks toward an active relationship with deceased friends and relatives. "Remember us after we have gone. Don't forget us," reads the *Popul Vuh*. "Conjure up our faces and our words. Our image will be as dew in the hearts of those who want to remember us." It is unknown who authored the *Popol Vuh*, which was translated into Spanish in the early 18th century by Father Francisco Ximénez, but the practices and myths of the sacred book of the Maya still make their way into the Day of the Dead celebrations across Guatemala.

The country's two most fascinating Day of the Dead celebrations take place in Santiago Sacatepéquez and Todos Santos Chuchumatán on November 1. In Santiago Sacatepéquez, a Cakchiquel town located 30 km (19 mi) from Antigua, the villagers gather in the early morning hours and have a procession through the narrow streets to the cemetery. Once there, they take part in what is one of Guatemala's most resplendent ceremonies, flying giant kites of up to 2 meters (61/2 feet) in diameter to communicate with those who have passed away. The villagers tie messages to the kite tails to let the dead know how they are doing and to ask God for special favors. The colorful celebration is finished with a lunch feast of *fiambre*, a traditional dish of cold cuts, boiled eggs, vegetables, olives, and other delicacies. The so-called "drunken horse race" in the remote mountain village of Todos Santos Cuchumatán, near Huehuetenango—the riders get plastered, not the horses—is not to everyone's taste, but is an integral part of that town's Day of the Dead celebration.

The color scheme of the cemeteries is more than just decorative: turquoise and green tombs signify an adult member of the family was recently interred in the above-ground crypts, whites and yellows indicating the passing of an elderly family member, and pinks and blues reserved for deceased children.

Just remember that although foreigners are welcome in the cemeteries, it's important to respect the traditions and dignity of those visiting deceased relatives—tread softly and leave your camera behind.

—Gregory Benchwick

WHERE TO STAY

¢ ⛄ **Hotel Ixil.** Nebaj doesn't have much in the way of lodging; the best bet is this friendly whitewashed hotel set around two courtyards. Some of the basic but spacious rooms overlook the garden. A few rooms in an annex next door have nicer furnishings and even toss in cable TV. ⊠*Nebaj* ☎*7755–1091* ⤶*12 rooms* ⌂*In-room: no a/c, no phone no TV (some). In-hotel: parking (no fee)* ▤*No credit cards.*

The drive north from Santa Cruz del Quiché takes about 90 minutes over a precipitously curving road at stretches. Regular bus service leaves from Santa Cruz throughout the day. The trip takes about two hours.

> **LANGUAGE SCHOOL IN NEBAJ**
>
> Almost no one here speaks anything but Spanish and Ixil—you can study Ixil, too, if you like—so learning the language in such a remote location virtually eliminates the temptation to lapse into English outside the classroom.
>
> **Nebaj Language School** (⊠*Nebaj* ☎*7832–6345 in Antigua* ⊕*www.nebajlanguageschool. com*).

QUETZALTENANGO (XELAJÚ)

91 km (56 mi) southwest of Chichicastenango.

Guatemala's second largest city might seem quite provincial if you've first visited the capital. But we'll take friendly, old Quetzaltenango any day. Historically, the city never entirely warmed to the idea of authority from far-away Guatemala City, and, in fact, was a hotbed of separatist sentiment during the 19th century. Those dreams have long faded, but you'll see Quetzaltenango's blue-white-red regional flag flying far more frequently here than the blue-white-blue national flag.

The first attraction of the place is the city itself. You won't find many must-see sights here, but Quetzaltenango's large student population gives it a cosmopolitan, politically astute, slightly bohemian feel, with a good selection of restaurants, cafés, and nightlife. It's no wonder that the city has become such a choice place to study Spanish.

The city anchors a valley guarded by the Volcán Santa María, with an economy based on agriculture. The rolling hills, enriched by fertile volcanic soil, are particularly good for growing coffee. The area attracts travelers, who come here to purchase the intricate weavings from the surrounding villages. The first Sunday of each month is the main market day in Quetzaltenango itself, and the central square is filled with women selling their wares. Many days a week, towns in the Quetzaltenango orbit play host to their own markets, and are well worth their easy day trips.

Streets in Quetzaltenango vaguely follow the Guatemala City organizational model. The city is divided into 11 zones, although nearly everything you need is in Zona 1. Avenidas run north–south; calles,

east–west. Outside the very heart of the city, hills interrupt the regular
grid system, and many streets need to be designated as *Diagonal*.

EXPLORING

❷ Catedral del Espíritu Santo/Catedral de los Altos. On the southeastern corner of Parque Centro América, this cathedral dates from 1535. All that
remains of the original building (Espíritu Santo) is the facade, which
features life-size saints that look down upon those headed here to pray
and is offset to the left of the newer cathedral (Los Altos), with its own
front, constructed in 1899. ✉ *11 Av. and 7 C., Zona 1.*

❺ Iglesia de San Nicolás. This bluish church, on the east side of Parque
Benito Juárez, is known for its unusual baroque design. Although
lovely, it looks a bit out of place in the town's mix of Greek and colonial structures. ✉ *15 Av. and 3 C., Zona 3.*

❸ Museo de Historia Natural. In the Casa de la Cultura on the south side of
Parque Centro América, the Museum of Natural History is interesting
mainly for its neoclassic flourishes. Inside are some examples of pre-
Columbian pottery. Your ticket also includes admission to the so-called
Museo de la Marimba, which, despite its name, has little to do with

QUETZALTENANGO OR XELAJÚ?

All the highway signs direct you to QUETZALTENANGO, but once you arrive, you'll hear many residents refer to their city by its one-time indigenous name, "Xelajú" (*Shay-la-HOO*) or, more commonly, "Xela" for short. The long version was *Xelajú Noj*, meaning "under 10 mountains." Originally part of the Mam empire, Quetzaltenango was captured in the 14th century by the Quiché people. It remained part of the Quiché kingdom until 1524, when Spanish conqueror Pedro de Alvarado captured and destroyed the city. He used the stones to build a new city called Quetzaltenango, which means "the place of many quetzals" in Mexico's Nahuatl language.

Nearly five centuries later, the new name still sticks in the collective craw of many residents. Some, as a matter of pride and tradition, would never let the word "Quetzaltenango" pass their lips. Others are more pragmatic: "Xela" is just quicker to say and write.

marimbas, and is more a hodgepodge collection of Quetzaltenango artifacts. ✉7 C. and 11 Av., Zona 1 ☎7761–6427 ✉Q6.

❹ **Parque Benito Juárez.** About 10 blocks north of Parque Centro América is this palm-lined park where many families spend their Sunday afternoons. Ice-cream stands are in glorious abundance. ✉15 Av. and 3 C., Zona 3 ✉Q6.

❶ **Parque Centro América.** The city's central plaza, ablaze with pepper trees, is one of the most beautiful in Central America. It is surrounded by neoclassical architectural masterpieces, most of which date from the early 20th century. (Earthquakes took their toll on older colonial structures.) such as the magnificent building called Pasaje Enríquez, built in 1900 in the style of a center-city European shopping arcade. Bees buzz around the park's numerous flower beds. Be careful if you're susceptible to harm from their stings. ✉12 Av. and 4 C., Zona 1.

NEED A BREAK? Anyone can buy a huipil as their souvenir of Guatemala. How about coming home with a few flashy moves that will wow your friends on the dance floor? The Salsa Rosa dance studio (✉ Diagonal 11 7–79, Zona 1 ☎5204–0404) gives group salsa lessons each weeknight at 6 PM, and the cost is a bargain Q25 per hour. (Instruction is in Spanish.) You can also opt for private lessons daily except Sunday for Q60 per hour—equally a bargain, we think—and delve into the fine art of salsa, merengue, cha-cha, or lambada. If you're new to Latin dancing, we recommend sticking with the relatively simpler merengue, which works well with an amazing variety of pop music back home. Call a couple of days in advance to make an appointment for private lessons and to arrange for an English-speaking instructor if you need one.

WHERE TO EAT

$–$$$ ✕**Il Cardinali.** For a home-style southern Italian atmosphere with checked tablecloths, opera music, and basketed Chianti bottles hanging from the rafters, head to Il Cardinali. The extensive, pasta-heavy menu also includes pizza and a decent wine selection. The service is friendly and quick. The front room gets chilly at night. Opt instead for the larger and bustling, but cozier back room. ⊠*14 Av. 3–25, Zona 1* ☎*7761–0924* ⊟*AE, DC, MC, V.*

$–$$ ✕**Dos Tejanos.** Tex-Mex food has come to Quetzaltenango in a big way with the 2007 opening of this restaurant inside the Pasaje Enríquez building on Parque Centro América. Look for the neon signs. Decor is that of an old, southwest cantina, with wood tables and stools in the room that also houses the bar, and chairs with backs in the amply sized room for nonsmokers. Barbecue ribs, fajitas, and nachos make up the hearty fare. ⊠*4 C. 12–3* ☎*7765–4360* ⊟*V* ⊗*BP.*

¢–$$ ✕**Royal Paris.** This bistro caters to foreign students, so the menu covers a lot of bases. Some dishes aren't the least bit Parisian, such as the succulent chicken-curry kebab. It's all prepared with flair, however. The ambience at this 2nd-floor restaurant is definitely imported, and slightly bohemian, courtesy of the paintings of cabaret scenes. There's also a bar with an extensive wine list. ■TIP➔ **Stop by on Tuesday evenings; it's movie night, with a French or Italian film (with Spanish subtitles).** ⊠*C. 14A 3–06, Zona 1* ☎*7761–1942* ⊟*AE, D, DC, MC, V* ⊗*No lunch Mon.*

¢–$ ✕**El Kopetín.** Good food, attentive service, and reasonable prices make this place popular with the locals, so it can be tough to get a table later in the evening. It couldn't be described as fancy, but this restaurant's long polished bar and wood paneling raise it above the usual neighborhood dive. The menu has a number of delicious appetizers, including traditional queso fundido and a selection of meat and seafood dishes that are smothered in rich sauces. Saturday, the place whips up its *caldo de mariscos* (seafood stew). ⊠*14 Av. 3–51, Zona 1* ☎*7761–8381* ⊟*AE, D, DC, MC, V.*

¢–$ ✕**Las Orquídeas.** You'll see the posters and leaflets for this small Thai restaurant—just a scant five tables and extremely informal—all over town, so by the time you get here, you feel you already know the place. Look for the circular orchid-symbol sign with no name at the front door. (Orquídea means "orchid.") The English–Spanish menu is a mix-and-match affair. All the dishes, whether pad thai, coconut-milk soup, or green- or red-curry stir-fry come with a choice of chicken, tofu, or shrimp. ⊠*4 C. 15–45, Zona 1* ☎*5247–5873* ⊗*Closed Sun. and Mon.*

WHERE TO STAY

$$ ▥**Casa Mañen.** This romantic little B&B, west of the central plaza, blends colonial comforts with modern conveniences. The rooms—most have fireplaces—are spacious and homey, with handmade wall hangings and throw rugs and the occasional rocking chair. On the roof is a two-level terrace with a fantastic view of the city. Complimentary

LANGUAGE SCHOOLS

Quetzaltenango has the greatest number of Spanish schools in Guatemala, and is widely known for having the country's most rigorous programs. As elsewhere, schools can line you up with homestays.

Casa Xelajú (⊠ *Callejón 15, Diagonal 13–02,Zona 1* ☎ *7761–5954* ⊕ *www.casaxelaju.com*).

CBA Spanish School (⊠ *12 Av. 10–27, Zona 1* ☎ *7761–8535* ⊕ *www.cbaspanishschool.com*).

Celas Maya Spanish School (⊠ *6 C. 14–55, Zona 1* ☎ *7761–4342* ⊕ *www.celasmaya.edu.gt*).

Centro de Estudios Español Pop Wuj (⊠ *1 C. 17–72, Zona 1* ☎ *7761–8286* ⊕ *www.pop-wuj.org*).

Centro Ligüístico El Baul (☎ *7765–8066*).

Educación para Todos (⊠ *Av. el Cenizal 0-58, Zona 5* ☎ *5935-3815* ⊕ *www.spanishschools.biz*).

El Anual Language Center (⊠ *27 Av. 8–68, Zona 1* ☎ *7765–2098* ⊕ *www.languageselnahual.com*).

El Mundo en Español (⊠ *8 Av. C. B A-61, Zona 1* ☎ *7761–6256* ⊕ *www.elmundoenespanol.org*).

El Portal Spanish School (⊠ *9 Callejón A 11–49, Zona 1* ☎ *7761–5275* ⊕ *www.spanishschoolelportal.com*).

El Quetzal Spanish School (⊠ *10 C. 10–29, Zona 1* ☎ *7765–1085* ⊕ *222.xelawho.com/elquetzal*).

Escuela de Español EVA (⊠ *Diagonal 12 6–39, Zona 1* ☎ *7765–3325* ⊕ *www.xelapages.com/vamosadelante*).

Eureka Spanish School (⊠ *12 Av. 8–21, Zona 1* ☎ *7761–5260*).

Inepas Spanish School (⊠ *15 Av. 4–59, Zona 1* ☎ *7765–1308* ⊕ *www.inepas.org*).

Ixim No'j (⊠ *1 Av. 7–34, Zona 1* ☎ *5977–1040* ⊕ *www.iximnoj.com*).

Kie Balam Spanish School (⊠ *Diagonal 12 4–46, Zona 1* ☎ *7761–1636* ⊕ *www.kiebalam.com*).

La Democracia Spanish School (⊠ *9 C. 15–05, Zona 3* ☎ *7763–6895* ⊕ *www.lademocracia.net*).

Madre Tierra Spanish School (⊠ *13 Av. 8–34* ☎ *7761–6105* ⊕ *www.madre-tierra.org*).

Miguel Ángel Asturias Spanish School (⊠ *8 C. 16–23, Zona 1* ☎ *7765–3707* ⊕ *www.spanish-school.com*).

Minerva Spanish School (⊠ *24 Av. 4–39, Zona 3* ☎ *7767–4427* ⊕ *www.minervaspanishschool.com*).

Proyecto Lingüístico Quetzalteco de Español (⊠ *5 C. 2–40, Zona 1* ☎ *7763–1061* ⊕ *www.hermandad.com*).

Proyecto Lingüístico Santa María (⊠ *3 C. 10–56, Zona 1* ☎ *7765–8136* ⊕ *www.spanishgua.net*).

Sakribal Spanish School (⊠ *6 C. 7–42, Zona 1* ☎ *7763–0717* ⊕ *www.sakribal.com*).

Ulew Tinamit Spanish School (⊠ *4 C. 15–23, Zona 1* ☎ *7761–6242* ⊕ *www.spanishguatemala.org*).

Utatlán Spanish School (⊠ *12 Av. 4–32, Zona 1* ☎ *7763–0446* ⊕ *www.xelapages.com/utatlan*).

breakfast is served in a small dining room downstairs. The staff is incredibly friendly and will be happy to help you with travel plans. You'll get a small discount if you pay in cash. ⊠9 *Av. 4–11, Zona 1* ☎*7765–0786* 🖷*7765–0678* ⊕*www.comeseeit.com* 🛏*7 rooms, 2 suites* 🔑*In-room: no a/c, no phone, safe, refrigerator (some). In-hotel: no elevator, laundry service, parking (no fee)* ☰*AE, D, DC, MC, V* ⎮⊙⎮*BP.*

$$ 🖥**Pensión Bonifaz.** Don't let the name fool you into thinking this is a modest establishment—Pensión Bonifáz is Quetzaltenango's most upscale hotel. Though housed in a stately old building at the central plaza's northeast corner, it has a modern interior that doesn't quite live up to its exterior. Still, it is a comfortable, well-run establishment. The nicest rooms are in the older building, where small balconies offer nice views of the plaza. A small café serves light fare for lunch, whereas the larger restaurant (¢–$$$) has a continental menu. ⊠*4 C. 10–50, Zona 1* ☎*7765–1111* 🖷*7763–0671* ✒*bonifaz@intellnet.net.gt* 🛏*74 rooms* 🔑*In-room: no a/c. In-hotel: restaurant, room service, bar, pool, laundry service, public Internet, public Wi-Fi, parking (no fee)* ☰*AE, D, DC, MC, V* ⎮⊙⎮*EP.*

$ 🖥**Hotel Modelo.** Founded in 1892, this family-run establishment is one of Guatemala's oldest, still-operating lodgings. Over the years the distinguished hotel has maintained its tradition of good service. The wood-floor rooms, furnished with antiques, surround a few small courtyards leading off the lobby. Dinner is served in a fine colonial-style restaurant. Rooms in the overflow annex on the next block (the Hotel Modelo Anexo) are far more basic. ⊠*14 Av. A 2–31, Zona 1* ☎*7763–0216* 🖷🖷*7763–1376* 🛏*32 rooms* 🔑*In-room: no a/c, safe (some). In-hotel: restaurant, bar, parking (no fee)* ☰*AE, D, DC, MC, V* ⎮⊙⎮*BP.*

$ 🖥**Hotel Villa Real Plaza.** Surrounding a covered courtyard illuminated by skylights, the spacious carpeted rooms at Hotel Villa Real Plaza all have fireplaces that you'll appreciate on cool evenings. Those in a newer wing are superior to those in the dimly lit older section. The restaurant (¢–$$) has an interesting menu whose offerings range from chicken cordon bleu to a variety of meaty stews. You'll receive a small discount if you pay with cash. ⊠*4 C. 12–22, Zona 1* ☎*7761–4045* 🖷*7761–6780* ⊕*www.xelapages.com/villarealplaza* 🛏*54 rooms* 🔑*In-room: no a/c. In-hotel: restaurant, room service, bar, laundry service, parking (no fee)* ☰*AE, DC, MC, V.*

$ 🖥**Villa de Don Andrés.** A turn-of-the-century building just a half-block off the Parque Centro América houses this charming budget find. Each of the five carpeted rooms is decorated with local artisan work and lines a long, wide, bright hall that serves as a sitting room, with rocking chairs and lots of plants. All have their own baths, although Room 1's bathroom is across the hall. The one triple room at the end of the hall is huge, with one stone wall and a nonoperating fireplace that has been converted into shelving. You'll receive a small discount if you pay in cash. ⊠*13 Av. 6–16, Zona 1* ☎*7761–2014* ⊕*www.villadedonandres. com* 🛏*5 rooms* 🔑*In-room: no a/c, no phone. In-hotel: laundry service, public Internet, parking (no fee)* ☰*AE, D, DC, MC, V* ⎮⊙⎮*BP.*

¢–$ ⊞ **The Black Cat.** This slightly ramshackle hotel, a few blocks off the plaza, is a popular spot with travelers on a budget. Rooms on two floors of a converted residence face a small courtyard overflowing with plants. Several are arranged dorm-style with bunks, and sleep eight to 10 people. Though simple, they're clean and comfortable. There's a separate lounge where you can chat with other guests. ⊠ *13 Av. 3–33, Zona 1* ☎ *7765-8591* ✉ *blackcatxela@gmail.com* ⇆ *14 rooms, none with bath* ⌂ *In-room: no a/c, no phone, no TV. In-hotel: restaurant, bar, public Internet, public Wi-Fi* ⊟ *No credit cards* ⦿| *BP.*

¢–$ ⊞ **Casa Doña Mercedes.** This longtime budget standby just two blocks off the Parque Centro América was undergoing a complete remodeling at press time to upgrade its furnishings and facilities. Spacious, carpeted rooms on the upper floor now contain private bathrooms; those on the 1st floor, all with partial brick walls, still offer shared baths. Everyone has access to shared kitchen facilities. ⊠ *6 C. 13–42, Zona 1* ☎ *7765–4687* ⊕ *www.geocities.com/guest_house_mercedes* ⇆ *8 rooms, 4 with bath* ⌂ *In-room: no a/c, no phone. In-hotel: no elevator, public Internet, parking (no fee)* ⊟ V ⦿| *EP.*

NIGHTLIFE

Guatemala's second city gets our first-place nod for a fun night out on the town. Although the center city is fine for walking in the evening, take a taxi back to your hotel if you plan to be out late.

Many places have no phone, other than a cell number belonging to someone on staff. For updates and the latest news, check the monthly, slightly irreverent English-language publication *Xela Who,* available around town.

BARS

Casa Babylon (⊠ *5 C. 12–54, Zona 1* ☎ *7761–2320*) attracts foreign students and Guatemalans alike. They have an extensive mixed drink list. Right off the central square, **Salón Tecún** (⊠ *12 Av. 4–40, Zona 1*) is a small pub inside the Pasaje Enríquez building on Parque Centro América that is popular with students.

Vegetarian restaurant **Asados Puente** (⊠ *7 C. 13–29, Zona 1* ☎ *7759–5077*) holds happy hour every night from 8 to 10 PM.

Complementing all the city's down-home offerings, classy bar **Bajo La Luna** (⊠ *8 Av. 4–11, Zona 1* ☎ *7761–2242*) serves wine by the glass, pitcher, or bottle.

CAFÉS

Grab a cup of coffee or a drink on the 2nd-floor outdoor balcony of **Balcón del Enríquez** (⊠ *12 Av. 4–40, Zona 1* ☎ *7765–2296*), in the Pasaje Enríquez building on Parque Centro América. **Blue Angel Video Café** (⊠ *7 C. 15–79, Zona 1*) serves up fruit and veggie drinks while you log in via Wi-Fi on your laptop. For a taste of Xela's bohemian scene, head to the oh-so-funky **La Luna** (⊠ *8 Av. 4–1, Zona 1*). Though they don't serve alcohol, the extensive hot-drink menu is enough to satisfy any espresso addict or chocophile.

LIVE MUSIC

Enjoy live music each Thursday evening at the mellow **Brooklyn Bar** (⌧*15 Av. 0–67, Zona 1*). **La Fonda del Ché** (⌧*15 Av. 7–43, Zona 1* ☎*5569–8827*) has trova, a genre of protest music popular in Latin America, Tuesday through Saturday night. Nurse a glass of wine and listen to live music or a poetry reading at **El Viñedo** (⌧*15 Av. A 3–05, Zona 1*) Tuesday through Saturday. **La Mansión Marilyn** (⌧*13 Av. 5–38, Zona 1*) offers live music with a lot of Marilyn Monroe decor in the background Tuesday through Sunday.

> **CHEERING ON THE GOATS**
>
> You'll have to look for it as XELAJÚ MC in the sports scores, but Quetzaltenango better knows its 2007 Guatemalan National League championship soccer team as the *Superchivos* ("supergoats"), the city being the center of an important goat-raising region.

FILMS

Enjoy a coffee, log in with your laptop, and enjoy the occasional movie night at **Cinema Coffee Shop** (⌧*12 Av. 8–21, Zona 1*). We like cozy **El Cuartito** (⌧*13 Av. 7–09, Zona 1*) for its coffee and veggie snacks. It has an outdoor patio, but the inside is a lot warmer. Tuesday's "Alternative Film Night" gets underway at 7 PM. **Cinema Paraíso** (⌧*1 C. and 2 Av., Zona 1*) is a small café that screens artsy films. **Cubatenango** (⌧*19 Av. 2–08, Zona 1* ☎*5508–3348*) screens Latin American films on DVD each Tuesday and Thursday at 7 PM, and serves two-for-one *Cuba Libres* (rum and cokes) each even from 6 to 8 PM.

DANCING

Catering to the university crowd, **El Duende** (⌧*14 Av., between 1 and 2 Cs., Zona 1*) is the place to go dancing on the weekends. Take your pick, depending on the night of the week, at **Kokoloko's** (⌧*15 Av. and 4 C., Zona 1* ☎*5904–9028*), and dance to salsa, reggae, or world music. Happy hour is from 7 to 9 every night. Dance the night away, Latin style, at **La Parranda** (⌧*6 C. and 14 Av., Zona 1*). Dance to a variety of music at **Pala Life Klishé** (⌧*4 C. and 15 Av., Zona 1*) Tuesday is reggae night; Friday means disco.

OUTDOOR ACTIVITIES

BICYCLING

There's great mountain biking through the hills and villages surrounding Xela. **Vrisa Bicicletas** (⌧*15 Av. 3–64, Zona 1* ☎*7761–3237*) rents both on-road and off-road bikes by the day or week and has maps so you can take self-guided tours of the countryside.

HIKING

Quetzaltrekkers (⌧*Casa Argentina, 12 Diagonal 8–67, Zona 1* ☎*7761–5865* ⊕*www.quetzaltrekkers.com*) is a nonprofit company that supports three major social-service programs by coordinating truly unforgettable hiking trips. The three-day trek to Lago Atitlán and the two-day ascent of Volcán Tajamulco both pass through spectacular countryside and several remote villages.

SHOPPING

BOOKS

Literary- and politically-minded Quetzaltenango has several fine book-stores, three with good selections in English. **El Libro Abierto** (⊠*15 Av. A 1–56, Zona 1* ☎*7761–5195*) deals in used books, as well as post-cards and organic coffee. **North & South Bookstore** (⊠*8 C. 13–77, Zona 1* ☎*7761–0589*) is strong in works dealing with history and politics. **Vrisa Bookstore** (⊠*15 Av. 3–64, Zona 1* ☎*7761–3237*) has many used books in English.

MARKETS

The bustling **Mercado Minerva** (⊠*6 C., Zona 3*), next to the main bus terminal, is the best of the city's markets. There are plenty of interest-ing handicrafts to be found here. But watch your pockets—groups of skillful thieves prey on tourists coming to and from the buses.

Artesanía from most of the villages in the region can be found in the **Mercado La Democracia** (⊠*1 C. and 15 Av., Zona 3*). Since there are rela-tively few shoppers, prices tend to be lower than elsewhere in the city.

Near Parque Centro América, the **Centro Comercial Municipal** (⊠*7 C. and 11 Av., Zona 1*) has a more limited selection of souvenirs.

SPECIALTY STORES

Trama Textiles (⊠*3 C. and 11 Av., Zona 1* ☎*7765–8564*) exhibits scarves, bags, and tablecloths woven by a local women's cooperative. Quetzaltenango is famous for its beautiful glass. **Vitra** (⊠*13 Av. 5–27, Zona 3* ☎*7767–1269*) is one of the city's most noted stores. You'll find excellent handblown glass at affordable prices.

Bazar de Café (⊠*13 Av. 5–38, Zona 1* ☎*7761–4980*) sells fine roasted coffee from here in the highlands (fair-trade, of course). Purchase cof-fee from area cooperatives at **Café Conciencia** (⊠*6 C. 7–31, Zona 1* ☎*7765–8761*), as well as peanut butter and macadamia nuts. The **Gallo Store** (⊠*12 Av. 3–35, Zona 1*) sells T-shirts, caps, and mugs with the logo of Guatemala's best-known beer, as well as the complete line of beer itself.

AROUND QUETZALTENANGO

SALCAJÁ

10 km (6 mi) northeast of Quetzaltenango.

Salcajá is at the turnoff at the Cuatro Caminos crossroads on the Pan-American Highway.

Quetzaltenango is hardly an urban jungle you'll need to escape, but a group of small towns clustered nearby make pleasant day- or half-day trips from the city. Each carves out its identity from its church, its cen-tral plaza, and, one or two days a week, its market. What you think is your first glimpse of Quetzaltenango is not Quetzaltenango at all, but actually the Quiche market town of Salcajá. With the growth of the metropolitan area, you'll barely know where one ends and the other begins these days, but Salcajá warrants a brief stop on your way into or out of Quetzaltenango.

The town's **Iglesia de San Jacinto** dates from 1524 and is said to be the oldest surviving church in Central America. It suffered severe structural damage in a 2001 earthquake.

Salcajá puts a different spin on Guatemalan textiles with its famous *jaspe* weavings. These are similar to the Asian *ikat* technique, and although the process is historically associated with Asia, it is assumed to have developed independently in Mesoamerica—and often likened to old-fashioned tie-dyeing. The artisan first colors strands of warp, the lengthwise yarns attached to a foot-operated treadle loom, in a resist-dyeing process, usually with hot wax that prevents exposure of some of the materials to the dye. The elaborate designs require painstaking, labor-intensive precision. You'll see the results at Salcajá's Tuesday market.

SAN MIGUEL TOTONICAPÁN

20 km (12 mi) northeast of Quetzaltenango, 10 km (6 mi) east of Salcajá.

This traditional highland village is famous for its wooden toys. "Toto" is full of workshops where a wide variety of handicrafts are actually produced. Come on Saturday for the market day when you can find hand-loomed textiles, wax figures, furniture, painted and glazed ceramics, and a year-round assortment of handcrafted Christmas decorations.

Totonicapán's main church, the **Iglesia San Miguel Arcángel,** dedicated to its patron, the archangel Michael, dates from 1545, although much of what you see is actually post-earthquake reconstruction done in the late 19th century.

SAN FRANCISCO EL ALTO

18 km (11 mi) northeast of Quetzaltenango, 8 km (5 mi) north of Salcajá.

What is Guatemala's largest market? Everyone guesses Chichicastenango, but it's actually the Friday affair at this highland town an easy drive from Quetzaltenango. You'll find far less of interest for visitors here than you will in Chichi, but the local color and the experience of its market, with its brilliant views and good buys on the textiles that are for sale, can't be beat. Make sure to leave time to visit the open-field animal market where everything from pigs to parrots are sold. This is pickpocket heaven, so be aware of your belongings and bring only the cash you'll need for the day.

128 < **The Highlands**

MOMOSTENANGO

30 km (18 mi) northeast of Quet-
zaltenango, 12 km (7 mi) north of
San Francisco El Alto.

It's "Momo" in local parlance and
on the front of the buses that shuttle you here from Quetzaltenango.
This is one of the few places left
in Guatemala where the 260-day
Mayan calendar still holds sway.
The small town has become Guatemala's Blanket Central. Townspeople turn out woolen blankets by
foot on treadle looms. The works
were historically undyed, bearing
simple designs and only the white,
black, and brown colors of natural

THE HOLIDAYS

Have a craving for holiday egg-
nog? There's no need to hang
on until December in this part of
Guatemala. Salcajá is the center
of distilling of *rompopo*, a concoc-
tion of egg yolks, honey, sugar,
cinnamon, and white rum. Many
households make their own in
small quantities, but the town is
also home to two rompopo factories. It goes down very easily...a
bit too easily, in fact.

wool; however, dyeing has become a new phenomenon, with all manner of colors to choose from. Check them out, as well as high-quality
woolen poncho's on Momo's Wednesday and Sunday market days.

SAN ANDRÉS XECUL

12 km (7 mi) northeast of Quetzaltenango, 2 km (1 mi) north of
Salcajá.

A quick detour from the Pan-American Highway brings you to San
Andrés Xecul, notable for its canary-yellow baroque church of the
same name, which is possibly the most ornate house of worship in the
country. The structure's facade contains more than 200 carved figures
that echo the designs found in the huipils worn by local women. San
Andrés' Thursday market begins on the plaza in front of the church and
spills onto the steep streets that lead away from the town center.

ALMOLONGA

5 km (3 mi)south of Quetzaltenango.

In this charming village just outside of Quetzaltenango, you'll find
women wearing bright orange huipils and beautiful headbands. At the
busy Wednesday and Saturday markets you can buy fruits cultivated at
the numerous orchards in the area. A few kilometers beyond the town
are several hot springs where you can relax for a few quetzals.

ZUNIL

9 km (5½ mi) south of Quetzaltenango, 4 km (2½ mi) south of
Almolonga.

★ At the base of an extinct volcano, the radiant village of Zunil is one
of the prettiest in the highlands. Mud and adobe houses are clustered

around the whitewashed church that marks the center of town. On the outskirts of the village you'll find the local cemetery, which is lined with tombstones painted in soft shades of pink and blue.

Zunil is surrounded by the most fertile land in the valley, so it's no surprise most people make their living off the land. The best day to visit is Monday, when women wearing vivid purple shawls hawk fruits and vegetables grown in their own gardens.

Zunil is a good place to pay your respects to the highland cigar-smoking deity Maximón. (Residents of Zunil call him "San Simón.") You can ask anyone in town where his likeness is—the site changes in an elaborate procession each November—as almost everyone asks a favor of him at some time or another. The idol has become a tourist attraction, and foreigners are charged a few quetzals to see him. Be sure to bring a small gift, preferably a cigar or a bit of rum. Unlike in Santiago Atitlán, here you can place the cigar in or pour the liquid into the figure's mouth.

High in the hills above Zunil are the wonderful hot springs of **Fuentes Georginas.** There are four pools, two of which remain in their natural basins. Unfortunately, the spring has been losing its potency over the years and is now only tepid throughout. Lounging near the rocky source in the natural pool will give you the most warmth. The springs are tucked in a lush ravine in the middle of a cloud forest, so hikers should take advantage of the beautiful trails that begin here. The complex is open from 8 AM to 6 PM; admission is Q20.

WHERE TO STAY

$ **Fuentes Georginas.** Although they're a bit run-down, these nine bungalows are adequate and have fireplaces that keep you cozy at night. The best part of staying here is having round-the-clock access to the hot springs, which close to the public at 6 PM. The cabins themselves have no hot water, though. ⊠ *8 km (5 mi) from main road* ☎ *5704–2959* ✇ *9 bungalows* ♻ *In-room: no a/c, no TV. In-hotel: restaurant, bar, pool, parking (no fee)* ▭ *No credit cards.*

HUEHUETENANGO

94 km (58 mi) north of Quetzaltenango.

At the foot of the Los Cuchumatanes mountain range, Huehuetenango was once part of the powerful Mam Empire, which dominated most of the highland area. It wasn't until much later that the Guatemalan Quiché came into the area to stir things up, pushing the Mam up into the mountains.

Today Huehuetenango ("place of the ancestors") is a quiet town in the midst of a fertile coffee region, with few real sights of its own. It serves as a gateway to the magnificent Cuchumatanes and the isolated villages scattered across them.

The town surrounds its **Parque Central,** where you'll find a pretty fountain, oyster-shaped bandstand, and relief map of the region.

The butter-yellow **Catedral de la Inmaculada Concepción** stands guard over the main square.

The ancient city of **Zaculeu**, 4 km (2 mi) from Huehuetenango, was built around AD 600 by the Mam people. The site was chosen for its strategic location, as it has natural barriers on three sides. The defenses worked all too well against the Spanish. Realizing they could not take the Zaculeu people by force, the Spaniards chose instead to starve them out. Within two months they surrendered. Today the ruins consist of a few pyramids, a ball court, and a two-room museum that gives a few insights into the world of the Mam. The site's restoration is said to be the worst in all of Guatemala, as the original archaeologists simply covered the pyramids with concrete, which was not a common building material in pre-Colombian Central America. Admission is Q25.

A short drive north of Huehuetenango, the dirt road begins to wind its way up into the mountains where traditional villages are set between massive rocky peaks. There's a **mirador,** or scenic view, about 6 km (4 mi) from Huehuetenango.

WHERE TO STAY & EAT

¢–$$ ✕**Las Brasas.** Grilled meats are the specialty at Huehuetenango's most elegant restaurant. Simple típica tablecloths are the only nod toward decor, actually making it the sole place in town with any atmosphere. The menu has a surprisingly broad range of options. There are even Chinese entrées, which you won't find anywhere else in town. ⊠*4 Av. 1–55, Zona 1* ☎*7764–2339* ▤*V.*

¢–$ ✕**Lekaf.** Definitely one of Huehue's better eateries, offering everything from filet mignon to pizza, which is reputed by many locals to be the best in town. All can be washed down with a nice selection of liquados (fruit or yogurt smoothies). With live music on the weekends, this is also a good place for after-dinner drinks. ⊠*6 C. 6–40, Zona 1* ☎*7764–3202* ▤*V.*

¢ ✕**Jardín Café.** This colorful little corner restaurant is friendly and popular among the locals. Come early for the excellent pancakes served at breakfast, or stop by for beef and chicken dishes—*pepín,* a fricassee in pumpkin and sesame sauce, or chile relleno are favorites here—at lunch or dinner. The menu includes a few Mexican favorites as well. ⊠*4 C. and 6 Av., Zona 1* ☎*7769–0769* ▤*No credit cards.*

$ 🛏**Hotel Casa Blanca.** Who would've thought that little Huehuetenango would have such a top-notch hotel? Spacious rooms, excellent service, and a central location make it the town's best lodging option. Third-floor rooms have great views, especially when the bougainvillea are in full bloom. At the restaurant you can choose between a table in the shady courtyard or in the cozy dining room warmed by a fireplace. ⊠*7 Av. 3–41, Zona 1* ☎*7769–0777* ✐*casablanca@intellnet.com* ⚲*13 rooms* ◒*In-room: no a/c. In-hotel: restaurant, public Internet, parking (no fee)* ▤*AE, DC, MC, V.*

¢ 🛏**Hotel Mary.** This four-story hotel in the heart of town offers clean, if spartan, accommodations. Ask to see a few rooms, as some are much better than others. ⊠*2 C. 3–52, Zona 1* ☎*7764–1618* 🖷*7764–7412*

Restaurants ▼
Jardín Cafe **2**
Las Brasas **1**
Lekaf **3**

Hotels ▼
Hotel
Casa Blanca **3**
Hotel Mary **1**
Hotel Zaculeu **2**

3

⤶26 rooms ⌂In-room: no a/c, no phone. In-hotel: restaurant, parking (no fee) ☰No credit cards.

¢ 🏨 **Hotel Zaculeu.** When you pass through the front doors of this hotel, north of the main square, you enter a courtyard overflowing with greenery. The older rooms, set around a portico, are brightened by locally made fabrics. They can be a bit noisy, however, especially those facing the street. The newer ones in the back are quieter, but lack character. ⊠5 Av. 1–14, Zona 1 ☎7764–1086 🖷7764–1575 ⤶39 rooms ⌂In-room: no a/c. In-hotel: restaurant, parking (no fee) ☰V.

SHOPPING

A few blocks to the east is the **Mercado Central,** where you can purchase local handicrafts.

TODOS SANTOS CUCHUMATÁN

40 km (24 mi) north of Huehuetenango.

Although it takes about three hours to cover the short distance from Huehuetenango to Todos Santos Cuchumatán, the bumpy ride is probably the best way to experience the tremendous height of the Los Cuchumatanes range. Whether you are driver or passenger, steel your nerves: the ride becomes anxiety-provoking at the many junctures where one side of the winding dirt road drops off into a deep ravine. Despite the arduous journey, Todos Santos is one of Guatemala's most frequently visited mountain villages. Though the town was one of Guatemala's hardest hit during the civil war, with a substantial portion of the population fleeing to the safety of nearby Mexico, most residents have now returned.

The town's big annual blowout revolves around the November 1 All Saints' Day holiday. (Todos Santos means "All Saints.") Many people come for the extended 10-day celebration between October 21 and November 1. The high point (or low point, depending on your perspective) of the celebration is a horse race in which the competitors ride bareback, but this is no Kentucky Derby. After each leg of the race, each rider takes a drink. His goal is not to cross a finish line, but to be the last one remaining on his horse. The booze flows copiously and, unfortunately, so does the blood from riders who tumble off their steeds (death is not uncommon). All in all, we recommend giving the race a pass.

Any other day of the year, Todos Santos, the spiritual heartland of the highland Mam culture, is one of those mystical, magical places in which you feel you've been transported to another world. Market days are Thursday and Saturday, with mostly produce for sale, and the attendant cacophony tossed in at no extra charge. This is one of the few remaining towns in Guatemala when men still wear traditional clothing, in this case candy-cane-stripe pants and woven shirts with long embroidered collars. The women wear stunning red, pink, and purple huipils with indigo skirts.

Logistics present difficulties in getting here. With only extremely spartan lodgings, Todos Santos realistically needs to be a day trip. If you have your own vehicle and want to brave the rough road from Huehuetenango yourself, be prepared for an exhausting drive that you'll have to make twice in one day. The vagaries of public-bus schedules don't make things any better. You no sooner arrive then you'll need to catch your bus back to Huehuetenango. We recommend an organized excursion. Tour operators in Quetzaltenango offer them. You'll leave very early in the morning and get back in the evening, and the minivan ride will still be hair-raising, but someone else takes care of all the details for you.

THE HIGHLANDS ESSENTIALS

TRANSPORTATION

BY AIR

There is no scheduled air service to the highlands. The Guatemalan government is retooling dormant airfields in Quetzaltenango (AAE) and Huehuetenango (HUE) at this writing, with plans to restore one-time domestic-air routes from Guatemala City. No date has been announced for resumption of such service. For now, Adrenalina Tours in Quetzatenango and Antigua charters air service between Guatemala City and Quetzaltenango.

Air Services **Adrenalina Tours** (☎ *7761–4509 in Quetzaltenango, 7832–1108 in Antigua* ⊕ *www.adrenalinatours.com).*

BY BOAT & FERRY

With the exception of the service between Panajachel and Santiago Atitlán, Lago Atitlán's public ferries have been replaced by private water taxis. Although they don't follow a schedule, the private boats are much faster and cost about the same. Panajachel has two primary docks, one at the end of Calle del Embarcadero and one at the end of Calle Rancho Grande. The first is for private boats on the San Pedro route, stopping at Santa Cruz, Jaibalito, San Marcos, Santa Clara, and San Pedro. It's about Q15, no matter where you get off.

The other dock is for hour-long journeys to Santiago, with departures at 6 AM, 8:30 AM, 9 AM, 9:30 AM, 10:30 AM, 1 PM, 3 PM, 4:30 PM, and 5 PM, and return trips at 6 AM, 7 AM, 11:45 AM, 12:30 PM, 1:30 PM, and 4:30 PM. The cost is about Q10. Private boats occasionally take passengers to Santiago in about half the time.

BY BUS

Transportes Rébuli travels from Guatemala City to Panajachel hourly from 5 AM to 4 PM daily. Buses bound for Guatemala City leave Panajachel hourly from 6 AM to 3 PM daily. The 6 AM and 3 PM buses are more expensive, but they're also much more comfortable. Count on a four-hour trip.

To get to Chichicastenango and Santa Cruz del Quiché, take Veloz Quichelense, which departs from the capital on the half hour between 5 AM and 6 PM and returns on a similar schedule. For Quetzaltenango, take Galgos buses, which leave Guatemala City at 5:30 AM, 8:30 AM, 11 AM, 12:45 PM, 2:30 PM, 5 PM, 6:30 PM, and 7 PM. They depart from Quetzaltenango at 4 AM, 5 AM, 8:15 AM, 9:45 AM, 11:45 AM, 2:45 PM, and 4:45 PM. The trip takes four hours.

To travel to Huehuetenango, you can choose from several companies for the five-hour run from Guatemala City. Los Halcones has departures at 7 AM and 2 PM. Rápidos Zaculeu runs buses at 6 AM and 3 PM. Transportes Velásquez also has daily departures at the same time.

Transportes Turisticos Atitrans and Turansa have buses that travel from Antigua to towns in the Western Highlands. You can also catch a public bus at the terminal, which is cheaper but much less comfortable. The one or two direct buses to Panajachel and Quetzaltenango each day, as well as five or six bound for Chichicastenango.

Information **Galgos** (⊠ *7 Av. 19–44, Zona 1, Guatemala City* ☎ *2232–3661).* **Los Halcones** (⊠ *Calzada Roosevelt, Zona 11* ☎ *2439–4911).* **Rápidos Zaculeu** (⊠ *9 C. 11–42, Zona 1* ☎ *2232–2858).* **Transportes Rébuli** (⊠ *21 C. 1–34, Zona 1, Guatemala City* ☎ *2230–2748).* **Transportes Velásquez** (⊠ *20 C. 1–37, Zona 1* ☎ *2221–1084).* **Veloz Quichelense** (⊠ *Terminal de Buses, Zona 4, Guatemala City* ☎ *No phone).*

BY CAR

The Pan-American Highway—part country road, part modern highway—heads northwest out of Guatemala City, where it is called the Calzada Roosevelt. It bypasses Antigua and passes through Chimaltenango before reaching a crossroads called Los Encuentros. Here you can head north to Chichicastenango, Santa Cruz del Quiché, and Nebaj. Continue on the Pan-American Highway, and you'll pass a turn-off to Panajachel and then another just beyond for San Marcos La Laguna and other towns on the north shore of Lago Atitlán. The Pan-American Highway continues over some impressive ridges and then descends to a crossroads called Cuatro Caminos, about 200 km (124 mi) from the capital. Here the road to Quetzaltenango heads off to the south. The Los Encuentros-Cuatro Caminos section of the highway is undergoing construction and expansion to four lanes at this writing. The end result will cut travel time considerably to this part of the country; in the meantime, expect some slow-going as you weave around construction barriers. Heading west, the 60-km (37-mi) section between Cuatro Caminosand Huehuetenango has been completed. Many roads to the north of Huehuetenango and Santa Cruz del Quiché are unpaved and pretty rough—this is nerve-racking mountain driving relieved intermittently by memorable views.

CAR RENTAL   There is only one national car-rental agency in the Western Highlands, Tabarini. It might be easier to rent a car in Guatemala City instead.

Local Agencies Tabarini (⊠ *9 C. 9–21, Zona 1, Quetzaltenango* ☎ *7763–0418* ⊠ *Hotel Los Cuchumatanes, Sector Brasil Zona 7, Huehuetenango* ☎ *7764–1951*).

CONTACTS & RESOURCES

EMERGENCIES

In Panajachel, Clínicas Médicas Pana Medic offers 24-hour medical attention. The physicians, Francisco Ordoñez and his wife, Zulma Buitrago, both speak English. Quetzaltenango is home to two fine private hospitals, the Hospital Privado de Quetzaltenango and Hospital La Democracia. The Hospital Nacional Dr. Jorge Vides Molina in Huehuetenango and Hospital Nacional in Panajachel are both public hospitals. Farmacia La Unión is a full-service pharmacy in Panajachel. Farmacia Batres is a chain with many pharmacies in the highlands

Emergency Services Ambulance (☎ *7762–4121 in Panajachel, 7761–2746 in Quetzaltenango*). **Police** (☎ *7756–1365 in Chichicastenango, 7764–8877 in Huehuetenango, 7762–1120 in Panajachel, 7761–4990 in Quetzaltenango, 7755–1325 in Santa Cruz del Quiché, 7766–4374 in Totonicapán*).

Hospitals Clínicas Médicas Pana Medic (⊠ *C. Principal 0–72, Panajachel* ☎ *7762–2174*). **Hosptial Nacional** (⊠ *Calzada Venancio Barrios, Sololá* ☎ *7762–4122*). **Hospital Privado de Quetzaltenango** (⊠ *5 C. 12–44, Zona 3, Quetzaltenango* ☎ *7763–4381*). **Hospital Nacional Dr. Jorge Vides Molina** (⊠ *Aldea Las Lagunas, Huehuetenango* ☎ *7764–3204*). **Hospital La Democracia** (⊠ *13 Av. 6–51, Zona 3, Quetzaltenango* ☎ *7763–6760*).

Pharmacies Farmacia Batres (✉ *6 Av. 6–05, Chichicastenango* ☎ *7756–1029* ✉ *4 C. 3–62, Zona 1, Huehuetenango* ☎ *7768–2325* ✉ *10 Av. and 6 C., Zona 1, Quetzaltenango* ☎ *7761–4531* ✉ *2 Av. 6–13, Zona 1, Santa Cruz del Quiché* ☎ *7755–3700* ✉ *C. Principal 0–32, Zona 2, Sololá* ☎ *7762–1485* ✉ *3 C. 11–09, Zona 2, Totonicapán* ☎ *7766–3978*). **Farmacia La Unión** (✉ *C. Santander near C. Principal, Panajachel* ☎ *7762–1138*).

INTERNET

Expect to pay Q6 to Q10 for an hour of Internet access in this part of the country.

Internet Cafés Café Digital (✉ *Diagonal 9 19–77 A, Zona 1, Quetzaltenango*). **Cyber Centro** (✉ *6 Av. and 4 C., Chichicastenango*). **Interhuehue** (✉ *3 C. 6–65, Zona 1, Panajachel*). **MayaNet** (✉ *C. Santander, Panajachel*).

MAIL & SHIPPING

All the villages in the Western Highlands have branches of El Correo, Guatemala's post office, but you are probably better off posting your letters from the larger towns, or better yet, back in Guatemala City. If you are sending something valuable, go with DHL, with branches in Panajachel and Quetzaltenango, or one of the local companies that will ship packages. Alternativas is in Quetzaltenango, and Get Guated Out is in Panajachel.

Overnight Services Alternativas (✉ *16 Av. 3–35, Zona 3, Quetzaltenango*). **DHL** (✉ *C. Santander, Panajachel* ☎ *7762–2333* ✉ *12 Av. C–35, Local 2, Zona 1 Quetzaltenango* ☎ *7763–1209*).

Get Guated Out (✉ *Comercial Pueblito, upstairs, Panajachel*).

Post Offices Chichicastenango (✉ *7 Av. 8–47*). **Panajachel** (✉ *Cs. Santander and 5 de Febrero*). **Quetzaltenango** (✉ *15 Av. and 4 C., Zona 1*).

MONEY MATTERS

All the larger towns in the Western Highlands have ATMs where you can use your bank card. Bancared has branches in Panajachel, Chichicastenango, Quetzaltenango, and Huehuetenango.

Banks Bancared (✉ *5 Av. and 6 C., Chichicastenango* ✉ *4 C. 6–81, Zona 1, Huehuetenango* ✉ *C. Principal 0–78, Zona 2, Panajachel* ✉ *4 Av. 17–40, Zona 3, Quetzaltenango*).

SAFETY

Several groups of travelers have been robbed while hiking around the Lago Atitlán area. It is always a good idea to hire a guide, especially when you are not familiar with your destination. In Quetzaltenango

---

A FASCINATION WITH FIRECRACKERS

First, rest reassured: that loud boom that jolts you out of your early-morning sleep is not a gun, and, despite the fact that they are called *bombas* in Spanish, is not a bomb. They are fireworks, and along with *cohetes* (homemade rockets), are a fact of life in Guatemala, set off to celebrate market day, a saint's day, a special mass, an ordinary mass, someone's wedding. Any observance that warrants celebration, warrants firecrackers.

and Chichicastenango it is best to avoid the areas outside the city center at night as gang activity is reportedly on the rise.

TOURS

In Panajachel, Atitrans is a reputable company with many area excursions. Union Travel in Panajachel also offers tours to just about everywhere in the region. Chichicastenango's only tour company, Chichi Turkaj–Tours, is well-regarded. In Quetzaltenango, Quetzaltrekkers supports social-service programs in the area. Adrenalina Tours in Quetzaltenango and a branch in Antigua leads trips to area volcanoes and surrounding towns on their market days.

Contacts **Adrenalina Tours** (✉ 12 Av. 4–25, Zona 1, Quetzaltenango ☎ 7761–4509 ⊕ www.adrenalinatours.com). **Atitrans** (✉ 3 Av. 3–47, Zona 2, Panajachel ☎ 7762–2246).

Chichi Turkaj–Tours (✉ 5 C. 4–42, Zona 1, Chichicastenango ☎ 7756–2111). **Kaqchiquel Tours** (✉ 7 C. 15–20, Zona 1, Quetzaltenango ☎ 5294–8828 ✍ kaqchikeltours@hotmail.com). **Quetzaltrekkers** (✉ Casa Argentina, Diagonal 12 8–67, Zona 1, Quetzaltenango ☎ 7765–5895 ⊕ www.quetzaltrekkers.com). **Union Travel** (✉ In Los Pinos Av. Santander, Zona 2, Panajachel ☎ 7762–2426).

VISITOR INFORMATION

The Guatemala tourism agency Inguat has offices in Panajachel, open daily 9 to 5, and in Quetzaltenango, open weekdays 9 to 5 and Saturday 9 to 1, and San Miguel Totonicapán. The staff at the office in Panajachel is particularly helpful.

Information **Inguat** (✉ Edificio San Rafael, C. Santander, Panajachel ☎ 7762–1106 ✉ Casa de la Cultura, Parque Centro América, 7 C. 11–35, Zona 1, Quetzaltenango ☎ 7761–4931).

Las Verapaces

WORD OF MOUTH

"The highlands around Cobán are less traveled from what I understand."

—Suzie2

"I've never been to the Verapaces, so maybe that will be on the table for the next trip."

—hopefulist

NORTHEAST OF GUATEMALA CITY YOU'LL find heavily forested mountains drained by wild rivers running through deep caverns. This region of central Guatemala, known collectively as Las Verapaces, is split between Baja Verapaz, to the south, and Alta Verapaz, to the north. The smaller Baja Verapaz is drier than Alta Verapaz, but mist-covered mountains are the norm in both. The area's humid climate, which often comes in the form of a drizzly rain called the *chipi-chipi,* has made it the cradle of Guatemala's cardamom and coffee production.

This part of the country has long been a haunt of European budget travelers, but remains relatively undiscovered by North Americans. The region's inhabitants are predominantly Pokomchí and Q'eqchí people, who over the years have lost much of their territory to expanding coffee plantations. As a result, they have abandoned some of their traditional ways of sustaining themselves. The region's largest city is workaday Cobán, which has an almost completely indigenous population. Here you'll find a handful of businesses catering to visitors, making it a good base for exploring the region.

ORIENTATION & PLANNING

ORIENTATION

Alta Verapaz, in the north, plus Baja Verapaz, in the south, make up this part of the country known as Las Verapaces. The small city of Cobán, the administrative center of Alta Verapaz, anchors this misty highland region. The major Baja Verapaz attractions are easily accessible, lying on or near the Guatemala City highway. The sites you'll visit in Alta Verapaz orbit around Cobán, some via less-than-ideal roads.

PLANNING

WHEN TO GO

Unlike the central part of Guatemala, Las Verapaces has rainy (May through October) and less-rainy (November through April) seasons, rather than a distinct dry time of year. Residents will tell you the rains aren't as strong as they used to be, but they're actually distributed throughout the year. ■TIP→ If you're planning on doing any spelunking (opportunities abound in this region) the drier months offer a more sure-footed hike through the caves.

Cobán's famous Rabin Ahau indigenous festival is held in late July, and a festival dedicated to its patron saint Santo Domingo follows in early August. Make reservations far in advance if you plan to be here during those times.

Las Verapaces makes a good halfway stopping point if you're traveling by road to El Petén. The region is four to five hours in either direction from Tikal or Guatemala City. Las Verapaces also has good

access to the Atlantic coast, and can easily be combined with a visit to that region.

GETTING AROUND

Having your own car is ideal for exploring Las Verapaces. Primary and secondary highways are in good shape, but beyond that, they can degenerate into gravel. Good networks of public buses are based in Cobán and serve the region with frequent runs to towns in the area. Relying on public transportation makes it difficult to visit some of the farther-flung attractions such as Semuc Champey or the caves at Lanquín. Signing on with a guided tour puts such sights in your reach if you have no car.

WHAT TO DO

A visit to Las Verapaces is the perfect, low-key, back-to-nature antidote to the hubbub of Antigua and the highlands. With its parks, forests, caverns, and rivers, this region is fast becoming Guatemala's destination for ecotourism. If hurtling down white-water rapids is not your thing, you can also enjoy more sedate activities such as bird-watching hikes. Tourism infrastructure is still small, although a growing number of outfitters are setting up shop up here. The region hasn't yet seen the throngs of visitors that pass through Antigua or the highlands, so you

A BIT OF HISTORY

In the history of a country with a frequently violent past, one man stands out for his devotion to peace. Dominican priest Bartolomé de Las Casas (1484–1566) crusaded tirelessly in opposition to the atrocities committed by Spanish colonists against indigenous peoples and advocated for an end to their use as slaves. Though more frequently associated with neighboring Mexico—in his honor, his name was appended to that of southern Mexico's indigenous city par excellence, San Cristóbal de las Casas—the priest's ideals were tested strongly here in Las Verapaces. As the home of the Rabinal Maya, one of the most feared indigenous groups in Mesoamerica, the region was the site of fierce fighting in the early 1500s. Spanish colonists were unable to overcome the Rabinal with brute force, but their atrocities against the original inhabitants of the land continued.

Las Casas struck an unusual bargain with his compatriots: if the military stayed away, he would deliver the land without spilling a single drop of blood. Spain reluctantly agreed, and Las Casas began translating hymns and scripture into local languages. The Rabinal chief, realizing the Spanish weren't going to go away, agreed to be baptized. His people followed suit, and the "conquest" of the region meant that the area was soon dotted with orderly Spanish-style villages. It became known as Las Verapaces, "The Lands of True Peace."

Historians debate Las Casas's legacy. He initially advocated replacing indigenous labor with African slaves, a position he later recanted when he saw the harsh treatment the Africans received at the hands of the Spanish. And the measures Las Casas proposed for bringing peace did dilute the strength and dominance of indigenous culture. However, during Guatemala's darkest years in the 1980s, those who yearned for true peace frequently invoked the memory of the iconic Dominican priest.

can usually find last-minute space on organized excursions, especially if you're staying in Cobán. That said, it never hurts to make plans a few days in advance to avoid disappointment if you have specific days in mind for rafting or spelunking.

RESTAURANTS & CUISINE

The region's most notable dish is *kaq'ik*, or in Spanish, *caldo de chunto*, which is a hearty turkey stew and the Verapaces' signature dish. You'll find it almost everywhere, although each establishment renders the Mayan spelling a bit differently: *K* might be *C* might be *Q*. Whether urban or rural, the region is mostly the realm of small, family-run restaurants, which dish up plenty of hearty food, such as venison and homemade breads.

ABOUT THE HOTELS

Think "small" when contemplating where you'll overnight in this region, both in terms of the number of options—there aren't a lot—and the size. With one exception, the typical Verapaces hostelry is a small, family-run place. For that reason, reservations are a good idea any time of the year. Air-conditioning is unheard of up here, but you won't miss it.

WHAT IT COSTS IN GUATEMALAN QUETZALES					
	¢	$	$$	$$$	$$$$
RESTAURANTS	under Q40	Q40–Q70	Q70–Q100	Q100–Q130	over Q130
HOTELS	under Q160	Q160–Q360	Q360–Q560	Q560–Q760	over Q760

Restaurant prices are per person for a main course at dinner. Hotel prices are for two people in a standard double room, including tax and service.

BAJA VERAPAZ

The lesser known of the two Verapaces, Baja Verapaz is a primarily agricultural region where farmers cultivate sugar and vegetables, but have begun branching out into nontraditional activities such as beekeeping. It gets fewer visitors than Alta Verapaz, but it does have Guatemala's only quetzal reserve.

BIOTOPO DEL QUETZAL

50 km (31 mi) south of Cobán; 166 km (100 mi) northeast of Guatemala City.

All Guatemala City–Cobán buses stop at the entrance to the reserve. Drivers know it as "el biotopo." You can get any Cobán tour operator to organize transportation or a guided tour. (*See Tours in Las Verapaces Essentials, below.*)

★ A 2,849-acre tract of cloud forest along the road to Cobán, the Biotopo del Quetzal was created to protect its namesake species. The resplendent quetzal, known for its brilliant plumage, is endangered because of the indiscriminate destruction of the country's forests.

The reserve offers the chance to see the quetzal in its natural habitat during its mating season, between April and June. Oddly enough, the best place to see the birds is not in the park itself, but in the parking lot of the Ranchito del Quetzal, 1½ km (1 mi) north. Since it is easier to spot quetzals around dawn or dusk, it's worth spending a night in the area. Even if you don't catch a glimpse of the legendary bird, there are plenty of other species to spot—you're actually far more likely to see a brilliant emerald toucan than you are a quetzal.

Expect rain here year-round, or at least the Verapaces' famed, drizzly chipi-chipi. (March and April clock in as the least-wet months.) At altitudes ranging from 1,500 to 2,300 meters (4,900 to 7500 feet), temperatures here average 16°C (60°F). The resulting luxuriant greenery of the cloud forest is gorgeous in its own right. One of the last remaining cloud forests in Guatemala, the Biotopo del Quetzal is a vital source of water for the region's rivers. Moisture that evaporates from Lago Izabal settles here as fog, which provides sustenance for the towering old-growth trees. Plants like lichens, hepaticas, bromeliads, and orchids abound.

CLOSE UP

The National Bird

Perhaps no bird is tied to the culture and symbolism of a country the way the resplendent quetzal is to Guatemala. As the national bird, it appears on the country's coat of arms and flag, and is the name of the currency. The elusive quetzal has been revered since the days of the ancient Maya, who called it the winged serpent. Though the Mayan often captured quetzals to remove their tail feathers, killing one was a capital offense.

Tradition holds that the quetzal was the spiritual guide of Maya warrior Tecún Umán, Guatemala's national hero. When Tecún Umán was mortally wounded in battle with Spanish explorers, the story says his quetzal alighted on his chest, staining itself with its dying master's blood, forever giving the male bird its distinctive scarlet breast. Legend also says that its sadness over Tecún Umán's death silenced the quetzal's once beautiful song. The quetzal has long symbol-ized freedom; it is said the bird cannot live in captivity, a fact that has been proven false by the quetzals that live and breed in Mexico City's zoo.

Central American cloud forests remain the natural habitat of the resplendent quetzal (*Pharomachrus mocinno*), one of six quetzal species. Misty Las Verapaces offers Guatemala's most likely place to spot one. Although the female quetzal is attractive, the male is spectacular, with its distinctive crimson belly, blue-green back and spectacularly long tail. (Think "robin" for the body size, but the tail more than doubles that length.) Its conspicuous appearance notwithstanding, the quetzal can be difficult to spot in the lush foliage of the cloud forest. April through June, the mating season, is your best bet. (In the spirit of equality between the sexes, male and female quetzals take turns incubating their eggs.)

If you're lucky, you can see howler monkeys swinging above the two well-maintained trails, the 2-km (1-mi) Los Helechos (The Ferns) and the 4-km (2-mi) Los Musgos (The Mosses). The latter takes a short detour past a series of beautiful waterfalls. Plan on 45 minutes to an hour for the shorter trail and about double that for the longer hike. Both trails cross a river with concrete bathing pools where you can swim if you don't mind the cold. An interpretive guide is available at the stand at the trailheads. At this writing, a third trail is being developed for people with disabilities.

Contact info: ☎5332–6942, 2331–0904 in Guatemala City 🖃Q20 ⏱*Daily 7–4.*

WHERE TO STAY & EAT

$ 🏠**Posada Montaña del Quetzal.** We like the one- and two-bedroom cabins in this roadside lodging near the Biotopo del Quetzal. All are set back from the road and can accommodate four to eight people. Each has a much-appreciated fireplace with ample wood supply for those chilly nights, of which there are many up here, making them much cozier than the simply furnished, stucco-wall, brick-floor rooms in the main building closer to the highway. The Posada operates its own small nature reserve; it's ideal for short hikes and is full of orchids, including the region's famed *monja blanca*. ✉*Km 156, Carretera a Cobán* ☎*5976–7689* ⊕*www.hposadaquetzal.com* 🛏*8 rooms, 18 cabins* ♿*In-room: no a/c, no phone, no TV. In-hotel: restaurant, bar, 2 pools, laundry service, parking (no fee)* ▤*AE, D, DC, MC, V* ❙○❙*EP.*

$ 🏨 **Ram Tzul.** Like little treehouse temples, the Ram Tzul's funky cabins
★   have rustic log-stump floors, and pitched pine and cedar ceilings—and terrific views of the surrounding private nature reserve. The octagonal stained-glass windows are a little incongruous, but the bamboo furniture and studied rusticity more than make up for it. The hotel has its own trail that leads to a magnificent 60-meter (197-foot) waterfall, which is worth the visit even if you're not a guest. ■**TIP**➔ We suggest an overnight stay; this is our favorite lodging along this stretch of highway. ✉*Km 158.5, Carretera a Cobán,* ☎*5908–4066* 🖷*2335–1802* ✏*ramtzul@intelnet.net.gt* 🛏*12 rooms* ♿*In-room: no a/c, no TV. In-hotel: restaurant, bar, no elevator, parking (no fee)* ▤*AE, MC, V.*

¢–$ ✕ **Café La Granja.** Homemade everything makes for a nice touch at this Swiss chalet-style roadside restaurant between the Biotopo del Quetzal and Cobán. The sauces, dressings, jellies, tortillas, and cheeses are all made on-site. The place comes into its own with its huge farm-style breakfasts of eggs, breads, plantains, and cheeses. It's a terrific place to stop if you're out early in the morning. If you stop for dinner, get here early: the place closes at 7:30 PM. ✉*Km 187, Carretera a Cobán* ☎*7953–9003* ▤*V.*

ALTA VERAPAZ

The *alta* (high) and *baja* (low) designations to the two Verapaces is a bit of a misnomer in that both are at relatively high elevations above the Atlantic lowlands to the east and El Petén to the north. The Alta Verapaz half to the twin regions sits high atop limestone rock with a mostly unexplored network of caverns underneath. You can explore a few of them.

COBÁN

214 km (133 mi) northeast of Guatemala City.

Spanish King Charles V dubbed Cobán *La Ciudad Imperial* ("the Imperial City"), a designation that generates pride among residents even today. Little remains of this highland town's regal past, however. It has fallen victim to the wrecking ball and an out-with-the-old, in-with-new mentality of successive city governments. This mostly indigenous city of 70,000 bustles with prosperity, thanks to its position as a center of the lucrative coffee and cardamom industries, and to its role as the center of a growing tourism region.

The longtime residents of Cobán are the Q'eqchí Maya. Though they are seldom featured in the tourism brochures, many still wear traditional clothing in a style quite different from those of the highlands. *Cortes* (woven skirts), each made of 8 meters (27 feet) of fabric, are gathered and usually worn to just below the knees. They are paired with embroidered *huipiles* fashioned from a rectangular piece of fabric, with a hole cut out for the neck and the sides sewn up.

Cobán is divided into 10 *zonas,* but your visit will likely be confined to the four central sectors. Numbered *avenidas* (avenues) run north–south; *calles* (streets) run east–west, and the same grid of addresses appears in each zone. 1 Calle, the main east–west downtown street, serves as the boundary between Zonas 1 and 2 west of the cathedral, and between Zonas 3 and 4 east of the cathedral.

> **MARIO DARY RIVERA**
>
> The Biotopo del Quetzal is officially known as the Biotopo Mario Dary Rivera in honor of the Guatemalan ecologist who fought for its creation. Dary Rivera accomplished much in his short life (1928–1981). A pharmaceutical chemist by training, he undertook postgraduate studies in biology, and founded that department at Guatemala City's Universidad de San Carlos. His tireless efforts led to the creation of the country's premier quetzal reserve here in Baja Verapaz in 1976.

4 The whitewashed **Catedral de Santo Domingo,** bordering the main square, is worth peeking into, although it is one of the more understated churches you'll see. To the right of the cathedral is the convent. Built in the late 1500s, it is one of Cobán's oldest surviving buildings, and now serves as the diocesan offices. In front, an odd, modern orange-and-yellow bandstand mars an otherwise lovely central park, and blocks your ability to get a good photo of the cathedral. Residents have dubbed it "the tortilla press," and most would be just as happy to see it torn down. ✉ *1 Av. and 1 C.* ☎ *7952–1941.*

2 **Parque National Las Victorias,** near Templo El Calvario, sits on what used to be a privately owned plantation. Today the park is filled with winding paths that have great views of the town. Robberies have occurred here; the gatekeeper will offer you a stick, not to employ as a walking aid, but to use instead in self-defense. We advise against making the visit without a guide. Aventuras Turísticas leads daily tours to the park. (*See Tours in Las Verapaces Essentials, below.*) ✉ *9 Av. and 3 C..*

5 The **Museo El Príncipe Maya,** a 10-minute walk from the plaza, has a private collection of ancient Mayan artifacts, mostly recovered from El Petén. Though the exhibit is relatively small, the variety of pieces is impressive. See fearsome masks, giant sacrificial pots, a reconstructed tomb, jade jewelry, and weapons. ✉ *6 Av. 4–26, Zona 3* ☎ *7952–1541* 💻 *Q10* 🕙 *Weekdays 9–6.*

For a nation so involved with the coffee industry, Guatemala offers few opportunities for visitors to watch its principal export being produced. **3** The **Finca Santa Margarita,** three blocks west of Cobán's Parque Central, is a pleasant exception to that rule. Here you can take a 45-minute tour of an operating coffee farm and witness the process of planting, growing, harvesting, and processing coffee beans. Owned by the Dieseldorff family, which has lived in Cobán for more than a century, the slatted wooden buildings have a distinct old-world feel. ✉ *3 C. 4–12,*

CLOSE UP

Let Sleeping Jaguars Lie

A short walk from the modern markets of central Cobán sits the city's best known sight, the **Templo El Calvario**, which offers one of the best views in the area.

Tradition holds that an indigenous hunter happened upon a pair of sleeping jaguars here, but decided not to kill them. He later returned to the location to find an image of Jesus in place of the jaguars. Town elders took this as a sign that a church should be built at the site. The present El Calvario is not that original church; the structure you see dates from 1810, and sits at the top of a cobblestone path with 130 steps, each representing a bead of the rosary. A series of

small shrines, each sheltering a cross, darkened with ash, lines the path up to the church. The lowest shrine is traditionally devoted to random prayers of any type. The middle stop is for requests of affairs of the heart. The highest shrine, near the church entrance is the stop to make to pray for good health.

If you light a votive candle, pay attention to the way the flame burns: local belief says an upright, vertical flame is a sure sign your prayer will be answered; any flickering of smoke or angling of the flame portends a less certain response.

✉ 3 C. and 7 Av. ☎ No phone 💲 Free ☉ Daily 7–7.

Zona 2 ☎ *7951–3067* 💲 *Q20* ☉ *Weekdays 8–12:30 and 1:30–5, Sat. 8–noon.*

Run by the friendly Millie Mittelstaedt de Hernández, the magnificent ❶ orchid farm **Viveros Verapaz** is a good place for an afternoon jaunt. Mittelstaedt clearly enjoys sharing her passion with visitors, pointing out breathtaking blossoms and describing the painstaking process of coaxing the temperamental ornamentals to bloom. Tours are given at 8, 9, 10, and 11 AM and 1, 2, 3, and 4 PM. Typically, orchids bloom in late November and early December, the height of the season, culminating in Cobán's International Orchid Festival held annually in early December. Orchid cultivators from as far as Japan come to show off their flowers. ✉ *Carretera Antigua, 2 km (1 mi) south of Cobán* ☎ *5442–5916* 💲 *Q25* ☉ *7–5.*

WHERE TO STAY & EAT

$ 🏨 **Casa Duranta.** The newish lodging in a century-old house offers great
FodorśChoice in-town value and promises to give old Cobán standby La Posada some
★ competition. The building is arranged, colonial-style, around a lovely garden. Rooms—all are nonsmoking—contain two queen-size beds, tile floors, huge bathrooms, and lots of wrought iron, echoed in the heads of beds and clothes and luggage racks. Enjoy the evenings on the chairs outside your room on the breezeway lining the perimeter of the garden. Top it all off with a knowledgeable owner, and you have one of our favorite lodgings in the country. The restaurant serves local cuisine and is open daily except Monday. ✉ *3 C. 4–46, Zona 3* ☎ *7951–4188* ⊕ *www.casaduranta.com* 🛏 *10 rooms* 🔑 *In-room: no a/c, no phone.*

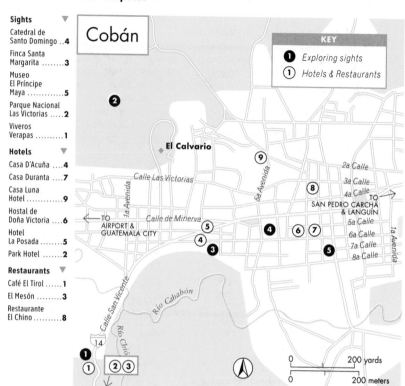

Cobán

KEY

1 *Exploring sights*

(1) *Hotels & Restaurants*

El Calvario

Calle Las Victorias

1a Avenida

5a Avenida

Calle de Minerva

TO
AIRPORT &
GUATEMALA CITY

2a Calle

3a Calle

4a Calle
TO
SAN PEDRO CARCHÁ
& LANGUÍN

5a Calle

6a Calle

7a Calle

8a Calle

1a Avenida

Río Cahabón

Calle San Vicente

Río Chió

14

0   200 yards

0   200 meters

In-hotel: restaurant, public Internet, public Wi-Fi, parking (no fee), no-smoking rooms ☰V ⏹EP ⊗Restaurant closed Mon.

$ 🏠 **Hostal de Doña Victoria.** The colonial-style Doña Victoria was built as a convent more than 400 years ago. It's filled with gorgeous antiques; rocking chairs and overstuffed couches line the stone porch encircling the gardens. Rooms are spacious and have beds piled high with blankets for the cold Cobán nights. ✉3 C. 2–38, Zona 3 ☎7951–4213 ☎7952–1388 ⊕www.hotelesco-ban.com ➺13 rooms, 11 with bath ♿In-room: no a/c. In-hotel: restaurant, public Internet, parking (no fee) ☰AE, DC, MC, V.

$ ✕🏠 **Hotel La Posada.** True charm
FodorśChoice   pervades La Posada, an attractive
★   colonial inn overlooking Cobán's central plaza. Rooms have wood floors and exposed beams and are furnished with antiques. Some have special touches like wardrobes and writing desks. Blue chairs and cloth

GOOD HABITS

Guatemala's national flower, the monja blanca (*white nun*), grows in abundance here. Legend holds that a colonial-era nobleman asked a young woman of meager means to marry him. She happily accepted, but her family saw the marriage as their ticket to riches, and placed incessant demands on their new son-in-law. She died of despair over her family's behavior and turned into a delicate white orchid with petals resembling a nun's habit.

The German Connection

CLOSE UP

The economic prosperity of Las Verapaces traces back to the wave of German immigrants who settled here in the 1870s. Invited by President Justo Rufino Barrios to inhabit and work the land, they turned the region into a center for coffee and cardamom production.

Subsequent generations of Germans never saw much need to assimilate, and kept their language, German citizenship, and ties to their homeland. That never bothered anyone until the 1930s, when a few swastika flags began fluttering over Cobán. When Guatemala declared war on Hitler in 1941, the Germans were given a choice: renounce their German citizenship or be expelled. Many chose to leave. Others stayed, became Guatemalan citizens, and continued working in the industries they had established. You can see evidence of their presence in the German surnames up here—you're as likely to meet a Schmidt as you are to encounter a Rodríguez—but there's no need to dust off your high-school German. They all speak Spanish these days.

4

hammocks fill the porch overlooking the small garden. A cozy restaurant (¢–$) with a fireplace serves international as well as Guatemalan favorites. ⊠1 C. 4–12, Zona 2 ☎7952–1495 🖷7951–0646 ⊕*www. laposadacoban.com* 🛏*16 rooms* ♿*In-room: no a/c, no phone, no TV (some). In-hotel: 2 restaurants, public Internet, public Wi-Fi, parking (no fee)* ⊟*AE, DC, MC, V.*

$ 🖥**Park Hotel.** You start seeing the signs advertising this hotel on the Atlantic Highway as you leave Guatemala City, and long before you get here you've memorized the name and location. The place, a few kilometers south of Cobán, is huge and, in that regard, very *un*-Verapaceslike, humming with all the activity—gym, shops, playground, meeting rooms—of a hotel that bills itself as a "resort and conference center." Rooms are scattered around the lush grounds, each with large windows and private patio or balcony. The larger rooms have fireplaces. The hotel has a lot of amenities and is a good value. ⊠*Km 196.5 Carretera a Cobán, Santa Cruz de Verapaz* ☎7952–0807 🖷7952–0831 ⊕*www.parkhotelresort.com* 🛏*132 rooms* ♿*In-room: no a/c, no phone (some). In hotel: 2 restaurants, room service, bar, gym, no elevator, public Internet, parking (no fee)* ⊟*AE, D, DC, MC, V* ❍|*EP.*

¢–$ ✕🖥**Casa D'Acuña.** The Restaurante Casa D'Acuña (¢) is a necessary stop when you're in Cobán, regardless of whether you're a guest at the hotel. Take a seat in the dining room or out in the garden and enjoy a variety of Italian dishes. Homemade carrot cake and a cup of locally grown coffee make a great dessert or midday snack. A small and clean hostel is adjacent to the restaurant. One room has a double bed; the rest have bunk beds. The proprietors—a lovely Guatemalan–American family—are an invaluable resource of information about the region. They run excellent two- to five-day ecoadventures to the Biotopo del Quetzal and other sights. ⊠*4 C. 3–11, Zona 2* ☎7951–0482 🖷7951–0449 ✎*casadeacuna@yahoo.com* 🛏*7 rooms without bath* ♿*In-room: no a/c, no phone, no TV. In-hotel: restaurant, parking (no fee), public Internet* ⊟*AE, DC, MC, V.*

¢–$ ✕**Restaurante El Chino.** Although the proprietor is of Chinese descent, and goes by "El Chino," there's no Asian food on the menu here. For an authentic taste of Cobán's gastronomic offerings, head to this small restaurant, which serves up the town's best *caldo de chunto*, a turkey stew, more commonly referred to in these parts by its Mayan name, *kaq'ik*. They also have excellent grilled meats and game dishes like *venado* (venison) and *tepescuintle*, a rain-forest rodent. On game day the television becomes the focal point for both servers and customers. ⊠*4 Av. 3–34, Zona 4* ☎*7951–3211* ⊟*No credit cards.*

> **THERE SHE IS . . .**
>
> The Rabin Ahau, Cobán's biggest festival of the year, takes place the last week in July, and gathers indigenous groups from around the country. It culminates in a Guatemalan-style beauty contest on Saturday night, in which the festival queen, the *Reina Rabin Ahau*, is crowned from among contestants representing their individual groups.

¢   ✕**Café El Tirol.** The owner of this popular café grew up on a coffee plantation near Cobán. Duly qualified, she serves the largest selection of caffeinated beverages in this coffee-growing region. Hot coffee, cold coffee, coffee with liquor, coffee with chocolate, and a wide assortment of teas make up most of the menu. She also whips up the best breakfasts in town. The café is on the grounds of the Viveros Verapaz. ⊠*Carretera Antigua, 2 km (1 mi) south of Cobán, Zona 1* ☎*5442–5916* ⊟*No credit cards.*

¢   🏠**Casa Luna.** If your tastes run toward the simple, then this modestly furnished, family-friendly lodging on a quiet street near the center of Cobán makes for a good, family-friendly budget find. Three of the six rooms are for one or two people; the other three have bunk beds and can sleep up to four; bathrooms are shared. Breakfast is served out on the interior garden on the patio but is not included in the room rate. Plenty of hammocks are hanging out in the garden and are nice to come back to at the end of a long day. ⊠*5 Av. 2–28, Zona 1* ☎*7952–3528* ⊕*www.cobantravels.com* ↪*6 rooms, none with bath* ⚷*In-room: no a/c, no phone, no TV. In hotel: public Internet, parking (fee)* ⊟*V* ⊘*EP.*

¢   ✕**El Mesón.** The lemon meringue pie alone is worth a trip to this unassuming log cabin–turned restaurant just south of Cobán, but you'll likely want to precede dessert with a full Verapaces-style meal. The ubiquitous regional turkey stew kaq'ik is on the menu, of course, but you can also try roast lamb, beef, or rosemary chicken. ⊠*Km 207.7, Carretera a Cobán* ☎*7951–0141* ⊟*AE, D, DC, MC, V.*

OUTDOOR ACTIVITIES

CAVING The Cuevas de Rey Marco, near the village of San Juan Chamelco, are relatively untouched caves. Tours take you into the caves only a few hundred yards, but the potential for further exploring is limitless, as the caverns stretch for many miles beneath the mountains of the Sierra Yalijux. Getting inside is difficult; expect to crawl through the entrance and cross a waist-high river.

CLOSE UP

The Magic Bean

When locusts destroyed Guatemala's blue-indigo and red-cochineal harvests in the early 19th century, ending its lucrative role in the dye-production process, no one imagined that a tentative, newfangled replacement crop called coffee would one day drive the country's economy. But Guatemala ranks today as the sixth largest exporter of coffee, providing 5% of the world's supply. The country possesses all the factors necessary—moderately high altitude, mineral-rich volcanic soil, adequate rainfall, and distinct rainy and dry seasons—to be a major player in the coffee world.

The Asociación Nacional del Café, the Guatemalan Coffee Association, recognizes and certifies eight regional coffees. Tasters wax poetic about **Antigua** in particular, using terms such as "spicy," "smoky," "flowery," and "chocolaty" to describe the highly nuanced flavors of Guatemala's arguably most famous coffee. Like Antigua, the nearby **Fraijanes** and **Acatenango**—the association added the latter as a designated region in 2007—are cultivated in soil enriched by volcanic ash, and are protected from the climatic vagaries of ocean air, giving these three coffees their well-known bright acidity. Volcanic soil is also the key to the flavor of **Atitlán** and **San Marcos,** but their wetter climates, particularly in San Marcos' case, make for softer, fuller-bodied coffees. Guatemala's three nonvolcanic regions—rainy **Cobán,** moderately wet **Oriente,** and dry, remote **Huehuetenango**—also give rise to full-bodied coffees.

Guatemala has become the darling of fair-trade advocates: Much of the industry here remains the province of small producers, especially around Lake Atitlán. The isolation of regions such as Huehuetenango necessitates close-by milling and drying of beans by local cooperatives, thereby keeping much of the labor in the community, and creating a sustainable product. Some 95% of Guatemalan coffee is shade-grown, an ecofriendly, migratory bird–sociable method of cultivating the product, requiring lower use of pesticides and fertilizers, and resulting in less soil erosion. However, production costs for many small operations have begun to exceed prices fetched on the world market—shade-grown means smaller yields, for example—forcing an increasing number of individual farmers off their land and to the cities. Still, coffee has helped transform historically poorer areas of the country, such as the Oriente, near the Honduran border. Producers look to fair-trade certification as a way to produce a finer product and reap a higher resulting price. The Germany-based Fairtrade Labelling firm presently certifies 20 producers here with its fair-trade imprimatur.

The rub for the coffee-loving visitor is that it's difficult to find a decent cup of the stuff here. True to the realities of economics in the developing world, the quality product goes for export, leaving a lower-grade bean behind for the local market. Nor does it help that Guatemalans heavily lace their coffee with sugar. Your best bet is an upscale hotel or restaurant, one in tune with international tastes and that will have export-quality coffee on hand. Souvenir shops also have good product for you to take home.

4

SOCCER   Cobán's more-than-respectable soccer team, Cobán Imperial, plays regularly in the hilltop **Estadio Verapaz**, five blocks northwest of the bus station. Sit in the bleachers or on the grassy hillside. Look for the sandwich board in the main square for information. Tickets are about Q20.

TO & FROM SAN PEDRO CARCHÁ
6 km (4 mi) east of Cobán.

TOURING TIP

The attractions out here are difficult to visit without your own vehicle. We recommend signing on for a day excursion with a tour operator in Cobán. Most do a daylong trip, spending the morning at Semuc Champey and the afternoon at Lanquín tour.

An interesting daily market is the highlight of San Pedro Carchá, a traditional little town 6 km (4 mi) east of Cobán. Nearby Las Islas, with a waterfall and pool, is a popular spot for picnics.

LANQUÍN

63 km (39 mi) east of Cobán.

This pretty village is on the doorstep of some impressive natural wonders, namely the caverns of Lanquín and the limpid pools of Semuc Champey.

Portions of the **Grutas de Lanquín,** a system of caves cut through by underground rivers, are easy to explore. The first 30 minutes of the hour-long hike consist of a trail with iron railings to help you keep your footing among the huge stalactites and stalagmites. Things get hairier toward the end, and you'll want an experienced guide who knows exactly how to help you navigate the path. Visit toward sunset and you'll see thousands of bats leave their dark dwellings and head for the starry night sky. The entrance is worth it, despite the garish labels painted on the formations. You could probably figure out what the formations are, but signs point them out to you: *sapo* (toad), *oveja* (sheep), *tigre* (tiger), or *señora* (woman). ■TIP→ **You'll get wet and dirty, so wear old clothes. The interiors of the caverns are illuminated, but you'll appreciate a small flashlight.** 🕾*No phone* 🎫*Q30; Q10 parking* 🕙*Daily 9–6.*

WHERE TO STAY & EAT

$ ✕🏨**Hotel El Recreo Lanquín Champey.** This concrete-block hotel at the mouth of the Grutas is a good choice for budget travelers. There are sparsely furnished single and double rooms in the main building and several bungalows out back. The hot water only runs sporadically, and some of the rooms share bathrooms. The restaurant (¢–$) was built with the expectation of more diners than it typically garners; it serves decent Guatemalan fare. ✉*Near Grutas de Lanquín* 🕾7983–0056 ⊕*www.hoteleselrecreo.com* ⇆*38 rooms, 24 with bath, 4 bungalows* ⚒*In-room: no a/c, no TV. In-hotel: restaurant, parking (no fee)* ▭*AE, DC, MC, V.*

OUTDOOR ACTIVITIES

WHITE-WATER RAFTING Rafting expeditions on the Río Cahabón, a challenging river near Lanquín, usually last from one to five days. The easiest sectors log in at Class III, but can go up to Class V. Guatemala City–based **Maya Expeditions** (⊠15 C. A 14–07, Zona 10, Guatemala City ☎2363–4955)

> **DID YOU KNOW?**
>
> A National Geographic team was able to map the entire underground system in 1993, when, in an exceptionally parched year, the water sank to record low levels.

arranges trips down the raging river. Local Cobán outfitter **Aventuras Turísticas** (⊠3 C. 3–25, Zona 3, Cobán ☎7951–4213 ⊕www.aventurasturisticas.com) arranges single- or multi-day expeditions on the Cahabón.

4

SEMUC CHAMPEY

Fodor'sChoice ★

10 km (6 mi) south of Lanquín.

Semuc Champey is pretty close to Lanquín, but as it's along a gravel road, you'll need a four-wheel-drive vehicle to reach it.

Often praised as the most beautiful spot in Guatemala, Semuc Champey lives up to that lofty billing. The site appears to be a series of emerald pools surrounded by dense forest and limestone canyon. On further investigation you'll notice that the pools are actually the top of a natural arch through which the raging Río Cahabón flows. Local legend has it that various explorers have tried to enter the underground passage by lowering themselves over the lip of the arch; many turned back right away, while some were swallowed up, their bodies never recovered.

You'll find a series of trails of various lengths here. Bring practical shoes. We recommend starting in the morning with the hour-long Mirador trail which takes you high above the site to give you a feel for the lay of the land (and the water). After that tiring trek, you'll appreciate the shorter, 20-minute Champey trail which leads you to the whirlpools for a refreshing swim. (There are no lifeguards here. You swim at your own risk.) The half-hour Cahabón trail takes you back to the park entrance past the point where the river emerges from the cave. ⊠10 km (6 mi) south of Lanquín ☎No phone ☎Q30; Q10 parking ⊗Daily 8–6.

■TIP→ For more info on Semuc Champey, check out www.semucchampey. com. The site has information on restaurants, hotels and sights, including helpful tips for Lanquín.

LAS VERAPACES ESSENTIALS

TRANSPORTATION

BY AIR

There are no airports in Las Verapaces. Most people headed for this region fly into Guatemala City's Aeropuerto Internacional La Aurora.

BY BUS

Transportes Monja Blanca runs comfortable buses between Guatemala City and Cobán, passing the Biotopo del Quetzal. The driver will let you off if you ask. Buses depart every hour or so from 4 to 4 at both ends of the route, and the trip takes five hours.

Information **Transportes Monja Blanca** (✉ *8 Av. 15–16, Zona 1, Guatemala City* ☎ *2238–1409* ✉ *2 C. 3–77, Zona 4, Cobán* ☎ *7952–1536*).

BY CAR

Several agencies in Cobán rent cars for about Q400 a day, which is a great deal if you want to spend some time exploring the area on your own. Companies with good reputations include Inque and Tabarini. Reserve ahead of time, especially on the weekends.

To get to Las Verapaces from Guatemala City, take the Carretera Atlántica to El Rancho, where you'll take Route 17 north to reach Cobán and Lanquín. Gas stations line the route. Fog frequently veils rural roads at night. Try to arrive at your destination before dark. Dotting the region are numerous green DISMINUYA SU VELOCIDAD signs with a silhouette of a leaping deer, warning you to slow down for deer crossings.

Local Agencies **Inque** (✉ *3 Av. 1–18, Zona 4, Cobán* ☎ *7952–1994*). **Tabarini** (✉ *Av. 227, Cobán* ☎ *7952–1504*).

LANGUAGE SCHOOLS

Centro de Idiomas Oxford (✉ *4 Av. 2–16, Zona 3, Cobán* ☎ *7951–2836* ⊕ *www.olcenglish.com*).

La Escuela para una América (✉ *C. del Cementerio 1–47, Zona 7, Cobán* ☎ *7951–3795* ⊕ *www. aschoolforoneamerica.com*).

School of Arts & Languages (✉ *16 Av. 2–50, Zona 1, Cobán* ☎ *7953–9062* ✎ *alftujab@ intelnett.com*).

Escuela de Español Muq'bil'Be (✉ *6 Av. 5–39, Zona 3* ☎ *7951–2459* ✎ *muqbilbe@yahoo.com*).

CONTACTS & RESOURCES

EMERGENCIES

Emergency Services **Police** (☎ *7951–2222 in Cobán, 7940–0050 in Salamá*).

Hospitals **Hospital Regional de Cobán** (✉ *8 C. 1–24, Zona 11, Cobán* ☎ *7952–1315*). **Hospital Nacional de Salamá** (✉ *1 C. 1–01, Zona 4, Salamá* ☎ *7952–1315*).

Pharmacies **Farmacia Central** (✉ *1 C., Zona 2, Cobán* ☎ *7951–0581*). **Farmacia Gloria** (✉ *5 Av. 2–5, Zona 1, Salamá* ☎ *7940–0381*).

MAIL & SHIPPING

Letters and packages can be shipped from El Correo, the post office in Cobán, but you're better off bringing them back to Guatemala City and mailing them from there.

Post Offices **El Correo** (✉ 3 C. 2–02, Zona 3, Cobán).

MONEY MATTERS

Currency and traveler's checks can be exchanged in Cobán, and you can get cash at the numerous ATMs. Some banks will give you cash advances on credit cards. Bancafé has a branch on the Parque Central.

Information **Bancafé** (✉ 1 Av. 2–66, Zona 1, Cobán ☎ 7952–1011).

TOURS

Aventuras Turísticas, Maya'ch Expeditions, and Cobán Travels organize tours of Cobán and the region. Proyecto Ecológico Quetzal specializes in tours of the region, and can arrange homestays with indigenous Q'eqchí families.

Contacts **Aventuras Turísticas** (✉ 3 C. 3–25, Zona 3, Cobán ☎ 7951–4213 ⊕ www.aventurasturisticas.com). **Cobán Travels** (✉ 1 C. 4–39, Zona 1, Cobán ☎ 7951–7371 ✍ cobantravels@yahoo.com). **Maya'ch Expeditions** (✉ 1 C. 3–25, Zona 1, Cobán ☎ 7951–4335). **Proyecto Ecológico Quetzal** (✉ 2 C. 14–36, Zona 1, Cobán ☎ 7952–1047).

VISITOR INFORMATION

There are no tourist offices in Las Verapaces, but most tour operators listed above can provide information on area attractions and arrange tours.

The Atlantic Lowlands

WORD OF MOUTH

"I haven't sailed on Lago Izabel (I looked at it as a possibility but didn't have enough time). What really caught my imagination was the much recommended trip from Río Dulce to Livingston or vice versa."

—fuzzy logic

"I recommend that one weekend you jump the border to Copán in Honduras. It's very different from Tikal and more accessible from Antigua by bus."

—RobertQuirk

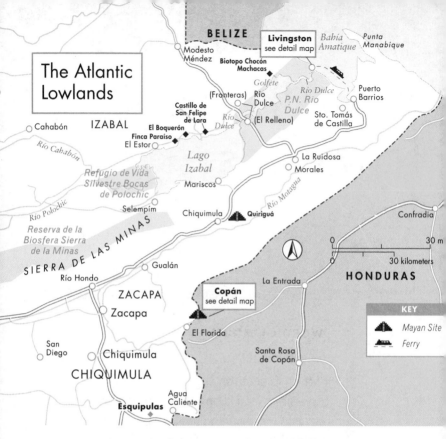

The Atlantic Lowlands

BELIZE

Modesto Méndez

Biotopo Chocón Machacas

Livingston
see detail map

Bahía Amatique

Punta Manabique

Golfete

(Fronteras) Río Dulce

Río Dulce

P.N. Río Dulce

Puerto Barrios

Cahabón

IZABAL

Castillo de San Felipe de Lara

El Boquerón

(El Relleno)

Sto. Tomás de Castilla

Río Dulce

Finca Paraíso

El Estor

Lago Izabal

La Ruidosa

Morales

Río Cahabón

Refugio de Vida Silvestre Bocas de Polochic

Mariscos

Río Polochic

Selempím

Chiquimula

Quiriguá

Río Motagua

Confradia

Reserva de la Biosfera Sierra de la Minas

SIERRA DE LAS MINAS

Gualán

Río Hondo

ZACAPA

Zacapa

La Entrada

HONDURAS

Copán
see detail map

San Diego

Chiquimula

El Florida

CHIQUIMULA

Santa Rosa de Copán

Agua Caliente

Esquipulas

0   30 m
0   30 kilometers

KEY

Mayan Site

Ferry

GUATEMALA'S SHORT CARIBBEAN SHORELINE DOESN'T generate the same buzz as that of neighboring Belize and Mexico. The coast—Guatemalans all call it the *Atlántico*, even though it's the Caribbean you're seeing—stretches a scant 123 km (74 mi). But whatever you call it, there's plenty to keep you occupied in the lowlands on this side of the country. Tourist brochures tout this coast as "The Other Guatemala" because predominantly indigenous and Spanish cultures of the highlands give way to an Afro-Caribbean tradition that listens to the rhythms of far-off Jamaica rather than taking its cue from Guatemala City.

Although the indigenous culture here isn't as striking as that in the highlands, traces of the Mayan empire, such as the impressive city of Quiriguá, mark the movement of this ancient people through the lowlands, and you'll run across many inland people who speak only their native Q'eqchí. Living in remote mountain villages, they sometimes must walk a full day or more to get to the market towns. The coastal towns of Livingston and Puerto Barrios are home to the Garífuna, an Afro-Caribbean people who speak a language all their own. In this region largely untouched by tourism is the stunning Lago Izabal, one of Guatemala's great, don't-miss excursions.

ORIENTATION & PLANNING

ORIENTATION

Think of this region as being laid out in a large oval-shaped loop oriented northeast and southwest. At the northeastern end on Guatemala's short Caribbean coast lie Puerto Barrios, the region's largest city, and its more fun, more interesting sibling, Livingston, which can be reached only by boat across the Bahía Amatique (Amatique Bay). The Río Dulce flows from Livingston southwest to Lago Izabal, Guatemala's largest lake. River and lake meet at the town also usually referred to as Río Dulce, the southwest curve of the loop. From there, a short drive brings you back to the Carretera Atlántica (Atlantic Highway), either southwest to Guatemala City, or northeast back to the coast. Off the route back to Puerto Barrios lie the Mayan ruins of Quiriguá, or the more famous Mayan city of Copán, just across the border in Honduras.

5

PLANNING

WHEN TO GO

This side of the country has less distinct rainy and dry seasons; rains are evenly spaced throughout the year. Ironically, June and July, when the rainy season is getting underway in the rest of the country, are the driest months in the Caribbean region. The best time to visit is November and December, when temperatures are most tolerable. It's best to avoid the region during March and April, when the heat is dizzying and farmers burning their fields in preparation for annual planting leave the skies thick with view-obliterating smoke.

The Atlantic Lowlands fit in nicely with a visit to Las Verapaces or El Petén. Either can be reached easily without heading back to Guatemala City.

WHAT TO DO

This region of the country is perfect for mixing planned activities with some unplanned down time. Visit the Mayan ruins of Quiriguá, hop across the border to Copán, Honduras, and take the de rigueur boat trip up or down the Río Dulce. Don't forget to enjoy the culture—it's an entirely different ethnic mix from what you've seen so far if you've just come from the highlands—leading to varied music and food.

GETTING AROUND

The Carretera Atlántica (Highway CA-9) forms the northeast–southwest transportation backbone of the region, starting out at Guatemala City and leading to the coast at Puerto Barrios. Perpendicular to this, Highway CA-13 intersects at La Ruidosa, leading northwest to the town of Río Dulce. Get much farther off this beaten path and you have the option to (or in some cases you must) travel by water. Río Dulce (the river) connects Río Dulce (the town) with Livingston on the coast. Livingston can be reached only via boat across Amatique Bay from Puerto Barrios.

RESTAURANTS & CUISINE

A warm climate means that restaurants here are bright, airy al fresco, or semiopen places. The outdoor seating is a refreshing change from the chill if you've been in the highlands. As for the food, think one word: coconut, or *coco* in Spanish. It pervades everything here. You might order *leche de coco* (coconut milk), or *pan de coco* (coconut bread). *Sere* is a hearty fish stew cooked in coconut milk. *Rice and beans*—the name is always in English—is the Caribbean adaptation on the beans and rice you've been eating elsewhere in Guatemala. This variation is steeped in (what else?) coconut milk. Another key ingredient here is cassava, locally known as *yuca*, which is used in a labor-intensive bread. This region is also where you'll find some of Guatemala's best seafood.

ABOUT THE HOTELS

The Atlantic Lowlands mix medium-size resort complexes—they may bill themselves as having a beach, but you'll more likely spend time in the hotel pool—and small, family-run lodgings. All do a brisk business on weekends when Guatemalans head out from the city; make reservations if you plan to be here then. Other than Christmas and Easter weeks, rates remain constant year-round.

WHAT IT COSTS IN GUATEMALAN QUETZALES				
	¢	$	$$	$$$	$$$$
RESTAURANTS	under Q40	Q40–Q70	Q70–Q100	Q100–Q130	over Q130
HOTELS	under Q160	Q160–Q360	Q360–Q560	Q560–Q760	over Q760

Restaurant prices are per person for a main course at dinner. Hotel prices are for two people in a standard double room, including tax and service.

LAGO IZABAL

Mention "Guatemala" and "lake" in the same sentence, and you'll likely think of the highlands' Lago Atitlán, but the famed Izabal deserves as much attention. The country's largest lake sits in the midst of a tropical-forested region alive with wildlife, and is connected to the Atlantic coast by the Río Dulce.

RÍO DULCE

30 km (19 mi) northwest of La Ruidosa, where the road to El Petén leaves the Carretera Atlántica.

The town serves as a major transportation hub. Drive south and you'll hit the road connecting Guatemala City with the Caribbean coast, head north and you'll eventually reach El Petén.

Fodor'sChoice   The term "Río Dulce" denotes two geographic entities. First and fore-
★   most, it is the name of the beautiful waterway connecting the coastal town of Livingston with Lake Izabal, and is one of Guatemala's signature sights. It also refers a the town of that name, although that isn't

actually its name at all. (Highway signs do direct you to RÍO DULCE however.) What everyone refers to as "Río Dulce" consists of two towns on opposite shores of the river—Fronteras on the north and El Relleno on the south—connected by the country's longest bridge clocking in at 850 meters (2,790 feet). At first glance, the town has little to keep you here, although unexpectedly good restaurants and hotels nearby are easily reached by road or water. The *lancheros* (captains) who congregate on the river will take you anywhere in the immediate area for under Q40.

> ### A GOOD OUTLOOK
>
> You'll enjoy your trip to the Atlantic Lowlands much more if you adapt to the local rhythm of life. Wake at sunrise and do most of your activities in the morning. With a good book in hand, find a hammock in which to relax during the steamy midday hours. Hit the street again in the late afternoon and evening, when the temperatures are a bit cooler.

Once an important Mayan trade route, the Río Dulce later became the route over which the conquistadors sent the gold and silver they plundered back to Spain. All this wealth attracted Dutch and English pirates, who attacked both the ships and the warehouses on shore. In hopes of curtailing these buccaneers, colonists built a series of fortresses on the river's northern banks. In 1955, the Guatemalan government reconstructed the ruined fortress of **Castillo de San Felipe de Lara** (✉*Southwest of Fronteras* ☎*No phone* 💲*Q10*). Spanish colonists constructed the fortress in 1595 to guard the inland waterway from pirate incursions. It was used as a prison between 1655 and 1660. You can reach it by the road leading west from Río Dulce or by a short boat ride. A 1999 earthquake in this region destroyed the river pier as well as damaging portions of the fort. If you wish to visit, rather than simply see the structure from the water, you'll need to approach the park overland rather than upriver.

The northern banks of the Golfete, an expansive body of water between Lago Izabal and Río Dulce, are covered by the 17,790-acre **Biotopo Chocón Machacas.** Among the stretches of virgin rain forest and the extensive mangrove swamp here are gentle manatees—shy marine mammals also known as sea cows because of their enormous size. Manatees are as elusive as quetzals, so as you boat through the reserve you're more likely to see other animals such as sea otters. Some of the creeks go through thick forests where giant mahogany, ceiba, and mangrove trees hang over the water to form tunnels so thick they block out the sun. A tiny island surrounded by the park's dozens of creeks and lagoons has a well-maintained 1-km (1/2-mi)nature trail that is easily walked by those with stiff boating legs. The trail has such interesting examples of old-growth trees as the San Juan, a tall, straight tree with yellow blossoms, and such exotic plants as orchids and bromeliads.

The only way to get to the reserve is a 45-minute boat trip from Río Dulce or Livingston. Most launches up and down the river will stop at the park entrance if requested, but they rarely enter the park. Most

THE BANANA TRILOGY

Although Rigoberta Menchú gets most of the attention as Guatemala's Nobel Prize laureate, the country has another novelist, diplomat, and journalist Miguel Ángel Asturias (1899–1974), who won the 1967 Nobel Prize for literature. Asturias spent his life and career alternately in Guatemala and abroad, living in forced or selfimposed exile during the tenures of the country's many right-wing military governments. He did a stint in Paris as a reporter for several Latin American newspapers during the 1920s, those "Lost Generation" years of Ernest Hemingway and Gertrude Stein.

Asturias never lived in the Atlantic Lowlands, but he is inexorably tied to the region, having immortalized the hot and humid eastern coast in 1950's *Viento Fuerte* ("Strong Wind," or in some translations, "The Cyclone"), 1954's *El Papa Verde* ("The Green Pope"), and 1960's *Los Ojos de los Enterrados* ("The Interred"). Known collectively as "The Banana Trilogy," these books chronicle the pain inflicted on the country by the United Fruit Company.

major hotels on the Río Dulce rent boats with guides for individual or group tours. ⊠ *Northeast of Fronteras* ☎ *No phone.*

WHERE TO STAY & EAT

$$$–$$$$ 🏨 **Hotel Banana Palms.** Río Dulce's largest resort is also one of its more luxurious properties. Guests flock for the weekend from Guatemala City, leaving the hotel relatively quiet during the week. It's set amid lovely forested grounds next door to the San Felipe fortress. Rooms are all suites, with small kitchens, living rooms, and bedrooms containing one or two queen-size beds. Second-floor suites have private decks with individual hot tubs. The Banana Palms is a good option for families, since it has a separate children's pool, and games such as foosball, Ping-Pong, and billiards. ⊠ *300 meters (984 feet) east of Castillo San Felipe* ☎ *7930–5022, 2334–2598 in Guatemala City* 📠 *2331–2815 in Guatemala City* ⊕ *www.bananapalms.com.gt* 🛏 *33 rooms, 11 villas* ₺ *In-room: kitchen, refrigerator. In-hotel: restaurant, bar, pool, beachfront, no elevator, laundry service, public Internet, parking (no fee)* ⊟ *AE, D, DC, MC, V.*

$$$ ✕🏨 **Catamaran Island Hotel.** On the north bank of the Río Dulce, this
Fodor's Choice   lovely resort takes advantage of its location with a restaurant (¢–$$)
★   built right over the water. The specialties are grilled steaks and fresh fish, including the delicious robalo plucked from the river. A string of spacious bungalows is cooled by river breezes, the nicest feature of which are the porches, perfect for watching boats. The staff can arrange boat trips along the river and to Livingston. Although the Banana Palms *above* is bigger and grander, we prefer Catamaran Island's more traditional resortlike experience. ⊠ *5 km (3 mi) east of Fronteras* ☎ *7930–5494, 2367–1545 in Guatemala City* 📠 *7930–5492, 2367–1633 in Guatemala City* ⊕ *www.catamaranisland.com* 🛏 *36 rooms* ₺ *In-room: no phone, no TV. In-hotel: restaurant, room service, bar, tennis court, pool, public Internet* ⊟ *AE, D, DC, MC, V* ❖❘ *BP.*

$ ✕▣ **Bruno's.** At this popular hangout for the yachting crowd, many of the regular patrons arrive by boat. Bruno's is best known for its lively restaurant (¢–$), featuring a great international menu. Expats enjoy sandwiches and other light fare as they watch football on the big-screen TV. The rooms, next to a pool, are spacious and clean. ✉ *Under bridge, on north side* ☎5692–7292 ☎☎7930–5174 ⊕*www.mayaparadise. com* ⤏*12 rooms, 7 with bath, 1 dormitory* ♨ *In-room: no a/c (some), no phone, no TV (some). In-hotel: restaurant, bar, pool, no eleva- tor, laundry service, public Internet, parking (no fee)* ▭*AE, MC, V* ▯○▯*EP.*

$ ✕▣ **Hacienda Tijax.** There is only very basic accommodation here, but people come for the ecoactivities, not the rooms. Built out over the water, this jungle lodge—the name is pronounced *Tee-HAHSH*—offers a number of types of accommodations, from cozy birdhouse-shape cabanas to large two-story bungalows with kitchens and dining rooms. A series of swinging bridges over a mangrove swamp lets you stroll to the adjacent nature reserve. Also nearby is a plantation where you can learn how rubber is extracted from trees. The lodge is also known for its restaurant (¢–$), which serves a variety of Italian dishes including homemade pesto. There are also plenty of vegetarian dishes. ✉*North- east of Fronteras* ☎7930–5505 ✎*tijax@directway.com* ⊕*www.tijax. com* ⤏*19 cabins, 10 with bath* ♨ *In-room: no a/c, no phone, kitchen (some), no TV. In-hotel: restaurant, bar, pool, water sports, no eleva- tor* ▭*MC, V.*

¢ ▣ **Posada del Río.** An in-town lodging on the Fronteras side of the bridge offers very simple rooms with a bed, television, chair, and little else. It's a good value if you don't need too many amenities. Reception is on the 1st floor; all rooms are on the 2nd, as well as a small com- munal balcony. ✉*Under bridge, Fronteras* ☎7930–5167 ⤏*6 rooms* ♨ *In-room: no a/c, no phone. In-hotel: no elevator, parking (no fee)* ▭*No credit cards* ▯○▯*EP.*

NIGHTLIFE

Head to **Hotel Backpackers** (✉*Under bridge, Ell Relleno* ☎7930–5480) for a beer at the waterfront bar. It's a fun place to while away the eve- ning, and it's a bar with a conscience to boot. All the proceeds go to benefit **Casa Guatemala Orphanage** (⊕*www.casa-guatemala.org*), so drink up. They also offer Río Dulce's most affordable accommodation, but rates (¢) are cheap for a reason. The accommodation is extremely basic, although a few of the rooms are being upgraded at this writing.

OUTDOOR ACTIVITIES

The natural crown jewel of this region is Río Dulce which winds its way between Lake Izabal and the coast through a 13,000-hectare (32,000- acre) national park. Excursions approach the park by land, but we recommend making the two- to three-hour trip up or down the river to immerse you in the experience and have fun feeling a bit like Indiana Jones. The *collectivos* (public boats) leave from Río Bravo Restaurant when they have at least eight passengers (the lancheros will keep you waiting all afternoon if the boat is not full). The rate is usually about Q100 per person. Private boats can also be hired, but they cost around

Q750 depending on how well you negotiate the price, really only useful if you have your own group. All public launches stop at Bird Island, a roosting place for several hundred cormorants, and Flower Lagoon, a small inlet covered in bobbing water lilies and magnolias. There's also a stop at a hot springs that tumbles into a shallow river. Definitely bring your bathing suit.

EL ESTOR

40 km (24 mi) southwest of Fronteras.

Although the vast majority of this little town's population is Q'eqchí, there's also a decidedly Caribbean influence. Locals describe El Estor as *tranquilo*, which means easygoing or laid-back, and this becomes evident as you stroll around the brick streets. The town, which grew up around the nickel mine to the west, seems to have drifted to sleep after the facility was shut down. There's a waterfront walk where you can look for birds along the banks of Lago Izabal. El Estor is on a migratory path, so hundreds of species can be spotted here.

The drive here from Río Dulce takes you past expansive banana plantations as well as cattle ranches. Look for the massive ceiba trees along the road. They are sacred to the Maya—the only reason they were left standing when the rest of the forest was cleared. Also try to spot strangler figs, which wrap themselves around the trunks of palms. Eventually they overcome the palms, which die from lack of sunlight.

Fodor's Choice
★

Perhaps the most beautiful of Guatemala's natural wonders, **El Boquerón** is a narrow limestone canyon whose 180-meter (590-foot) walls are covered in foliage heavy with hanging moss. Hummingbirds dance around lavish blooms, blue morpho butterflies flutter between branches, and kingfishers dive at minnows. Sometimes howler monkeys visit the trees nearby—listen for their thunderous cries in the late afternoon. All along the canyon you can climb rocks and explore caves filled with clinging bats. Close to the entrance is a turnoff past a giant ceiba tree that leads to several thatch huts along the river; the proprietors, Antonio and Miguel, provide roughly fashioned *kayukos* (canoes) that you can rent for a ride through the canyon. The water is clean and cool and great for swimming except after a heavy rain, when all the local rivers turn a muddy brown. ⌧ *3 km (2 mi) east of El Estor.*

Known for its steaming waterfall, think of **Finca El Paraíso** as a natural spa for the tired traveler. (The entire complex is technically a mixed-use farm, with livestock and crops.) Don't be dissuaded from a trip here even if the weather is hot and humid, as the falls descend into an icy cold river. A trail from the front gate leads to a short yet somewhat bumpy climb to the falls—be careful, as the rocks can be slippery. Around the falls are small indentations in the rock that serve as natural saunas. You can also hike upstream to the narrow cave at the source of the river. The rock formations here are otherworldly. About 2 km (1 mi) downstream from the hot springs is a simple restaurant that serves hearty meals. From here you can also rent horses and ride to the springs. ⊠16 km (10 mi) east of El Estor ☎7949–7122 or 7949–7131 🚲Q10.

Declared a protected area in 1997, **Refugio de Vida Silvestre Bocas del Polochic** is home to more than 250 species of birds, including blue herons, kingfishers, and snowy egrets. If you're lucky, you'll spot the blue-throated motmot. On the western end of Lago Izabal, the country's largest wetland encompasses more than 51,000 acres. An organization called Fundación Defensores de la Naturaleza manages the private reserve. From the office in El Estor you can arrange a guided boat trip to the reserve and a visit to the Q'eqchí village of Selempín, with meals prepared by local women. The organization also runs a remote ecolodge at the base of the Sierra de las Minas. The thatch-roof lodge has rooms with bunk beds and a full kitchen. ■TIP→ **A midnight thunderstorm is magical, but regardless of the weather you'll hear the roar of howler monkeys well into the evening. Rates are \$25.** ⊠Defensores de la Naturaleza, 10 km (6 mi) south of El Estor ☎7949–7237, 2440–8138 in Guatemala City ⊕www.defensores.org.gt.

WHERE TO STAY & EAT

¢–\$ ✕**Restaurante Chaabil.** The name means "beautiful" in the language of the Q'eqchí, and that's an apt description for the best eatery in El Estor. Built over the water, the palm-thatched building is the perfect place for a breakfast with a view of the majestic Sierra de las Minas or for a dinner accompanied by a spectacular sunset over Lago Izabal. You may even get a chance to snap a photo of a fisherman delivering the catch of the day. Call ahead of time to enjoy a bowl of seafood *tapado,* a hearty stew prepared with coconut milk and plantains, or stop by anytime for lake perch or river robalo. For dessert try a pineapple smoothie. ⊠West of main square ☎7949–7272 ☐No credit cards.

¢–\$ ✕🏠**Hotel Marisabela.** This hotel has clean, simply furnished rooms overlooking the lake. A 3rd-floor balcony with wooden lounge chairs is the best place in town for an afternoon siesta. Although the restaurant (¢–\$) always looks closed, it's open for business. Just call out "¡Buenas tardes!" until one of the workers appears. The Italian dishes are authentic and filling. ⊠8 Av. and 1 C. ☎7949–7206 🚲12 rooms ♨In-room: no phone, no TV. In-hotel: restaurant, no elevator, parking (no fee) ☐No credit cards.

¢ 🏠**Hotel Vista al Lago.** This hotel was once the general store that gave El Estor its name. Now run by the loquacious Oscar Paz, it has clean, cozy rooms. The wide wooden balcony is a great place to observe the town's waterfront. Before checking in, make sure the town hall next door has no plans for a dance; otherwise the thumping music will keep you awake until 4 AM. ⊠Next to town hall, 6 Av. 1–13 ☎7949–7205 ✑vistalago@intelnett.com 🚲21 rooms ♨In-room: no a/c, no TV. In-hotel: no elevator, parking (no fee) ☐AE, DC, MC, V.

SHOPPING

You can watch how the beautiful weavings of Guatemala are made at the **Q'eqchí Women's Weaving Workshop** (⊠North of main square ☎No phone ⏰Mon.–Sat. 8–noon and 3–5). Every year small numbers of women come from their villages to live at the workshop, where they spend a year learning the age-old crafts of loom and belt weaving. Every woman who successfully completes the course is given a loom to take back to her village and is encouraged to teach other women how to weave.

QUIRIGUÁ

186 km (115 mi) northeast of Guatemala City, 96 km (60 mi) south-west of Puerto Barrios. To get here, take the turnoff on Km 203 of the Atlantic Highway, near Chiquimula.

FodorśChoice Unlike the hazy remnants of chiseled images you see at most other
★ archaeological sites in Central America, Quiriguá has some that are seemingly untouched by winds and rain. They emerge from the rock faces in breathtaking detail. Quiriguá, a Mayan city that dates from the Classic period, is famous for the amazingly well-preserved stelae, or carved pillars, which are the largest yet discovered, and dwarf those of Copán, Honduras, some 50 km (30 mi) south. Construction began on the Guatemalan lowlands' most important Mayan ruins about AD 500. Its hieroglyphics tell its story: Quiriguá served at the time as a satellite state under the control of Copán. By the height of its power in the 7th century, Quiriguá had overpowered Copán, but just as quickly fell back into submissive status.

The stelae depict Quiriguá's ruling dynasty, especially the powerful Cauac Chan (Jade Sky), whose visage appears on nine of the structures circling the Great Plaza. Stela E, the largest of these, towers 10 meters (33 feet) high and weighs 65 tons. Several monuments, covered with interesting zoomorphic figures, still stand. The most interesting of these depicts Cauac Chan's conquest of Copán and the subsequent behead-ing of its then-ruler, 18 Rabbit. The remains of an acropolis and other structures have been partially restored.

In ancient times Quiriguá was an important Mayan trading center that stood on the banks of the Río Motagua (the river has since changed its course). The ruins are surrounded by a stand of rain forest—an untouched wilderness in the heart of banana country. Quiriguá still lives in the shadow of its more well-known neighbor across the bor-der, and of Tikal in the Petén in northern Guatemala, but it is one of Guatemala's most accessible Mayan sites. A small museum on-site gives insight into the history of Cauac Chan and his contemporaries. ☎*No phone* ▣*Q25* ☾*Daily 7:30–5.*

ALONG THE ATLANTIC COAST

If you've made it this far, you've arrived at Guatemala's Caribbean coast. The sultry air, the swaying coconut palms, and the banana freighters that ply the Bahía de Amatique are a world away from the highlands that everyone comes to see. To borrow the adjective from the tourist brochures, this is Guatemala at its most "different."

OFF TO NEW YORK?

American diplomat and explorer John Lloyd Stephens (1805–1852) visited Quiriguá in 1841 and hatched an ambitious plan to dismantle the site's structures, float them down the Motagua River, and ship them to New York for permanent exhibition. Stephens had visited Copán two years earlier and purchased that site for a mere $50, with plans to remove its structures in the same manner. He argued that a museum could better protect the stelae from the ravages of rain and sun. Fortunately for history, the asking price for Quiriguá was far more than Stephens was willing to pay.

Despite the questionable scheme, historians today consider Stephens one of the great Mayanists of the 19th century. His *Incidents of Travel in Central America, Chiapas and Yucatán* and his extensive mapping of regional ruins are regarded as important period contributions to this field of knowledge.

LIVINGSTON

37 km (23 mi) northeast of Río Dulce.

The only way to get to or from the town is by boat.

Visitors always compare Livingston with Puerto Barrios across the bay, and the former wins hands down, for its sultry, seductive Caribbean flavor. Wooden houses, many on stilts, congregate in this old fishing town, once an important railroad hub, but today inaccessible by land from the outside world. Although it sits on the mainland, Livingston might as well be a Caribbean island—the culture seems closer to that of Jamaica than to the rest of Guatemala. Livingston proudly wears its Garífuna heritage on its sleeve. The culture is unique to Central America's eastern coast and descends from the intermarriage of African slaves with Caribbean indigenous peoples.

Livingston's single paved road is the only evidence left of its heyday as a major port for coffee and other crops during the late 19th century. Livingston's population now makes its living mostly from fishing. By day the soft lick of waves on the shore measures out the slow pace that makes this laid-back community so attractive. At night roving bands of musicians take to the streets.

Anyone expecting white-sand beaches and azure waters is bound to be disappointed. The narrow beach that stretches north from the river mouth is not especially attractive. It is, however, a great place to explore, as it is home to several bars and a little shop where Pablo Marino sells handmade drums, shakers, and wood carvings. Afternoon breezes off the ocean make resting on the beach a good place to pass the torrid afternoons. Once you arrive here, shed your worries and settle under a coconut palm.

■ TIP→ Livingston's streets have official names. However, other than the main street, called Calle Principal, no one uses them or even seems to know them.

WHERE TO STAY & EAT

$–$$ ✕ **Happy Fish.** The thatch roof and painfully slow-turning ceiling fans are right out of *Night of the Iguana* or any other tropical movie of your choice. The seafood is phenomenal here at one of the town's most popular restaurants, which draws locals and tourists in equal numbers. We like the seafood *tapado,* a sweet fish stew. You can check your e-mail at the Internet terminal while you're waiting. ✉*C. Principal* ☎*7947–0303* ▭*V.*

¢–$ ✕ **Restaurante Bahía Azul.** The walls are literally covered with travel information at Bahía Azul, the most popular tourist restaurant in town. If you're thinking about a trip, you can probably arrange it here. At the curve on the main street, its porch is a great place to watch people stroll past. The large menu includes everything from sandwiches to lobster. Most nights include live drumming by a local band. ✉*C. Principal* ☎*7947–0151* 🖷*7947–0136* ▭*AE, D, DC, MC, V* ☾*BP.*

¢–$ ✕ **Restaurante Margoth.** Presided over by the charming, well-respected lady the entire town knows as "Doña Margoth," this longtime favorite serves the usual fish dishes. It's famous, however, for its delicious *caldo de mariscos* seafood stew. The dish is a challenge to eat, so tuck your napkin into your collar. Margoth keeps a sharp eye on her workers, so the service in this bright and bustling café is speedy. Dinner is a casual

CLOSE UP

Dance the Punta

You won't quite be able to put your finger on what it is: It's not reggae. It's not salsa. It's not hip-hop. But the punta resembles all three, and you'll hear the music everywhere along the Caribbean coast, here and in neighboring Belize and Honduras.

Scholars surmise that the name *punta* is actually a corruption of the word *bunda,* meaning "buttocks" in the Mandé language of West Africa, from where the music was imported. The name fits: dancers remain nearly stationary from the waist up, but engage in intense hip gyrations, right to left in a circular motion, while dancing on the balls of their feet. Historically, drums, rattles, and turtle shells provided the percussion-only accompaniment; these days, synthesizers and guitars have taken over that role, creating an all-the-rage style of music known as punta rock. Garífuna lyrics were the one-time norm; English and Spanish have become more common, helping to propel the punta beyond this region to prominence in World Music playlists.

affair, and sometimes doesn't start until 7 PM. ⊠*North of C. Principal* ☎*7947–0019* ⊟*No credit cards.*

¢–$ ✕**Tilingo Lindo.** For the best curry this side of the Darién Gap head to this small bistro, which sits near the beach. The menu features such international favorites as Israeli *shockshuka* (an egg soup), chow mein, and chicken a l'orange. Meals all come with tasty salads and garlic bread. The intimate, rustic feel will keep you content while you wait for your meal, which takes awhile to arrive. ⊠*North end of C. Principal at the beach* ☎*No phone* ⊟*No credit cards.*

$$$$ ✕🖼 **Hotel Villa Caribe.** Livingston's finest hotel, the Villa Caribe has
Fodor'sChoice some great views of the Caribbean from its hilltop perch. The exten-
★ sive grounds overflow with foliage. Spacious rooms, in a thatch-roof building, all have private balconies and ocean views. Palm trees surround the large pool, where you can relax in one of the lounge chairs or order a drink at the bar. The restaurant ($–$$$) serves seafood dishes, such as coconut shrimp and robalo, but is almost always empty. The staff can arrange trips up the Río Dulce and to spots around the Bahía de Amatique. ⊠*On the main street* ☎*2334–1818 in Guatemala City* 🖷*2334–8134 in Guatemala City* ⊕*www.villasdeguatemala.com* 🛏*42 rooms, 2 suites* ♻*In-room: no phone, refrigerator. In-hotel: 2 restaurants, room service, bar, pool, beachfront, no elevator, laundry service, public Internet* ⊟*AE, D, DC, MC, V.*

¢ ✕🖼 **Casa Rosada.** This string of waterfront bungalows can best be
Fodor'sChoice described as Guatemala's most luxurious way of roughing it. Each is
★ furnished with bright highland furniture and a pair of beds draped with mosquito nets. Don't be scared off by the shared baths; they're clean and comfortable, and the showers have hot water. The main building houses a restaurant (¢–$) serving excellent meals on a pretty patio overlooking the water. The dinner menu changes daily but always includes lobster and other favorites. Dinner, at 7 sharp, is by candlelight. ⊠*Near public dock* ☎*7947–0303* 🖷*7947–0304* ⊕*www.hotelcasa-rosada.com* 🛏*10 bungalows, none with bath* ♻*In-room: no a/c, no*

CLOSE UP

The Garífuna

Guatemala's Atlantic coast contains a different ethnic makeup than the rest of the country. It has a substantial percentage of mixed indigenous and African descent known as the Garífuna. They speak one of Guatemala's 23 constitutionally recognized non-Spanish (and one of two non-Mayan-based) languages.

The Garífuna word for Garífuna is "Garinagu," but British-colonial powers called them the "Black Caribs," a term which sounds decidedly politically incorrect today. In the eyes of the British, "black" distinguished them from the "good" (from a British perspective) "Yellow Caribs," indigenous Arawak peoples in the British West Indies that had not intermarried with African slaves. Following a 1797 revolt on the Caribbean island of St. Vincent, British authorities exiled the Garífuna to the island of Roatán, off the coast of Honduras, then under British control. From there they dispersed to the mainland, settling Central America's Caribbean coast from Belize through northern Nicaragua.

Some 17,000 of their descendents live today in Guatemala. Music, dance traditions, and the Garífuna language remain here on the coast, even if old-timers lament the creeping outside influences, namely Spanish, rap, and reggae. Migration from Central America (largely in the 1980s) means that today the United States contains the world's largest Garífuna population.

phone, no TV. In-hotel: restaurant, no elevator, laundry service ▤*No credit cards* ⦿*EP.*

¢ ▦**Finca Tatín.** A rustic bed-and-breakfast run by a friendly Argentine family, Finca Tatín is far off the beaten path, 20 minutes by boat from Livingston. The inn, which doubles as a Spanish school, rents canoes, which are a great way to see the river without the roar of a motor. A generator supplies the electricity here from 6 to 11 PM; the rest of the day, solar panels take their turn. ✉*8 km (5 mi) south of Livingston* ☎*5902–0831* ⊕*www.fincatatin.centramerica.com* ⟿*3 bungalows, 4 rooms without bath* ⚘*In-room: no a/c, no phone, no TV. In-hotel: restaurant* ▤*No credit cards.*

¢ ▦**Hotel Garífuna.** Run by a cordial Livingston family, Hotel Garífuna puts you in the heart of a lively neighborhood. The rooms in this two-story building open onto a porch overlooking the street or a tree-filled backyard. ✉*Off the main st.* ☎*7947–0183* 🖷*7947–0184* ⟿*8 rooms* ⚘*In-room: no a/c, no TV. In-hotel: no elevator, laundry service, public Internet* ▤*No credit cards.*

NIGHTLIFE

Nightlife in Livingston has always been synonymous with one word: Ubafu. Everyone, resident and visitor alike, stops by this popular bar on the Calle Principal to enjoy the distinctive punta music. Your other option is to stop by various hotels and restaurants—namely the Villa Caribe and Bahía Azule—which also present shows of Garífuna music many evenings. These places are lively and enjoyable, but fall a bit into the watered-down-for-tourists category.

BARS The **Ubafu,** a Rasta-inspired shack (note the Bob Marley posters) on the main street is Livingston's most famous and enduring bar, and the best place to see punta rock music as the locals enjoy it.

OUTDOOR ACTIVITIES

A short hike or boat ride (5 km/3 mi) north of Livingston takes you to a gorgeous little jungle river called Siete Altares, a series of deep pools that are ideal for swimming. The name translates as "Seven

> **TIP**
>
> Be aware that young men wait on the town dock to "escort" you to your hotel. They may even tell you your chosen lodging is "full" or "closed," and recommend an alternative, from which they get a commission. Don't buy it. "Tipping" them to leave you alone is your prerogative.

Altars," the altars of which are seven lovely waterfalls. Arrange for a guided tour with the friendly folks at **Bahía Azul** (☎7947–0151) or **Happy Fish** (☎7947–0303). A walking tour costs about Q100, and usually takes in a stroll through Livingston; a bag lunch is included. Other tours replace the hike with a boat ride and cost about double. The one-way walk takes about 90 minutes, but is a fantastic way to experience nature here. ■TIP➡**There have been numerous robberies of tourists on the way to Siete Altares, so be sure to go with a guide. Never walk in the countryside around Livingston alone or, especially, after dark.**

PUERTO BARRIOS

295 km (183 mi) from Guatemala City. Puerto Barrios is 2 hours by ferry from Livingston.

The friendly but down-at-the-heels port city of Puerto Barrios conserves the atmosphere of an old banana town. Its wide streets, mostly detached buildings—many are old stilt houses built in the traditional Caribbean style—and heavy tropical air give it a small-town feel, belying its population of 40,000. Nearby Santo Tomás de Castilla has now replaced it as the country's largest port, but the city still serves as the region's administrative, economic, and transportation center.

"Barrios," as everyone calls it, was once a thriving port for the United Fruit Company, thanks to the formerly operating railroad that connected it with Guatemala City. The commercial boom, however, has long since subsided; its port still functions, but most operations have been transferred to Santo Tomás. Officially, there's little to keep you here—the thriving market, while interesting, is geared to the workaday needs of the populace rather than any must-have souvenirs—but because transportation schedules don't always mesh well in this region, you may find yourself here for a night.

WHERE TO STAY & EAT

¢–$$ ✕ **Restaurante Safari.** A longtime favorite in Puerto Barrios, this grass-roof restaurant is one of the few right on the water. On a hot afternoon or steamy night the ocean breezes are a tremendous relief. ✉*End of 5 Av. at water* ☎7948–0563 ▭*AE, D, DC, MC, V.*

THE BANANA REPUBLIC

From the docks in Puerto Barrios gigantic freight-liners leave daily with enormous crates of bananas stacked like children's blocks. Groups of farmworkers can be spotted along the roadside, each carrying nothing more than a small knit bag. Men from one village often seek work as a group to increase their chances of being hired. Although the minimum wage is about $3.50 a day, some will work for half that amount. They usually return home on Sunday, the one day of the week they don't live on the farms.

Most of what is written about the banana industry in Guatemala focuses on the bad old days of the legendary United Fruit Company. The term "banana republic" was coined to describe neighboring Honduras, but it could just as easily have described Guatemala during the first half of the 20th century. The company got its start here in 1901 when financier and United head Minor Keith won the right to transport mail between Guatemala and the United States. That expanded into telegraph services and the construction of the Atlantic railroad between Guatemala City and Puerto Barrios, all in addition to their traditional activities of growing and processing fruit. United Fruit and its rival Standard Fruit gradually became dominant political and economic forces in the country, pulling strings and dictating policy.

Those days are gone. United Fruit ceased operations under that name in 1970, and, through a series of mergers and acquisitions, became Chiquita Brands International in 1984. Standard Fruit became Dole about the same time. Bananas are still big business here—Guatemala's $270 million industry accounts for 5.8% of the world's banana supply—and Dole and Chiquita remain owners of huge plantations in the lowlands. But neither company exercises the control over Guatemalan affairs they once wielded.

$$$$ 🛏**Amatique Bay Resort & Marina.** Sprawling resorts like this waterfront complex are the newest trend in Guatemala. The beautiful natural surroundings are somewhat diminished by all the effort to make things luxurious. The impressive pool, complete with a replica of a Spanish galleon that shoots water from its cannons, has slides for children and an island bar for adults. Few of the sunny suites have views of the ocean, but they are equipped with everything you would find in a well-furnished apartment, including washers and dryers. ⊠*North of Puerto Barrios* ☎*7948–1800, 2421–3333 Ext. 563 in Guatemala City* 🖷*2363–5396* ⊕*www.amatiquebay.net* ⥀*57 rooms* ♿*In-room: kitchen. In-hotel: 2 restaurants, bar, pools, bicycles, no elevator, public Internet* ⊟*AE, D, DC, MC, V* 🍴*All meals included.*

$$$ 🛏**Hotel Green Bay.** Set amid a tropical garden, this string of thatch bungalows faces the expansive waters of the Bahía de Amatique. The grounds are adjacent to a forest-draped hill with a small waterfall. You can relax by the pool or the private beach, or arrange a cruise on the bay and up the Río Dulce. Boats pick up guests at the dock in Puerto Barrios; phone ahead to let them know you're coming. ⊠*8 km (5 mi) west of Puerto Barrios* ☎*7948–2361, 2337–2500 Ext. 8 in Guatemala*

City ☎*7948–2361* ⊕*www.greenbay.com* ☞*50 rooms* ♿*In-hotel: restaurant, bar, pool, beachfront* ⊟*AE, D, DC, MC, V* ⦿|*BP.*

COPÁN (HONDURAS)

Explorer Christopher Columbus landed on the northern coast of Honduras in 1502, claiming the region for Spain. He was far from the first person to set foot here, however. This land had already seen great civilizations rise and fall. Nowhere is this more evident than in Copán, one of the most breathtaking archaeological sites in Central America. What makes Copán so fascinating to archaeologists is not just its astounding size, but its small details. Here they have uncovered carvings that tell the history of this great city, as well as that of others in the region. If you want to understand the ancient civilizations of Quiriguá in Guatemala or Teotihuacán in Mexico, first come to Copán.

For 2,000 years the Maya resided in what is now western Honduras, creating the distinctive art and architecture that can still be seen at the ancient city of Copán. The Lenca, who are believed to have lived alongside the Maya, had an equally vibrant, although less well-known, culture. Dominating the region after the fall of the Maya, the Lanca had no intention of being subjugated when the Spanish arrived in the 16th century. Chief Lempira brought tribes together to battle the conquistadors; his murder at the hands of the Spanish at a "peace conference" provided Honduras with its first national hero. The country's currency is named for the great warrior.

COPÁN RUINAS

168 km (104 mi) south of San Pedro Sula, Honduras.

With a squat colonial church watching over its eastern edge, the central square of Copán Ruinas calls to mind an era long past. You may think you've gone back in time, as horse-drawn wagons are not an uncommon sight on the surrounding cobblestone streets.

Although most visitors come here to see the astounding Mayan ruins east of town, you can also learn a bit about that culture at the **Museo Copán Ruinas.** Though most of this charming little museum's descriptions are in Spanish, the ancient tools and artworks speak for themselves. The exhibit on *el brujo* ("the witch") is especially striking, displaying the skeleton and religious artifacts of a Mayan shaman. ⊠ *West side of Parque Ctl.* ☎*No phone* ☞*L40* ⊙*Daily 8–noon and 1–4.*

EXPLORING

A cadre of colorful parrots greets you at the gate to Copán, one of the most breathtaking archaeological sites in Central America. Down a tree-lined path you'll find a series of beautifully reconstructed temples. The intricate carvings on the stone structures, especially along the Hieroglyphic Stairway, are remarkably well preserved. Here you can marvel at the artistry of a city that many have called the "Athens of Central America."

CRUISE DAY AT SANTO TOMÁS

Take one sleepy town. Turn it into Guatemala's largest commercial port. Make it the headquarters of the country's navy. Then build a cruise-ship terminal. The result is a small boom, the likes of which the village of Santo Tomás de Castilla never thought possible.

During the October to May cruise season, boats dock at the port's modern, spacious Terminal de Cruceros (cruise terminal). The facility offers money exchange—you can get by with U.S. dollars if you go on an organized shore excursion—post office, telephones, Internet computers, a lively crafts market, and an office of INGUAT, the national tourist office. Most passengers opt for an organized shore excursion.

Few visitors spend much time in Santo Tomás itself. In the mid-19th century Belgian immigrants settled the town, but scant evidence of their presence remains save for the preponderance of French and Flemish names in the local cemetery.

For urban life, Guatemala–Caribbean style, Puerto Barrios beckons, a quick taxi ride away. Livingston is a 30-minute water-taxi jaunt across the bay. Many passengers go for resort-chic and spend their shore time at the nearby Amatique Bay Resort, swimming, watersliding, kayaking, horseback riding, or bicycling. Boat rides from Livingston up the Río Dulce are also popular.

The Mayan ruins at Quiriguá are the most accessible in this part of the country, but operators can also fly you from Puerto Barrios's airstrip to Copán, across the border in Honduras, and all the way up to Tikal, for about $500.

The area open to the public covers only a small part of the city's ceremonial center. Copán once extended for nearly 2 km (1¼ mi) along the river, making it as large as many Mayan archaeological sites in Guatemala. It's also just as old—more than 3,000 years ago there was an Olmec settlement on this site. Because new structures were usually built on top of existing ones, the great temples that are visible today were built during the reigns of the city's last few rulers.

As you stroll past cieba trees on your way to the archaeological site, you'll find the **Great Plaza** to your left. The stelae standing about the plaza were monuments erected to glorify rulers. Some stelae on the periphery are dedicated to Smoke Jaguar, but the most impressive, located in the middle of the plaza, depict 18 Rabbit. Besides stroking the egos of the kings, these monuments had religious significance. Vaults for ritual offerings have been found beneath most of them.

The city's most important **ball court** lies south of the Great Plaza. One of the largest of its kind in Central America, it was used for more than simple entertainment. Players had to keep a hard rubber ball from touching the ground, perhaps symbolizing the sun's battle to stay aloft. Stylized carvings of macaw heads that line either side of the court may have been used as markers for keeping score—and the score was worth keeping, since the losers were probably put to death.

Near the ball court is one of the highlights of Copán, the **Hieroglyphic Stairway**. This amazing structure, covered with a canopy to protect it from the weather, contains the world's largest collection of hieroglyphs. The 63 steps immortalize the battles won by Copán's kings, especially those of the much revered King Smoke Jaguar. Once placed chronologically, the history can no longer be read because an earthquake knocked many steps free, and archaeologists replaced them in a random order. All may not be lost: experts have located an early photograph of the stairway that helps unlock the proper sequence.

The **Western Court** is thought to have represented the underworld. The structures, with doors that lead to blank walls, appear symbolic. On the east side of the plaza is a reproduction of Altar Q, a key to understanding the history of Copán. The squat platform shows a long line of Copán's rulers passing power down to their heirs. It ends with the last great king, Dawning Sun, facing the first king, Yax Kuk Mo.

The **Acropolis** was partly washed away by the Río Copán, which has since been routed away from the ruins. Dawning Sun was credited with the construction of many of the buildings surrounding this grand plaza. Below the Acropolis are tunnels that lead to some fascinating discoveries. Underneath Structure 16 are the near-perfect remains of an older building, called the **Rosalila Temple**. This structure, dating from 571, was subsequently buried below taller structures. Uncovered in 1989, the Rosalila was notable in part because of the paint remains on its surface—rose and lilac—for which it was named. Another tunnel called **Los Jaguares** takes you past tombs, a system of aqueducts, and even an ancient bathroom.

Two other parts of Copán that served as residential and administrative areas are open to the public, and they offer a glimpse into the daily lives of ordinary people. **El Bosque** (literally, "the Forest") lies in the woods off the trail to the west of the Principal Group. **Las Sepulturas** ("the graves"), which lies 2 km (1 mi) down the main road, is a revealing look into Mayan society. Excavations have shown that the Maya had a highly-stratified-social system, where the elite owned houses with many rooms.

East of the main entrance to Copán, the marvelous **Museo de Escultura Maya** provides a close-up look at the best of Mayan artistry. All the sculptures and replicas are accompanied by informative signs in English as well as Spanish. Here you'll find a full-scale replica of the Rosalila Temple. The structure, in eye-popping shades of red and green, offers an educated guess at what the ceremonial and political structures of Copán must have looked like at the time they were in use.

PRACTICALITIES
The entrance fee covers admission to the ruins, as well as to nearby sites like El Bosque and Las Sepulturas. Admission to the tunnels to Rosalila and Los Jaguares is extra, as is admission to the Museo de Escultura Maya. It's a good idea to hire a guide, as they are very knowledgeable about the site. English-speaking ones charge about L300 for a two-hour tour, whereas Spanish-speaking guides charge about half that. A

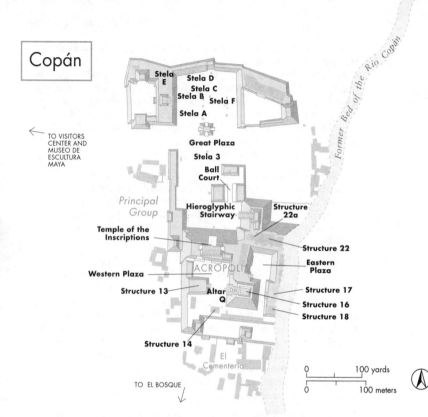

Copán

Stela E
Stela D
Stela C
Stela B Stela F
Stela A

← TO VISITORS
CENTER AND
MUSEO DE
ESCULTURA
MAYA

Former Bed of the Río Copán

Great Plaza

Stela 3
Ball Court

Principal Group

Hieroglyphic Stairway

Structure 22a

Temple of the Inscriptions

Structure 22

ACROPOLIS

Eastern Plaza

Western Plaza

Structure 13   Altar Q

Structure 17

Structure 16

Structure 18

Structure 14

El Cementerio

0   100 yards
0   100 meters

TO EL BOSQUE

small cafeteria and gift shop are near the entrance ⊠ *1 km (½ mi) east of Copán Ruinas* ☎ *No phone* ᯤ *L150* ☉ *Daily 8–4.*

BORDER CROSSING Many Guatemala-based travelers do cross-border jaunts as organized day trips out of Guatemala City or Antigua. Guatemala's border post is El Florido, a town with no real lodging or dining options, other than a few food stands. If Copán is your only Honduras destination, formalities are minimal: $3 to exit Guatemala, and a free visa that lets you stay in Honduras up to five days. You must not travel any farther than Copán and its nearby town of Copán Ruinas, and must return to Guatemala the same way you came.

WHAT IT COSTS IN HONDURAS (LEMPIRAS)			
$	$$	$$$	$$$$
RESTAURANTS under L75	L75–L150	L150–L225	over L225
HOTELS under L750	L750–L1,500	L1,500–L2,250	over L2,250

Restaurant prices are per person, for a main course at dinner. Hotel prices are for two people in a standard double room in high season, excluding tax.

CLOSE UP

Copán History

The first king during the Classic Period, Yax Kuk Mo (or "Blue-Green Quetzal Macaw") came to power around AD 435. Very little is known about him or his successors until the rise of the 12th king, Smoke Jaguar (628–695). Under his rule Copán grew to be one of the largest cities in the region. His successor, King 18 Rabbit (695–738), continued the quest for complete control of the region. The city's political structure was shaken, however, when he was captured by the soldiers of Quiriguá, a city in what is today part of Guatemala. He was brought to that city and beheaded.

During his short reign, Smoke Monkey (738–749) was increasingly challenged by powerful noble families. Smoke Monkey's son, Smoke Shell (749–763), tried to justify his power by playing up the historical importance of great warrior kings. He ordered the construction of the elaborate Hieroglyphic Stairway, the longest Classic Mayan inscription yet to be discovered, which emphasized the supremacy in battle of Copán's rulers. The 16th king, Dawning Sun (763–820), continued to glorify warfare in his architecture, but it was too late. By this time, Copán and its political authority were in decline.

5

WHERE TO EAT

$–$$ ✕**Carnitas Nía Lola.** Housed in a charming wooden building, this long-time favorite has sweeping views of the valley from its second-story dining room. Wonderful smells emanate from the meats on the grill, which is crowned with a stone skull reminiscent of those at the nearby ruins. One of the favorite dishes here is the *carne encebollado*, sizzling beef topped with onions and accompanied by a mound of french fries. ⊠*2 blocks south of the Parque Ctl.* ☎*No phone* ⊟*AE, MC, V.*

WHERE TO STAY

$$ ⊞**Hotel Marina Copán.** Facing Parque Central, this colonial-era building has been lovingly converted into the town's prettiest hotel. The second-story restaurant overlooks the sparkling pool, shaded by clusters of banana trees. Brilliant bougainvillea lines the paths to the rooms, which are filled with hand-hewn wood furniture and cooled by lazily turning ceiling fans. At the bar you can listen to mariachi music on Friday and Saturday night. ⊠*Northwest corner of Parque Ctl.* ☎*651–4070* ⊟*651–4477* ⊕*www.hotelmarinacopan.com* ➪*48 rooms, 2 suites* ⊘*In-hotel: restaurant, room service, bar, pool, gym, spa, laundry service, parking (no fee)* ⊟*AE, MC, V.*

$$ ⊞**Hotel Posada Real de Copán.** The closest lodging to the archaeological site, this Spanish-style hotel is in the hills just outside of town. The open-air lobby, filled with tropical flowers, adds to the ambience. Inside the tile-roof buildings are generously proportioned rooms with views of the lush gardens. After a day exploring the dusty ruins, swim a few laps in the palm-shaded pool or relax in the nearby hot tub. ⊠*2 km (1 mi) east of Copán Ruinas* ☎*651–4480* ⊟*651–4497* ⊕*www. posadarealdecopan.com* ➪*80 rooms* ⊘*In-hotel: restaurant, room service, bar, pool, parking* ⊟*AE, MC, V.*

$$ □ **Plaza Copán.** Watch horses clip-clop around the cobbled streets of Copán Ruinas from your terrace at this hotel on Parque Central. Ask for one of the rooms on the top floor, which have views of the town's red-tile roofs. Relax with a drink by the little pool in the central courtyard, which is shaded by tall palm trees. The restaurant, set behind a lovely colonnade, appropriately called Los Arcos, serves traditional fare. ⊠*Southeast corner of Parque Ctl.* ☎*651–4508* 🖷*651–4039* ↪*21 rooms* ⚇*In-room: refrigerator. In-hotel: restaurant, bar, pool* ☰*AE, MC, V.*

$ □ **Hacienda San Lucas.** In a century-old hacienda, this country inn is one
★ of the most charming lodgings in the area. Flavia Cueva's tender care shows in all the details, from the carefully crafted wooden furniture in the simple but elegant rooms to the hammocks swinging from the porch outside. The restaurant serves steaming tamales, tasty adobo sauce, and aromatic coffee. Take a walk to Los Sapos, a Mayan archaeological site where huge stones were carved into the shape of frogs, or go horseback riding through the cool Copán Valley. ⊠*1½ km (1 mi) south of Copán* ☎*651–4106* ⊕*www.geocities.com/sanlucascopan* ↪*4 rooms* ⚇*In-hotel: restaurant* ☰No credit cards.*

SANTA ROSA DE COPÁN

153 km (95 mi) south of San Pedro Sula.

Set in one of the most beautiful regions of Honduras, Santa Rosa de Copán has a friendliness that makes you long to linger. It is the kind of highland town that still feels like a village—you get the sense you would know everybody in town within a week or so. The hilltop *casco histórico* (historic center) is being renovated with care, with much work being put into preserving the splendid colonial-era buildings lining the narrow cobbled streets.

Tobacco still runs the local economy, and nearly everyone seems to be hard at work rolling cigars. Some prefer the strong Don Melo or the smoother Santa Rosa, but the pride of the area is the Zino, made by **Flor de Copán** (⊠*C. Real Centenario 168, between 2 and 3 Avs.* ☎*662–0111*). A seductively sweet odor engulfs you as you enter the decrepit old factory west of Parque Central. In the dimly-lit space you can watch workers piling tobacco leaves into *pilones* (bales). The neat shop at the entrance stocks the different brands made by the company. The factory is open weekdays 7:30 to noon and 2 to 4.

Coffee lovers should head to **Beneficio Maya** (⊠*Between 11 and 12 Avs. Norte, Colonia San Martín* ☎*662–1665*) where they can watch the roasting and grading process. Fresh export-grade coffee is for sale on the premises. The factory is open weekdays 7 to noon and 2 to 5. Take a taxi, as it's difficult to find.

Set in a restored building, the **Casa de Cultura** (⊠*Av. Alvaro Contreras, Barrio El Centro* ☎*662–0800*) buzzes with music lessons, theater, ballet, and modern dance and may well have one of Central America's best children's libraries. The patio is a pleasant place to relax.

THE ATLANTIC LOWLANDS ESSENTIALS

TRANSPORTATION

AIR TRAVEL

There are presently no flights to the Atlantic Lowlands. The government is refurbishing dormant airfields at Puerto Barrios (PBR) and Río Dulce (LCF) with the eventual goal of restoring air service, but at press time no target date had been set.

BOAT TRAVEL

Daily ferry service leaves Puerto Barrios at 10:30 AM and 5 PM and Livingston at 5 AM and 2 PM. The trip takes about two hours. Launches that connect the two cities take about 30 minutes, but they don't depart until they are full. This can really dent your plans, especially if you are leaving late in the day. (You usually don't need to wait more than 45 minutes.) There is boat service from Puerto Barrios to Honduras and Livingston. There is also boat service from Livingston to Río Dulce for approximately Q100.

BUS TRAVEL

Litegua operates comfortable buses from Guatemala City to Puerto Barrios. Trips to the capital from Puerto Barrios also leave approximately hourly during the day, and slightly less frequently in the evening. Be sure to ask for the comfortable *clase* service on the company's double-decker buses, which run three times daily.

Litegua also has direct service to Río Dulce from the capital. Linea Dorada runs between Guatemala City and Flores in El Petén, passing through Río Dulce. Buses leave the capital daily at 10. The trip to Río Dulce takes about six hours.

Information **Linea Dorada** (✉ *16 C. 10–03, Zona 1, Guatemala City* ☏ *2290–7990).* **Litegua** (✉ *15 C. 10–40, Zona 1, Guatemala City* ☏ *2220–8840* ✉ *6 Av. 9–10, Puerto Barrios* ☏ *7948–1172* ✉ *C. Principal, Fronteras (Río Dulce* ☏ *7930–5251* ⊕ *www.litegua.com).*

CAR TRAVEL

From Guatemala City most people drive to the Atlantic Lowlands via the Carretera Atlántica. The journey to Río Dulce or Puerto Barrios is about five hours on a good day. Descending the curving roads through the mountains you can feel the temperature and humidity rising.

CONTACTS & RESOURCES

EMERGENCIES

Emergency Services **Police** (☏ *7948–7943–2074 in Esquipulas, 7643 in Puerto Barrios, 7948–3244 in Santo Tomás de Castilla).*

Hospital **Hospital Nacional** (✉ *Colonia San Manuel, Puerto Barrios* ☏ *7948–3073).*

HEALTH

The heat and sun in the Atlantic Lowlands can be intense. Be prepared with a good sun hat and lightweight clothing that covers your arms and legs. Shorts don't protect legs from the sun, tall grass, insects, and dust. Also pack plenty of sunscreen and insect repellent.

MAIL & SHIPPING

Most towns in the Atlantic Lowlands have post offices, but you should wait to post letters in Puerto Barrios. The main post office here is about four blocks from the bay.

Post Office **Puerto Barrios** (✉ *6 C. and 6 Av.*).

MONEY MATTERS

If you need to exchange cash in the Atlantic Lowlands, the place to do it is Puerto Barrios. There are several banks that will be happy to help you, including Banco Industrial.

Contacts **Banco Industrial** (✉ *7 Av. Norte 73, Puerto Barrios*).

SAFETY

Robberies have been known to occur in Puerto Barrios and Livingston, so be on your guard. Use the same precautions you would anywhere else—don't wear flashy jewelry and watches, keep your camera in a secure bag, and don't handle money in public. Remain alert for pickpockets, especially in crowded markets. Only hike in the countryside with a reputable guide. Women should never hike alone.

TOURS

A few tour operators have set up shop in this area. Gray Line Guatemala operates in Puerto Barrios and Río Dulce, running shuttles to Guatemala City and Antigua. Río Dulce–based agency Otitours runs shuttles to the capital, Antigua, Tikal, and Copán, Honduras. Asotransali represents 50 private boat drivers in Livingston and can help you arrange á la carte tours on the Río Dulce or to Siete Altares. Happy Fish Travel, affiliated with the restaurant of the same name in Livingston, arranges area tours. Transportes El Chato, in Puerto Barrios, can set you up with transport and tours to nearby Belize.

Contacts **Asotransali** (✉ *Municipal docks, Livingston* ☎ *7947-0870*). **Gray Line Guatemala** (✉ *16 C. and 7 Av., Puerto Barrios* ☎ *7948-1254* ✉ *C. Principal, Fronteras (Río Dulce* ☎ *7930-5196* ⊕ *www.graylineguatemala.com*). **Happy Fish Travel** (✉ *C. Principal, Livingston* ☎ *7947-0661*). **Otitours** (✉ *Parque Las Brisas, Fronteras, Río Dulce* ☎ *7930-7674*). **Transportes El Chato** (✉ *1 Av. and 10 C., Puerto Barrios* ☎ *7948-5525* ⊕ *www.transporteselchato.com*).

VISITOR INFORMATION

There are no official visitor-information offices in the area, but heading to a restaurant, tour operator, or hotel will certainly get you on the right path.

The Pacific Lowlands

WORD OF MOUTH

"I find myself shivering sometimes at night in Antigua and the Highlands, but just an hour away, toward the Pacific coast, I discovered I can bask in the warmth of the tropics. It's so easy to get here, but nobody (except Guatemalans) knows about the region. I especially like Monterrico, this cool, kind of funky little beach town, sort of on the cusp of its very own Jimmy Buffett era."

—Jeffrey Van Fleet

GUATEMALA'S 266-KM (160-MI) PACIFIC SHORELINE *could* lay the groundwork for a string of beach resorts like those in neighboring Mexico, but a rugged coast, dark-sand beaches, and water too rough for swimming conspire to make things otherwise. Except for the beach town of Monterrico, a fun-in-the-sun vacation culture has barely developed here. This highland country has historically looked inward rather than to the sea.

This is Guatemala's breadbasket, and agriculture—primarily cattle raising and sugar and cotton production—has brought a level of prosperity to the Pacific Lowlands little seen elsewhere in the country. The region is also the country's hot new real-estate market. Condominiums and vacation homes are springing up, not just on the coast, but inland, too. With Guatemala City hemmed in by mountains north and west, south provides the path of least resistance for metro-area growth to spill.

Paradoxically, travelers most familiar with this region are those with little interest in Guatemala at all. For drivers traveling to and through Central America, this region's Highway CA-2 makes for a faster, straighter, flatter route through the country than the parallel Pan-American Highway (CA-1) through the mountainous highlands to the north. If you have the time, consider spending some time here.

ORIENTATION & PLANNING

ORIENTATION

Guatemala's mountainous highlands front the Pacific Lowlands on the north, with the landscape tumbling down to the ocean in less than two hours. The small cities of Retalhuleu and Santa Lucía Cotzumalguapa anchor the western part of this region. The old port city of Puerto San José and the lively beach town of Monterrico sit on the far eastern end of the coast, not far from the border with El Salvador. In the middle of the lowlands sits the not-so-interesting city of Escuintla, the region's economic hub, a place you may pass through, but will likely not stay.

PLANNING

WHEN TO GO

The year here divides into rainy (June to October) and dry (November to May) seasons. Unlike in most of the rest of Guatemala, hotels here do observe high and low seasons corresponding to the weather, and set rates accordingly. Beach lodgings also raise rates on weekends. Even though comparatively few travelers come here, the Pacific Lowlands fit nicely into a visit to points just north. A good highway connects the eastern coast at Puerto Quetzal with Guatemala City and Antigua, putting you here in about 90 minutes, and Retalhuleu is a one-hour drive south (and downhill all the way) from Quetzaltenango in the highlands.

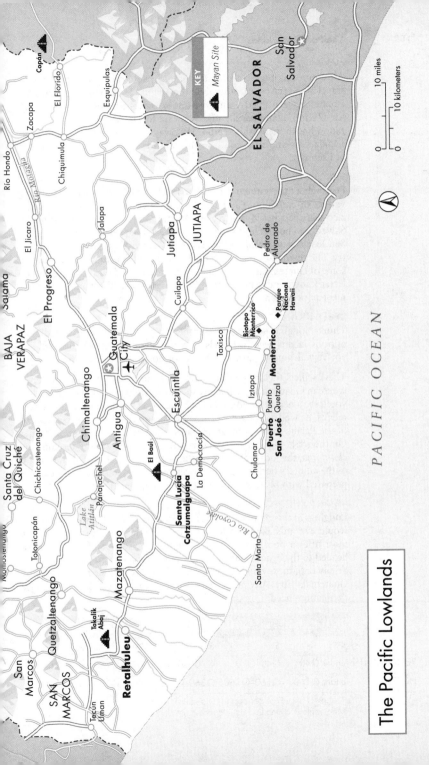

The Pacific Lowlands

GETTING AROUND

Although this region fronts the ocean, you'll find very little way to travel along the coast, other than the 40 km (24 mi) road that hugs the Pacific between Puerto San José and Monterrico. Highway CA-2, 45 km (27 mi) inland parallel to the ocean, forms the east–west transportation backbone of this region. Highway CA-9, which begins in Guatemala City and runs south to the coast at Puerto Quetzal, intersects at Escuintla.

WHAT TO DO

For such a little-known region, the Pacific Lowlands offer a surprising variety of activities. The beach is your obvious choice, with Monterrico your best bet in that regard. Monterrico and the coast east to the Salvadoran border host sea-turtle conservation projects. Nearby Puerto San José is developing as the center of Guatemala's sportfishing industry. The region around Santa Lucí Cotzumalguapa and Retalhuleu has some of Guatemala's best white-water rafting, and two of the country's lesser known indigenous ruins. Retalhuleu is also Guatemala's amusement-park center.

RESTAURANTS & CUISINE

Think "lodging"—yours or another—when considering your dining options in this region. Hotels tend to have the best restaurants, and you're welcome to partake whether or not you're staying there.

The Pacific Lowlands bring together a number of dishes from elsewhere in Guatemala, with a few specialties of its own. No surprise that you'll see a hearty *caldo de mariscos* (seafood stew) on most restaurant menus, as well as *sopa de tortuga* (turtle soup). Given the fragile state of the Pacific turtle population, we suggest avoiding that second one. On the topic of what to avoid, you might also be on the lookout for *chanfaina,* the local variation on the Spanish lamb stew that uses many of the animal's body parts. In this region of Guatemala, it's more likely prepared with beef, but still with everything tossed in.

ABOUT THE HOTELS

Lodgings in this region go for the resort look and feel, although no one would ever mistake them for a Club Med. They tend to be small, but most offer a pool, always appreciated in the lowland heat. If you're headed to the beach, make advance reservations if you plan to be here Friday or Saturday night—the weekend is getaway time for residents of Guatemala City. Any other night of the week, you can probably show up unannounced.

WHAT IT COSTS IN GUATEMALAN QUETZALES				
¢	$	$$	$$$	$$$$
RESTAURANTS	under Q40	Q40–Q70	Q70–Q100	Q100–Q130	over Q130
HOTELS	under Q160	Q160–Q360	Q360–Q560	Q560–Q760	over Q760

Restaurant prices are per person for a main course at dinner. Hotel prices are for two people in a standard double room, including tax and service.

THEME-PARK CENTRAL

Retalhuleu is home to two well-designed, Disney-like theme parks operated by IRTRA, a Guatemalan labor organization. Both sit just north of town on the highway to Quetzaltenango.Wet and wild, **Xocomil**, is a water park of which there are many in this part of the country. The Mayan-themed structures tend a bit toward the cheesy side, but it's a well-integrated design that encompasses waterslides, wave pools, and children's pools in the park.(✉ *Km 180.5, Carretera a Quetzaltenango* ☎ *7722–9400, 2423–* 9000 *in Guatemala City* ⊕ *www.irtra. org.gt* ⊕ *Tues.–Sun. 9–5* 💲*Q75; Q50, kids 5–12, under 5 free*).

We'll call the adjoining **Xetulul** a bit more "Epcot Center-y." It expands on Xocomil's Maya theme, but incorporates pavilions devoted to colonial Guatemala, as well as Spain, Italy, and France into its complex, with several fun amusement rides to boot. (✉ *Km 180.5, Carretera a Quetzaltenango* ☎ *7722–9450, 2423–9000 in Guatemala City* ⊕ *www.irtra.org.gt* ⊕ *Thurs–Sun. 10–6* 💲*Q200*)

RETALHULEU

6

62 km (74 mi) south of Quetzaltenango, 192 km (115 mi) southwest of Guatemala City.

Guatemala has some pretty complex place names, but no one even bothers trying to pronounce this one. It's *ray-tahl-hoo-LAY-oo* if you care to venture a try—that means "sign of hollows in the earth"—but everyone just goes with "Reu" (*RAY-oo*) for short. This friendly, one-time cacao town has become Guatemala's very own Orlando, with two huge amusement parks just outside town. Water sports beckon between here and the coast, and on the way east to neighboring Santa Lucía Cotzumalguapa. The nearby indigenous ruins of Takalik Abaj are just a short trip west toward the Mexican border.

WHERE TO STAY

$ 🏨 **Hotel Posada de Don José.** Retalhuleu's prestige address is this medium-size, colonial-style hotel a couple of blocks from the Central Park. It is frequented by business travelers during the week, and vacationing families on the weekend. The large rooms are arranged on 2 floors around the pool area and contain dark-wood furnishings and two beds each. Ask for a room that doesn't overlook the busy 5 Calle. ■TIP➔**The poolside restaurant is the best in town.** ✉ *5 C. 3–67, Zona 1* ☎ *7771–0180* 🖨 *7771–4176* ⊕ *www.hotelposadadedonjose.com* 🛏 *23 rooms* ⌂ *In-hotel: restaurant, room service, bar, pool, no elevator, laundry service, public Internet, parking (no fee)* 🚪 *AE, D, DC, MC, V.*

TAKALIK ABAJ

11 km (61/2 mi] northwest of Retalhuleu.

Olmec meets Mayan at this little-known complex of ruins tucked away in the southwestern corner of the country. Historically, this lowland location gave far better access to central and southern Mexico than did sites elsewhere in Guatemala, and the Olmec influence was stronger here than other places around the country. Inhabitants of Takalik Abaj also formed strong commercial ties with Kaminaljuyú, on the site of present-day Guatemala City.

The name means "standing stones" in Quiché, a moniker given to the site by those who uncovered it in the 1880s. (No one is certain what its original inhabitants called the place, as is the case with the majority of Guatemala's indigenous ruins.) What is known is that the site dates from the Preclassic period, and was inhabited from the 8th century BC to AD 9th century, peaking about AD 200. The standing-stone name is apt: Takalik Abaj is home to almost 300 well-preserved stelae, made of granite, unlike the limestone used at ruins in northern Guatemala's Petén region. Several small pyramids round out the offerings on the site.

Guides staff the booth at the site entrance, and can provide you with a tour. These folks don't see a lot of visitors, so a Q15 tip is always appreciated. Alternatively, the nearby Takalik Maya Lodge can set you up with a tour. ☒ *11 km (6½ mi) northwest of Retalhuleu* ☎ *No phone* ⏱ *Daily 10–6* ☒ *Q25.*

WHERE TO STAY

$$–$$$$ 🏨 **Takalik Maya Lodge.** You negotiate a rough road to get here—it's a few kilometers north of the entrance to its namesake ruins—but a stay on this working coffee, rubber, and macadamia plantation is worth the trip. The colonial-style rooms are in the plantation house, and, except for the shared bathrooms, are quite nice. Two large, newer, separate bungalows are designed to be their own mini-Mayan palaces. The lodge has a lot of mix-and-match packages that contain lodging only, all meals, or several tours, among them horse and bicycle rides, as well as tours of the nearby ruins. ☒🚗 *Turn at Km 190.5 on Pacific Hwy* ☎ *5651–1094, 2337–0037 in Guatemala City* 🌐 *www.takalik. com* 🛏 *7 rooms, none with bath, 2 bungalows* 🔧 *In-room: no a/c, no phone, no TV. In-hotel: restaurant, bar, pool, parking (no fee)* 🍴 *AE, D, DC, MC, V* ⎮🍴*Breakfast included; all meals included.*

SANTA LUCÍA COTZUMALGUAPA

104 km (82 mi) east of Retalhuleu, 88 km (53 mi) southwest of Guatemala City.

Tidy, prosperous Santa Lucía Cotzumalguapa is the town that sugar built. The small city is worth a stop to visit a couple of lesser known indigenous ruins. Several nearby rivers also put Santa Lucía in the midst of one of the country's best white-water regions. However, you'll have to hook up with a trip in Guatemala City, as none depart from here.

In the midst of working fields of sugarcane north of town, **Finca El Baúl** clumps together a collection of stelae from the Preclassic to Late Classic periods (AD 250–900). The site shows influences of the indigenous

SUGAR IS ENERGY

Guatemala's $500-million-sugar industry centers around Santa Lucía Cotzumalguapa. The annual *zafra*, or cutting of cane, lasts from November to May, roughly corresponding to the dry season. The 2006 to 2007 season generated 47.1 million *quintales* of sugarcane (one quintal = 46 kg. = 100 lb., the traditional unit used to measure output in the industry.) Guatemala's 14 *ingenios* (sugar producers) go through various stages in the process of converting cane to refined sugar, and the heat and moisture generated produce about 750 gigawatt-hours of electricity—enough excess energy to supply their own needs as well as 10% of the country's power. That packet of sugar you put in your Guatemalan coffee, another of the country's signature agricultural products, just might have generated the electricity needed to brew your morning cup.

Pipil people, who spoke the Nahuatl language of central Mexico, as well as the Maya. Though billed as an outdoor museum, you'll find little explanation of what you're seeing at El Baúl. Most visitors come here, rather, to observe the occasional Mayan rituals that still take place on the site. There's no fixed schedule, but if you do stumble upon an observance, be unobtrusive. A few robberies have occurred of visitors wandering aimlessly through the fields. We recommend a taxi to get here and back. Most drivers know the place and are happy to serve as your guide and protector (⊠*4 km [2½ mi] north of Santa Lucía Contzumalguapa* ☎*No phone* ☉*Daily 8–4* ⌨*Free*). For a far better grounding in the Mayan history of the region than you can get at El Baúl, head to the Finca Las Ilusiones, also a one-time sugarcane plantation. The site is officially known as the **Museo de Cultura Cotzumalguapa,** and takes in a collection of stelae and stones gathered from nearby archaeological sites. Most of these come from Bilbao, on the northern edge of Santa Lucía, which housed a collection of carved stones. The 80-ton, so-called Monument 21 remains at the Bilbao site, and has been copied in fiberglass for display at this museum. The remainder of the Bilbao stones are here in person (⊠*Km 87.5, Carretera al Pacífico, on eastern edge of Santa Lucía Contzumalguapa* ☎*No phone* ☉*Daily 8–noon and 2–4* ⌨*Q10*).

OUTDOOR ACTIVITIES

June through October is the season for daylong rafting excursions to the beginners' Río Coyolate (Class II–III), the slightly more difficult Río Nahualate (Class III), and the Río Naranjo (Class III–IV) for experienced rafters only. All are within striking distance of Santa Lucía Cotzumalguapa and Retalhuleu, but excursions leave from Guatemala City. **Maya Expeditions** (⊠*15 C. A 14–07, Zona 10* ☎*2363–4955* ⊕*www.mayaexpeditions.com*) offers trips that range from easy to challenging.

PUERTO SAN JOSÉ

42 km (25 mi) south of Escuintla, 99 km (59 mi) south of Guatemala City.

Guatemala's oldest port dates from 1853, its construction spurred by the then-nascent coffee trade. Its importance has been eclipsed since the 1980s by the more modern Puerto Quetzal, next door to the east. Puerto San José serves as the westernmost mainland point on the Canal de Chiquimulilla, a waterway separating a sliver of land from the rest of Guatemala. Puerto San José is the center of the Pacific coast's just-beginning-to-burgeon sportfishing trade. It has also been a traditional beach-vacation destination for residents of Guatemala City, but is being supplanted by nearby Monterrico.

> ## THE LADINOS
>
> In Guatemala's historically stratified society, a vaguely defined group called the *Ladinos* occupies the middle rungs of the socioeconomic ladder. The word very generally describes anyone with mixed European-indigenous blood—neighboring Mexico uses the term *mestizo* to express the same phenomenon—and the Pacific Lowlands and Guatemala City are the most Ladino-populated areas of the country. People entirely of Mayan ancestry, but who live in an urban area, speak Spanish at home, and wear Western clothing, may choose to identify themselves as "Ladino."

WHERE TO STAY & EAT

$$$ ✕⬚ **Hotel Martita.** At first blush, you wouldn't choose a hotel near the center of a port town, but this hotel in the center of Puerto San José does things up big and draws a ton of weekend vacationers from Guatemala City. The place is thoroughly sparkling and modern with air-conditioned comfort, a great pool, with one for the kids on the side, and a yummy restaurant. If you find yourself needing to stop in Puerto San José—we admit that's far from a likely possibility—this is a good bet. ⊠ *Av. del Comercio* ☎ *7881–1337, 2474–1383 in Guatemala City* 🖷 *7881–1337, 2474–1337 in Guatemala City* 🛏 *38 rooms, 13 villas* ⚒ *In-hotel: restaurant, room service, bar, pool, laundry service, public Internet, parking (no fee)* ☰ *AE, D, DC, MC, V* ⧖⦀*BP.*

FISHING

Guatemala's southern coast is one of the best bill-fishing spots in the world, especially during fall and spring. Several world records have been recorded here. The targets are sailfish that can reach up to 150 pounds, but enormous yellow tuna and blue marlin are often caught in the outer waters. November through May is prime season here, but anglers say you're likely to reel something in all year long. **Sailfish Bay Lodge** (☎ *2426–3909 in Guatemala City, 800/638–7405 in U.S.* ⊕ *www.sailfishbaylodge.com*) is one of the best companies in the area, offering a variety of excursions from Iztapa, near Puerto San José. Only multiday packages are offered, beginning at $1,824 per person, double occupancy in the lodge's two-story bungalows, including meals, airport transfers, chartered boats, and last-night accommodation in Guatemala City.

CRUISE DAY AT PUERTO QUETZAL

The port of Puerto Quetzal has nudged out next-door Puerto San José as the Pacific coast's largest container port. Its newest incarnation is that of a port for call ships of several cruise lines during the October to May season. Some 30 ships visited during 2006 and 2007, about half the number that called at Santo Tomás de Castilla on the Caribbean coast (*see Cruise Day at Santo Tomás de Castilla box, in Chapter 5*). Puerto Quetzal offers a distinct advantage that its competing Atlantic port does not: the proximity here to the central and western highlands means that Antigua, Lake Atitlán, and Chichicastenango all appear on the list of shore excursions offered—that last one is an option on Thursday and Sunday market days only—all too far to reach from the Caribbean as a day trip. (Operators have jettisoned Guatemala City tours due to lack of interest.) Holland America, Oceania, Princess, P&O, and Silversea call at Puerto Quetzal on select Panama Canal– and South America–cruise itineraries.

MONTERRICO

35 km (21 mi) east of Puerto San José, 134 km (80 mi) south of Guatemala City.

Don't forget that Monterrico is on an island, separated from the mainland by the Canal of Chiquimulilla. The most direct route from Guatemala City and points north takes you to Escuintla, then southeast to the town of Taxisco. From there, head south to the tiny hamlet of Avellanas, where you board a ferry—the flat-bed boats are called a *lanchón,* and most are big enough for only one or two vehicles at a time—to cross the canal.

Just east of Puerto San José is the small town of Iztapa, also on the mainland side of the canal, and also served by lanchónes. A bridge is under construction at this writing, and is expected to open in 2008. From the island side of this crossing, it's a 30-minute drive to Monterrico.

Look up "laid-back beach town" in the dictionary, and you just might find a picture of Monterrico, the only town in the country with such a vibe. Don't expect Puerto Vallarta, but Monterrico is a wonderful little place with a growing selection of lodgings, and even the upscale hotels aren't too pricey. Weekends are usually full here—you can be here from Guatemala City in just two hours, and a huge number of the capital's residents do exactly that—but come during the week and you'll likely have the place to yourself.

Drawbacks include black volcanic sand that is very hot on bare feet at midday (wear sandals), and a wicked undertow that can pull you out to sea before you realize what is happening. (Lifeguards watch over a small section of beach on weekends only. Exercise extreme caution, and never swim alone, good advice anywhere, but especially here.)

The only named street—and the only paved street, for that matter—is Calle Principal, which ends at the beach. Lodgings are scattered a block inland from the beach along dirt streets leading east and west.

The **Biotopo Monterrico,** officially, the Monterrico Natural Reserve for Multiple Uses, encompasses 6,916 acres along Guatemala's Pacific coast and includes everything from mangrove swamps to dense tropical forests. This is a haven for ornithologists, as the reserve is home to more than 100 species of migratory and indigenous birds. Marine turtles swim ashore from July to January, and you can often see them digging nests for their eggs at night. We recommend an organized tour of the reserve. Although the visitor's center sits in town a couple of blocks east of Calle Principal, visiting on your own is logistically difficult. **Naturaltours** (⊠ *East of C. Principal* ☎ *5958–9491*) leads boat tours—in Spanish only—of the canal, mangroves, and lagoons. Rise and shine, for they begin at 5 AM, an hour necessary to take advantage of the best wildlife-viewing opportunities. ⊠ *Southeast of Monterrico* ☎ *No phone* ⌂ *Free.*

WHERE TO STAY & EAT

$–$$ ✕ **La Taberna del Pelícano.** The thatch-roof place a couple of blocks east of Calle Principal with two resident pelicans on the premises—hence the name—is our favorite stand-alone restaurant in Monterrico. You'll appreciate when the server lights a mosquito coil under your wooden table, and you'll dine on a yummy selection of pastas and seafood, all to the accompaniment of soft music. Peruse the book-exchange shelf while you wait. ⊠ *Beach road east of Monterrico* ☎ *5584–2400* ▤ *No credit cards* ⌂ *Closed Mon. and Tues.*

$$ ✕⌂ **Hotel Pez de Oro.** The hotel whose name translates as "fish of gold" is best known for its Italian restaurant. Stop by for dinner even you aren't staying here. Thatch-roof, tile-floor bungalows are scattered around the grounds, each with carved-wood furniture and ceiling fans that keep each unit surprisingly cool. ⊠ *Beach road east of Monterrico* ☎ *7920–9785, 2368–2684 in Guatemala City* ⌂ *18 cabins* ⌂ *In-room: no a/c, no phone, no TV. In-hotel: restaurant, bar, pool, beachfront, parking (no fee)* ▤ *V* ⌂ *EP.*

$$$ ⌂ **Dos Mundos Pacific Resort.** Set a bit outside the center of town, Monterrico's most sumptuous lodging comes courtesy of the folks who brought you Panajachel's Hotel Dos Mundos. It's another winner, even if such luxury seems a bit out of place in this funky beach town. Bungalows are arranged around the beachfront grounds, and contain tile floors, carved-wood furniture, and individual porches. The combination of ceiling fans and air-conditioning keeps things delightfully cool, as do a dip in the pool or a refreshing drink at the large rancho-style restaurant and bar. ⊠ *La Curvina, beach road east of Monterrico* ☎ *5847–4840* ⊕ *www.dosmundospacific.com* ⌂ *14 rooms* ⌂ *In-room: no phone, no TV. In-hotel: restaurant, room service, bar, pool, parking (no fee)* ▤ *AE, D, DC, MC, V* ⌂ *BP.*

$$$ ⌂ **Utz Tzaba Beach Hotel.** This is a realistic option only if you have a car, but the Utz Tzaba is a good small-resort choice. (The name means "beautiful coast.") Rooms make a semicircle around the lush green

grounds fronting the beach, and have high ceilings and tile floors. Bungalows sleep up to seven people, and come with one or two bedrooms and fully equipped kitchenettes. (The bungalow rate does not include breakfast for that reason, but rooms do.) A separate kids' pool and playground make this a good option if you're traveling with the family. Internet access is difficult in this part of the country. These folks offer Wi-Fi. ⊠ *Km 21.8, Carretera a Monterrico* ☎ *5318–9452* 🖷 *7848–1479* ⊕ *www.utz-tzaba.com* ⤢ *10 rooms, 4 bungalows* & *In-room: refrigerator (some), kitchen (some). In-hotel: restaurant, bar, pool, public Internet, public Wi-Fi, parking (no fee)* ▭ *AE, D, DC, MC, V* ⦿| *BP, EP.*

$–$$ ⊞ **Johnny's Place.** Traditionally Monterrico's most happening place gives you several lodging options that will work out, no matter what your budget. They range from multi-person dorm rooms, to fully equipped bungalows—they're made of concrete and are still a bit on the basic side, but comfortable, nonetheless. If you're feeling flush with your quetzals, and are here with a small group, opt for the two-story, stone-and-brick deluxe bungalow, the only unit here with air-conditioning, hot water, and television. ■ TIP→ **Even if you don't stay here, stop by for a meal**—everybody in town usually does at some point during their stay. ⊠ *Beach road east of C. Principal* ☎ *5812–0409* ⊕ *www.playademonterrico.com* ⤢ *5 rooms, 7 bungalows* & *In-room: no a/c (some), no phone, no TV (some). In-hotel: restaurant, bar, pool, beachfront, no elevator, parking (no fee)* ▭ *V* ⦿| *EP.*

$ ⊞ **Atelie del Mar.** A wonderfully friendly Finnish–Guatemalan couple operates this bright, cheery hotel on the beach-road west of town. The Guatemalan half of the pair brings her artist's talents—ask for a tour of her on-premises studio—to the rooms, which are decorated in bright tropical colors, with one or two beds per room, two chairs, small armoire, and a stone-basin sink and shower in the bathroom. A small staff whips up great food and serves it out in the thatch-roof rancho next to the pool. ⊠ *Beach road west of Monterrico* ☎ *5752– 5528* ⊕ *www.hotelateliedelmar.com* ⤢ *8 rooms* & *In-room: no a/c, no phone, no TV. In-hotel: restaurant, bar, pool, no elevator, parking (no fee)* ▭ *No credit cards.*

THE PACIFIC LOWLANDS ESSENTIALS

TRANSPORTATION

AIR TRAVEL

The Pacific Lowlands have no airport, but the capital's Aeropuerto Internacional La Aurora on the south side of Guatemala City puts you within an hour or two of most places in this region.

BOAT TRAVEL

Boat travel does not exist through the rough waters along this stretch of coast. Your only experience on boats will be the quick ride on the *lanchón* ferries that transport you and your vehicle across the Canal de Chiquimulilla that separates Monterrico and environs from the main-

GUATEMALAN SEA TURTLES

This far eastern stretch of Guatemala's Pacific coast is home to three species of marine turtle: the green, the leatherback, and, most prominently, the olive ridley turtle. For thousands of years, all three have engaged in an elaborate nesting ritual here, usually July to January, with peak-nesting season taking place in August and September.

Every two to four years, female turtles come ashore, nesting 2 to 5 times in a 12-day period. Each turtle digs a pit with her flippers and scoops out a chamber for depositing about 100 eggs. She fills and conceals the chamber before heading back out to sea. After a 60-day incubation period, the hatchlings emerge. In the ultimate team effort, they scurry up the sides of the chamber, kicking sand down to the bottom, and gradually raising the level of the base of the pit, from which they escape and make a mad dash to the sea. Biologists believe that the nesting site's sand leaves an imprint on the hatchlings—though it's not known exactly how—that draws the females back as adults to the same stretch of beach to continue the millennia-old ritual.

Unfortunately, turtle eggs are prized by poachers. (Walk into a bar and you'll probably see them on the appetizer menu.) Guatemalan authorities have struck a pragmatic bargain: egg harvesting can continue, as long as the harvesters donate 20% of their eggs to local hatcheries. Two organizations based here lead those conservation efforts, incubating donated eggs and, when the hatchlings emerge, returning them to the sea. Even with such conservation efforts, many of the hatchlings will not make it to adulthood. Many fall victim to sharks, boat rudders, and fishing nets. The fact that the turtle population survives at all is a remarkable feat of nature.

CECON (*The Center for Conservation Studies* ✉ *2 blocks, east of C. Principal, Monterrico* ☎ *5847–7777, 2331–0914 in Guatemala City* ⊕ *www.usac.edu.gt/cecon.html* ✉ *Q8* ⊙ *Daily 7–5*), based at Guatemala City's Universidad de San Carlos, operates the Biotopo Monterrico and an interesting visitor's center that documents the life cycle of the turtles, as well as iguanas and caimans. It also manages Monterrico's most popular event: the weekly turtle release during the July to January nesting season. Each Saturday at 5:30 PM, the week's hatchlings return to the sea in a well-attended event. For a Q10 ticket, you can sponsor a turtle, and release it at the starting line, and watch it scurry across the sand and make it to the finish line. The tide is the goal, of course—whoever said turtles are slow never witnessed this race—where it is washed out to sea to initiate the age-old life cycle. If your turtle wins, you win a prize, usually dinner at a local eating establishment. Win or lose, your Q10 goes to a good cause.

The Petén-based **ARCAS** (✉ *Parque Nacional Hawaii, 8 km [5 mi] east of Monterrico* ☎ *2478–4096 in Guatemala City* ⊕ *www.arcasguatemala. com*), whose name is the Spanish acronym for "Association for Rescue and Conservation of Wildlife," maintains an operation in Hawaii National Park, east of Monterrico near the Salvadoran border. ARCAS is always looking for volunteers with a passion for conservation.

land. Even that will begin to vanish with the expected opening of a bridge at Iztapa in 2008.

BUS TRAVEL

Transportes Esmeralda operates service between Guatemala's main bus terminal in Zona 4 and Puerto San José every half hour throughout the day. Travel time is about two hours.

Autobuses Fuente del Norte operates comfortable hourly buses between its own terminal in Retalhuleu and the capital. The trip takes three hours.

Public bus connections to Monterrico are complicated. You need to transfer in Escuintla, then take a smaller bus to the administrative capital of Taxisco, and then board a final bus to Monterrico, when you negotiate the ferry at Avellanas. Virtually every tour operator in Guatemala City and Antigua can set you up with a minivan shuttle to the beach.

Information **Autobuses Fuente del Norte** (☎ *5540–9989 in Retalhuleu, 2471–0952 in Guatemala City*). **Transportes Esmeralda** (✉ *Terminal de Buses, Zona 4, Guatemala City* ☎ *2232–3643 in Guatemala City*).

CAR TRAVEL

A fine four-lane highway—it's the country's best—connects Guatemala City with Puerto Quetzal on the coast. You'll pay a Q12 toll at Km 51 north of the hub city of Escuintla. Highway CA-2 intersects at Escuintla, heading west to Santa Lucía Cotzumalguapa and Retalhuleu.

CONTACTS & RESOURCES

EMERGENCIES

Both Escuintla and Retalhuleu are home to large public hospitals.

Hospital **Hospital Nacional** (✉ *Carretera a Taxisco, Km 59.5, Escuintla* ☎ *7889–5146*).

Hospital Nacional (✉ *Blvd. Centenario and 3 Av., Zona 2, Retalhuleu* ☎ *7771–0116*).

Police **Police** (☎ *7888–1120 in Escuintla, 7881–1333 in Puerto San José, 7771–0002 in Retalhuleu, 7882–5032 in Sant Lucía Cotzumalguapa*).

HEALTH

The heat and sun in the Pacific Lowlands can be intense. Be prepared with a good sun hat and lightweight clothing that covers your arms and legs. Shorts don't protect legs from the sun, tall grass, insects, and dust. Also pack plenty of sunscreen and insect repellent. The mosquitoes are voracious at the beach. Replenish regularly with lots of fluids.

MAIL & SHIPPING

Most towns in the region have branches of El Correo, Guatemala's post office, but you should post letters in Retalhuleu, or when you get back to Guatemala City.

Post Office **Retalhuleu** (✉ *Parque Ctl.*).

MONEY MATTERS

If you need to exchange cash in the Pacific Lowlands, the place to do it is Escuintla, Retalhuleu or Santa Lucía Cotzumalguapa. Monterrico has no bank, but you'll find the sole ATM at the Super Monte Rico on the Calle Principal. It frequently runs out of cash.

Contacts **Banco Agromercantil** (✉ 7 C. 3–07, Zona 1, Escuintla ✉ 5 Av. and 5 C., Zona 1, Retalhuleu ✉ 3 Av. 6–78, Zona 1, Santa Lucía Cotzumalguapa).

SAFETY

This is a mostly safe region of the country, and with standard travel precautions—no flashy jewelry, keep valuables well hidden—you should be fine. Strong undercurrents mean swimming poses a risk along the entire coast. Exercise extreme caution, and never swim alone.

VISITOR INFORMATION

There are no official visitor-information offices in the area, but heading to a restaurant, tour operator or hotel will certainly get you on the right path.

El Petén

WORD OF MOUTH

"I would definitely recommend staying in Las Flores or Santa Elena (which is less expensive) and then from there getting a minibus to Tikál. Las Flores is fun; a great place to pick up presents for the family (Flores is the best place to buy hammocks if you cannot make it down to the street fairs at Chichicastenango)."

—Christina

"You will certainly want to stay right at Tikál. There's nothing like entering the ruins early morning and late afternoon/early evening to enjoy the tremendous light and the abundance of birds and animals. Whatever you do, be sure to pack some good binoculars!"

—SharonNRayMc

THE JUNGLES OF EL PETÉN were the one-time heartland of the Mayan civilization. The sprawling empire—including parts of present-day Mexico, Belize, Honduras, and El Salvador—once encompassed a network of cities that was home to hundreds of thousands of people, but a millennium ago this fascinating civilization suddenly vanished without a trace. The temples that dominated the horizon were swallowed up by the jungle, not to be rediscovered by outsiders until the late 19th and early 20th centuries.

El Petén still has a bit of a backwater bent to it—the region comprises one-third of Guatemala but is its least populated region—but tourism-fueled development is slowly beginning to change things. Nature reigns supreme, with vines and other plants quickly covering everything that stands still a little too long.

ORIENTATION & PLANNING

ORIENTATION

The Petén may be vast and remote, but the traveler's focus takes in a far more limited area. Ruins dot the entire region, but excavation has begun on only a few of them. In the center of the region on Lago Petén Itzá sits Flores, its administrative center, and its twin town of Santa Elena, the site of the regional airport. Northeast lie the famed ruins of Tikal. The complexes of Yaxhá, Nakúm, Uaxactún, and El Zotz are scattered around Tikal. They're all close, but poor roads limit the number of visitors, especially during the rainy season. Farther removed, southwest of Flores, off the road to Cobá in Las Verapaces, are the town of Sayaxché and its nearby Ceibal ruins.

PLANNING

GETTING AROUND
Roads in El Petén are either great or atrocious. It can be slow going beyond the smooth highways connecting Flores and Santa Elena with Tikal, the Belize border at Melchor de Mencos, Río Dulce and Cobán. Four-wheel-drive vehicles are required to get to many of the sites, whereas others are reachable only by boat or on foot. The difficulty doesn't just enhance the adventure, it gives you time to take in the exotic scenery.

WHEN TO GO
It's warm here year-round. The rainy season (May to November) lasts about a month longer than that farther south in central Guatemala. Occasional showers are a possibility the rest of the year, but shouldn't interfere with your plans. March and April are the hottest months, with December and January a few degrees cooler than the rest of the year. July and August see an influx of visitors during prime North American and European vacation time.

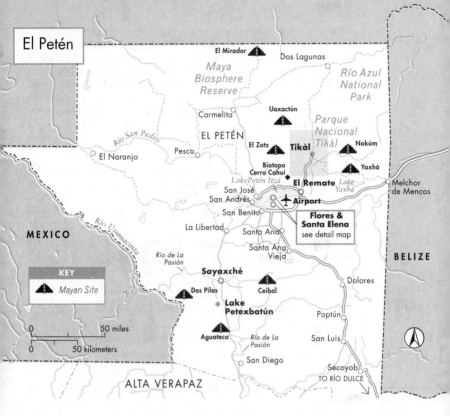

Proximity to Las Verapaces and the Atlantic Lowlands—it's four to five hours from either region—make the Petén a reasonable overland combination with either, and air links to Guatemala City simplify travel here from almost any other region of the country.

WHAT TO DO
In a word, ruins. Tikal is the most accessible Mayan complex up here, but, believe it or not, you'll find several others. None is as easily visited as Tikal, but that limited access translates into fewer crowds. Whatever your primary interest—archaeology, history, birding, biking—you'll find plenty to do and see in this remote region.

RESTAURANTS & CUISINE
Outside Flores, you'll find few separate stand-alone restaurants. Most visitors take their meals in hotel dining rooms. Guest or not, everyone is welcome in most places. El Petén has a few regional specialties, namely *palmito* (heart of palm)—it shows up in salads and other dishes such as *langostinos* (freshwater prawns) and *escabeche de pescado,* fish with a pickled vegetable relish.

ABOUT THE HOTELS

You'll find the largest concentration of lodgings in the twin towns of
Flores and Santa Elena. There are a few more in the small village of
El Remate, and along the north shore of Lago Petén Itzá. Three hotels
stand at the visitor's center complex on the grounds of Tikal itself.
Most of these are small, family-run affairs, although you have the
option of a couple of medium-size resort complexes, too. Despite the
heat, a surprising number of hotels don't offer air-conditioning, especially the ones that bill themselves as "ecofriendly," relying instead on
ceiling fans and good ventilation.

■TIP→ Unlike most in other regions in Guatemala, lodgings here do
observe low and high seasons, charge higher rates during the December
to –April dry season, and again during the busy July to August vacation season. Advance reservations are always a good idea during those
periods.

WHAT IT COSTS IN GUATEMALAN QUETZALES				
¢	$	$$	$$$	$$$$
RESTAURANTS under Q40	Q40–Q70	Q70–Q100	Q100–Q130	over Q130
HOTELS under Q160	Q160–Q360	Q360–Q560	Q560–Q760	over Q760

Restaurant prices are per person for a main course at dinner. Hotel prices are for
two people in a standard double room, including tax and service.

FLORES

*206 km (133 mi) north of Río Dulce, 61 km (38 mi) northeast of
Sayaxché.*

The red-roof town of Flores, on an island surrounded by the waters of
Lago Petén Itzá, sits on the site of the ancient city of Tayasal. This was
the region's last unconquered outpost of Mayan civilization, until it
finally fell to the Spanish in 1697. The conquerors destroyed the city's
huge pyramids.

Today the regional capital is one of Guatemala's most beguiling towns,
a pleasant place to explore, with its narrow streets lined with thick-
walled buildings painted pink, blue, and purple. Flowering plants
droop over gingerbread balconies. There's a central square presided
over by a colonial church. Connected to the mainland by a bridge,
Flores serves as a base for travelers to El Petén. It's also the center of
many nongovernmental organizations working for the preservation of
the Mayan Biosphere, an endangered area covering nearly all of northern Petén. Flores is also one of the last remaining homes of the Itzá, the
people who built Mexico's monumental Chichén Itzá.

In the 1800s, long before it was a departure point for travelers headed
for the ruins, remote Flores was called Devil's Island because of the
prison on top of the hill (a church stands there now). Since 1994 the
building has been home to the **Centro de Información sobre la Naturaleza,
Cultura, y Artesanía de Petén** (⊠*North side of Parque Ctl.* ☎7867–5209

A BIT OF HISTORY

The first major Mayan society dates to 2000 BC, based largely on the traditions of the Olmecs, a people living in what is now Mexico. Over the next 2,000 years the Maya proved to be an intellectually curious people. They developed a type of writing (one of the earliest) and a sophisticated system of mathematics (the first to use a zero). The Maya were particularly adept astronomers, mapping the orbits of the sun, moon, and planets with incredible accuracy—the Mayan lunar cycle differs from today's calculations by only seven minutes.

From about 250 BC to AD 900 the Maya developed complex social systems, agricultural practices, and religious beliefs, reaching their zenith with the construction of temples like Tikal. Around AD 1000, the Maya suffered repeated attacks from rival civilizations, followed by a sudden and mysterious period of decline. The

arrival of conquistadors like Hernán Cortés and Pedro de Alvarado in the early 1500s marked the beginning of the subjugation of what was left of the Mayan people.

The region remained isolated until the mid-20th century. Mexican and British currency circulated here far more than Guatemala's quetzal. Traveling to Guatemala City meant an arduous overland journey to Belize (then British Honduras), a boat trip to the Caribbean port of Puerto Barrios, and a rail journey to the capital. Modern roads began to open up the region in the 1940s, with the completion of the highway from Guatemala City to Flores via Cobán. Today's most commonly used highway access, the route via Río Dulce, was not paved until 1999. That road and commercial air links make El Petén seem less remote than it once was.

⊙ *Weekdays 8–5; shop, daily 9–9*). This center has a small museum with photographs of the region and information about local resources, such as allspice, chewing-gum base *chicle* (*see Chewing Gum box, below*) and *xate* (a shade palm used in floral decorations). A gift shop sells wood carvings, woven baskets, corn-husk dolls, and even locally made peanut butter.

WHERE TO STAY & EAT

$–$$$
Fodor's Choice
★

✕ **La Luna.** With its homemade-paper-lamp shades illuminating lovely blue walls in a converted century-old house, La Luna inspires romance on any moonlit night, but you can just as easily fall in love with the place when you stop in for a delicious lunch. Choose from inventive dishes, including wonderful vegetarian options like the stuffed squash in white sauce. Many people drop by for a drink at the bar. ⊠ *C. 30 de Junio* ☎ *7867–5443* ⊟ *AE, D, DC, MC, V* ⊙ *Closed Sun.*

¢–$$$
✕ **Capitán Tortuga.** The large, cartoonlike Capitán Tortuga sign may fool you into thinking this restaurant is just for kids, but the excellent grilled steak and seafood options make this one of Flores' best restaurants. The *pinchos* (grilled kebabs) are cooked on an open barbecue, sending enticing aromas throughout the restaurant. There's a nice patio and a 2nd-floor balcony out back, both of which offer tremendous sunset views of the lake. ⊠ *C. 30 de Junio and Callejón San Pedrito* ☎ *7926–0247* ⊟ *MC, V.*

Flores &
Santa Elena

FLORES

Centro de Información
de la Naturaleza, Cultura, y
Artesanía de Petén (CINCP)

Parque
Central

Calle Union

Calle Fraternidad

Calle 15 de Septiembre

El Carmen

Avenida Flores

El Rosario

Calle 10 de Novembre

Calle El Rosario

Calle

Calle 15 de Septiembre

Av. La Reforma

Av. Barrios

Calle 30 de Junio

Calle Centro América

Lago de
Petén Itzá

Causeway

KEY

① *Hotels*

❶ *Restaurants*

SANTA
ELENA

TO
AIRPORT →

0 _____ 1/4 mile
0 _____ 1/4 kilometer

THE MAYAN CALENDAR

The Maya devised an intricate calendar system whose dates you'll see on monuments in the Petén. Though most Mayan-descended peoples have fully adopted the Western Gregorian calendar, a few communities in the highlands, most notably Momostenango, still use the old system. The calendar plays a role in various rituals: the famous *palo volador* dance, so integral to Chichicastenango's December Santo Tomás celebrations, bases the number of aerial spins "danced" around a pole on the Mayan calendar's figures (*see Spinning Around the Maypole box, in Chapter 3*).

The system is technically a three-in-one interlocking calendar. The Maya didn't entirely develop the scheme, but refined it during the Late Preclassic period earlier conventions of dating developed by the Olmec civilization of Mexico. Some scholars surmise that the calendar marks the beginning of the world at what would correspond to our August 11, 3114 BC.

At the system's base is the Tzolkin calendar made up of 13 cycles of 20 days. Each of the resulting 260 days bears a unique name, combining day and cycle. Why 13 and 20? Theories abound. The human body contains 13 major joints (three for each limb plus the neck). The domain of the gods also contained 13 levels. The Maya used a base-20-numbering system (as opposed to ours, which is based on 10). Other experts suggest that 260 days roughly corresponds to the nine months of human pregnancy, and that midwives may have developed the Tzolkin system to aid in prediction of birth dates.

Running parallel to the Tzolkin system is the Haab calendar, approximately matching the solar year, with 18 months of 20 days each, plus 5 unnamed days, considered dangerous for many activities. Though Mayan astronomers were able to calculate an accurate length of the solar year, those calculations did not form part of the Haab calendar, which remained fixed at 365 days, and had no leap-year fixes to even things out.

Combine the two to get a cycle of 18,980 days that lasts 52 solar years. Cycles were marked in what scholars today refer to as the Long Count Calendar. The approaching end of each 52-year cycle caused great consternation in Mayan circles, for it was never known if the gods would permit the renewal of another cycle. The present Long Count cycle will conclude on December 21, 2012. We'll see what happens.

¢–$$ ✕**El Tucán.** Toucans and parrots, part of the menagerie belonging to the owner, share the breezy terrace with diners. The small dining room, decorated with highland weavings, also has good views of one of Flores's cobblestone streets. The menu includes a variety of traditional meals, though Mexican cuisine is the specialty here. The bread is baked on the premises. ⊠ *Cs. 15 de Septiembre and Centroamérica* ☎ *7867–5137* ▭ *AE, D, DC, MC, V* ☉ *Closed Sun.*

¢–$ ✕**Pizzeria Picasso.** If you find yourself returning to Pizzeria Picasso, it's because the brick-oven pizza is incomparably hot and delicious. The decor, featuring prints of various Picasso works is another draw. If you're not in the mood for pizza, there are a variety of pastas as well. Save room for cheesecake or tiramisu and a cup of steaming cappuccino. ✉ *C. Centroamérica* ☎ *7867–5137* ⊟ *AE, D, DC, MC, V* ⊘ *Closed Mon.*

¢–$ ✕ **Las Puertas.** On a quiet side street, Las Puertas was named for its six screened doors. It's a favorite hangout for locals and travelers alike. The friendly couple who run the place take great pride in serving only the freshest foods. Notable are the delicious sandwiches made with homemade bread and mozzarella cheese and the giant goblets of incredible iced coffee. In the afternoon you can relax with a fruit drink—the freshly made orangeades and lemonades go down very easily—as you play one of the many board games. Don't forget to stop back at night for a hearty dinner and live music. ✉ *C. Ctl. at Av. Santa Ana* ☎ *7867–5242* ⊟ *AE, D, DC, MC, V* ⊘ *Closed Sun.*

> ### LUCKY LINDY
>
> Famed aviator Charles Lindbergh flew to the Petén in late December 1927 as part of a goodwill tour of Mexico and Central America. He was fresh from being named *Time* magazine's first Man of the Year in recognition of his solo transatlantic flight on his plane, *The Spirit of St. Louis*, several months earlier. Later trips brought Lindbergh back to the Petén, where he played an instrumental role in early aerial mapping of the region.

$$$$ ✕⊡ **Ni'tun Ecolodge.** After hiking through the jungle, you'll love returning
Fodor'sChoice   to this charming cluster of cabins. The point is to disturb the envi-
★   ronment as little as possible, so the buildings are constructed of stone and wood left behind by farmers clearing land for fields. The common areas, including an enormous kitchen downstairs and an airy bar and reading room upstairs, are delightful. Multi-day packages are available. The owners also run Monkey Eco Tours, so you can choose from itineraries ranging from one-day trips to nearby villages to a seven-day journey to El Mirador. ✉ *2 km (1 mi) west of San Andrés* ☎ *5201–0759* ⊕ *www.nitun.com* ⤳ *4 cabins* ♿ *In-room: no a/c, no phone, no TV. In-hotel: restaurant, bar, no elevator, airport shuttle, parking (no fee)* ⊟ *AE, D, DC, MC, V* ⦿*BP.*

$ ⊡ **Hotel Petén.** An arabesque plunge pool graces the central courtyard of this lovely lodging. Taking a dip to escape the midday heat is a treat not to be missed. The rooms are simply furnished. Ask for one facing the lake, as the views are incredible. ✉ *Off C. 30 de Junio* ☎ *7926–0692* ⊕ *www.hotelesdepeten.com* ⤳ *20 rooms* ♿ *In-hotel: restaurant, bar, pool, laundry service, public Internet* ⊟ *AE, D, DC, MC, V* ⦿*BP.*

$ ✕⊡ **Hotel Sabana.** This small hotel offers simple rooms that open onto a terrace overlooking the pool. A sundeck has nice views of the lake. This is a good choice if you require a few creature comforts like air-conditioning and television. ✉ *C. Unión and Av. Libertad* ☎ *7926–1248* ⊕ *www.hotelsabana.com* ⤳ *28 rooms* ♿ *In-room: no phone. In-hotel: restaurant, bar, pool, no elevator* ⊟ *AE, D, DC, MC, V.*

$ ✕⊡ **Hotel Santana.** Sitting right on the water, this bright pink hotel is the
Fodor'sChoice   best lodging on the island. All the rooms open up onto wide balconies
★   with wicker chairs where you can enjoy the view. The sunny central courtyard surrounds a pleasant pool. ✉ *C. 30 de Junio* ☎ *7926–0262*

ONE-DAY PETÉN

After the market in the highlands' Chichicastenango, Guatemala's most popular excursion is Tikal. Tour operators around the country pack round-trip transportation and a visit into a day.

Tours begin with an early-morning flight from Guatemala City to the Aeropuerto Internacional Mundo Maya outside Santa Elena. From there it's a 65-km (39-mi) ride to Tikal, followed by a morning of sightseeing, lunch, and a bus ride to the airport for the late-afternoon flight back to the capital. People do this from even Antigua or Panajachel, adding that transit time onto either end of the day. The cost runs $250 to $300 per person.

If this is the amount of time you have to spend at Tikal, so be it. However, if you can spend at least an overnight up here, you can do the trip and the ruins much more leisurely.

⊕ *www.santanapeten.com* ⤸*32 rooms* ♨*In-room: safe. In-hotel: restaurant, bar, pool, no elevator, public Internet* ☰*AE, D, DC, MC, V.*

¢ ✕⊞**Hospedaje Doña Goya.** A rooftop terrace with hammocks swinging in the breeze is the best part of this budget lodging. If you prefer, grab a good book and sink into one of the comfortable lounge chairs. The hotel is clean and well run, which explains why it is so popular. Arrive early in the day to secure a room. ⊠*C. Unión* ☎*7926–3538* ⤸*6 rooms, 3 with bath, dormitory* ♨*In-room: no a/c, no phone, no TV. In-hotel: no elevator* ☰*No credit cards.*

NIGHTLIFE

The bar at the **Maya Princess** (⊠*Av. La Reforma and Av. 14 de Noviembre* ☎*7926–3797*) shows nightly movies on a big-screen TV.**Las Puertas** (⊠*C. Ctl. at Av. Santa Ana* ☎*7926–1061*) has live music many evenings.The artsy **La Luna** (⊠*C. 30 de Junio* ☎*7867–5443*) morphs into a pleasant café as the night goes on, and is a pleasant place to stop by for a drink or coffee.

OUTDOOR ACTIVITIES

BOATING Boat trips on Lake Petén Itzá can be arranged through most hotels in Flores or by haggling with boat owners who congregate behind the Hotel Santana. Tours often include a stop at Paraíso Escondido, a small mainland park northwest of Flores.

SANTA ELENA

½ km (¼ mi) south of Flores.

Tuk-tuks—the motorized three-wheeled Bajaj RE taxis manufactured in India have seen many places in Guatemala—ply the streets of Flores and Santa Elena. Five minutes and Q5 will get you between the two.

Although it lacks the charms of neighboring Flores, gritty Santa Elena is pretty much unavoidable. Most services that you'll need for your trip around El Petén, from currency exchange to travel planning, are usually offered here. There are also nicer hotels here than in Flores.

FLORES OR SANTA ELENA?

A classic question confronts you if you wish to lodge in the Petén's "metropolis": Should I stay in Flores or Santa Elena? Officially, the entire municipal entity is Flores, but colloquially, everyone distinguishes between Flores (the island) and Santa Elena (the mainland). Whichever town you choose, you're not far from the other.

The island of Flores sits a few hundred meters offshore in the Lago Petén Itzá, connected to the shore by a causeway. In a word, the place is sweet, with its hilly streets and narrow alleyways. It's on its way to achieving that place-to-hang-out cachet you find in Panajachel at Lake Atitlán, and makes a pleasant stop for a couple of days. Smaller hotels have set up shop here, as have some pretty good restaurants. Onshore Santa Elena resembles any other lowland Guatemalan town, and at first glance seems less attractive. But you'll find more upscale lodgings here, a few of them like mini-resorts.

WHERE TO STAY & EAT

$$$$ ×⊞ **Villa Maya.** You could lie in bed and count the birds flying by your window at these modern villas on beautiful Lago Petén Itzá. Some 50 species have been spotted in the region. If you're more interested in wildlife, ask an attendant where to find the troop of spider monkeys that roams the grounds and the adjacent rain forest. All the rooms, tastefully decorated with colorful weavings and mahogany accents, have terrific views. Vans shuttle you to and from Tikal. ⊠ *12 km (7 mi) east of Santa Elena* ☎ *5415–1592, 2334–1818 in Guatemala City* ⊠ *5514–0226, 2334–8134 in Guatemala City* ⊕ *www.villasdeguatemala.com* 🛏 *56 rooms* ⌂ *In-room: no phone, no TV. In-hotel: restaurant, bar, pool, bicycles, laundry service, public Internet, airport shuttle, parking (no fee)* ⊟ *AE, D, DC, MC, V.*

$$$ ×⊞ **Petén Espléndido.** You're not on Flores, but the views of that pretty island from your private balcony are the next best thing. The pool, surrounded by palm trees, is a great place to spend an afternoon sunbathing. Sit at one of the shaded tables on the terrace or in the attractive dining room and enjoy the *especial del día* (daily special). The hotel is popular among business travelers, who appreciate the fully equipped convention center. Families enjoy the paddleboats on the lake. ⊠ *C. 5, at foot of bridge leading to Flores* ☎ *7926–0880, 2360–8140 in Guatemala City* ⊠ *7926–0866, 2334–4651 in Guatemala City* ⊕ *www.petenesplendido.com* 🛏 *62 rooms* ⌂ *In-room: safe. In-hotel: 2 restaurants, room service, bar, pool, public Internet, public Wi-Fi, airport shuttle, parking (no fee)* ⊟ *AE, D, DC, MC, V* ⊺⊙⊺ *EP.*

$$ ⊞ **Hotel La Casona del Lago.** The style looks a tad out of place here (think Caribbean pastels), but no matter. Santa Elena's newest, spiffiest hotel sits on the lakeshore and has splendid views of Flores across the water, especially from the top-floor restaurant and bar. Rooms are bright and spacious, with large windows, tile floors, two double beds each and a desk, and are arranged around three sides of the pool. This place also tosses in amenities such as Wi-Fi, rarely seen in this part of the country. ⊠ *1 C.* ☎ *7952–8700, 2336–2841 in Guatemala City* ⊕ *www.hoteles-*

GUATEMALA & BELIZE

One of the hemisphere's longest-running territorial disputes involves Guatemala and its eastern neighbor, Belize. The disagreement has its roots a 1763 decision by Spain to grant British settlers the right to cut timber in what is now Belize. The British gradually encroached on the territory, establishing the colony of British Honduras in the 19th century. Guatemala maintains that it inherited Spain's claim to the territory upon its 1821 independence. However, Belize itself, a nation of 250,000 people, became independent in 1981.

A series of negotiations brought about Guatemalan recognition of Belizean independence and establishment of diplomatic relations in 1991. Gone are the BELICE ES GUATEMALA ("Belize is Guatemala") signs on the Guatemalan side of the border. Maps can be a different story, with Guatemala maintaining that borders have yet to be defined. Old publications clearly show Belize as just another political division of Guatemala. Newer maps often choose not to address the issue by showing Belize as a blank, unidentified region. Such is the case with the free map you'll get from the Inguat tourist office here. It clearly names Mexico, Honduras, and El Salvador, but for Belize, no name; just a FRONTERA NO DEFINIDA (border not defined) designation.

The disagreement need not concern you as a visitor. You'll breeze through immigration at the single land border post at Melchor de Mencos or via the air routes that link the Petén's Mundo Maya International Airport with Belize.

depeten.com ⤴33 rooms △In-hotel: restaurant, bar, pool, laundry service, public Internet, public Wi-Fi, parking (no fee) ≡AE, D, DC, MC, V ⏀EP.

$$ 🏨**Hotel del Patio-Tikàl.** Built in traditional Spanish style, this modern hotel is easily recognizable by its stone walls and barrel-tile roof. Rooms face a small patio with a trickling fountain. Ask for a room on the 1st floor, as these have much larger windows. The patio restaurant sits under big arches leading to a grassy courtyard, making it a much more pleasant place to relax than the musty bar. ⊠2 C. and 8 Av., Santa Elena ☎7926–1229 🖷7926–3030 ⊕www.caminoreal.com.gt ⤴21 rooms △In-room: no a/c. In-hotel: restaurant, bar, pool, gym, no elevator, laundry service, parking (no fee) ≡AE, D, DC, MC, V ⏀BP.

$ ✕🏨**Casa Elena Hotel.** An attractive lobby paneled with lots of dark wood welcomes you to this centrally located hotel. Just beyond the entrance is a restaurant that lets the breeze in through lace curtains. There's a wide range of dinner options, from fresh fish to grilled steak. The rooms lack the charm of others in the area, but they are clean and comfortable. There are no balconies—for a view, head to the meeting room on the top floor. The pool has a small waterslide that kids love. ⊠6 Av. ☎7926–2238 🖷7926–0097 ⊕www.casaelena.com ⤴28 rooms △In-hotel: restaurant, bar, pool, no elevator, laundry service, parking (no fee) ≡AE, D, DC, MC, V.

OUTDOOR ACTIVITIES

There are several caves in the hills behind Santa Elena with interesting stalactite and stalagmite formations and subterranean rivers. The easiest to visit is Aktun Kan, just south of town.

🕐 **Ixpanpajul Parque Natural** (✉ *Km 468, Ruta a Santa Elena* ☎ *2336–0576* 🌐 *www.ixpanpajul.com* 💲 *Q200*) is a private nature reserve sitting on a large stand of primary rain forest. Hiking the suspended bridges of the skyway will give you a bird's-eye view of the indigenous flora and fauna that make the rain forest the most biodiverse ecosystem on the planet. You'll also get a Tarzan-eye view at the park's canopy tour, a series of zip-line cables that you navigate via a secure harness, but think of it more as an amusement-park ride, rather than an up-close view of nature. The park also offers myriad adventure opportunities from nighttime ATV tours to horseback rides to mountain-bike excursions. The entrance to the reserve is 10 km (6mi) south of Santa Elena.

EL REMATE

30 km (18½ mi) northeast of Flores.

El Remate is about an hour away from Tikal.

A mellow little town on the eastern shore of Lago Petén Itzá, El Remate is known mostly for its wood carvings, made by families that have dedicated themselves to this craft for generations. Because it's less than one hour from both Tikal and Yaxhá, El Remate makes a good base for exploring the area.

With more than 1,500 acres of rain forest, **Biotopo Cerro Cahuí** is one of the most accessible wildlife reserves in El Petén. It protects a portion of a mountain that extends to the eastern edge of Lago Petén Itzá, so there are plenty of opportunities for hiking. Two well-maintained trails put you in proximity of birds like oscillated turkeys, toucans, and parrots. As for mammals, look up to spot the long-armed spider monkeys or down to see squat rodents called *tepezcuintles*. Tzu'unte, a 6-km (4-mi) trail, leads to two lookouts with views of nearby lakes. The upper lookout, Mirador Moreletii, is known by locals as Crocodile Hill because, from the other side of the lake, it looks like the eye of a half-submerged crocodile. Los Ujuxtes, a 5-km (3-mi) trail, offers a panoramic view of three lakes. Both hikes begin at a ranger station, where English-speaking guides are sporadically available. ■ TIP→ **Do go with a guide in any case; there are occasional tales of visitors getting robbed.** ✉ *West of El Remate* 💲 *Q20* 🕐 *Daily 7:30–4.*

WHERE TO STAY & EAT

¢–$ ✕ **La Estancia Cafetería.** Owner Victor Morales's specialty is an exquisite whitefish served with vegetables sautéed in butter on a wooden platter. Every once in a while he cooks up some fresh venison. Even though the driveway is usually filled with cars, this eatery is easy to miss—look for the orange crush sign. ✉ *2 km (1¼ mi) south of El Remate* ☎ *No phone* 🚫 *No credit cards.*

CHEWING GUM

October through February marks the busy *chicle* season in the forests of the Petén in an industry that supports about 2,500 families here. The latex-like substance that has historically been used in chewing gum—the brand Chiclets takes its name from the substance—is extracted from the tropical evergreen chicozapote tree (*Manikara zapota*). Harvesters known as *chicleros* make zigzag cuts in the tree trunks. They collect the sap in bags and then boil it, just as their Mayan ancestors did centuries ago to make their own precursor to chewing gum.

At one time, the Wrigley Company of Chicago imported almost all of Guatemala's chicle for use in its gum. Economics and tastes have changed that fact, and since the 1970s, U.S. companies have mostly replaced chicle with oil-based polymers. These days, nearly all of Guatemala's product goes to Japan and Italy—markets that prefer natural chicle in their chewing gums. Numbers are down from the Wrigley heyday, but about 500-metric tons (1.1-million pounds) of chicle is collected each year and pumps $2 million into the region's economy.

$$$$ ╳⊞ **Camino Real Tikal.** To experience the natural beauty of the jungles surrounding Lago Petén Itzá without sacrificing creature comforts, many people head to Camino Real Tikal. It's possible to spend several days at the hotel without exhausting the possibilities—kayaking on the lake, hiking in a private reserve, swimming in the pool, lounging in the lakeside hammocks, and experiencing a traditional Mayan sauna. A dozen thatch-roof villas set high on the hillside hold the rooms, all of which have porches with views of the sparkling lake. ⊠*5 km (3 mi) west of El Remate* ☎*7926–0204, 2337–4402 in Guatemala City* ☎*7926–0222, 2368–3741 in Guatemala City* ⊕*www.camino-realtikal.com.gt* ⌦*72 rooms* ♿*In-room: safe, refrigerator. In-hotel: 2 restaurants, bar, pool, gym, beachfront, bicycles, no elevator, airport shuttle, parking (no fee)* ☰*AE, DC, MC, V* ⌶◉⌶*BP.*

$$$$ ⊞ **La Lancha.** Here's the third of film director Francis Ford Coppola's
Fodor's Choice   hotel forays into Central America (Blancaneaux Lodge and Turtle Inn
★   in Belize are the others) and it's another winner. Rooms are arranged as duplex units that scatter down the hill toward the lake. Both rooms per unit share a deck divided by a curtain. Higher units have gorgeous lake views and are more spacious, with marble-and-tile bathrooms, and a mix of Balinese and Guatemalan furnishings. Heading down the hill—and the paths do seem steep if you're making the trek up and down a few times a day—are the rain-forest-view rooms, slightly more snug, but cozy nevertheless, with similar, if a bit less, furniture. The restaurant prides itself on serving 100% Guatemalan cuisine; it's technically open to the public, but since hotel guests always get priority, call ahead if you're not staying here. ⊠*Jobompiche, 15 km (9 mi) west of El Remate* ☎*7928–8331, 800/746–3743 in North America* ⊕*www.lalancha.com* ⌦*10 rooms* ♿*In-room: no a/c, no phone, no TV. In-hotel: restaurant, bar, pool, beachfront, parking (no fee)* ☰*AE, D, DC, MC, V* ⌶◉⌶*CB.*

7

$$$ ✕⊞**La Mansión del Pájaro Serpiente.**
Perched high on a small hillside on the main road heading into El Remate, La Mansión del Pájaro Serpiente has some of the prettiest accommodations in El Petén. Canopy beds grace the bedrooms, which are furnished in dark tropical woods and have big windows that let in lots of light. You can throw open the windows to catch the lake breezes, so sleeping is comfortable. Up a nearby hill. is a swimming pool, and farther up you'll find a covered terrace with several hammocks. The open-air restaurant serves local and international dishes. ⊠ *On main hwy south of El Remate* ☎ *7928–8498* ✐ *tikalnancy@hotmail.com* ⤶ *10 rooms* ⌂ *In-room: no a/c, no phone, no TV. In-hotel: restaurant, pool, no elevator, parking (no fee)* ▭ *No credit cards.*

ON SET AT TIKAL
The *Star Wars* films used footage from some pretty far-flung locations—Guatemala among them. Remember the secret rebel base on Yavin IV that the Death Star was thwarted in destroying at the end of *A New Hope*? Forested Tikal served as the exterior. Tikal also appeared in the 1979 James Bond film *Moonraker.* In true rakish Bond style, Roger Moore cavorted with voluptuous women outside the pyramids.

$–$$ ✕⊞**La Casa de Don David.** Owner David Kuhn was the original *Gringo Perdido* ("lost gringo"), who gave his name to the nearby lodging over 25 years ago. About a decade ago, Kuhn set up shop at this cluster of bungalows, and is a great source of travel tips. Rooms are simple and clean, with private baths. The hotel is perhaps most famous for its second-story restaurant, which has good home cooking. Have dinner for two in a booth, or eat at the "friendship table" and make some new acquaintances. ⊠ *On road to Biotopo Cerro Cahuí* ☎ *5306–2190 or 7928–8469* ⊕ *www.lacasadedondavid.com* ⤶ *15 rooms* ⌂ *In-room: no a/c (some), no phone, no TV. In-hotel: restaurant, beachfront, no elevator, laundry service, public Internet, parking (no fee)* ▭ *MC, V accepted for Internet reservations* ⍟ *All meals included.*

$ ⊞**Gringo Perdido.** One of the Petén's oldest lodgings sits on the shore of Lago Petén Itzá and offers simply furnished, and quite affordable accommodation. Though there's no air-conditioning here, ceiling fans and the lush, forested grounds keep things cool. ⊠ *3 km (2 mi) west of El Remate* ☎ *5404–6822* ⊕ *www.hotelgringoperdido.com* ⤶ *15 rooms, 11 with bath* ⌂ *In-room: no a/c, no phone, no TV. In-hotel: restaurant, bar, beachfront, parking (no fee)* ▭ *MC, V* ⍟ *EP.*

SHOPPING

Although most souvenirs here are similar to those found elsewhere in Guatemala, the beautiful wood carvings are unique to El Petén. More than 70 families in this small town dedicate themselves to this craft. Their wares are on display on the side of the highway right before the turnoff for the Camino Real hotel on the road to Tikal.

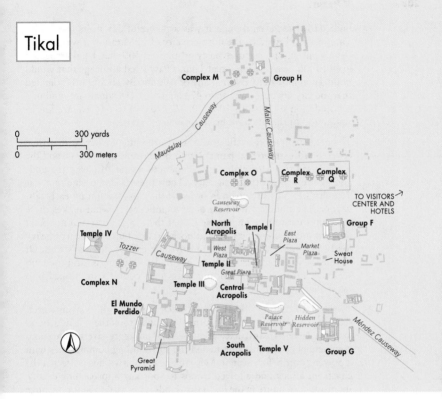

Tikal

TIKÀL

35 km (22 mi) north of El Remate, 68 km (42 mi) northeast of Flores.

A good, well-patrolled highway connects the two, passing through the town of El Remate at about its halfway point

Fodor'sChoice
★
⚠

The high point of any trip to Guatemala is a visit to Central America's most impressive ruins. Tikal is one of the most popular tourist attractions in Central America—and with good reason. Smack in the middle of the 575-square-km (222-square-mi) Parque Nacional Tikal, the towering temples are ringed on all sides by miles of virgin forest. The area around the ruins is great for checking out creatures that spend their entire lives hundreds of feet above the forest floor in the dense canopy of trees. Colorful birds like yellow toucans and scarlet macaws are common sights.

Although the region was home to Mayan communities as early as 600 BC, Tikal itself wasn't established until sometime around 200 BC. One of the first structures to be built here was a version of the North Acropolis. Others were added at a dizzying pace for the next three centuries. By AD 100 impressive structures like the Great Plaza had already been built. However, even though it was a powerful city in its own right, Tikal was still ruled by the northern city of El Mirador. It wasn't until the arrival of a powerful dynasty around AD 300 that Tikal arrogated itself to full power. King Great Jaguar Paw sired a lineage that would build Tikal into a city rivaling any of its time. By AD 500 it's estimated that the city covered more than 47 square km (18 square mi) and had a population of close to 100,000. (Approximately 16 square km [6 square mi] of the site have been excavated to date.)

The great temples that still tower above the jungle were at that time covered with stucco and painted with bright reds and greens, and the priests used them for elaborate ceremonies meant to please the gods and assure prosperity for the city. (Their present-day designations as Temples I to VI were given in order of their excavation by early surveyors. The numbers hold no other significance.) What makes these structures even more impressive is that the Maya possessed no metal tools to aid in construction, had no beasts of burden to carry heavy loads, and never used wheels for anything except children's toys. Of course, as a hierarchical culture they had a slave class, and the land was rich in obsidian, a volcanic glass that could be fashioned into razor-sharp tools.

By the sixth century Tikal governed a large part of the Mayan world, thanks to leader Caan Chac (Stormy Sky), who took the throne around AD 426. Under Caan Chac, Tikal became an aggressive military and commercial center that dominated the surrounding communities with a power never before seen in Mesoamerica. The swamps protected the city from attack and allowed troops to spot any approaching enemy. Intensive agriculture in the *bajos* (lowlands) provided food for the huge population. A valuable obsidian trade sprang up, aided by the city's strategic position near two rivers.

Tikal thrived for more than a millennium, forming strong ties with two powerful centers: Kaminaljuyú, in what is now Guatemala City, and Teotihuacán, on the site of present-day Mexico City. Some evidence exists of a hiatus in the seventh century, a term used by anthropologists to denote a stalling of development. Date inscriptions indicate no new construction for about a century, a phenomenon historians now attribute to the temporary conquering of Tikal by the Caracol people in what is now Belize. The city reentered a golden age when Ah-Cacao (Lord Chocolate) ascended the throne in AD 682. It was Ah-Cacao and his successors who commissioned the construction of most of the city's most important temples. Continuing the tradition of great structures, Ah-Cacao's son commissioned Temple I, which he dedicated to his father, who is buried beneath it. He also ordered the construction of Temple IV, the tallest temple at Tikal. By the time of Ah-Cacao's death in 768, Tikal was at the peak of its power. It would remain so until its mysterious abandonment around AD 900.

For almost 1,000 years Tikal remained engulfed by the jungle. The conquistadors who came here searching for gold and silver must have passed right by the overgrown ruins, mistaking them for rocky hills.

Local Peténeros certainly knew of the ancient city's existence, but no one else ventured near until 1848, when the Guatemalan government dispatched archaeologists to the region. Tikal began to receive international attention in 1877, when Dr. Gustav Bernoulli commissioned locals to remove the carved wooden lintels from across the doorways of Temples I and IV. These items were sent to a museum in Basel, Switzerland.

In 1881 and 1882 English archaeologist Alfred Percival Maudslay made the first map showing the architectural features of this vast city. As he began to unearth the major temples, he recorded his work in dramatic photographs—you can see copies in the museum at Tikal. His work was continued by Teobert Maler, who came in 1895 and 1904. Both Maler and Maudslay have causeways named in their honor. In 1951 the Guatemalan air force cleared an airstrip near the ruins to improve access for large-scale archaeological work. Today, after more than 150 years of digging, researchers say that Tikal includes some 3,000 buildings. Countless more are still covered by the jungle.

> **FADED COLOR**
>
> Mayan structures around Meso-america were not always the faded gray you see today. In ancient times El Petén's vibrant cities sported building facades covered in stucco painted vivid shades of red and green. If you wonder what a temple might have looked like, head to the ruins of Copán in Honduras. There you can see the remains of the Rosalila Temple, then head to the nearby museum to see a re-creation of that structure.

✉ *Parque Nacional Tikal* ☎ *No phone* 💲 *Q50* ☉ *Daily 6–6.*

EXPLORING

Doing justice to a complete tour of Tikal means a walk of about 10 km (6 mi), which, realistically, can take a full day or more. Most organized tours of the site last about four hours and take place during the cooler morning hours. If you have the time, two successive mornings are ideal, with hot afternoons spent visiting the site's museums or relaxing back at your hotel.

TIPS

Tikal adheres fairly strictly to its 6 AM to 6 PM opening hours, and visitors are no longer allowed inside the ruins outside those times. We do hear tales of tourists sneaking in or slipping guards bribes to pass, but we advise against that. The trails are not lit and climbing the pyramids entails a certain risk during daylight hours, let alone in the dark. There's also a slight menace of robbery. ■ TIP→ **If you stay at one of the three lodgings on the grounds, you get a jump-start on the day-tour visitors. You also have the advantage of being here late in the afternoon, after everyone else has left.** If you purchase your entrance ticket after 3 PM, you can use the same ticket for your next day's entry.

TOURING

To take in the highlights, and keep things to the standard half-day tour-group itinerary, follow the itinerary set out below:

As you enter from the visitor's center complex, keep to the middle trail. You'll soon arrive at the ancient city's center, filled with awe-inspiring temples and intricate acropolises. Tikal's six Roman numeral–denoted step pyramids, usually referred to as the "Great Temples," each contain a one- to three-room temple sitting on the top platform. A lintel (a carved wooden sculpture) stands guard over the entrance to four of the temples (those over Temples I and IV have been removed).

The pyramid that you approach from behind is Tikal's most famous structure, the 44-meter (145-foot) **Temple I**, known as the Temple of the Great Jaguar because of the feline represented on one of its carved lintels. It's in what is referred to as the **Great Plaza**, which is one of the most beautiful and dramatic in Tikal, primarily due to its high elevation. The Great Plaza was built around AD 700 by Ah-Cacao, one of the wealthiest rulers of his time. His tomb, comparable in magnitude to that of Pa Cal at the ruins of Palenque in southern Mexico, was discovered beneath the Temple of the Great Jaguar in the 1960s. The theory is that his queen, Lady Twelve Macaw, who died at a young age, is buried beneath **Temple II**, called the Temple of the Masks for the decorations on its facade. Tradition holds that Ah-Cacao wished to gaze at his wife from his tomb for eternity. Temple II lies just to the west of Temple I, and is its twin, but a few feet shorter. Construction of matching pyramids distinguishes Tikal from other Mayan sites. Visitors are no longer permitted to climb Temple I, a measure implemented to prevent continual wear and tear on the surface. Temple II may still be climbed.

The **North Acropolis,** to the west of Ah-Cacao's temple, is a mind-boggling conglomeration of temples built over layers and layers of previous construction. Excavations have revealed that the base of this structure is more than 2,000 years old. Be sure to see the stone mask of the rain god at Temple 33. The **Central Acropolis,** south of the Great Plaza, is an immense series of structures assumed to have served as administrative centers.

If you climb to the top of one of the pyramids, you'll see the gray roof combs of others rising above the rain forest's canopy but still trapped within it. **Temple V,** to the south, underwent a $3-million-restoration project and is now open to the public. **Temple IV,** to the west, is the tallest-known structure built by the Maya, clocking in at 64 meters (212 feet). It is frequently referred to as the Temple of the Two-headed Serpent. Although the climb to the top is difficult—you make the ascent via a series of wooden ladders—the view is unforgettable.

To the southwest of Temple V and the plaza lies the **South Acropolis,** which hasn't been reconstructed, and a 32-meter (105-foot) pyramid, similar in construction to those at central Mexico's Teotihuacán, and comparable in size to the north and central acropolises here at Tikal. A few jungle trails, including the marked Interpretative Benil-ha Trail, offer a chance to see spider monkeys and other wildlife. Outside the park, a somewhat overgrown trail halfway down the old airplane runway on the left leads to the remnants of old rubber-tappers' camps and is a good spot for bird-watching.

Just west of the South Acropolis is the so-called **Lost World** complex, with a radial pyramid, frequently called by the same name. The structures are assumed to have been built for astronomical observations, and the pyramid is Tikal's signature spot to watch the sun set. Explorers in the 1950s gave the collection of structures the name of an Arthur Conan Doyle novel, and even in Spanish, the name (*Mundo Perdido*) is commonly used.

Immediately north of the Lost World, and directly west of Temple II, sits **Temple III**, whose lintel depicts a head on a plate. Nearby is the so-called **Palace of Windows,** which is colloquially referred to as the Palace of the Bats, a name given in recognition of its one-time bat colonies.

Beyond "central" Tikal, lie several less-visited sites. If you have time left over after a thorough exploration of the sights above, these are worth a visit. Rather than head down the middle trail when you enter from park headquarters, bear right to head to a series of letter-named complexes, most of which have undergone minimal excavation. Two pyramids grace each of **Complexes Q and R.** Their purposes have not yet been determined. A collection of stelae populate **Complex P,** the most northerly point in Tikal. Beyond the Great Plaza, southwest, you come to **Temple VI,** the last excavated of the six great temples here, and frequently referred to as the Temple of the Inscriptions, because of its extensive use of hieroglyphics. Temple VI is far enough off the beaten path that your opportunities for spotting wildlife, especially spider monkeys, will be good. However, "off the beaten path" has also translated into occasional robbery, so only go with a guide.

A series of causeways, named for Tikal's early re-discoverers, connects the various complexes: Maler (visitor's center to Complex P); Maudslay (Complex P to Temple IV); Tozzer (Temple IV to Great Plaza); and Méndez (Great Plaza to Temple VI). The well-trodden path from the visitor's center to the Great Plaza is unnamed.

Also falling into the only-if-you-have-extra-time category are two archaeological museums that display Mayan artifacts. These are at park headquarters and are a good resource for information on the enigmatic rise and fall of the Mayan people. The so-called Tikal Museum, officially the **Museo Sylvanus Morley,** contains a small collection of pottery. It's between the Jungle Lodge and Jaguar Inn. The larger **Stelae Museum** is in the modern visitor's center building and contains a collection of stelae taken from around Tikal. They are open daily from 9 to 5, and a Q10 ticket admits you to both museums.

WHERE TO STAY & EAT

$$–$$$$ ✕⊞ **Tikal Inn.** This cluster of comfortable bungalows wraps around a well-manicured garden and a pool. It's set apart from the other lodgings, affording a bit of privacy. The rooms have a modern look, yet they have thatch roofs and stucco walls decorated with traditional fabrics. A small restaurant has a menu that changes daily. Hot water and electricity are on for only a few hours in the morning and evening. ⊠*Parque Nacional Tikal* ☎*7926–1917 or 7926–0065* ✐*hoteltikalinn@itelgua.com* ↩*18 rooms, 18 bungalows* ⌂*In-room: no a/c, no phone, no TV. In-hotel: restaurant, pool, parking (no fee)* ⊟*AE, D, DC, MC, V* ⚍◎*MP.*

> ### WATCH FOR THE ANIMALS!
>
> Obey Tikal's 45 kph (27 mph) speed limit; it's designed to give you time to stop for animals that cross the road within the confines of the park. Be particularly careful of the raccoon-like animal locals call a *pizote*, which scurries with abandon across the road. At the park entrance, a guard gives you a time-stamped ticket to be collected by another guard when you arrive at the visitor center. If you cover the 15-km (9-mi) distance in less than 20 minutes, you'll be deemed to have been speeding and possibly fined.

$–$$$$ ⊞ **Jungle Lodge.** Originally built to house archaeologists working at Tikal, the Jungle Lodge is the largest and nicest of the lodgings on the grounds. If your budget is flush, opt for one of the spacious bungalows with double beds, tile floors, and ceiling fans, or the new suites, each with hot tub and private patio. The oldest rooms are cute duplexes, with a noticeable lack of privacy—the dividing wall between the rooms does not meet the ceiling—clean, though the furnishings are dated. ⊠*Parque Nacional Tikal* ☎*2477–0570 in Guatemala City* ⊕*www.junglelodge.guate.com* ↩*12 rooms, none with bath, 2 suites, 34 bungalows* ⌂*In-room: no a/c, no phone, no TV. In-hotel: restaurant, bar, pool, public Internet, parking (no fee)* ⊟*V* ⚍◎*MP.*

$$ ⊞ **Jaguar Inn.** The most basic of the lodgings at the visitor's center complex nevertheless offers bright and spacious, if simply furnished, rooms. All come with two beds and a small porch with a hammock. The electricity here goes off at 11 PM and again for a few hours at midday. ⊠*Parque Nacional Tikal* ☎*7926–0002* ⊕*www.jaguartikal.com* ↩*13 rooms* ⌂*In-room: no a/c, no phone, no TV. In-hotel: no elevator, public Internet, parking (no fee)* ⊟*AE, D, DC, MC, V* ⚍◎*EP.*

MONUMENTO NATURAL YAXHÁ-NAKÚM-NARANJO

Southwest of Tikal.

Southwest of Tikal lies a 1,200-square-km (430-square-mi) complex of three ruins from the Late Classic period. Yaxhá is the most easily visited of these, with Nakúm and Naranjo realistically accessible only during the dry season. All three are part of the Proyecto Triángulo (Triangle Project), an ongoing German-led excavation funded by Deutsche Bank. All three ruins have suffered looting throughout their histories. Naranjo has endured the worst problems.

Overlooking a beautiful lake of the same name, the ruins of **Yaxhá** are divided into two sections of rectangular structures that form plazas and streets. Although this is the best excavated of the three complexes here, that's all relative, and the labors at Yaxhá remain a work in progress. ■TIP→ A guide is a good idea here, since it is not obvious what the structures are. Here's what is known: the city was probably inhabited between the Preclassic and Classic periods, and at its peak contained 20,000 people. It was also an important ally of nearby Tikal. Only a portion of the estimated 500 structures are visible at present, the most famous of which is designated Templo 216, Yaxhá's highest edifice with splendid views of the adjoining lake and rain forest.

Lake Yaxhá—the name, pronounced *Yah-SHAH*, translates as "green waters"—surrounded by virgin rain forest, is a good bird-watching spot. In the middle of the lake sit the ruins of **Isla Topoxté**, a fortress dating from the Postclassic period about AD 1000, and the site of one of the last strongholds against Spanish invaders. Ask the staff here about transportation. Someone can take you if you pay for the boat's gas. (Crocodiles inhabit the lake. Beware.)

✉48 km (29 mi) east of Flores, 30 km (19 mi) southeast of Tikal ☎Q10 ⌚Daily 6–6.

The ceremonial center of **Nakúm** lies deep within the forest, connected to Tikal via jungle trails that are sometimes used for horseback expeditions. You can't visit during the rainy season, as you'll sink into mud up to your ankles. Even during the dry season, a four-wheel-drive vehicle with high clearance is a good idea. Explorer Alfred Tozzer rediscovered Nakúm in 1909, and began to assign certain structures descriptive names, some of which may not be accurate. Two building complexes, designated "North" and "South," and separated by a causeway, are visible. The south side has more excavated structures, including a 44-room "palace" (to use Tozzer's old terminology). ✉26 km (16 mi) east of Tikal ☎Q10 ⌚Daily 6–6.

WHERE TO STAY

$ ⬚**El Sombrero Campamento Ecológico.** This cluster of wooden cabins is a restful place to spend the night. There's only three hours of electricity a day, but the lakefront views and ample opportunities for bird-watching more than make up for it. The friendly Italian owner Gabriella Moretti goes out of her way to arrange trips for her guests. There are rooms with shared bathrooms for very reasonable rates. ✉Yaxká ☎7861–1687 or 7861–1688 ⊕www.ecosombrero.com 🛏6 rooms, 7 without bath ♨In-room: no a/c, no TV. In-hotel: restaurant, bar, parking (no fee) ▭No credit cards.

UAXACTÚN

35 km (22 mi) north of El Remate, 68 km (42 mi) northeast of Flores.

Uaxactún is surrounded by thick rain forest, so the trip can be difficult. The rock-and-dirt road is passable during the drier seasons and nearly impossible at other times without a four-wheel-drive vehicle.

DID YOU KNOW?

Explorer Sylvannus Morley redis-covered the ruins in 1916, and gave them their modern name, pronounced *Wah-shahk-TOON*, meaning "eight stones." Morley may also have been forming a pun on the name of Washington, D.C., the site of the Carnegie Institution, which funded his explorations.

The 4,000-year-old city of Uaxactún once rivaled Tikal's supremacy in the region. It was conquered by Tikal in the fourth century and lived in the shadow of that great city for centuries. Inscriptions show that Uaxactun existed longer than any other Mayan city, which may account for the wide variety of structures. Here, among the stelae and palaces, you'll find a Mayan astronomical observatory, thought to be the oldest in Mesoamerica. It is designated "Structure E-VII-B." From the observatory, the sun lines up precisely on the solstices and equinoxes.

As it's difficult to get here, you most likely won't have to fight the crowds as you do at neighboring Tikal, leaving you free to enjoy the quiet and mystic air of the ruins. You'll need to secure a permit to visit Uaxactún. The administration building in Tikal is on the road between the Jaguar Inn and the Jungle Lodge. Obtaining a permit is sometimes easier said than done, but with a little persistence and perhaps a small *mordida* (bribe), you should be able to get past the guards into the administration area where they grant the free permits. Sometimes police will ask to accompany you on the trip, which is helpful for two reasons: it prevents potential robberies and, most important, will give you an extra person to push if your vehicle gets stuck. The police may ask you for some money; a Q20 tip goes a long way toward making your trip smooth. ⊠ *24 km (16 mi) north of Tikal* 🚃 *Q10* 🕙 *Daily 6–6.*

EL ZOTZ

A popular ecotourism destination, El Zotz is where you'll find the remnants of a Mayan city. On a clear day you can see the tallest of the ruins at Tikal from these unexcavated ruins. The odd name, which means "the bat" in Q'eqchí, refers to a cave from which thousands of bats make a nightly exodus. Troops of hyperactive spider monkeys seem to have claimed this place for themselves, swinging through the treetops and scrambling after each other like children playing a game of tag. Unlike those in Tikal, however, these long-limbed creatures are not used to people and will shake branches and throw twigs and fruit to try to scare you away. During the rainy season the mosquitoes can be fierce, so bring your strongest repellent. ■ TIP➡ **Getting here is an arduous journey, best done with an organized excursion from Flores or Santa Elena. Trips are usually two days and one night.** ⊠ *24 km (15 mi) west of Tikal.*

SAYAXCHÉ & CEIBAL

61 km (38 mi) southwest of Flores.

Though Ceibal can be reached via a dirt road that floods during the rainy season, it's best accessed by boat on the Río de la Pasión, followed by a half-hour ascent through the forest.

Down a newly paved road from Flores, this muddy frontier town on the southern bank of the Río de La Pasión is a good base for exploring the southern reaches of El Petén. This is river country, and the La Pasión and Petexbatún rivers lead to a number of important yet largely unvisited ruins in various stages of excavation.

Upriver from Sayaxché are the impressive ruins of **Ceibal,** frequently rendered "Seibal" in English. The site takes its name from the many canopylike ceiba trees in the area. Ceibal achieved prominence serving as a tollgate collecting tribute from barges plying the La Pasión river. Its archaeological attractions are several restored temples, including the only circular one known to exist. Here you will also find intricately carved stelae—31 in all—some of the best preserved in the region. Interestingly, a number of anomalies were found in these monuments, which hint at a foreign influence, most likely from the Toltecs of central Mexico. Carvings on structures here show dates corresponding to about AD 900, and are some of the latest among Mayan ruins in Mesoamerica. Ceibal is now thought to have undergone two distinct periods of growth, one in the Late Preclassic period and another in the Late Classic period, the two interrupted by a centuries of abandonment. The area is quite marshy, and rife with mosquitoes; lather up with insect repellent. ⊠ *On the Río de la Pasión* 🖃*Free* 🕓*Daily 6–6.*

WHERE TO STAY

$ ⬚ **Hotel Guayacán.** By the south bank of the Río de La Pasión, this place looks run-down but has clean, comfortable rooms on the 2nd floor. Some rooms even have air-conditioning, a real rarity in these parts. The owner can arrange boat trips to nearby Mayan ruins. ⊠*Sayaxché* 🖀*7928–6111* 📞*19 rooms* 🛏*In-room: no a/c (some), no phone, no TV. In-hotel: no elevator, parking (no fee)* 🖃*No credit cards.*

OUTDOOR ACTIVITIES

The lowland Río de la Pasión flows into the Usumacinta, which winds for countless miles through the rain forest. Both rivers were important Mayan trade routes and thus pass numerous archaeological sites. Local agencies book expeditions to the sites that can last from a day to more than a week. Along the way you can catch a glimpse of the area's many animal inhabitants, including turtles, crocodiles, and a vast array of birds.

A day trip to one of the ruins costs Q300 to Q500, depending on the number of passengers. The rate is not set in stone, so feel free to bargain. A reputable company in Sayaxché is **Viajes Don Pedro** (🖀*7928–6109*).

LAKE PETEXBATÚN

2 hrs by boat from Ceibal.

This impressive rain-forest lagoon was the seat of a 6th-century kingdom that extended south as far as the Verapaces and east to present-day Belize. It was ruled by a power-hungry prince whom historians designate simply as Ruler I. He is thought to have fled Tikal and engaged in battles for territory from two twin capitals, Dos Pilas and Aguateca.

A three-hour hike from Sayaxché brings you to **Dos Pilas.** Recent archaeological finds here indicate that continual warfare may have caused an ecological imbalance that led to the collapse of the Mayan civilization. Most spectacular of the ancient structures found here is a limestone staircase covered with carvings that recount the battles the upstart ruler waged against his brother at Tikal. Unlike most other Mayan cities, this one was surrounded by a defensive wall. ☒*Free* ⊙*Daily 6–6. .*

On the southern shore of the lake lies **Aguateca,** a small site by a 61-meter (200-foot) escarpment. It was likely the final capital after Dos Pilas was subsumed by Tikal. Few of the ruins have been excavated, but the trip here is a wonderful adventure. ☒*Free* ⊙*Daily 6–6.*

The fortress of **Punta de Chimino,** 4-km (2½-mi) north of Aguateca, was the last residence of the area's besieged royal family. The defenders dug several moats into the peninsula where the fort stood, turning it into an island.

WHERE TO STAY & EAT

$$$$ ✕🖭 **Chiminos Island Lodge.** Archaeologists speculate that Punta de Chimino was once the retreat of Mayan nobility. Beautiful cabins are scattered along the peninsula's edges, with private views of the lake and the jungle beyond, and will let you live almost like nobility, at least for these parts. Rooms have hardwood floors and screened walls that keep the jungle near and the insects at bay. Delicious meals using local ingredients are served in an open-air restaurant. Tours of nearby archaeological sites for both the hearty and the delicate are included. Transportation (a 1½-hour boat ride) is arranged from Sayaxché. ☒*Punta de Chimino* ☎*2471–0855 in Guatemala City* ⊕*www.chiminosisland. com* ⇆*6 bungalows* ⚑*In-room: no a/c, no phone, no TV. In-hotel: restaurant, pool* ▭*No credit cards* ¶⊙*All meals included.*

EL PETÉN ESSENTIALS

TRANSPORTATION

BY AIR

Taca and TAG operate flights from Guatemala City to Santa Elena that take less than an hour and cost $60 to $100 each way. Air service between Santa Elena and the Mexican resort of Cancún is offered by Taca. Tropic Air flies twice daily between Santa Elena and Belize City.

Aeropuerto Internacional Mundo Maya (FRS) is less than 1 km (½ mi) outside Santa Elena. Taxis and shuttles meet every plane and charge about Q20 to take you into town.

Contacts **Taca** (☎ *7926–1238, 2470–8222 in Guatemala City* ⊕ *www.taca.com*). **TAG** (☎ *2360–3038* ⊕ *www.tag.com.gt*). **Tropic Air** (☎ *7926–0348, 800/422-3435 in North America* ⊕ *www.tropicair.com*).

BY BUS

Linea Dorada offers direct bus service between Guatemala City and Santa Elena and Flores. The 10-hour trip on air-conditioned buses

> PROTECTING
> AGRICULTURE
>
> El Petén is one of Guatemala's two protected agricultural regions. (El Quiché in the highlands is the other.) Entering via land or air, you'll need to surrender any fresh fruit in your possession.

with comfortable reclining seats, TVs, and bathrooms costs $30 to $50 round-trip. Call at least one day ahead for reservations. Inexpensive local service is available, but those buses stop in every village along the way, which adds hours to the trip.

In Santa Elena the San Juan Hotel serves as the local bus terminal. Here you can catch a bus operated by San Juan Travel that makes the two-hour trip to Tikal at 6, 8, and 10 AM and return trips at 2, 4 and 5 PM. Local buses serving other destinations like Sayaxché depart from the market in Santa Elena. They are inexpensive but very slow.

Information **Linea Dorada** (✉ *C. Principal, Santa Elena* ☎ *7926–0528* ✉ *16 C. 10–03, Zona 1, Guatemala City* ☎ *2290–7990*).

BY CAR

Roads in El Petén are often in poor repair and not very well marked. Some roads are impassable during the rainy season, so check with the tourist office before heading out on seldom-traveled roads, such as those to the more-remote ruins surrounding Tikal. A four-wheel-drive vehicle is highly recommended.

To be on the safe side, never travel at night. If you come upon a fallen tree across the road, do not get out of your car to remove the debris. Robbers have been known to fell trees to get tourists to stop. Turn around as quickly as possible.

If you're not booked on a tour, the best way to get around El Petén is by renting a four-wheel-drive vehicle. Hertz has an office in the Santa Elena suburb of San Benito. Guatemalan agencies Koka and Tabarini have offices at Aeropuerto Internacional Mundo Maya.

Local Agencies **Hertz** (✉ *10 A C. 1–47, San Benito* ☎ *7950–0204*). **Koka** (✉ *Aeropuerto Internacional Mundo Maya* ☎ *7926–1233*). **Tabarini** (✉ *Aeropuerto Internacional Mundo Maya* ☎ *7926–0277*).

CONTACTS & RESOURCES

EMERGENCIES

El Petén's only hospital is in San Benito, a suburb of Santa Elena.

Emergency Services **Police** (☎ *7926–1365*). **Hospital Nacional** (✉ *San Benito* ☎ *7926–1333*). **Farmacia Nueva** (✉ *Av. Santa Ana, Flores* ☎ *7926–1387*).

MAIL & SHIPPING

The main post office in Flores is a half block east of the main square. In Santa Elena the post office is a block east of the bridge leading to Flores. Mail service is slow, so expect to get back home before your letter does.

Post Offices Flores (⊠ *C. 10 de Noviembre, Flores*). **Santa Elena** (⊠ *2 C. and 7 Av., Flores*).

MONEY MATTERS

There are several banks in Santa Elena, but none anywhere else in the region. Make sure to exchange your money before heading off on your jungle adventure. Some high-end hotels will exchange dollars for a small commission.

LANGUAGE SCHOOLS IN EL PETÉN

Though Spanish schools up here may promote themselves with images of you studying at Tikal, you're actually on the north shore of Lago Petén Itzá, and can combine your language study with optional excursions to visit area ruins—all in all, a nice deal.

Bio-Itzá Spanish School (⊠ *San José* ☎ *7928–8142* ⊕ *www.eco-bioitza.org*).

Eco-Escuela de Español (⊠ *1 San Andrés* ☎ *5940–1235*).

TOURS

Flores-based Martsam Travel, run by Lileana and Benedicto Grijalva, offers many different types of tours in the area. Guatemala City–based Adventuras Naturales and Flores-based Expedition Panamundo specialize in tours of the Mayan world and bird-watching expeditions. Guatemala City–based Maya Expeditions has trips down Sayaxché area rivers and the nearby archaeological sites. From Antigua, Inter Quetzal, and Sin Fronteras all offer tours of El Petén.

Contacts Adventuras Naturales (⊠ *9 C. 18–17, Zona 14, Guatemala City* ☎☎ *2333–6051 or 7832–3328* ⊕ *aventurasnaturales.tripod.com*). **Expedition Panamundo** (⊠ *2 C. and 4 Av., Zona 1, Santa Elena* ☎ *7926–0501, 2331–7588 in Guatemala City* ✐ *panamundo@guate.net*). **Inter Quetzal** (⊠ *7 Av. 1–20, Zona 4, Guatemala City* ☎ *2360–1422*). **Martsam Travel** (⊠ *C. Centroamérica and Av. 30 de Junio, Flores* ☎ *7926–0346* ⊕ *www.martsam.com*). **Maya Expeditions** (⊠ *15 C. 1–91, Zona 10, Guatemala City* ☎ *2363–4965* ⊕ *www.mayaexpeditions.com*). **Sin Fronteras** (⊠ *5 Av. Norte 15, Antigua* ☎ *7832–1226* ⊕ *www.sinfront.com*).

VISITOR INFORMATION

Arcas, which returns illegally captured animals to the wild, is a great resource on the flora and fauna of El Petén. The Centro de Información sobre la Naturaleza, Cultura, y Artesanía de Petén in the center of Flores is a wealth of information about the region's nature, history, and culture. Inguat has two offices in El Petén, one outside Santa Elena on the highway to Tikal, open daily 8 to 1 and 2 to 6, and one open for all arriving flights at Aeropuerto Internacional Mundo Maya.

Information Arcas (⊠ *10 km [6 mi] east of Santa Elena in San Benito* ⊕ *www. arcasguatemala.com*). **Centro de Información sobre la Naturaleza, Cultura, y Artesanía de Petén** (CINCAP) (⊠ *North side of Parque Ctl.* ☎ *7867–5209*). **Inguat** (⊠ *Km 8, Hwy to Tikal* ☎ *7926–0669* ⊠ *Aeropuerto Internacional Mundo Maya* ☎ *7926–0533*).

Mayan Sites

WORD OF MOUTH

"We had to walk a mile through a jungle trail to get to the [Tikal] ruins. The weather was perfect: 75°, cloudy. Wow, what a site! The courtyard area in the grand Plaza was surrounded by temples and Mayan housing. [We] saw spider monkeys, colorful birds, coatimundis, and finally, howler monkeys. The howlers were so loud. Just amazing how the Mayans built these magnificent temples in 600 AD without our modern ways."

—puckettt

By Lan Sluder   **VISITING CENTRAL AMERICA WITHOUT TOURING** any Mayan sites is like going to Greece and not seeing the Acropolis and the Parthenon. For at least five millennia, the Maya left their imprint on the region, and today some of the Mayan world's most awe-inspiring ruins are yours to explore. Even the most accessible sites aren't overrun with hordes of travelers—at some you may be the only visitor, other than perhaps a troop of howler monkeys or a flock of parrots. This chapter fills you in on the fascinating history of the Maya, exposes some of the secrets of their great architecture, suggests itineraries for visiting the most interesting sites, and provides tips for touring the ruins.

A MAYAN PRIMER

CHRONOLOGY

The **Preclassic** (circa 3,000 BC to AD 250) period is characterized by the influence of the Olmec, a civilization centered on the Gulf Coast of present-day Mexico. During this period, cities began to grow, especially in the southern highlands of Guatemala and in Belize, and it's at this time that Belize's Cuello, Lamanai, Santa Rita, Cahal Pech, Pacbitun, and Altun Ha sites were first settled.

By the **Late Preclassic** (circa 300 BC to AD 250) period, the Maya had developed an advanced mathematical system, an impressively precise calendar, and one of the world's five original writing systems.

During the **Classic** (circa 250 BC to AD 900) period, Mayan artistic, intellectual, and architectural achievements literally reached for the stars. Vast city-states were crisscrossed by a large number of paved roadways, some of which still exist today. The great cities of Caracol (Belize), Palenque (Mexico), Tikal (Guatemala), and Quirigu (Guatemala) were just a few of the powerful centers that controlled the Classic Mayan world. In AD 562, Caracol—which, at its height, was the largest city-state in Belize, with a population of about 150,000—conquered Tikal. Other notable Classic-period sites in Belize include Xunantunich, El Pilar, and Lubaantun.

The single largest unsolved mystery about the Maya is their rapid decline during the **Terminal Classic** (AD 800 to AD 900) period and the centuries following. Scholars have postulated that climate change, pandemic disease, drought, stresses in the social structure, overpopulation, deforestation, and changes in the trade routes could have been responsible. Rather than a single factor, several events taking place over time could well have been the cause.

The Maya of the **Postclassic** (AD 900 to early AD 1500s) period were heavily affected by growing powers in central Mexico. Architecture, ceramics, and carvings from this period show considerable outside influence. Although still dramatic, Postclassic cities such as Chichén Itzá and Uxmal pale in comparison to their Classic predecessors. By the time the Spanish conquest reached the Yucatán, the Maya were scattered, feuding, and easy to conquer.

KEY DATES

Here are some key dates in the history of the Maya in the El Petén area of Guatemala and in Belize. Most of the dates are approximate, and some are disputed.

BC

3114	Date of the creation of the world, or 0.0.0.0.0 according to the Long Count calendar
3000	Early Olmec and Mayan civilizations thought to have begun
2500	Cuello established
2000	Santa Rita established
1500	Lamanai established
1000	Cahal Pech established
900	Olmec writing system developed; Caracol established
800	Tikal established
700	First written Mayan language
500	First Mayan calendars carved in stone
250	Altun Ha established
200	First monumental buildings erected at Tikal and El Mirador

AD

400–600	Tikal becomes leading city-state, with population of perhaps 200,000
553	Accession of Lord Water as Caracol ruler
562	Caracol conquers Tikal
599	Accession of Lord Smoke Ahau as Caracol ruler
618	Accession of Kan II as Caracol ruler
631	Caracol defeats Naranjo; Caracol's population is 150,000
700	Lubaantun established
800	Cahal Pech abandoned
895	Xunantunich abandoned
899	Tikal abandoned
900	Classic period of Mayan history ends
900–1500	Maya civilization in decline, many cities abandoned
1000	Southern Belize Mayan centers mostly abandoned
1050	Caracol abandoned
1517	Spanish arrive in Yucatán and begin conquest of Maya
1517–1625	Diseases introduced from Europe cause death of majority of Maya
1524–25	Hernán Cortés passed through Belize en route to Honduras, after leading expeditions to conquer the Aztecs in Mexico
1546–1600S	Maya in Belize rebel against Spanish
1695	Tikal ruins rediscovered by Spanish
1700S	Lamanai continuously occupied over 3,000 years
1724	Spanish abolish *encomienda* system of forced Mayan labor
1847	Caste Wars in Yucatán begin
1881	Early archaeological work begins at Tikal, by Alfred Maudslay
1894	Thomas Gann begins exploring Xunantunich and other ruins
1936	Caracol ruins rediscovered by a lumberman

1956 William Coe and others begin excavations at Tikal
1992 Rigoberta Menchú, a Maya from Guatemala, wins Nobel Prize for Peace
2006 Mel Gibson's *Apocolypto,* set in a crumbling Mayan civilization, and with actors speaking Yucatec Maya, was filmed in Veracruz
2012 The end of the world, 13.0.0.0.0 in the Long Count calendar

HISTORY IN BRIEF

Anthropologists believe that humans from Asia crossed a land bridge, in what is now the Bering Strait in Alaska, into North America more than 25,000 years ago. Gradually these Paleoindians, or "Old Indians," whose ancestors probably were Mongoloid peoples, made their way down the continent, establishing Native American or First Nation settlements in what is now the United States and Canada. Groups of them are thought to have reached Mesoamerica, which includes much of central Mexico, Guatemala, Belize, Honduras, and Nicaragua, around 20,000 to 22,000 years ago.

These early peoples were hunter-gatherers. The Olmec civilization, considered the mother culture of later Mesoamerican civilizations including that of the Maya, arose in central and southern Mexico 3,000 to 4,000 years ago. The Olmecs developed the first writing system in the New World, dating from at least 900 BC. They also had sophisticated mathematics and created complex calendars. The Olmecs built irrigation systems to water their crops.

As long ago as around 3000 BC—the exact date is in question and has changed as archaeologists have made new discoveries—the Maya began to settle in small villages in the region. They developed an agriculture based on the cultivation of maize (corn), squash, and other fruits and vegetables. What would become the great city-states of the region, including Tikal in today's Petén region of Guatemala and Caracol in Cayo, was first settled around 900 to 700 BC.

Two or three centuries before the time of Christ, several Mayan villages grew into sizeable cities. The Maya began to construct large-scale stone buildings at Tikal and elsewhere. Eventually, Tikal, Caracol, and other urban centers each would have thousands of structures—palaces, temples, residences, monuments, ball courts, even prisons. Although the Maya never had the wheel, and thus no carts or wagons, they built paved streets and causeways, and they developed crop-irrigation systems.

At its height, in what is known as the Classic period (250 BC to AD 900), the Mayan civilization consisted of about 50 cities, much like ancient Greek city-states. Each had a population of 5,000 to 100,000 or more. Tikal, the premier city in the region, may have had 200,000 residents in and around the city during its heyday, and Caracol in Belize probably had nearly as many. The peak population of the Mayan civilization possibly reached 2 million or more.

The Mayan culture put a heavy emphasis on religion, which was based on a pantheon of nature gods, including those of the sun, moon, and rain. The Mayan view of life was cyclical, and Mayan religion was based on accommodating human life to the cycles of the universe.

Contrary to what scholars long believed, however, Mayan society had many aspects beyond religion. Politics, the arts, business, and trade were all important and dynamic aspects of Mayan life. Dynastic leaders waged brutal wars on rival city-states. Under its ruler Lord Smoke Ahau, Caracol, the largest city-state in Belize, conquered Tikal in AD 562, and less than a hundred years later, conquered another large city, Naranjo (also in Guatemala).

The Maya developed sophisticated mathematics. They understood the concept of zero and used a base-20-numbering system. Astronomy was the basis of a complex Mayan calendar system involving an accurately determined solar year (18 months of 20 days, plus a 5-day period), a sacred year of 260 days (13 cycles of 20 days), and a variety of longer cycles culminating in the Long Count, based on a zero date in 3114 BC, or 0.0.0.0.0—the date that the Maya believed was the beginning of the current cycle of the world.

The Mayan writing system is considered the most advanced of any developed in Mesoamerica. The Maya used more than 800 "glyphs," small pictures or signs, paired in columns that read from left to right and top to bottom. The glyphs represent syllables and, in some cases, entire words, that can be combined to form any word or concept. There is no Mayan alphabet. Mayan glyphs can represent either sounds or ideas, or both, making them difficult to accurately interpret. The unit of the writing system is the cartouche, a series of 3 to 50 glyphs, the equivalent of a word or sentence in a modern language.

As in most societies, it's likely that the large majority of the Maya spent much of their time simply trying to eke out a living. In each urban area the common people lived in simple thatch dwellings, similar to those seen in the region today. They practiced a slash-and-burn agriculture. Farmers cleared their small plots by burning the bush, then planting maize, squash, sunflowers, and other crops in the rich ash. After two or three years, when the soil was depleted, the plot was left fallow for several years before it could be planted again.

Beginning around AD 800, parts of the Mayan civilization began to decline. In most areas the decline didn't happen suddenly, but over decades and even centuries, and it took place at different times. For example, the cities in the Northern Lowlands of the Yucatán, such as Chichén Itzá, flourished for several more centuries after Tikal and Caracol were abandoned.

Scholars are still debating the reasons for the decline. Climatic change, lengthy droughts, overpopulation, depletion of arable land, social revolutions by the common people against the elites, epidemics, and the impact of extended periods of warfare all have been put forth as reasons. It may well have been a combination of factors, or there may have been different causes in different regions.

Whatever the reasons, the Mayan civilization never regained its Classic-period glory. By the time the Spanish arrived in the early 1500s, only a few of the Mayan cities, mainly in the Highlands of Guatemala, were still thriving. Most of the great cities and trading centers of Belize and Guatemala, including Caracol and Tikal, had long been abandoned. Lamanai and a few other urban settlements were still inhabited.

Seeking gold and other plunder, the Spanish began their conquest of the Maya in the 1520s. Some Mayan states offered fierce resistance, and the last Mayan kingdom, in Mexico, was not vanquished until almost 1700. The Maya in Belize rebelled against the Spanish several times, but there was one enemy against which the Maya were defenseless: European disease. Smallpox, chicken pox, measles, flu, and other infectious diseases swept through the Mayan settlements. Scientists believe that within a century, nearly 90% of the Maya had been wiped out by "imported" diseases. Mayan resistance to European control continued from time to time. In 1847 Mayan Indians in the Yucatán rose up against Europeans in the bloody Caste Wars, which lasted until 1904.

Much of the Mayan civilization was buried under the tropical jungles for centuries, and Westerners knew little about it. In the process of trying to convert the Maya to Christianity in the 16th century, the Spanish burned most of the codices, Mayan "books" made of deer hide or bleached fig-tree paper. Only in the last few decades have scholars made progress in deciphering Mayan glyphic writing.

In 1839 two British adventurers, John Lloyd Stephens and Frederick Catherwood, visited Central America, and explored a number of the Mayan sites. Their books, especially *Incidents of Travel in Central America, Chiapas, and Yucatán,* with text by Stephens and illustrations by Catherwood, brought the attention of the world to the Mayan past.

In the late 1800s the first systematic archaeological excavations of Tikal and Mayan sites in Belize were begun. Alfred Maudslay, an Englishman, conducted excavations at Tikal in 1881–82, and Harvard's Peabody Museum did fieldwork there between 1895 and 1904. Sylvanus Morley, a well-known Mayan expert conducted work at Tikal at times between 1914 and 1928. In 1956 the University of Pennsylvania began the first large-scale excavation project at Tikal. Since then, many university and museum teams have conducted extensive fieldwork.

The end of the world, or at least its current cycle, will take place on December 21, 2012, according to the Long Count calendar of the ancient Maya.

DOS & DON'TS FOR VISITING RUINS

Don't ever take any artifact from a Mayan site, not even a tiny pottery shard. The theft of Mayan antiquities is a serious crime. Luggage is often searched at the international airport, and if any Mayan artifacts are found, you could be in hot water.

Do climb the temples and enjoy the views from the top. At most sites, you're free to climb the ruins. The views from El Castillo at Xunantunich, from structures at Cerros of Chetumal Bay, and from Lubaantun to the sea, are among the most memorable. Be warned, though: most of the steps are very steep.

Do descend into Xilbalda. The Maya called the underworld Xilbalda. You can experience it by visiting one of the caves once used by the Maya. Actun Tunichil Muknal, The Cave of the Stone Sepulture, near Belmopan, is our favorite. Che Chem Ha near San Ignacio is another cave with many Mayan artifacts. Both require a guide. Private land, especially in Cayo and Toledo, often contains caves with Mayan artifacts.

Do look for wildlife at the ruins and en route. One of the best things about the ruins and their surroundings is that they're home to many birds and wild creatures. On the long drive to Caracol, for example, you'll pass through pine ridge and broadleaf jungle, and you may see brocket deer, oscellated turkey, and coatimundi. En route to Caracol, we once saw a small crocodile sunning at the bridge over the Macal River and, on another occasion, a fer-de-lance at DiSilva village. You're sure to see many beautiful butterflies. The trip up the New River to Lamanai is another good opportunity to see birds and wildlife on the riverbanks, and once you get to Lamanai, chances are good that you'll spot howler monkeys.

8

ARCHITECTURE

One look at the monumental architecture of the Maya, and you might feel transported to another world. The breathtaking structures are even more impressive when you consider that they were built 1,000 to 2,000 years ago or more, without iron tools, wheels, or pulleys. The following is a brief explanation of the architecture you see at a Mayan ruin.

INFLUENCES

Mayan architecture, even the great temples, may echo the design of the typical thatch hut ordinary Maya used for thousands of years. The rectangular huts had short walls made of a limestone mud and were topped by a steeply tilted two-sided thatch roof. Caves—everimportant Mayan ceremonial sites—were also influential. Many aboveground Mayan temples and other monumental structures have cavelike chambers, and the layout of Mayan cities probably reflected the Mayan cosmology, in which caves played a critical role.

BUILDING MATERIALS

With few exceptions, the large buildings in Mayan cities were constructed mostly from limestone, which was widely available in this area. Quarries were often established close to a building site so that workers didn't have to haul stone long distances. The Maya used limestone for mortar, stucco, and plaster. Limestone was crushed and burned in wood-fired kilns to make lime. A cementlike mortar was made by combining one part lime with one part of a white soil called *sahcab,* and then adding water.

The Maya also used wood, which was plentiful in Mesoamerica. In fact, some of the early temples were probably constructed of wood poles and thatch, much like the small houses of the Maya; unfortunately, these buildings are now lost.

TOOLS

The Maya were behind the curve with their tool technology. They didn't have iron tools, pulleys to move heavy weights, or wheels to build carts. They didn't have horses or other large animals to help them move materials. Instead, they used large numbers of laborers to tote and haul stones, mortar, and other building materials.

Obsidian, jade, flint, and other hard rocks were used to make axes, knives, and saws. The Maya had mason's kits to cut and finish limestone, and they had the equivalent of a plumb bob and other tools to align and level stones. The Maya were skilled stoneworkers, although the degree of finish varied from city to city.

CITY LAYOUT

In most Mayan cities, large plazas were surrounded by temples and large pyramids, probably used for religious ceremonies and other important public events. Paved causeways connected the plazas. Away from the city center were sprawls of "suburbs"—smaller stone buildings and traditional thatch huts. Most cities had ball courts, and although the exact rules are unclear, players used a ball of natural rubber (rubber was discovered by the Olmecs) and scored points by getting the ball through a hoop or goalpost. "Sudden death" had a special meaning—the leader of the losing team was sometimes killed by decapitation.

Adventure & Learning Vacations

WORD OF MOUTH

"Guatemala is amazing! We stayed at a lakeside resort and boated, trekked up an active volcano and saw red-hot lava a meter below our feet, stayed in a lodge and took a sunrise hike to Tikal, zip lined in the jungle "Tarzan style," and spent three nights on a catamaran."

—Smgapp

"Travel agencies all over Antigua sell trips ($6–$8) to Pacaya Volcano that leave at about 6 AM and return around 1 PM. The 1 hour and 15 minute drive could be in a van, a minibus, or a schoolbus. You also need to pay the Q40 ($6) park admission. Buy the walking stick for Q5—it's the best 75 cents you'll ever spend."

—Happy LC

By Nicholas
Gill

THIS CHAPTER IS MEANT TO help you find the best tour operators for your adventure vacation. In Guatemala you can experience Mayan culture in the jungle-covered ruins at Tikal; at Copán just across the border in Honduras; and at several sites in neighboring Belize. Antigua is known for language-study and volunteer-vacation opportunities. There are also volcanoes to explore; adventure sports to try; and endless wildlife to view. Many companies organize trips that will take you to more than one country.

PLANNING YOUR ADVENTURE

CHOOSING A TRIP

With hundreds of choices for special-interest trips to Guatemala, there are a number of factors to keep in mind when deciding which company and package will be right for you.

How strenuous do you want your trip to be? Adventure vacations are commonly split into "soft" and "hard" adventures. Hard adventures, such as strenuous treks (often at high altitudes) or Class IV or V rafting, generally require excellent physical conditioning and previous experience. Most hiking, biking, canoeing/kayaking, and similar soft adventures can be enjoyed by persons of all ages who are in good health and are accustomed to a reasonable amount of exercise. A little honesty goes a long way—recognize your own level of physical fitness and discuss it with the tour operator before signing on.

How far off the beaten path do you want to go? Depending on your tour operator and itinerary, you'll often have a choice between relatively easy travel and comfortable accommodations or more strenuous daily activities accompanied by overnights spent in basic lodgings or at campsites. Ask yourself if it's the *reality* or the *image* of roughing it that appeals to you. Be honest, and go with a company that can provide what you're looking for.

Is sensitivity to the environment important to you? If so, determine if it is equally important to your operator. Does the company protect the fragile environments you'll be visiting? Are some of the company's profits designated for conservation efforts or put back into the communities visited? Does it encourage indigenous people to dress up (or dress down) so that your group can get great photos, or does it respect their cultures as they are? Many of the companies included in this chapter are actively involved in environmental conservation and projects with indigenous communities. Their business' future depends on keeping this fragile ecological and cultural mix alive.

What sort of group is best for you? At its best, group travel offers curious, like-minded people companions with which to share the day's experiences. Do you enjoy mixing with people from other backgrounds, or would you prefer to travel with people of different ages and backgrounds? Inquire about group size; many companies have a maximum of 10 to 16 members, but 30 or more is not unknown. The larger the group, the more time spent (or wasted) at rest stops, meals, and hotel arrivals and departures.

If groups aren't your thing, most companies will customize a trip for you. In fact, this has become a major part of many tour operators' business. Your itinerary can be as flexible or as rigid as you choose. Such travel offers all the conveniences of a package tour, but the "group" is composed of only you and those you've chosen as travel companions. Responding to a renewed interest in multigenerational travel, many tour operators also offer family trips, with itineraries carefully crafted to appeal both to children and adults.

How much extra pretrip help do you want? Gorgeous photos and well-written tour descriptions go a long way toward selling a company's trips. Once you've chosen your trip, though, there's a lot of room for your operator to help you out, or leave you out in the cold. For example, does the operator provide useful information about health (suggested or required inoculations, tips for dealing with high altitudes)? A list of frequently asked questions and their answers? Recommended readings? Equipment needed for sports trips? Visa requirements? A list of client referrals? All of these things can make or break a trip, and you should know before you choose an operator whether or not you want their help getting answers to all these questions.

Are there hidden costs? Make sure you know what is and is not included in basic trip costs when comparing companies. International airfare is usually extra. Sometimes domestic flights in-country are too. Is trip insurance required, and if so, is it included? Are airport transfers included? Visa fees? Departure taxes? Gratuities? Although some travelers prefer the option of an excursion or free time, many, especially those visiting a destination for the first time, want to see as much as possible. Paying extra for a number of excursions can significantly increase the total cost of the trip. Many factors affect the price, and the trip that looks cheapest in the brochure could well turn out to be the most expensive. Don't assume that roughing it will save you money, as prices rise when limited access and a lack of essential supplies on-site require costly special arrangements.

MONEY MATTERS

Tours in Central America can be found at all price points, but local operators are usually the best deal. Tours that are run by as many local people and resources as possible are generally cheaper, and also give the greatest monetary benefit to the local economy. These types of tours are not always listed in guidebooks or on the Internet, so often they have to be found in person or by word of mouth. Safety and date specificity can fluctuate. Guides don't always speak English, and are not always certified. Amenities such as lodging and transportation may be very basic in this category. Some agencies pay attention to the environment, whereas others do not. You really have to do your research on every operator, no matter the cost, to be sure you get what you need. When you find the right match, the payoff in terms of price and quality of experience will be.

On the other end of the spectrum, the large (often international) tour agencies are generally the most expensive; however, they provide the greatest range of itinerary choices and highest quality of services. They use the best transportation, like private planes, buses, and boats, which rarely break down. First-rate equipment and safe, reliable guides are the norm. Dates and times are set in stone, so you can plan your trip down to the time you step in and out of the airport. Guides are usually English-speaking, certified, and well paid. When food and lodging is provided it is generally of high quality. If you are a traveler who likes to have every creature comfort provided for, look for tour operators more toward this end of the spectrum.

LODGING

Overnight stays can cost as much or as little as you want them to. Independent travelers tend to favor budget hotels and hostels costing little more than a few dollars a night, whereas luxurious five-star hotels geared to package tourists are becoming common. Your preference will help determine what type of tour operator is best for you.

Most multiday tours include lodging, often at a discounted rate, and they generally have options that accommodate most budgets through a number of hotels. On the other hand, many hotels have their own tour agency or will sell tours at a discounted rate to particular agencies. You can book through either one—it just depends on the specific tours and hotels that interest you. In many instances you don't have to book accommodation through your tour agency; however, you will often save money if you are combining services such as transportation, food, tours, and guides. If you are interested in specific hotels, such as beach resorts or ecolodges, in many cases your best tour options will be directly through these establishments. Considering the small size of most countries in Central America, almost any single sight in a country can be seen on a one-day tour, which allows you to leave your luggage at the hotel for less hassle.

WHAT TYPE OF TRIP

Adventure Tours. Adrenaline-pumping sports and thrills for the active traveler.

Beaches & Relaxation. Find a place to hang your hammock after a volcanic-mud bath.

Diving Trips. Central America's Caribbean coastline is one of the top diving destinations in the world.

Ecotourism. Spot a resplendent Quetzal while staying at a thatched jungle lodge in pristine cloud forests.

Cultural Tourism. Living and learning with a native culture.

Language Schools. Learn Spanish while staying with a local family.

Mayan Ruins. Trek to pyramids hidden by lush jungle and surrounded by the roar of Howler monkeys.

Volunteer Vacations. Get your hands dirty helping save the rain forest or protect the leatherback-turtle breeding grounds.

EQUIPMENT

Good gear is essential. Sturdy shoes, a small flashlight or headlamp, rain gear, mosquito protection, and medicine are all things you should bring with you no matter what kind of tour you're taking. For more technical sports, your choice of tour operator will determine whether you bring your own gear, buy new gear, or rent what they already have. The decision will probably be yours in most cases. Tour operators can generally provide equipment, but the quality of this equipment varies a great deal. If you're going to use equipment that will be provided, ask your operator for a written statement of the gear to be used.

When you arrive, check that your expectations have been met, and complain if they haven't. Many companies do use top-of-the-line equipment; however, the occasional company will cut corners. Prices on equipment purchased in Central America tend to be significantly more expensive (roughly 20 to 40% higher) than in North America or Europe. If you prefer or require a specific brand of equipment, bringing your own is a good idea. Airlines accommodate most types of equipment and will likely have packing suggestions if you call ahead. For instance, most bicycle shops can take apart and box up your bike for plane transport. Airlines may charge additional fees for surpassing size and weight limits. Shipping equipment to Central America tends to be expensive, and if you're not using an agency such as FedEx or DHL (actually, even if you are!) expect the unexpected.

ADVENTURE & LEARNING VACATIONS

ADVENTURE TOURS

If you're looking for a heart-thumping adrenaline rush, Central America has a lot to offer you. From biking down active volcanoes to rafting down raging Class IV rapids, every country here has an abundance of adventure tours. Wherever you go, you're never very far from a zip line through the rain forest or sport fishing for a 900-pound black marlin.

GUATEMALA
Season: Year-round
Locations: Antigua, Lake Atitlán, Río Dulce, Livingstone
Cost: From $395 for four days from Guatemala City
Tour Operators: Old Town Outfitters, Guatemala Ventures

If lava is what you seek, Old Town Outfitters will take you climbing to the best of Guatemala's 33 volcanoes on their 7-day tour. The highly active Pacaya and the dormant Agua volcanoes near Antigua are the first ascents, and the multiple night climbs of Acatenango and Fuego volcanoes make up the latter part of the trip. The climb to the top of Central America's highest peak, Tajamulco Volcano (4218 meters/13,840 feet), is an optional three-day addition. For something a bit cooler, try their four-day kayak trip down the Río Dulce, which ends on the Caribbean, at Guatemala's only Garifuna village. If you're interested in high-adrenaline sports, try Guatemala Adventures' Pacific coast to Atlantic coast tour, which combines hiking, biking, and rafting on an eight-day journey across Guatemala's most stunning landscapes. Exact destinations are tailored to meet your skill level.

ECOTOURISM

Ecotourism, a style of touring natural habitats to see flora and fauna while minimizing one's ecological impact, really began in the jungles of Costa Rica. It quickly spread across Central America and around the world. There are plenty of opportunities to spot wildlife or get in tune with nature in each of the Central American nations.

BELIZE

Season: Year-round
Locations: Tikal, San Ignacio, Cay Caulker, Cockscomb Jaguar Reserve
Cost: From $895 for 15 days from Belize City
Tour Operators: G.A.P. Adventures, Wildland Adventures

Many come to Belize for diving, but the inland jungle has unique opportunities for spotting diverse wildlife. More than 70% of the country is covered with forest. G.A.P. Adventures' Hummingbird Highway itinerary combines beaches, ruins, and jungle to bring you the best ecological experiences in Belize and Guatemala. First you visit the lush jungles surrounding Tikal, where you'll explore the ruins and hike through the forests. Back in Belize, you'll visit San Ignacio, then paddle the Belize River by canoe, ending with a snorkeling trip around Cay Caulker. Wildland Adventures offers similar combination tours.

GUATEMALA

Season: Year-round
Locations: Flores, Petexbatun Lake, Aguateca, Yaxhá, Tikal, Ixpanpanajul Natural Park
Cost: From $1,280 for eight days from Guatemala City
Tour Operators: Guatemala Ventures, Adventure Life, Old Town Outfitters, Abercrombie & Kent

The volcanic slopes, cloud forests, and lowland jungle regions of Guatemala are home to many rare-bird species such as quetzals, the mountain trogon, blue-throated green motmot, hairy woodpecker, hummingbirds, toucans, and macaws. Nineteen ecosystems in total can be found here, and they are home to not just birds, but more than 250 species of mammals and 200 species of reptiles and amphibians. Many are only found in isolated pockets around the country. Adventure Life explores the Petén jungle region heavily, bringing you to Flores, Petexbatun Lake, the Aguateca, Yaxhá, and Tikal ruins, as well as Ixpanpajul Natural Park. Guatemala Ventures has one-day tours to many of the parks and other locations throughout the country. Old Town Outfitters offers hiking, biking, and kayaking trips to a number of these regions. Abercrombie & Kent's Marco Polo Club has a photographic tour lead by photographer and explorer Roger Moore that extends into Honduras, offered only on select dates in January.

CULTURAL TOURISM

From ancient civilizations and indigenous groups to small pueblos rebounding from decades of civil war, there's no shortage of interest in Central America's diverse people. Here are some of the many tour companies that can take you to encounter groups that rarely meet the outside world and have remained unchanged for centuries. Always do your research before taking tours like this—it's important that your operator conduct business with the local people in an ethical, respectful way.

BELIZE
Season: May
Locations: Punta Gorda, Lubaantun, Río Blanco National Park
Cost: From $1,382 for eight days from Punta Gorda
Tour Operators: Cotton Tree Lodge, Wildland Adventures

The Maya are believed to have started eating chocolate as long as 2,600 years ago, and many of the area people still use the same production processes. Now, so can you. Cotton Tree Lodge has an annual one-week workshop to walk you through Belize's entire chocolate-making process. You begin with Cacao on the tree and end with the finished product. You'll be taught traditional techniques by local Maya, as well as attend lectures on the history and politics of chocolate with members of the local Toledo Cacao Grower's Association. Also, Wildland Adventures has a rich cultural tour of Belize that visits a Mayan harp-player's workshop, an organic cacao plantation, and a Garifuna feast and drumming performance, as well as the Mayan ruins at Lubaantun and Rio Blanco National Park.

GUATEMALA
Season: March and July
Locations: Guatemala City, Quiche, San Lucas Toliman, Lake Atitlán, Antigua
Cost: From $1,175 for 10 days from Guatemala City
Tour Operators: GATE Travel

The Maya are the living soul of Guatemala, but many difficulties surround their adaptation to the modern world. GATE's program helps you understand Mayan roots and spirituality, as well as the history and politics of Guatemala. Human-rights issues, poverty, community leadership, and migration are touched upon as you meet with human-rights advocates, theologians, and many of the country's indigenous people.

LANGUAGE SCHOOLS

You can study a day of Spanish with room and board in Central America for about the same price as a martini in a London club, which is why the activity has caught on. Prices are much lower than in Spain or in universities and many of the courses are accredited. People in their teens to retirees come for weeks or even months at a time to places like Antigua, Guatemala, where the number of students seems to outnumber traditional tourists. Some never end up leaving.

GUATEMALA

Season: Year-round
Locations: Antigua, Quetzaltenango
Cost: From $595 for one week from Guatemala City
Tour Operators: G.A.P. Adventures, Tucan Travel, Pop-Wuj

Guatemala is one of Latin America's language hot spots, where thousands of foreigners of all ages can be found practicing Spanish in the country at any given time. Antigua alone has more than 75 language programs with more opening up all of the time. G.A.P.'s 14-day Guatemala Spanish Adventure teaches you Spanish as you visit locations such as Antigua, Lake Atitlán, Tikal, and Poptún, using hands-on learning as you bargain at the Chichicastenango market or chat up locals at a Salsa bar. Tucan Travel's eight-day Spanish program is more typical of Guatemalan schools. Like many others, it's based in Antigua, where you will have 20 hours of classes per week, area tours, and local homestays. Volunteer community work projects are a must for all Pop-Wuj Spanish studies in Quetzaltenango. The projects are divided between community/social and medical/health care and will differ based on the type of language skills you want to learn.

MAYAN RUINS

Centered in northeastern Guatemala, the Mayan civilization once stretched from Mexico to as far south as Costa Rica. Ruins of their magnificent stelae, temples, and ballcourts are scattered throughout the region, with Tikal being the most prominent, but others such as Copán and Palenque leave visitors just as breathless. Lesser-known ruins such as the many pyramids in El Salvador are still being excavated.

BELIZE

Season: Year-round
Locations: Lamanai, Caracol, Altun Ha, Hol Chan Marine Reserve, Cahal Pech, Tikal
Cost: From $2,590 for nine days from Belize City
Tour Operators: Tropical Expeditions Belize, Journeys International

Although most history buffs head to Copán or Tikal to get their Mayan fix, Belize has many fascinating ruins. Many are encircled by dense jungle and were only discovered in the past few decades. Caracol, meaning snail in Spanish, was one of the most important cities of the Mayan classical period and is home to the 143-foot tall Caana pyramid. Much of the site is still under excavation and visitor permits are needed from the Belize Department of Archaeology, which your tour operator will hopefully arrange. Lamanai in north–central Belize, otherwise known as the submerged crocodile, was occupied for more than 1,000 years, making it one of the longest continuously occupied Mayan cities. There are more than 940 structures on the site, including two 16th-century Spanish churches that were evacuated after a Mayan revolt shortly after they were built. Tropical Expeditions brings you to both ancient cities, as well as the Mayan site of Altun Ha and the Hol Chan Marine Reserve on their eight-day Ancient Maya Cites & Coral Islands excursion. Journeys International's nine-day Mystery of the Maya program brings you to Caracol, Cahal Pech, and Tikal.

GUATEMALA
Season: Year-round
Locations: Playa del Carmen, Tulúm, Cay Caulker, Palenque, San Ignacio, Flores, Tikal, Río Dulce, Antigua, Panajachel, Lake Atitlán, Chichicastenango, Totonicapan
Cost: From $1,895 for 14 days from Guatemala City
Tour Operators: G.A.P. Adventures, Journeys Latin America, Adventuresmith Explorations, Wildland Adventures, Adventure Life, Geographic Expeditions, Maya Tours, Saca Tours, AIA

A wide range of tour companies operate in the region, and infinite combinations of ruins and other sightseeing tours are possible. G.A.P. Adventures' Mayan Explorer program, among many others, gives you 14 days visiting the Mayan ruins on Mexico's Yucatán peninsula, such as Chichen Itza and Palenque, moving all the way south to Guatemala and Tikal. En route you will explore traditional villages along Lake Atitlán and visit the market at Chichicastenango. Journeys Latin America's Hidden Maya brings you to the best ruins and sites in northeast Guatemala, plus Copán in Honduras, with a few days in exploring the reed at Cay Caulker in Belize. You can also add a three-day trip to Tikal to any of their excursions in Belize and Guatemala. Adventure Smith Explorations offers a five-day excursion between Tikal and Palenque stopping at lesser known ruins such as Yaxchilan and Bonampak along the way. Wildland Adventures extends the previous trip seven more days to add travels to Lake Atitlán and Copán, Honduras.

With Adventure Life's Mundo Maya you visit Tikal and Lake Atitlán like may other trips, but also the isolated and off-the-beaten-track highland town of Totonicapan. While there, you'll visit local artisans' workshops and indigenous markets, and even the home of a Mayan family. Geographic Expeditions combines Tikal, Antigua, Lake Atitlán, and Copán with luxury resorts including Coppola's La Lancha lodge. Maya Tours nine-day New Discoveries Tour takes you to the newest and littlest known Mayan ruins in Guatemala, such as Canceun, Aguateca, Waka, La Joyanaca, Holmul, and Yaha. The tours are lead by top archaeologists and include overnights in scenic lodges. Saca Tours has shorter two- to three-day excursions that combine a visit to Tikal with a lesser known ruins such as Uaxactun and Ceibal. AIA explores six of the greatest Mayan sites: Copán, Quirigua, Tikal, Yaxchilan, Bonampak, and Palenque. This expert-lead tour gives you the time to enjoy each site, while staying at five jungle lodges close to each set of ruins.

HONDURAS
Season: Year-round
Locations: Copán
Cost: From $455 for three days from Guatemala City
Tour Operators: Journeys Latin America, Grayline Tours, Garifuna Tours

Only one ruin in Honduras approaches the scale of other Central American sites: Copán. Discovered in 1839 and still hidden by dense vegetation, the importance of the enormous site is still emerging. Journeys Latin America can combine almost any of their tours with a three-day, standard trip to Copán from Guatemala City, which gives you approximately two full days at the ruins. Grayline tours have an eight-day guided excursion with several days exploring the ruins at Copán followed by Roatán for the remainder of your trip. Garifuna Tours includes the ruin on their 11-day trip that also covers bird-watching in two national parks and relaxation at Roatán.

VOLUNTEER VACATIONS

Whether you help protect endangered sea turtles or help a struggling community build houses and schools, volunteering can be one of the most rewarding travel experiences you could ever have—plus there are plenty of opportunities to practice your Spanish and see some sights along the way.

GUATEMALA

Season: Year-round
Locations: Antigua, Lake Atitlán, Tikal, Flores
Cost: From $1,450 for four weeks from Guatemala City
Tour Operators: G.A.P. Adventures, Global Crossroads

G.A.P. Adventures' Project Guatemala is a 13-day odyssey to help a remote village in the eastern highlands improve basic living conditions, while saving some time to visit Antigua, Lake Atitlán, and Tikal. Another option is to volunteer with Global Crossroads' Wildlife Rescue program at ARCS, a Wildlife Rescue Center in the Mayan Biosphere Reserve, to take care and rehabilitate rare and wild animals that were confiscated from the black market. The programs start at one-month in length and the initial weeks include Spanish-language study.

CLOSE UP

Tour Operators

There are far more adventure-tour operators in Central America than it's possible to include here. Most are small and local; to get more information about them, you can either stop by their storefront locations, or contact the relevant tourist office.

Abercrombie & Kent ✉ 1520 Kensington Rd., Oak Brook, IL 59801 ☎ 630/954–2944 or 800/323–7308 ⊕ www.abercrombiekent.com.

Adventure Life ✉ 1655 S. 3rd St. W, Missoula, MT 59801 ☎ 800/344–6118 ⊕ www.adventure-life.com.

Adventuresmith Explorations ✉ 3090 N. Lake Blvd., Tahoe City, CA 96145 ☎ 800/728—2875 or 530/583–1775 ⊕ www.adventure-smith.com.

Archaeological Institute of America (AIA) ✉ Box 938, 47 Main St., Walpole, NH 03608 ☎ 800/748–6262 ⊕ www.archaeological.org.

Cotton Tree Lodge ✉ Moho River, San Felipe, Toledo, Belize ☎ 501/670–0557 ⊕ www.cottontree-lodge.com.

G.A.P. Adventures ✉ E. 19 Charlotte St., Toronto, Ontario M5V 2H5 ☎ 416/260–0999 or 800/465–5600 ⊕ www.gapadventures.com.

Garifuna Tours ⊕ www.garifuna-tours.com.

GATE Travel ✉ 912 Market St., La Crosse, WI 54601 ☎ 608/791–5283 ⊕ www.gate-travel.com .

Geographic Expeditions ✉ 1008 General Kennedy Ave., Box 29902, San Francisco, CA 94129 ☎ 415/922–0448 or 800/777–8183 ⊕ www.geoex.com.

Global Crossroad ✉ 11822 Justice Ave., Suite A-5, Baton Rouge, LA 70816 ☎ 972/252–4191 ⊕ www.globalcrossroad.com.

Grayline Tours ✉ 1835 Gaylord St., Denver, CO 80206 ☎ 303/394–6920 ⊕ www.grayline.com

Guatemala Ventures ☎ 866/464–8183 ⊕ www.guatemalaventures.com.

Journeys International ✉ E. 107 April Dr., Suite 3, Ann Arbor, MI 48103 ☎ 734/665–4407 or 800/255–8735 ⊕ www.journeys-intl.com.

Journeys Latin America ✉ 12 & 13 Heathfield Terr., Chiswick, London, UK W4 4JE ☎ 020/8747–8315 ⊕ www.journeylatinamerica.co.uk.

Maya Tour ✉ 207 Beach Breeze La., Arverne, NY 11692 ☎ 800/690–2072 ⊕ www.mayatour.com.

Old Town Outfitters ✉ 5a Av. Sur 12, Antigua, Guatemala ☎ 502/5399–0440 ⊕ www.adventureguatemala.com.

Pop-Wuj ✉ Primera C., 17-72, Zona 1, Quetzaltenango, Guatemala ☎ 502/7761–8286 ⊕ www.pop-wuj.org.

Saca Tours ✉ 44 Pond St., Nahant, MA 01908 ☎ 781/581–0844 ⊕ www.saca.com.

Tropical Expeditions Belize ✉ 1449 Coney Dr., Belize City, Belize ☎ 501/223–6939 ⊕ www.tropical-expeditionsbelize.com.

Tucan Travel ✉ 316 Uxbridge Rd., Acton, London, UK W3 9QP ☎ 020/8896–1600 ⊕ www.tucantravel.com.

Wildland Adventures ✉ 3516 N.E. 155th St., Beulah, WA 98155 ☎ 800/345–4453 or 206/365–0686 ⊕ www.wildland.com.

9

Guatemala Essentials

There are planners and there are those who, excuse the pun, fly by the seat of their pants. We happily place ourselves among the planners. Our writers and editors try to anticipate all the issues you may face before and during any journey, and then they do their research. This section is the product of their efforts. Use it to get excited about your trip to Guatemala, to inform your travel planning, or to guide you on the road should the seat of your pants start to feel threadbare.

GETTING STARTED

We're really proud of our Web site: Fodors.com is a great place to begin any journey. Scan "Travel Wire" for suggested itineraries, travel deals, restaurant and hotel openings, and other up-to-the-minute info. Check out "Booking" to research prices and book plane tickets, hotel rooms, rental cars, and vacation packages. Head to "Talk" for on-the-ground pointers from travelers who frequent our message boards. You can also link to loads of other travel-related resources.

▌ RESOURCES

ONLINE TRAVEL TOOLS

ALL ABOUT GUATEMALA

Guatemala Tourist Commission (⊕*www.visitguatemala.com*): Guatemala's official tourism site has overviews of different destinations in Guatemala and is a useful pretrip planning resource. **Guatemalaweb** (⊕*www.guatemalaweb.com*) is run by a local travel agent, and has useful advice about Guatemala's different regions. **Turansa** (⊕*www.turansa.com*) has general information about travel in Guatemala and some good maps.

Currency Conversion Google (⊕www.google.com) does currency conversion. Just type in the amount you want to convert and an explanation of how you want it converted (e.g., "14 Swiss francs in dollars"), and then voilà. **Oanda.com** (⊕www.oanda.com) also allows you to print out a handy table with the current day's conversion rates. **XE.com** (⊕www.xe.com) is a good currency-conversion Web site.

Media Prensa Libre (⊕www.prensalibre.com) is the country's highest-circulating local daily newspaper (in Spanish). **Revue Magazine** (⊕www.revuemag.com), the online version of a monthly English-language magazine, has articles on travel as well as local news and culture. **Siglo XXI** (⊕www.sigloxxi.com) is a Spanish-language daily newspaper.

Safety Transportation Security Administration (TSA; ⊕www.tsa.gov).

Time Zones Timeanddate.com (⊕www.timeanddate.com/worldclock) can help you figure out the correct time anywhere.

Weather Accuweather.com (⊕www.accuweather.com) is an independent weather-forecasting service with good coverage of hurricanes. **Weather.com** (⊕www.weather.com) is the Web site for the Weather Channel.

Other Resources CIA World Factbook (⊕www.odci.gov/cia/publications/factbook/index.html) has profiles of every country in the world. It's a good source if you need some quick facts and figures.

VISITOR INFORMATION

The Guatemala Tourist Commission, known as Inguat, has offices in Guatemala City, Antigua, Panajachel, Quetzaltenango, and Flores. Staff members are helpful but have few resources beyond free maps to hand out. The offices can also put you in contact with the Tourist Police, who run a free escort services to visit popular sights.

Tourist Information Guatemala Tourist Commission (Inguat) (☎800/464–8281 in U.S., 801/464–8281 in Guatemala ⊕www.visitguatemala.com).

▌THINGS TO CONSIDER

GOVERNMENT ADVISORIES

As different countries have different worldviews, look at travel advisories from a range of governments to get more of a sense of what's going on out there. And be sure to parse the language carefully. For example, a warning to "avoid all travel" carries more weight than one urging you to "avoid nonessential travel," and both are much stronger than a plea to "exercise caution." A U.S. government travel warning is more permanent (though not necessarily more serious) than a so-called public announcement, which carries an expiration date.

The U.S. Department of State's Web site has more than just travel warnings and advisories. The consular information sheets issued for every country have general safety tips, entry requirements (though be sure to verify these with the country's embassy), and other useful details.

Violent crime is a serious issue in Guatemala and tourists are frequently victims. *For more information see Safety below.*

Guatemala has four active volcanoes and earthquakes are a constant possibility. You can check the tectonic situation before your trip at **The U.S. Government Federal Management Agency (FEMA)** (⊕*www. fema.gov*). June through November is hurricane season: both the Caribbean and Pacific coasts are often affected. During this time heavy rain frequently causes landslides, blocking roads and occasionally causing more serious accidents.

General Information & Warnings U.S. **Department of State** (⊕www.travel.state.gov).

GEAR

Whatever you do, pack light—casual, comfortable, hand-washable clothing. T-shirts and shorts are acceptable near the beach, while more conservative attire is appropriate in smaller towns. If you're heading into the Cayo, the mountains, or the highlands, especially during the win-

---

---

ter months, bring a sweater or jacket, as nights and early mornings can be chilly. Sturdy sneakers or hiking shoes or boots with rubber soles are essential. A pair of sandals (preferably ones that can be worn in the water) are indispensable, too. Jewelry—even the fake stuff—only attracts the wrong sort of attention. Scarves or beads are safer accessories.

"Insect repellent, sunscreen, sunglasses" is your packing mantra, and an umbrella or stashable raincoat are handy, too. Long-sleeve shirts and long pants will also protect your skin from the relentless sun and ferocious mosquitoes. Tissues and antibacterial hand wipes make trips to public toilets that bit more pleasant. A handbag-sized flashlight is also very useful: blackouts and streets without proper lighting are commonplace. In the jungle, a camping mosquito net is invaluable when staying at places with no screens on the windows (or no windows at all). Snorkelers should try to bring their own equipment if there's room in the suitcase. You're unlikely to find your favorite brand of condoms and tampons in Guatemala, so bring necessary supplies of both.

PASSPORTS & VISAS

As a U.S. citizen, all you need to enter Guatemala is a passport valid for at least six months after your arrival. This goes for children and teenagers, too. You are automatically granted a 90-day tourist visa at immigration. If you plan to stay longer, you either need to leave the country for 72 hours, or renew your visa at the Inguat office in Guatemala City: this takes five days, and you'll need to leave your passport there.

Info **Inguat** (✉ 7a Av. 1–17, Zona 4, Guatemala City ☎ 800/464–8281 in U.S., 801/464–8281 in Guatemala ☎ 331–4416 ⊕ www.inguat.gob.gt).

U.S. Passport Information **U.S. Department of State** (☎ 877/487–2778 ⊕ http://travel.state.gov/passport).

GUATEMALA REQUIREMENTS	
Passport	Must be valid for 6 months after date of arrival.
Visa	Issued automatically to Americans on arrival.
Vaccinations & Medication	No vaccinations required; antimalarial medication advised for areas below 1,500 meters (4,900 feet).
Driving	U.S. driver's license accepted; CDW is compulsory on car rentals and will be included in the quoted price.
Departure Tax	US$30, usually included in ticket price, and Q20, payable in cash at the airport.

SHOTS & MEDICATIONS

Malaria is prevalent in areas below 1,500 meters (4,900 feet)—both Antigua and Atitlán are too high to be at risk. Another mosquito-borne disease, dengue, is also rife, particularly on the Pacific coast. The best way to prevent both is to avoid being bitten: cover up your arms and legs and use ample repellent, preferably one containing DEET. The CDC recommends chloroquine as a preventative antimalarial for adults and infants in Guatemala. To be effective, the weekly doses must start a week before you travel and continue four weeks after your return. There is no preventative medication for dengue.

■ TIP→ If you travel a lot internationally—particularly to developing nations—refer to the CDC's Health Information for International Travel (aka Traveler's Health Yellow Book). Info from it is posted on the CDC Web site (www.cdc.gov/travel/yb), or you can buy a copy from your local bookstore for $24.95.

For more information see Health under On the Ground in Guatemala, below.

Health Warnings **National Centers for Disease Control & Prevention** (CDC ☎ 877/394–8747 international travelers' health line ⊕ www.cdc.gov/travel). **World Health Organization** (WHO ⊕ www.who.int).

TRIP INSURANCE

■ TIP→ Guatemalan public hospitals sometimes refuse to treat travelers without insurance. As they often lack basic supplies, you're best going to a private clinic, which means medical insurance is a must.

We believe that comprehensive trip insurance is especially valuable if you're booking a very expensive or complicated trip (particularly to an isolated region) or if you're booking far in advance. Who knows what could happen six months down the road? But whether or not you get insurance has more to do with how comfortable you are assuming all that risk yourself.

Comprehensive travel policies typically cover trip-cancellation and interruption, letting you cancel or cut your trip short because of a personal emergency, illness, or, in some cases, acts of terrorism in your destination. Such policies also cover evacuation and medical care. Some also cover you for trip delays because of bad weather or mechanical problems as well as for lost or delayed baggage. Another type of coverage to look for is financial default—that is, when your trip is disrupted because a tour operator, airline, or cruise line goes out of business. Generally you must buy this when you book your trip or shortly thereafter, and it's

Trip-Insurance Resources

INSURANCE-COMPARISON SITES		
Insure My Trip.com	800/487–4722	www.insuremytrip.com
Square Mouth.com	800/240–0369 or 727/490–5803	www.squaremouth.com
COMPREHENSIVE TRAVEL INSURERS		
Access America	800/729–6021	www.accessamerica.com
CSA Travel Protection	800/873–9855	www.csatravelprotection.com
HTH Worldwide	610/254–8700 or 888/243–2358	www.hthworldwide.com
Travelex Insurance	800/228–9792	www.travelex-insurance.com
Travel Guard International	715/345–0505 or 800/826–4919	www.travelguard.com
Travel Insured International	800/243–3174	www.travelinsured.com
MEDICAL-ONLY INSURERS		
International Medical Group	800/628–4664	www.imglobal.com
International SOS		www.internationalsos.com
Wallach & Company	800/237–6615 or 540/687–3166	www.wallach.com

only available to you if your operator isn't on a list of excluded companies.

If you're going abroad, consider buying medical-only coverage at the very least. Neither Medicare nor some private insurers cover medical expenses anywhere outside of the United States (including time aboard a cruise ship, even if it leaves from a U.S. port). Medical-only policies typically reimburse you for medical care (excluding that related to preexisting conditions) and hospitalization abroad, and provide for evacuation. You still have to pay the bills and await reimbursement from the insurer, though.

Expect comprehensive travel-insurance policies to cost about 4% to 7% or 8% of the total price of your trip (it's more like 8% to 12% if you're over age 70). A medical-only policy may or may not be cheaper than a comprehensive policy. Always read the fine print of your policy to make sure that you are covered for the risks that are of most concern to you.

Compare several policies to make sure you're getting the best price and range of coverage available.

■TIP→ **OK. You know you can save a bundle on trips to warm-weather destinations by traveling in rainy season. But there's also a chance that a severe storm will disrupt your plans. The solution? Look for hotels and resorts that offer storm/hurricane guarantees. Although they rarely allow refunds, most guarantees do let you rebook later if a storm strikes.**

BOOKING YOUR TRIP

Unless your cousin is a travel agent, you're probably among the millions of people who make most of their travel arrangements online.

But have you ever wondered just what the differences are between an online travel agent (a Web site through which you make reservations instead of going directly to the airline, hotel, or car-rental company), a discounter (a firm that does a high volume of business with a hotel chain or airline and accordingly gets good prices), a wholesaler (one that makes cheap reservations in bulk and then re-sells them to people like you), and an aggregator (one that compares all the offerings so you don't have to)?

Is it truly better to book directly on an airline or hotel Web site? And when does a real live travel agent come in handy?

ONLINE

You really have to shop around. A travel wholesaler such as Hotels.com or Hotel-Club.net can be a source of good rates, as can discounters such as Hotwire or Priceline, particularly if you can bid for your hotel room or airfare. Indeed, such sites sometimes have deals that are unavailable elsewhere. They do, however, tend to work only with hotel chains (which makes them just plain useless for getting hotel reservations outside of major cities) or big airlines (so that often leaves out upstarts like jetBlue and some foreign carriers like Air India).

Also, with discounters and wholesalers you must generally prepay, and everything is nonrefundable. And before you fork over the dough, be sure to check the terms and conditions, so you know what a given company will do for you if there's a problem and what you'll have to deal with on your own.

■TIP➜ **To be absolutely sure everything was processed correctly, confirm reserva-tions made through online travel agents, discounters, and wholesalers directly with your hotel before leaving home.**

Booking engines like Expedia, Travelocity, and Orbitz are actually travel agents, albeit high-volume, online ones. And airline travel packagers like AmericanAirlines Vacations and Virgin Vacations—well, they're travel agents, too. But they may still not work with all the world's hotels.

An aggregator site will search many sites and pull the best prices for airfares, hotels, and rental cars from them. Most aggregators compare the major travel-booking sites such as Expedia, Travelocity, and Orbitz; some also look at airline Web sites, though rarely the sites of smaller budget airlines. Some aggregators also compare other travel products, including complex packages—a good thing, as you can sometimes get the best overall deal by booking an air-and-hotel package.

WITH A TRAVEL AGENT

If you use an agent—brick-and-mortar or virtual—you'll pay a fee for the service. And know that the service you get from some online agents isn't comprehensive. For example Expedia and Travelocity don't search for prices on most budget airlines like jetBlue, Southwest, or small foreign carriers. That said, some agents (online or not) *do* have access to fares that are difficult to find otherwise, and the savings can more than make up for any surcharge.

A knowledgeable brick-and-mortar travel agent can be a godsend if you're booking a cruise, a package trip that's not available to you directly, an air pass, or a complicated itinerary including several overseas flights. What's more, travel agents that specialize in a destination may have exclusive access to certain deals and insider information on things such as charter flights. Agents who specialize in

Online-Booking Resources

AGGREGATORS

Kayak	www.kayak.com	looks at cruises and vacation packages.
Mobissimo	www.mobissimo.com	examines airfare, hotels, cars, and tons of activities.
Qixo	www.qixo.com	compares cruises, vacation packages, and even travel insurance.
Sidestep	www.sidestep.com	compares vacation packages and lists travel deals and some activities.
Travelgrove	www.travelgrove.com	compares cruises and vacation packages and lets you search by themes.

BOOKING ENGINES

Cheap Tickets	www.cheaptickets.com	discounter.
Expedia	www.expedia.com	large online agency that charges a booking fee for airline tickets.
Hotwire	www.hotwire.com	discounter.
lastminute.com	www.lastminute.com	specializes in last-minute travel; the main site is for the U.K., but it has a link to a U.S. site.
Luxury Link	www.luxurylink.com	has auctions (surprisingly good deals) as well as offers on the high-end side of travel.
Onetravel.com	www.onetravel.com	discounter for hotels, car rentals, airfares, and packages.
Orbitz	www.orbitz.com	charges a booking fee for airline tickets, but gives a clear breakdown of fees and taxes before you book.
Priceline.com	www.priceline.com	discounter that also allows bidding.
Travel.com	www.travel.com	allows you to compare its rates with those of other booking engines.
Travelocity	www.travelocity.com	charges a booking fee for airline tickets, but promises good problem resolution.

ONLINE ACCOMMODATIONS

Hotelbook.com	www.hotelbook.com	focuses on independent hotels worldwide.
Hotel Club	www.hotelclub.net	good for major cities and some resort areas.
Hotels.com	www.hotels.com	big Expedia-owned wholesaler that offers rooms all over the world.
Quikbook	www.quikbook.com	offers "pay when you stay" reservations that allow you to settle your bill when you check out; best for trips to U.S. and Canadian cities.

OTHER RESOURCES

Bidding For Travel	www.biddingfortravel.com	shows what you can get and for how much before you start bidding on, say, Priceline.

types of travelers (senior citizens, gays and lesbians, naturists) or types of trips (cruises, luxury travel, safaris) can also be invaluable.

■**TIP→ Remember that Expedia, Travelocity, and Orbitz are travel agents, not just booking engines. To resolve any problems with a reservation made through these companies, contact them first.**

Agent Resources **American Society of Travel Agents** (☎703/739–2782 ⊕www. travelsense.org).

Guatemala Travel Agents **Aventuras Vacacionales** (☎7832–6056 ⊕www.sailing-diving-guatemala.com). **Turansa** (☎2435–3575 ⊕www.turansa.com). **Mundo Guatemala** (☎7832–9017 ⊕www. mundo-guatemala.com).

■ ACCOMMODATIONS

Guatemala now has lodging options that go well beyond the needs of the backpacker, in the forms of reliable international hotels, far-flung ecolodges, classy colonial charmers, and rustic retreats with local flair.

Hotel isn't the only tag you'll find on accommodation: *hospedaje, pensionán, casa de huespedes,* and *posada* also denominate somewhere to stay. Unfortunately, there are no hard and fast rules as to what each name means, though hotel and *posada* tend to be higher-end places. Lodging prices are controlled by Inguat, the state tourism agency, and should be clearly visible in the reception. Breakfast isn't usually included in the room price.

The usual big international chain hotels have rooms and facilities equal to those at home, but usually lack atmosphere compared to locally owned options. You don't always have to sacrifice hot water or room service for a touch of culture—Antigua and Guatemala City have five-star guesthouses and boutique hotels that combine colonial class with modern amenities. At Lago Atitlán's hotels you get comfort and

culture in utter isolation: hammocks with stunning views of the lake beat television sets every time.

If five-star luxury isn't your top priority, the best deals are undoubtedly with midrange local hotels. Granted, there's no gym or conference center, but comfortable rooms with private bathrooms, hot water, and much more local character often come at a fraction of the cost of a big chain. Lodges—both eco- and not-quite-so—are the thing in Petén, near Tikal. Some are incredibly luxurious, others more back-to-nature; all are way off the beaten path, so plan on staying a few nights to offset travel time.

Most hotels and other lodgings require you to give your credit-card details before they will confirm your reservation. If you don't feel comfortable e-mailing this information, ask if you can fax it (some places even prefer faxes). However you book, get confirmation in writing and have a copy of it handy when you check in.

Be sure you understand the hotel's cancellation policy. Some places allow you to cancel without any kind of penalty—even if you prepaid to secure a discounted rate—if you cancel at least 24 hours in advance. Others require you to cancel a week in advance or penalize you the cost of one night. Small inns and B&Bs are most likely to require you to cancel far in advance. Most hotels allow children under a certain age to stay in their parents' room at no extra charge, but others charge for them as extra adults; find out the cutoff age for discounts.

■**TIP→ Assume that hotels operate on the European Plan (EP, no meals) unless we specify that they use the Breakfast Plan (BP, with full breakfast), Continental Plan (CP, continental breakfast), Full American Plan (FAP, all meals), Modified American Plan (MAP, breakfast and dinner), or are all-inclusive (AI, all meals and most activities).**

APARTMENT & HOUSE RENTALS

Short-term furnished rentals aren't common in Guatemala, and colonial-style villas in Antigua and occasionally Atitlán make up the bulk of the options. Usually luxurious, their prices are around $1,500 a week. The biggest selection is at Ah! Guatemala, whereas Great Rentals has more unusual properties. Sublet.com and Vacation Rentals By Owner deal with more modest, run-of-the-mill apartments, often as cheap as $300 a week.

ONLINE-BOOKING RESOURCES

Contacts **Ah! Guatemala** (⊕www.ahguatemala.com/travel_and_tourism). **Great Rentals** (☏512/493–0368 ⊕www.greatrentals.com). **Sublet.com** (⊕www.sublet.com). **Villas International** (☏415/499–9490 or 800/221–2260 ⊕www.villasintl.com). **Vacation Rentals By Owner** (⊕www.vrbo.com).

BED & BREAKFASTS

The Guatemalan definition of B&B might not coincide with yours. The term is frequently extended to luxury hotels that happen to include breakfast in their price; indeed, these make up most of the pickings at Bed & Breakfast.com and Bed & Breakfast Inns Online. The longer lists at Ah! Guatemala and A Thousand Inns include both these and homelier mid-range establishments. For cheap, family-run places, try Traveller's Point.

Reservation Services **A Thousand Inns**
(⊕www.1000inns.com). **Ah! Guatemala** (⊕www.ahguatemala.com/travel_and_tourism/bed_and_breakfast). **Bed & Breakfast. com** (☏512/322–2710 or 800/462–2632 ⊕www.bedandbreakfast.com) also sends out an online newsletter. **Bed & Breakfast Inns Online** (☏615/868–1946 or 800/215–7365 ⊕www.bbonline.com). **Traveller's Point** (⊕www.travellerspoint.com).

Exchange Clubs **Home Exchange.com**
(☏800/877–8723 ⊕www.homeexchange. com); $59.95 for a 1-year online listing. **Home For Exchange** (⊕www.homeforexchange. com). **Intervac U.S.** (☏800/756–4663 ⊕www.intervacus.com); $78.88 for Web-only

membership; $126 includes Web access and a catalog.

HOSTELS

Hostels offer bare-bones lodging at low, low prices—often in shared dorm rooms with shared baths—to people of all ages, though the primary market is young travelers, especially students. Most hostels serve breakfast; dinner and/or shared cooking facilities may also be available. In some hostels you aren't allowed to be in your room during the day, and there may be a curfew at night. Nevertheless, hostels provide a sense of community, with public rooms where travelers often gather to share stories. Many hostels are affiliated with Hostelling International (HI), an umbrella group of hostel associations with some 4,500 member properties in more than 70 countries. Other hostels are completely independent and may be nothing more than a really cheap hotel.

Guatemala has a good selection of cheap, shared accommodation. Budget lodging terminology varies: hostel, *hostal* and *la casa de . . .* are commonplace names, and some places are just listed as a hotel or *pensionán*.

Staff in most Guatemalan hostels are young, enthusiastic, and knowledgeable, and can usually inform you about Spanish classes and excursions—many have in-house travel agencies. Hostels proper do tend to cater to party animals, so if you're traveling with kids, a family-run hotel might be quieter.

Guatemala has no HI-affiliates, but Traveller's Point and Hostel World have ample listings and booking services. Consider sorting out your first few nights in advance, then get recommendations from fellow travelers for your next port of call.

Information **Hostels.com** (⊕www.hostels. com). **Hostel World.com** (⊕www.hostelworld. com). **Travellers' Point** (⊕www.travellers-point.com).

ECOLODGES

In addition to hotels and hostels, Guatemala does a brisk trade in so-called ecolodges, most of which are in El Petén. If you're seriously interested in sustainable accommodation, it pays to do your research. The term is used very flexibly, sometimes simply to describe a property in a rural or jungle location, rather than somewhere that is truly ecologically friendly. The International Ecotourism Society has online resources to help you pick somewhere really green. Responsible Travel is an online travel agency for ethical holidays.

Information **International Ecotourism Society** (⊕ www.ecotourism.org). **Responsible Travel** (⊕ www.responsibletravel.com).

▌AIRLINE TICKETS

Most domestic airline tickets are electronic; international tickets may be either electronic or paper. With an e-ticket the only thing you receive is an e-mailed receipt citing your itinerary and reservation and ticket numbers.

The greatest advantage of an e-ticket is that if you lose your receipt, you can simply print out another copy or ask the airline to do it for you at check-in. You usually pay a surcharge (up to $50) to get a paper ticket, if you can get one at all.

The sole advantage of a paper ticket is that it may be easier to endorse over to another airline if your flight is canceled and the airline with which you booked can't accommodate you on another flight.

▌RENTAL CARS

Driving in Guatemala is not for the faint of heart. Speed limits and road signs are routinely ignored, drivers overtake on blind corners without batting an eyelid, and indicating turns seems to be for sissies. However, a car can be a real asset to your trip. You don't have to worry about unreliable bus schedules, you can control your itinerary and the pace of your trip, and you can head off to explore on a whim. Drive defensively, maintain your distance, and assume that other drivers will make unexpected—often downright dangerous—maneuvers. Wearing a seat belt is compulsory, though many locals flaunt the rule.

The roads in urban areas and between big cities are generally paved, and in reasonable condition. Guatemalan road signs aren't always clear, so make sure you have a good road map (all rental agencies provide them). Avoid driving at night: it's easier to get lost, and the chances of carjacking and robbery skyrocket. The road to the airport is often targeted: in the event of a robbery, never put up a struggle. In cities, always park your car in guarded lots or hotels with private parking, never on the street.

For safaris into the mountains, or for exploring smaller roads in areas like Petén, a *doble tracción* or *cuatro por cuatro* (four-wheel-drive vehicle) stands you in good stead. If money isn't an object, consider renting one no matter where you go: unpaved roads, mud slides in rainy season, and a general off-the-beaten-path landscape are status quo here. Note that most Belize agencies do not permit you to take their vehicles over the border into Guatemala or Mexico, and vice versa.

Compact cars like a Kia Pianto or VW Fox start at around $32 a day; for $40 to $50 you can rent a Mitsubishi Lancer, a VW Golf or a Polo. Four-wheel-drive pickups start at $70 a day, though for a full cabin you pay up to $120. International agencies sometimes have cheaper per-day rates, but locals undercut them on longer rentals. Stick shifts are the norm in Guatemala, so check with the rental agency if you only drive automatics.

Rental-car companies routinely accept driver's licenses from the United States, Canada, and most European countries.

Most agencies require a major credit card for a deposit, and some require you be over 25, or charge extra insurance if you're not.

CAR-RENTAL RESOURCES

Automobile Associations U.S.: **American Automobile Association** (AAA ☎315/797–5000 ⊕www.aaa.com).; most contact with the organization is through state and regional members. **National Automobile Club** (☎650/294–7000 ⊕www.thenac.com); membership is open to California residents only.

Local Agencies Tabarini (☎2331–2643 ⊕www.tabarini.com) **Ahorrent** (☎2383–2802 ⊕www.ahorrent.com).

Major Agencies Alamo (☎800/522–9696 ⊕www.alamo.com). **Avis** (☎800/331–1084 ⊕www.avis.com). **Budget** (☎800/472–3325 ⊕www.budget.com). **Hertz** (☎800/654–3001 ⊕www.hertz.com). **National Car Rental** (☎800/227–7368 ⊕www.nationalcar.com).

CAR-RENTAL INSURANCE

Guatemalan car-rental agencies generally require collision- or loss-damage waiver (CDW), which also covers you if the car is stolen. There's generally a deductible (around $2,000) you have to pay, so consider adding on the extra fee to reduce your liability: it's often as low as $6 a day.

■TIP➡ You can decline the insurance from the rental company and purchase it through a third-party provider such as Travel Guard (www.travelguard.com)—$9 per day for $35,000 of coverage. That's sometimes just under half the price of the CDW offered by some car-rental companies.

■ VACATION PACKAGES

Packages *are not* guided excursions. Packages combine airfare, accommodations, and perhaps a rental car or other extras (theater tickets, guided excursions, boat trips, reserved entry to popular museums, transit passes), but they let you do your own thing. During busy periods packages may be your only option, as flights and rooms may be sold out otherwise.

There's no real reason to visit Guatemala on a package tour—in fact, doing so will probably cost you considerably more. Consider hunting for flights yourself (the cheapest deals are often online) and getting a Guatemalan agent to arrange accommodation and internal flights, instead.

Organizations American Society of Travel Agents (ASTA ☎703/739–2782 or 800/965–2782 ⊕www.astanet.com). **United States Tour Operators Association** (USTOA ☎212/599–6599 ⊕www.ustoa.com).
■TIP➡ Local tourism boards can provide information about lesser-known and small-niche operators that sell packages to only a few destinations.

■ GUIDED TOURS

Guided tours are a good option when you don't want to do it all yourself. You travel along with a group (sometimes large, sometimes small), stay in prebooked hotels, eat with your fellow travelers (the cost of meals sometimes included in the price of your tour, sometimes not), and follow a schedule.

But not all guided tours are an if-it's-Tuesday-this-must-be-Belgium experience. A knowledgeable guide can take you places that you might never discover on your own, and you may be pushed to see more than you would have otherwise. Tours aren't for everyone, but they can be just the thing for trips to places where making travel arrangements is difficult or time-consuming (particularly when you don't speak the language).

Whenever you book a guided tour, find out what's included and what isn't. A land-only tour includes all your travel (by bus, in most cases) in the destination, but not necessarily your flights to and from or even within it. Also, in most cases prices in tour brochures don't include fees and taxes. And remember that you'll be expected to tip your guide (in cash) at the end of the tour.

BEST BETS FOR TOURS

Wildland Adventures pride themselves on culturally and ecologically sensitive trips. They have two Guatemala tours, both of which emphasize learning about Mayan culture. One of AdventureSmith Explorations' nine-day Guatemala trips focuses exclusively on El Petén, and another focuses on the highlands; their five-day Tikal and Palenque escape takes in two Mayan ruins in a very short time.

British-based company Responsible Travel has many Guatemala trips: the range includes low-budget packages and combinations with other Central American countries. Small groups and low-impact touring are also an important part of Intrepid Travel's holidays. They have 12 Guatemala trips, all aimed at independent travelers, that include a 10-day mountain-biking holiday, ecotours, language programs, and multi-week volunteer opportunities.

The Adventure Center's trips usually involve a little bit of action (rafting, hiking, or cycling) as well as more standard touring. Guatemala is often combined with Mexico, Belize, and Costa Rica on their longer holidays. Canoe, foot, bike, and even zip-line are some of the modes of transport on The World Outdoors' Guatemala Multi-Sport holiday.

Overseas Adventure Travel takes pride in small groups and excellent guides. One of their tours combines Guatemala with Honduras, El Salvador, and Belize.

Recommended Companies **Adventure-Smith** (☎800/728–2875 ⊕www.adventuresmithexplorations.com). **Intrepid Travel** (☎61/3/9473—2626 (Australia) ⊕www.intrepidtravel.com).

Overseas Adventure Travel (☎800/493–6824 ⊕www.oattravel.com). **Responsible Travel** (☎44/1273/600030 [UK] ⊕www.responsibletravel.com). **The World Outdoors** (☎800/488-8483 ⊕www.theworldoutdoors.com). **Wildland Adventures** (☎800/645–4453 ⊕www.wildland.com).

BIRD-WATCHING

Cayaya Birding is a Guatemalan company. Their 8 set-itinerary birding tours last from 4 to 16 days; they can also arrange personalized tours.

Contacts **Cayaya Birding** (☎502/5308–5160 ⊕www.cayaya-birding.com).

CULTURE

Culture Xplorers' Guatemala trip focuses on grassroots culture, includes visits to indigenous communities and coffee-farmers, and introduces you to Mayan textiles.

Contacts **Culture Xplorers** (☎866/877–2507 ⊕www.culturexplorers.com).

FISHING

The Great Sailfishing Company has a range of escorted fishing packages based at villas or resorts on Guatemala's Pacific coast.

Contacts **The Great Sailfishing Company** (☎877/763-0851 ⊕www.greatsailfishing.com).

▌ CRUISES

Guatemala isn't a major cruise destination, but some ships on Panama Canal cruises call in at its only cruise port, Puerto Quetzal, on the Pacific coast.

Cruise Lines **Holland America Line** (☎206/281–3535 or 877/932–4259 ⊕www.hollandamerica.com). **Norwegian Cruise Line** (☎305/436–4000 or 800/327–7030 ⊕www.ncl.com). **Princess Cruises** (☎661/753–0000 or 800/774–6237 ⊕www.princess.com). **Silversea Cruises** (☎954/522–4477 or 800/722–9955 ⊕www.silversea.com).

TRANSPORTATION

Roughly the same size as Tennessee, Guatemala occupies the full breadth of Central America and has both Pacific and Caribbean coastlines. The main bulk of the country is the mountainous southern half, which contains 21 of Guatemala's 22 departments. Guatemala City, the country's capital, is in the south. It's the biggest urban area in Central America, and opinions of both visitors and locals are divided on whether *la ciudad* (the city), as it's often called, is a chaotic nightmare or a taste of the real Guatemala. Although most international flights land here, many visitors go straight to nearby Antigua (only 45 km [28 mi] away) or Lake Atitlán (60 km away) rather than staying in the city.

TRAVEL TIMES FROM GUATEMALA CITY		
To	By Air	By Bus
Antigua	n/a	1 hour
Panajachel	n/a	3 hours
Quet-zaltenango	n/a	3½ hours
Flores	¾ hour to 1 hour	7 to 9 hours
Lago Izabal	n/a	4 hours
Puerto Barrios	n/a	6 hours
Monterrico	n/a	3 hours
Cobán	n/a	4 hours

▌ BY AIR

Guatemala City is the country's main hub: from Dallas or Houston the flying time is 2 hours; from Miami, 2½ hours; from Los Angeles, 7 hours; from New York or Chicago, 5½ hours; from Toronto via Miami or Mexico City, about 7 hours.

Airlines & Airports Airline and Airport Links.com (⊕www.airlineandairportlinks.com) has links to many of the world's airlines and airports.

Airline Security Issues Transportation Security Administration (⊕www.tsa.gov) has answers for almost every question that might come up.

AIRPORTS

Nearly all international flights arrive at Aeropuerto Internacional La Aurora (GUA) in Guatemala City, the country's main air hub. It's currently undergoing a massive overhaul, aimed at transforming it into Central America's biggest airport. Works are slated to end in mid-2008, but for the moment La Aurora is slow, noisy, and chaotic. Its few shops and restaurants may be affected by the works, so bring ample entertainment and snacks if you expect to spend much time there waiting for a flight.

The arrivals hall has a temperamental ATM which is frequently out of money or out of order. You can buy quetzals at an exchange office, open until about 9 PM, when the airport begins to shut down operations for the night, but passengers with a valid ticket can stay there overnight to wait for early flights.

The road between the airport and Guatemala City is often targeted by thieves and carjackers, especially at night. Try to choose a flight that arrives in daylight hours. If you do travel into Guatemala City after dark, ask your hotel if they have a transfer service. Otherwise arrange a private shuttle or take a registered taxi or the shuttle bus, never the public bus.

⚠ **Construction work and traffic on the road between Antigua and Guatemala City can change the 1-hour trip into a 2 ½-hour one. Consult your hotel or shuttle service about the current situation, and leave plenty of time to arrive.**

Tikal is served by the smaller Aeropuerto del Mundo Maya (FRS), just outside Flores. More commonly known as Aeropuerto Internacional Santa Elena, it's mainly for internal flights from Guatemala City, although some flights from other Central American countries, notably Belize, also land here.

There are several other small airports in Guatemala—Puerto Barrios, for example—but these are usually served by private jets or island-hoppers, rather than scheduled flights.

In Guatemala there's a $30 departure tax on all international flights, but it's often included in your ticket price. All the same, you have to pay a so-called airport security fee of Q20 in cash at the airport. For local flights, departure tax is Q5.

AIRPORT INFORMATION
Aeropuerto Internacional La Aurora
(⊠Guatemala City ☎2331–8192).

GROUND TRANSPORTATION
La Aurora airport is about 61/2 km (4 mi) from Guatemala City and 24 km (15 mi) from Antigua. The easiest and safest way to reach both cities from the airport is by registered taxi or private shuttle. Taxis to Guatemala City cost about $13 and take between 15 and 30 minutes; the trip to Antigua can take anything between 40 minutes and 2½ hours, depending on traffic, and costs about $25. Only take a numbered cab from the official booth, never one touting for service.

Shuttles are private minibus services. You can either book a shuttle in advance for yourself, or you can share one with other passengers going in the same direction. Shuttles to Antigua leave regularly and cost $35 for a private service, or $12 to $15 per person on a shared service. STA is one of the best-known local shuttle services.

Public buses connect the airport to Guatemala City, but have a bad reputation for safety.

The 2-km-taxi ride between Aeropuerto del Mundo Maya and Flores costs around $3.

Contacts Servicios Turísticos Atitlán (☎7762–2246 ⊕www.visit-antigua.com/vans.htm).

FLIGHTS

TO & FROM GUATEMALA
All scheduled international flights into Guatemala land at Guatemala City, with the exception of flights between Flores and Belize City. Continental and Mexicana have operated services to Flores in the past, but at this writing these services had been suspended.

Central American airline TACA flies direct from Los Angeles, Chicago, New York, Miami, and Washington's Dulles. TACA flights are usually punctual and include a meal service, though missing luggage is an oft-reported problem.

There are daily flights from Dallas and Miami on American and from Houston on Continental. Los Angeles is served by United and Delta, which also flies to Atlanta. Mexicana flies direct to Mexico City, and Iberia has flights to Madrid.

Some of the best deals around are with Spirit Air, a low-cost airline that flies daily from Fort Lauderdale and Los Angeles to Guatemala. US Airways, which flies direct to Charlotte, North Carolina, also has good prices.

Tropic Air and Maya Island Air, both from Belize, each have two daily flights from Flores to Belize City.

Airline Contacts AmericanAirlines (☎800/433–7300 ⊕www.aa.com). **Continental Airlines** (☎800/523–3273 for U.S. and Mexico reservations, 800/231–0856 for international reservations ⊕www.continental.com). **Delta Airlines** (☎800/221–1212 for U.S. reservations, 800/241–4141 for international reservations ⊕www.delta.com). **Iberia** (☎800/772–4642 ⊕www.iberia.com). **Maya Island Air** (☎800/225–6732 ⊕www.mayaairways.com). **Mexicana** (☎800/531–7921 ⊕www.mexicana.com). **Spirit Airlines** (☎800/772–7117 ⊕www.spiritair.com). **TACA** (☎800/400–8222 ⊕www.taca.com). **Tropic**

Air (☎800/422-3435 ⊕www.tropicair.com).
United Airlines (☎800/864-8331 for U.S.
reservations, 800/538-2929 for international
reservations ⊕www.united.com). **USAirways**
(☎800/428-4322 for U.S. and Canada reservations, 800/622-1015 for international reservations ⊕www.usairways.com).

WITHIN GUATEMALA

TACA has both morning and afternoon
departures between Guatemala City and
Flores. You can buy flights online before
your trip, but booking through a Guatemalan travel agent can often reduce costs
by almost half. Standard return fares usually cost around $200. TAG operates the
same route once a day.

Airline Contacts **TACA** (☎800/400-8222 in
U.S., 2470-8222 in Guatemala ⊕www.taca.
com). **TAG** (☎2360-3038 ⊕www.tag.com.gt).

▌BY BOAT

There's a daily water taxi service at 9 AM
from Punta Gorda, in Belize, to Puerto
Barrios in Guatemala. The trip takes
about 1½ hours and returns at around
2 PM; tickets costs $15 to $18 each way.
A similar service operates between Livingston and Punta Gorda on Tuesday and
Friday; it's a 50-minute trip. Requena's
Charter Services are a reputable Belize-based outfit. Other operators have booths
on the waterfronts of all three towns: you
turn up and buy a ticket on the spot.

Note that life jackets are typically not
provided on boats and that the seas can be
rough. Postpone your trip if the weather
looks bad, and don't be shy about waiting
for another boat if the one offered looks
unseaworthy or overcrowded.

Information **Requena's Charter Service**
(☎501/722-2070 in Punta Gorda, Belize
⊕www.belizenet.com/requena).

▌BY BUS

ARRIVING & DEPARTING

Many travelers arrive and depart Guatemala by bus. The services listed here are
all so-called "first-class" buses, which
means little more than that there is a toilet on-board and air-conditioning, though
there are never guarantees as to whether
either will work. Despite this, departures
are usually punctual. Several second-class
buses operate international routes, but
have neither Web sites, reliable enquiry
numbers nor, at this writing, fixed terminals, due to the Guatemala City transport
authority's chaotic attempt at terminal
reorganization.

Popular with budget travelers, Ticabus is
a international bus company connecting
all of Central America. They have direct
daily services from Guatemala City to
Tapachula in Mexico ($17; five hours)
and El Salvador ($11; four hours). Connecting services go to Nicaragua, Honduras, Costa Rica, and Panama but usually
involve one or two overnight stops. Hedman Alas is a Honduran company that
connects Guatemala and Antigua with
Tegucigalpa in Honduras ($68). Línea
Dorada runs services from Guatemala
City to Tapachula, Mexico; and from
Flores to Belize City and Chetumal,
Mexico. They offer connecting services
to other Mexican cities.

Contacts **Hedman Alas** (☎2362-5072
⊕www.hedmanalas.com). **Línea Dorada**
(☎2232-5506 ⊕www.tikalmayanworld.com).
Ticabus (☎2366-4038 ⊕www.ticabus.com).

GETTING AROUND GUATEMALA

Guatemalan buses come in three very different subspecies. Locals still favor the
recycled Bluebird school buses known as
camionetas; but the newer, dearer *pullmans*—once Greyhound coaches—are
gaining popularity, especially for longer
trips. Quicker and more comfortable are
private minibus shuttle services: you can
hire one to yourself or buy a seat on services with scheduled departures.

Dressed up in the gaudiest paint jobs around and blaring merengue, camionetas whiz along at breakneck speeds. They often start out from terminals near a market, but will screech to a halt whenever a potential passenger appears on the roadside. People pile in like hens in a coop, giving rise to the tourist nickname "chicken buses." Camionetas can get you just about anywhere cheaply and quickly, making them great for short trips. Tightly-squeezed seating, short routes and their drivers' disregard for basic road rules means they probably aren't a good idea on longer journeys. Their schedules are also loose, sometimes delaying departures until buses fill up. Be aware that on some routes the last bus of the day isn't always a sure thing, so always ask before waiting around.

Drivers and their assistants, called *cobradors* or *ayudantes,* are often a bit gruff but really know their stuff: they can tell you if you're on the right bus and remind you when and where to get off. Within cities, you pay the cobrador as you board (Q2 to Q4 is the norm); on intercity buses a fare collector passes through the bus periodically to take your fare, showing an amazing ability to keep track of riders who haven't paid. Large bags are typically stowed on top—this may make you nervous, but thefts aren't common. Except for occasional pickpocketings, incidents involving foreign travelers on public buses are rare.

Several companies operate long-distance pullmans, the self-styled first-class service, between Guatemala's main cities. On a few routes there are *de lujo* (deluxe) express buses with air-conditioning and other comforts, which cost a few dollars more. Take the pictures shown at bus terminals and on Web sites with a pinch of salt, and keep your comfort expectations low even on deluxe routes: maintenance standards fluctuate wildly and you never really know what you're getting until you board the bus. You can buy tickets in advance at bus terminals, but it's usually

unnecessary for routes within Guatemala: arrive at bus terminals about a half hour before your departure.

From Guatemala City ADN (Autobuses del Norte) has services to Flores and Río Dulce. Litegua operates many daily regular and first-class services between Guatemala City and Puerto Barrios. Línea Dorada offers direct bus service between Guatemala City and Flores. Servicios Turísticos Atitlán, known as STA, is one of the best-known shuttle companies.

Bus Information **ADN** (☎2251–0050 ⊕www.adnautobusesdelnorte.com). **Litegua** (☎2289–4041 ⊕www.litegua.com). **Línea Dorada** (☎2232–5506 ⊕www.tikalmayanworld.com). **Servicios Turísticos Atitlán** (☎7762–2246 ⊕www.visit-antigua.com/vans.htm).

▌BY CAR

Although it's easy to get around Guatemala without a car, it's much easier to visit small villages and explore the countryside if you have one. Taking to Guatemala's roads requires some courage, however. Local drivers pay scant attention to speed limits or traffic rules. Outside the big cities potholed road surfaces are common and mountain roads are often bordered by sheer drops. If you are not used to driving very defensively, taking buses or private shuttles may be a better idea. Always allow extra travel time for unpredictable events, making sure to bring along snacks and drinks.

It's possible to enter Guatemala by land from Mexico, Belize, El Salvador, and Honduras. The Pan-American Highway, which passes through most major cities, connects the country with Mexico at La Mesilla and with El Salvador at San Cristobal Frontera. It's also possible to travel to El Salvador via the coastal highway, crossing at Ciudad Pedro de Alvarado, or Valle Nuevo. Pacific routes to Mexico pass through Tecún Umán and El Carmen–Talismán.

To reach Belize, take the highway east from Flores, passing El Cruce before reaching the border town of Melchor de Mencos. There are also two routes into Honduras, through El Florido or Esquipulas.

Travelers often get harassed or swindled at border towns. There is no entry fee, although you may be asked for a bribe. Rental agencies sometimes allow you to cross the border with their car, but you usually have to pay a fee to do so.

You can drive in Guatemala with a valid U.S. license. Most roads leading to larger towns and cities are paved; those leading to small towns and villages are generally dirt roads. *Doble-tracción*, or four-wheel drive, is a necessity in many remote areas, especially at the height of the rainy season. Gas stations can also be scarce, so be sure to fill up before heading into rural areas. Consider bringing some extra fuel along with you. Don't count on finding repair shops outside the major towns.

Many locals ignore traffic laws, so you should be on your guard. *Alto* means "stop" and *Frene con motor* ("use engine to break" or downshift) means that a steep descent lies ahead. Travel only by day, especially if you are driving alone. Keep your eyes peeled for children or animals on the road. If you arrive at a roadblock such as a downed tree, do not attempt to remove the roadblock, simply turn around. Highway robbers often deliberately fell trees to ensnare drivers.

GASOLINE

There are plenty of gas stations in and near big cities in Guatemala. On long trips fill your tank whenever you can, even if you've still got gas left, as the next station could be a long way away. An attendant always pumps the gas and doesn't expect a tip, though a small one is always appreciated. Plan to use cash, as credit cards are rarely accepted.

Most rental cars run on premium unleaded gas, which costs about Q28 a gallon.

PARKING

On-street parking generally isn't a good idea in Guatemala as car theft is very common. Instead, park in a guarded parking lot. Many hotels have their own guarded parking lots.

ROAD CONDITIONS

Immense improvements have been made to Guatemala's ravaged roads. All the same, potholed and unpaved surfaces are common. Mountain roads are peppered with hairpin bends, and often don't have guardrails; conditions are particularly tough in the rainy season. Always pick a four-wheel-drive vehicle for travel off the beaten path.

Ongoing roadworks and the sheer volume of traffic can double journey times between major cities. Don't count on going any faster than 50 mph on paved roads; 15 to 20 mph is more normal on dirt roads.

Guatemalan road signage is far from perfect. There are usually signs pointing to large towns, but routes to smaller towns may not be clearly marked. Look for intersections where people seem to be waiting for a bus—that's a good sign that there's an important turnoff nearby.

FROM	TO	DISTANCE
Guatemala City	Antigua	24 km (15 mi)
Antigua	Panajachel	60 km (37 mi)
Antigua	Quetzaltenango	215 km (134 mi)
Guatemala City	Cobán	212 km (132 mi)
Cobán	Flores	190 km (118 mi)
Flores	Tikal	60 km (37 mi)
Flores	Puerto Barrios	284 km (176 mi)
Guatemala City	Puerto Barrios	296 km (184 mi)

ROADSIDE EMERGENCIES

Guatemala has no private roadside assistance clubs—ask rental agencies carefully about what you should do if you break down. You can also call the police or Provial, the state roadside assistance team, but expect both to take a long time to arrive. Operators on both lines usually only speak Spanish.

Emergency Services Guatemalan National Police (☎110 or 120). **Provial** (☎2422–7878).

RULES OF THE ROAD

Drivers in Guatemala stick to the right. Seat belts are required, and the law is now enforced. There are few speed-limit signs, and police sometimes ignore speeders, though enforcement of all traffic laws is becoming more routine. As you approach small towns, watch out for *topes,* the local name for speed bumps.

Guatemala's highways are an adventure, especially when they run along the edges of cliffs soaring high above a valley. Trucks and buses drive unbelievably fast along these routes; if you don't feel comfortable keeping up the pace, pull over periodically to let them pass. The narrow roads mean you can be stuck motionless on the road for an hour while a construction crew stands around a hole in the ground. If you observe the rules you follow at home, you should be fine. Just don't expect everyone else to follow them.

▌ BY SHUTTLE

Shuttles in Guatemala are private minivans that can seat eight. You can either hire one for yourself, or pay for a seat on a shared service. They're faster and more comfortable than public buses and maintain a fairly reliable schedule. Advance reservations are usually required.

Shuttles can be arranged at the airport, at travel agencies, and through most hotels and hostels. Popular routes, like those between Guatemala City, Antigua, Chichicastenango, Panajachel, and Quetzaltenango run three to five times daily; other routes may have less frequent departures.

A private shuttle between Antigua and Guatemala airport costs $35 to $40; a seat on the same shuttle is $12. Atitrans and Servicios Turísticos Atitlán are two reputable companies that operate shuttles throughout the country.

Guatemala Companies Atitrans (☎7832–3371 ⊕www.atitrans.com). **Servicios Turísticos Atitlán** (☎7762–2246 ⊕www.visit-antigua.com/vans.htm).

▌ BY TAXI

Most Guatemalan cities are small enough to walk around, but taxis can be a good idea late at night or for longer trips. Meters are the norm in Guatemala City; everywhere else you need to agree upon your fare in advance. Wherever possible, get your hotel or restaurant to call you a cab, otherwise try to pick vehicles with a clearly painted number on the side, which means they're registered. You can often hire a taxi for a day or half-day trip, and many willingly shuttle you between Guatemala City and Antigua for $35. Taxi drivers aren't generally willing to change large bills, so carry enough for your trip and a small tip.

ON THE GROUND

▮ COMMUNICATIONS

INTERNET

Internet access is widely available to travelers in Guatemala. Many high-end hotels offer some kind of in-room access for laptop users (often Wi-Fi), but note that you are sometimes charged extra for using this. Many hostels and language-schools are also well-connected and usually charge reasonable rates.

All big cities have a choice of cybercafés, and even remote locations usually have at least one. Rates range between Q3 to Q8 an hour. Many have Internet-phone services.

Contacts **Cybercafes** (⊕ www.cybercafes. com) lists over 4,000 Internet cafés worldwide.

PHONES

The good news is that you can now make a direct-dial telephone call from virtually any point on earth. The bad news? You can't always do so cheaply. Calling from a hotel is almost always the most expensive option; hotels usually add huge surcharges to all calls, particularly international ones. In some countries you can phone from call centers or even the post office. Calling cards usually keep costs to a minimum, but only if you purchase them locally. And then there are mobile phones (⇨ below), which are sometimes more prevalent—particularly in the developing world—than landlines; as expensive as mobile phone calls can be, they are still usually a much cheaper option than calling from your hotel.

The country code for Guatemala is 502. To call Guatemala from the United States, dial the international access code (011) followed by the country code (502), and the eight-digit phone number, in that order. Guatemala does not use area codes.

CALLING WITHIN GUATEMALA

Guatemala's phone system is usually reliable. You can make local and long-distance calls from your hotel—usually with a surcharge—and from any public phone box or call center (known as *locutorios*). All Guatemalan phone numbers have eight digits.

Local calls in Guatemala are cheap. Most pay phones operate with phone cards, so it's worth buying one if you plan to make many local calls. You can buy a phone card in most grocery stores, or at Telgua offices. You can also make calls from these. ▮ TIP → **Do not use the black, red, or blue wall-mounted phones with signs that read FREE COLLECT CALL. They charge a whopping $10-per minute and have a 5-minute minimum.**

Useful Numbers **Local Directory Assistance (in Spanish) (☎ 124). Operator Assistance (in Spanish) (☎ 121).**

CALLING OUTSIDE GUATEMALA

To make international calls from Guatemala, dial 00, then the country code, area code, and number. Many public call centers (*locutorios*) use Internet telephony and so have very cheap rates, but communication quality can vary. Midrange and budget hotels sometimes have similarly competitive services. You can also make international calls from pay phones using a prepaid calling card. You can make collect calls to North America through the international operator.

The country code for the United States is 1.

You can use AT&T, Sprint, and MCI services from Guatemalan phones, though some pay phones require you to put coins in to make the call. Using a prepaid calling card is generally cheaper.

Useful Numbers **International Operator (for collect calls) (☎ 147–120).**

258 <   On the Ground

LOCAL DO'S AND TABOOS

CUSTOMS OF THE COUNTRY

■ Guatemala has a large indigenous population, who maintain many Mayan traditions and religious rites. Be judicious when taking photographs at such events, and if in doubt, ask for permission. There are few taboos to worry about when interacting with Ladinos (nonindigenous Guatemalans).

■ Ask when someone or something is due to arrive and you're likely to get "*ahorita*" (now-ish) as a reply. Guatemalan timing is rather more flexible than North American, and you should be prepared to be patient. Buses and airplanes are usually fairly punctual, however. In Guatemala it is acceptable to make a quick hiss or whistle to get someone's attention—you may find that you even take up the habit yourself, particularly with waiters. You also may hear men catcall women in this way, which, unfortunately, is not considered terribly rude either.

GREETINGS

■ Guatemalans use formal salutations (*buenos días, buenas tardes,* and *buenas noches*) to greet strangers, business associates, and people with whom they don't have a close relationship. The formal "you" form, *usted,* is also common in such situations. Women often greet each other with a kiss on the cheek. Among men, hand-shaking is the norm, sometimes accompanied by a friendly backslap.

SIGHTSEEING

■ In Guatemala's major cities, you can dress pretty much as you would at home. In smaller villages, however, people are more conservative, so ditch the microminis and hotpants in favor of less revealing clothing.

■ With the exception of luxury buses and shuttles, the seats on Guatemalan buses are expected to fit three abreast. Always make room for others on buses. It's perfectly fine to step into the aisle to let someone take a middle or window seat.

OUT ON THE TOWN

■ Although drinking alcohol—especially beer—is very normal for Guatemalan men, Guatemalan women tend not to drink very much, if at all. Smoking is prohibited on public transport and in some enclosed public spaces.

■ Public displays of affection are fine between heterosexual couples in big cities, but expect conservative—or even aggressive—reactions to same-sex couples.

■ If you are invited to someone's house for a meal, take along a small gift for the hostess.

LANGUAGE

■ Spanish is spoken by the majority of Guatemalans, many of whom also speak Mayan languages. Wherever tourist traffic is heavy, English speakers are plentiful. Spanish is the only way to communicate off the beaten path. Language schools are a huge business in Guatemala, and many offer quick "crash" courses which can help start you off on the right linguistic foot. Be aware than many Guatemalans will answer "yes" even if they don't understand your question, so as not to appear unkind or unhelpful. To minimize such confusion, try posing questions as "Where is so-and-so?" rather than "Is so-and-so this way?"

■ A phrase book and language-tape set can help get you started.

■ *Fodor's Spanish for Travelers* (available at bookstores everywhere) is excellent.

Access Codes **AT&T** (☎From Guatemala City 138–126, from the rest of Guatemala 9999–190). **MCI** (☎9999–189). **Sprint** (☎9999–195).

CALLING CARDS

Guatemala's public pay phones use pre-paid calling cards, which you can purchase at small markets, pharmacies, and Telgua offices. Ask for a *tarjeta telefónica*. They come in denominations of Q20, Q30, and Q50; calls within Guatemala cost 50 centavos per minute.

MOBILE PHONES

Mobile phones are immensely popular in Guatemala—landlines are hard to get and expensive to maintain so locals rely heavily on their cells for basic communication needs. Guatemalan mobile phones use the GSM network. If you have an unlocked triband phone, and intend to call local numbers, it makes sense to buy a prepaid Guatemalan SIM card on arrival—rates will be much better than using your U.S. network.

There are three main mobile companies in Guatemala. Movistar, owned by Telefónica, has the cheapest rates: Q0.50 to Q1 per minute for local calls and Q1 to the U.S. Claro, owned by Telgua, is more expensive (Q1 for local calls and Q4 for U.S. calls) but has better coverage. Tigo is a happy medium. Prepaid SIM cards from all three companies cost between Q150 to Q200; prepaid phone packages start at around Q225 to Q500. You can then top up your credit with cards sold at most small grocery stores. Occasionally there are so-called half-price-minute sales, where you are credited twice the face value of your top-up card. Shops and stands from all three companies abound in the big cities, with more opening all the time.

■ TIP→ **Many language schools rent mobile phones to their students, or have special deals for buying one.**

Contacts **Cellular Abroad** (☎800/287–5072 ⊕www.cellularabroad.com) rents and sells

GMS phones and sells SIM cards that work in many countries. **Claro** (⊕www.claro.com.gt).

Mobal (☎888/888–9162 ⊕www.mobalrental.com) rents mobiles and sells GSM phones (starting at $49) that will operate in 140 countries. Per-call rates vary throughout the world. **Movistar** (⊕www.movistar.com.gt).

Planet Fone (☎888/988–4777 ⊕www.planetfone.com) rents cell phones, but the per-minute rates are expensive. **Tigo** (⊕www.comcel.com.gt).

▮ CUSTOMS & DUTIES

You're always allowed to bring goods of a certain value back home without having to pay any duty or import tax. But there's a limit on the amount of tobacco and liquor you can bring back duty-free, and some countries have separate limits for perfumes; for exact figures, check with your customs department. The values of so-called "duty-free" goods are included in these amounts. When you shop abroad, save all your receipts, as customs inspectors may ask to see them as well as the items you purchased. If the total value of your goods is more than the duty-free limit, you'll have to pay a tax (most often a flat percentage) on the value of everything beyond that limit.

Visitors may enter Guatemala duty-free with a camera, up to six rolls of film, any clothes and articles needed while traveling, 500 grams of tobacco, 3 liters of alcoholic beverages, 2 bottles of perfume, and 2 kg of candy. Unless you bring in a lot of merchandise, customs officers probably won't even check your luggage, although a laptop may attract some attention.

It's illegal to export most Mayan artifacts. If you plan on buying such goods, do so only at reputable stores, and keep the receipt. You may not take fruits or vegetables out of Guatemala.

U.S. Information **U.S. Customs and Border Protection** (⊕www.cbp.gov).

▌EATING OUT

When it comes to food, Guatemala seems eclipsed by its neighbor, Mexico. It's an unfair oversight, though: there are plenty of delicious dishes unique to the country. As most top-end restaurants specialize in European or American fare, you'll have to look to cheaper places (including markets and street vendors) for truly Guatemalan flavors.

As in the rest of Central America, refried black beans, eggs, and thick corn tortillas play a big role in many Guatemalan dishes. Tamales, tacos, and tostadas (toasted corn tortillas with a variety of fillings) make quick and tasty snacks. Other street-side dishes include fried chicken and french fries, or *churrasquitos* (sliced beef or chorizo served with pickled cabbage and tortillas). *Huevos motuleños* (layers of fried eggs served on a crispy tortilla with cheese, beans, hot sauce, and sometimes ham) make an amazing breakfast.

Some of Guatemala's standout dishes include *róbalo* (a fish called snook elsewhere); *ceviche* (chilled marinated seafood "cooked" using lime juice, rather than heat), and chiles rellenos (bell peppers stuffed with meat and vegetables). Two excellent local sauces which accompany meat or chicken are *jocón* (made of green tomato and coriander) and *pepián* (a bitter sauce made with pumpkin seeds). More unusual specialities include *tepisquintle* (the world's largest rodent) and *sopa de tortuga* (turtle soup). Guatemalans don't each huge quantities of meat, but a little shredded chicken, ground beef, chorizo, or ham seems to make its way into just about every dish, so vegetarian options can be limited. In big cities, Chinese and Italian restaurants abound, and are a good way for veggies to stop feeling "beaned out." All the same, *ensalada de aguacate* (avocado salad), *pan de banana* (banana bread), and flan (a crème caramel dessert) never get dull.

Only the most expensive restaurants in Guatemala accept credit cards and traveler's checks. The restaurants that we list (all of which are indicated by a ✕ symbol) are the cream of the crop in each price category. Properties indicated by a ✕▥ are lodging establishments whose restaurant warrants a special trip.

MEALS & MEALTIMES

A typical Guatemalan breakfast (*desayuno*) consists of tortillas, fried or scrambled eggs and refried beans, washed down with weak coffee. Most hotels catering to foreigners also offer fresh fruit, toast, and cereal, and you can expect full breakfast buffets at five-star hotels.

Lunch (*comida* or *almuerzo*) is the main meal, and runs from noon to 2 or 3. Many restaurants do set-price meals of two or three courses at lunchtime. For Guatemalans, dinner is less important, and often is just a light snack not long after sundown. Restaurants in major tourist areas offer more substantial fare and stay open later, but most places are all but deserted by 9.

Unless otherwise noted, the restaurants listed in this guide are open daily for lunch and dinner.

PAYING

In restaurants with waiter service, you pay the check (*la cuenta*) at the end of the meal. At street food stands and in markets, you sometimes pay upfront. Credit cards are accepted in more expensive restaurants, but it's always a good idea to check before you order, especially as some establishments only accept one kind of credit card.

For guidelines on tipping see Tipping, below.

RESERVATIONS & DRESS

Regardless of where you are, it's a good idea to make a reservation if you can. We only mention them specifically when reservations are essential (there's no other way you'll ever get a table) or when they are not accepted. For popular restaurants, book as far ahead as you can (often 30 days), and reconfirm as soon as you arrive. (Large parties should always call ahead to check the reservations policy.) We mention dress only when men are required to wear a jacket or a jacket and tie.

WINES, BEER & SPIRITS

Alcohol is available in just about every restaurant in Guatemala, though cheaper places have much more limited choice. Beer is the local alcoholic drink of choice. Lager is the most popular style, usually served ice-cold. Good local brands include Gallo, Dorada, and Cabro. Gallo also brews a dark beer called Moza.

Guatemala has no real wine market to speak of, but restaurants catering to tourists often have imported bottles from the United States or Chile and Argentina. Imported liquor is easy to find in supermarkets; *ron* (rum) and *aguardiente* ("firewater" distilled from sugarcane) are favorite local tipples.

The official drinking age in Guatemala is 20, but this is rarely enforced.

▌ELECTRICITY

You won't need a converter or adapter as the electrical current in Guatemala is 110 volts, the same as in the United States. Outlets in both countries take U.S.–style plugs. ▌TIP➔ **Power surges are fairly common, so consider carrying a surge stabilizer if you travel with expensive electrical items, such as a laptop.** In a few remote areas lodges and hotels may generate their own electricity. After the generators are turned off at night, light comes only from kerosene lanterns or your flashlight.

Contacts Steve Kropla's Help for World Traveler's (⊕www.kropla.com) has information on electrical and telephone plugs around the world. **Walkabout Travel Gear** (⊕www.walkabouttravelgear.com) has a good coverage of electricity under "adapters."

▌EMERGENCIES

In a medical or dental emergency, ask your hotel staff for information on and directions to the nearest private hospital or clinic. Taxi drivers should also know how to find one, and taking a taxi is often quicker than an ambulance. If you do need an ambulance, it's best to call for one from the hospital you want to go for; alternatively, you can call the Red Cross. Many private medical insurers provide online lists of hospitals and clinics in different towns. It's a good idea to print out a copy of these before you travel.

For theft, wallet loss, small road accidents, and minor emergencies, contact the nearest police station. Expect all dealings with the police to be a lengthy, bureaucratic business—it's probably only worth bothering if you need the report for insurance claims.

Pack a basic first-aid kit, especially if you're venturing into more remote areas. If you'll be carrying any medication, bring your doctor's contact information and prescription authorizations. Getting your prescription filled in Guatemala might be problematic, so bring enough medication for your entire trip—and extras in case of travel delays.

Foreign Embassies United States (✉Av. La Reforma 7–01, Zona 10, Guatemala City ☎2326–4000, 2331–2354 for after-hours emergency assistance ⊕http://.guatemala.usembassy.gov).

General Emergency Contacts Municipal Fire Department (☎123). **Police** (☎110 or 120). **Red Cross Ambulances** (☎125).

▌HEALTH

Guatemala's public hospitals are chronically underfunded, under-equipped, and understaffed. Although they will tend to you in an emergency, wherever possible, seek private medical care. Most big cities have at least a couple of private clinics or hospitals; there's usually at least one English-speaker on the staff. Treatment at such clinics can be very expensive, so medical insurance is a necessity.

In Guatemala it's best to drink only bottled water, called *agua purificada* or *agua mineral* in Spanish. It is available even at the smallest stores and is much cheaper than in North America.

The major health risk in Guatemala is traveler's diarrhea, so skip uncooked foods and unpasteurized milk and milk products. Ask for your drinks *sin hielo*, meaning "without ice." In Belize most resort areas have ice that's perfectly safe. Pepto-Bismol or Imodium (known generically as loperamide) can be purchased over the counter in Guatemala, but bring along your own stash in case you aren't near a pharmacy. Drink plenty of purified water or tea—chamomile is a good folk remedy. Pharmacies also sell sachets of rehydration salts (*suero oral*), or you can purify your own: ½-teaspoon salt (*sal*) and 4-tablespoons sugar (*azúcar*) dissolved in a quart of water.

Two mosquito-borne diseases are prevalent in Guatemala: dengue fever (along the Pacific coast and in Petén province) and malaria (in areas below 1,500 meteres [4,921 feet]). Prevention is better than a cure: cover up your arms and legs and use a strong insect repellent containing a high concentration of DEET. Don't hang around outside at sunset, and sleep under a mosquito net in jungle areas. Preventative antimalarial medication may also be necessary, so consult your doctor well before you travel. There are no preventative drugs for dengue.

▌HOURS OF OPERATION

Most banks are open 9 to 4 but many stay open until 7 PM. Many museums are closed Monday. Most have normal business hours, but some close for a few hours in the afternoon. Tikal opens daily 8 to 6. Shops are generally open 10 to 7, with many closing for a 1 to 3 lunch break. Small grocery stores known as *tiendas* usually open much later than this.

HOLIDAYS

Año Nuevo (**New Year's Day**), January 1; *Semana Santa* (**Easter Week**), March 20–23, 2008, and April 9–13, 2009; *Día del Trabajador* (**Labor Day**), May 1; *Día del Ejército* (**Army Day**), June 30; *Día de la Independencia* (**Independence Day**), September 15; *Día de la Raza* (**Discovery of America**), October 12; *Día de la Revolución* (**Revolution Day**), October 20; *Todos los Santos* (**All Saints' Day**), November 1; *Navidad* (**Christmas**), December 25. Each town and region also have their own *fiesta* (festival), where carnival-like celebrations can last a whole week.

▌MAIL

Most Guatemalan towns have a post office. El Correo, the Guatemalan mail system, has a bad reputation for losing letters—especially if they are sent from more remote locations in the country. Most post offices open from 8:30 to 5:30. Airmail letters to North America cost Q5 and take a week or two to arrive. High-end hotels can usually send your mail for you, too.

Your hotel may be willing to receive mail for you. American Express also offers free mail collection at its main city offices for its cardholders.

Contacts El Correo (☎1-801/267-7367 ⊕www.elcorreo.com.gt).

SHIPPING PACKAGES

Expect packages you send through the Guatemalan mail system to take a very long time to arrive. They usually get there in the end, but it's worth paying extra for recorded delivery (*correo registrado*). Many stores can ship your purchases for you, for a cost. Valuable items are best send with private express services. Couriers operating in Guatemala include DHL, UPS, and Federal Express. Delivery within two to three days for a 1-kg. (2.2 lb) package starts at about Q500.

Express Services **DHL Worldwide Express** (☎2379–1111 ⊕www.dhl.com.gt). **Federal Express** (☎1–801/FEDEX ⊕www.fedex.com/gt). **UPS** (☎2630–6460 ⊕www.ups.com).

∎ MONEY

Guatemala can be remarkably cheap, especially when you're traveling in the villages of the highlands. Mid-range hotels and restaurants where locals eat are excellent value for money. Rooms at first-class hotels and meals at the best restaurants, however, approach those in developed countries. Trips into remote parts of the jungle and specialty travel like river rafting and deep-sea fishing are also relatively expensive.

You can plan your trip around ATMs—cash is king for day-to-day dealings—and credit cards (for bigger spending). U.S. dollars can be changed at any bank and are widely accepted as payment; leave all other currencies at home. Traveler's checks are useful only as a reserve.

Prices throughout this guide are given for adults. Substantially reduced fees are almost always available for children, students, and senior citizens.

∎TIP➔ **Banks never have every foreign currency on hand, and it may take as long as a week to order. If you're planning to exchange funds before leaving home, don't wait 'til the last minute.**

SAMPLE COSTS	
Item	Average Cost
Cup of Coffee	Q2 to Q4
Glass of Beer	Q8
Sandwich	Q10
Museum Admission	Free to Q25
Set-price lunch	Q15 to Q20

ATMS & BANKS

ATMs—known as locally as *cajeros automáticos*—are easy to find in Guatemalan cities. Cards on the Cirrus and Plus networks can be used in ATMs bearing these signs: CREDOMATIC, BANCARED, BI, and 5B. Major banks in Guatemala include BAC, Banco Industrial, and Banco Occidente. In some smaller cities, finding an ATM is trickier. Technically, you should be able to go into the bank to withdraw money through a teller using your ATM card, but it's easier just to take ample cash supplies with you. ∎TIP➔ **ATMs often empty out before holiday weekends, so withdraw your cash beforehand.** Be sure your pin number only has four digits, as most Guatemalan ATMS don't accept longer ones. Make withdrawals from ATMs in daylight, never at night. Where possible, choose ATMs inside banks rather than freestanding ones.

CREDIT CARDS

Throughout this guide, the following abbreviations are used: **AE**, American Express; D, Discover; **DC**, Diners Club; **MC**, MasterCard; and **V**, Visa.

Visa is the most widely-accepted credit card in Guatemala, followed by MasterCard and American Express. Diners Club and Discover might not even be recognized. If possible, bring more than one credit card, as some establishments accept only one type. You can usually pay by credit card in top-end restaurants, hotels and stores; the latter sometimes charge a small surcharge for using credit cards. Many transportation and tour companies also take plastic.

It's a good idea to inform your credit-card company before you travel, especially if you're going abroad and don't travel internationally very often. Otherwise, the credit-card company might put a hold on your card owing to unusual activity—not a good thing halfway through your trip. Record all your credit-card numbers—as well as the phone numbers to call if your cards are lost or stolen—in a safe place, so you're prepared should something go wrong. Both MasterCard and Visa have general numbers you can call (collect if you're abroad) if your card is lost, but you're better off calling the number of your issuing bank, since MasterCard and Visa usually just transfer you to your bank; your bank's number is usually printed on your card.

■TIP➔ **Before you charge something, ask the merchant whether or not he or she plans to do a dynamic currency conversion (DCC). In such a transaction the credit-card** *processor* **(shop, restaurant, or hotel, not Visa or MasterCard) converts the currency and charges you in dollars. In most cases you'll pay the merchant a 3% fee for this service in addition to any credit-card company and issuing-bank foreign-transaction surcharges.**

Dynamic currency conversion programs are becoming increasingly widespread. Merchants who participate in them are supposed to ask whether you want to be charged in dollars or the local currency, but they don't always do so. And even if they do offer you a choice, they may well avoid mentioning the additional surcharges. The good news is that you *do* have a choice. And if this practice really gets your goat, you can avoid it entirely thanks to American Express; with its cards, DCC simply isn't an option.

Reporting Lost Cards **American Express** (☎800/528–4800 in the U.S. or 336/393–1111 collect from abroad ⊕www.american-

express.com). **Diners Club** (☎800/234–6377 in the U.S. or 303/799–1504 collect from abroad ⊕www.dinersclub.com). **MasterCard** (☎800/627–8372 in the U.S. or 636/722–7111 collect from abroad ⊕www.mastercard.com). **Visa** (☎800/847–2911 in the U.S. or 410/581–9994 collect from abroad ⊕www.visa.com).

CURRENCY & EXCHANGE

Guatemala's currency is the quetzal, named after the national bird, and is equal to 100 centavos. Single quetzals come as both coins and bills. There are also 1-, 5-, 10-, and 25-centavo coins. Bills come in denominations of ½ (brown), 1 (green), 5 (purple), 10 (red), 20 (blue), 50 (vermilion), and 100 (brown). At this writing the exchange rate is 7.6 quetzals to the U.S. dollar.

U.S. dollars are widely accepted in Guatemalan shops and restaurants, though the conversion rate might not be quite as good as at banks. Street-side money changers abound, but you'll be safer from scams if you change your money at a bank, even though the rates aren't quite as good. You can exchange money easily at the airport and at border crossings.

TRAVELER'S CHECKS & CARDS

U.S. dollar American Express traveler's checks are the only ones you can change in Guatemala. By all means take some along as an emergency fall-back option, but plan your trip around cash, ATMs and credit cards—you'll save a whole lot of time and headaches, not to mention commission charges.

American Express now offers a stored-value card called a Travelers Cheque Card, which you can use wherever American Express credit cards are accepted, including ATMs. The card can carry a minimum of $300 and a maximum of $2,700, and it's a very safe way to carry your funds. Although you can get replacement funds in 24 hours if your card is lost or stolen, it doesn't really strike us as a very good deal. In addition to a high initial cost ($14.95 to set up the card, plus $5 each time you "reload"), you still have to pay a 2% fee for each purchase in a foreign currency (similar to that of any credit card). Further, each time you use the card in an ATM you pay a transaction fee of $2.50 on top of the 2% transaction fee for the conversion—add it all up and it can be considerably more than you would pay when simply using your own ATM card. Regular traveler's checks are just as secure and cost less.

Contacts **American Express** (☎888/412–6945 in the U.S., 801/945–9450 collect outside of the U.S. to add value or speak to customer service ⊕www.americanexpress.com).

▌RESTROOMS

Guatemalan restrooms use Western-style toilets; cleanliness standards are often low, especially in public facilities such as bus and gas stations. Despite this, you often have to pay a small fee (a quetzal or two) to use these toilets. ■TIP➡ **Toilet paper is a rarity, so carry tissues with you.** Antibacterial hand wipes are also useful. Guatemalan plumbing generally can't handle toilet paper; throw it in the basket by the toilet instead.

▌SAFETY

Guatemala has a bad reputation for safety, and it's true that pickpocketings, muggings, and thefts from cars are common. However, most Central Americans are extremely honest and trustworthy. It's not uncommon for a vendor to chase you down if you accidentally leave without your change. Taking a few simple precautions when traveling in Guatemala is usually enough to avoid being a target.

Attitude is essential: strive to look aware and purposeful at all times. Look at maps before you go outside, not on a street corner. Hire taxis only from official stands at the airport, and ask hotels or restaurants to order you a cab. If you do hail

one on the street, do so only at major intersections.

Don't wear anything that looks—or is—valuable. Even small items attract attention (your wedding ring, for example), and are best left behind. Limit your accessories to cheap beads and the like. Whipping out a flashy camera on a busy city street isn't a good idea either. Keep a very firm hold of handbags when out and about, and keep them on your lap in restaurants, not dangling off your chair.

Take special care when driving. If you can avoid it, don't drive after sunset. A common ploy used by highway robbers is to construct a roadblock, such as logs strewn

WORST-CASE SCENARIO

All your money and credit cards have just been stolen. In these days of real-time transactions, this isn't a predicament that should destroy your vacation. First, report the theft of the credit cards. Then get any traveler's checks you were carrying replaced. This can usually be done almost immediately, provided that you kept a record of the serial numbers separate from the checks themselves. If you bank at a large international bank like Citibank or HSBC, go to the closest branch; if you know your account number, chances are you can get a new ATM card and withdraw money right away. **Western Union** (☎800/325–6000 ⊕www.westernunion.com) sends money almost anywhere. Have someone back home order a transfer online, over the phone, or at one of the company's offices, which is the cheapest option. The U.S. State Department's **Overseas Citizens Services** (⊕www.travel.state.gov/travel ☎202/501–4444) can wire money to any U.S. consulate or embassy abroad for a fee of $30. Just have someone back home wire money or send a money order or cashier's check to the state department, which will then disburse the funds as soon as the next working day after it receives them.

across the road, and then hide nearby. When unsuspecting motorists get out of their cars to remove the obstruction, they are waylaid. If you come upon a deserted roadblock, don't stop; turn around. In cities, always park in car parks, never on the street; and remove the front of the stereo, if possible.

Many popular destinations have a special tourist police service, known as the *Policía Turística* or just "Politur." Aimed at reducing crimes against tourists, they're more like a private security service than a police force. As well as keeping a lookout at street corners, they'll accompany you on hikes and walks in places where safety is an issue.

The lonely slopes of some of the volcanoes near Antigua and Lago Atitlán have been frequented by muggers, so go with a group of people, a reputable guide, or a member of the Tourist Police, and carry only minimal valuables.

The increase in adoption of Guatemalan children has provoked the fear by many here, particularly rural villagers, that children will be abducted by foreigners. Limit your interaction with children you do not know, and never take photos of children without asking permission of their parents first.

Guatemalans don't have much faith in their regular police force: many officers are involved in highway robbery and protection rackets. At best the police are well-meaning but under-equipped, so don't count on them to come to your rescue in a difficult situation.

The most important advice we can give you is that, in the unlikely event of being mugged or robbed, do not put up a struggle. Nearly all physical attacks on tourists are the direct result of them resisting would-be pickpockets or muggers. Comply with demands, hand over your stuff, and try to get the situation over with as quickly as possible—then let your travel insurance take care of it.

> ## WORD OF MOUTH
>
> "I was nervous. We were going to be riding on a lot of roads between Atitlàn, Antigua, and Tikal, but there were no problems at all. Now that the civil war is over the country is working to make things better for tourists. In many of the larger cities there are tourist police that you can ask to go hiking with you if you are nervous. There are still advisories about some areas, but we never ever felt threatened at all."
>
> —Suzie2

PICKPOCKETS

Pickpockets are the most common threat in Guatemala. They typically work in pairs or in threes: one will distract you while another slips a hand into your pocket or backpack during the commotion. Distractions could include someone bumping into you, spilling something on you, or asking you for the time. Crowded markets or street corners are hot spots for this, especially if your hands are full with your luggage or purchases. Remember that children and old women are just as likely to be pickpockets as men; many are so skillful you won't realize you've been robbed until later.

Keep your money in a pocket rather than a wallet, which is easier to steal. If you carry a purse, choose one with a zipper and a thick strap that you can drape across your body; adjust the length so that the purse sits in front of you at or above hip level. On buses and in crowded areas, hold purses or handbags close to your body; thieves use knives to slice the bottom of a bag and catch the contents as they fall out.

Try to keep your cash and credit cards in different places, so that if one gets stolen you can fall back on the other. Avoid carrying large sums of money around, but always keep enough to have something to hand over if you do get mugged. Another good idea is to keep a dummy wallet (an old one containing an expired credit card and a small amount of cash) in your pocket, with your real cash in an inside or vest pocket: if your "wallet" gets stolen you have little to lose.

WOMEN

Traveling alone as a woman in Guatemala can be tiring. Catcalling single females, especially foreign ones, is practically routine. The best reaction is to make like local girls and ignore it. Going to a bar alone will be seen as an open invitation for attention.

Unfortunately, Guatemala has also been the site of some disturbing assaults on women. These have occurred on buses, usually late at night in remote areas, so avoid traveling alone at night. There's very little crime outside the major cities, but it does happen. Hiring a guide through the local tourist office or through a respectable tour agency can help to avoid such situations.

▌TAXES

Guatemala has an international departure tax of $30—check your air ticket carefully as it's sometimes included in the price—and a domestic departure tax of Q5. You also have to pay a Q20 airport security fee.

Most Guatemalan hotels and some tourist restaurants charge an additional 10% tourist tax. There is a 10% V.A.T. on most consumer products but it is already included in the display price. There is no tax refund scheme for visitors.

▌TIME

Guatemala is six hours behind G.M.T., the same as U.S. central standard time. Daylight saving time is not observed.

▌TIPPING

In Guatemala, tipping is a question of rewarding good service rather than an obligation. Restaurant bills don't include gratuities; adding 10% is customary. Bellhops and maids expect tips only in the most expensive hotels, where a tip in dollars is appreciated. You should also give a small tip to tour guides, or to guards who show you around ruins. Rounding up taxi fares is a way of showing your appreciation to the driver, but it's not expected.

Rice, beans, and tortillas are the heart of Guatemala's *comida típica* (typical food). It's possible to order everything from sushi to crepes in Guatemala City and Antigua, but most Guatemalans have a simple diet built around rice, beans, and the myriad fruits and vegetables that flourish here. Guatemalan food isn't spicy, certainly not like that of neighboring Mexico, but the Highlands' ubiquitous *pepián* can pack a kick. But many dishes are seasoned with the same five ingredients—onion, salt, garlic, cilantro, and red bell pepper.

SPANISH	ENGLISH
GENERAL DINING	
Almuerzo	Lunch
Bocas	Appetizers or snacks (literally "mouth-fuls") served with drinks in the tradition of Spanish tapas.
Cena	Dinner
Comedor	An inexpensive café; a plato de día is always found at a comedor
Desayuno	Breakfast
Plato del día	Heaping plate of rice, beans, fried plantains, cabbage salad, tomatoes, *macarrones* (noodles), and fish, chicken, or meat—or any variation thereof
ESPECIALIDADES (SPECIALTIES)	
Arroz con frijoles	Rice sautéed with black beans
Arroz con mariscos	Fried rice with fish, shrimp, octopus, and clams, or whatever's fresh that day
Arroz con pollo	Chicken with rice
Caldo de chunto	Turkey stew
Caldo de mariscos	Seafood stew
Camarones	Shrimp
Ceviche	Chilled, raw seafood marinated in lime juice, served with chopped onion and garlic
Chicharrones	Fried pork rinds
Chilaquiles	Meat-stuffed tortillas
Chile relleno	Stuffed bell pepper

Chorreados	Corn pancakes, served with *natilla* (sour cream)
Corvina	Sea bass
Empanadas	Savory or sweet pastry turnover filled with fruit or meat and vegetables
Empanaditas	Small empanadas
Escabeche	Pickled relish, usually served with fish
Fiambre	Salad with cold cuts and vegetables, frequently served on All Saints' Day
Kaq'ik	Turkey stew, interchangeable with caldo de chunto
Langosta	Lobster
Langostino	Prawns
Palmitos	Hearts of palm, served in salads or as a side dish
Pepián	Chicken fricassee in pumpkin and sesame sauce
Pescado ahumado	Smoked marlin
Picadillo	Chayote squash, potatoes, carrots, or other vegetables chopped into small cubes and combined with onions, garlic, and ground beef
Pozol	Corn soup
Rice and beans	A Caribbean dish cooked in coconut milk, not to be confused with arroz con frijoles
Salsa caribeño	A combination of tomatoes, onions, and spices that accompanies most fish dishes on the Caribbean coast
Sere	Fish stew cooked in coconut milk

POSTRES (DESSERTS) & DULCES (SWEETS)

Cajeta de coco	Fudge made with coconut and orange peel
Cajeta	Molasses-flavored fudge
Dulce de leche	Thick syrup of boiled milk and sugar
Flan	Caramel-topped egg custard
Mazamorra	Cornstarch pudding

Pan de maiz	Sweet corn bread
Torta chilena	Flaky, multilayered cake with dulce de leche filling
Tres leches cake	"Three milks" cake, made with condensed and evaporated milk and cream

FRUTAS (FRUITS)

Aguacate	Avocado
Anón	Sugar apple; sweet white flesh; resembles an artichoke with a thick rind
Banano	Banana
Bilimbi	Looks like a miniature cucumber crossed with a star fruit; ground into a savory relish
Carambola	Star fruit
Cas	A smaller guava
Coco	Coconut
Fresa	Strawberry
Granadilla	Passion fruit
Guanábana	Soursop; large, spiky yellow fruit with white flesh and a musky taste
Guayaba	Guava
Mango	Many varieties, from sour green to succulently sweet Oro (golden); March is the height of mango season
Manzana de agua	Water apple, shaped like a pear; juicy but not very sweet
Marañon	Cashew fruit; used in juices
Melocotón	Peach
Melón	Cantaloupe
Mora	Raspberry
Naranja	Orange
Palmito	Heart of palm
Papaya	One of the most popular and ubiquitous fruits
Pera	Pear
Piña	Pineapple

Plátano	Plaintain
Sandía	Watermelon

BEBIDAS (BEVERAGES)

Agua pura	Purified water
Café con leche	Coffee with hot milk
Café negro	Black coffee
Cerveza	Beer
Fresco natural	Fresh-squeezed juice
Horchata	Cinnamon-flavored rice drink
Leche de coco	Coconut milk
Licuado	Fruit shake made with milk (con leche) or water (con agua)
Refrescos	Tropical fruit smoothie with ice and sugar
Ron	Rum

VOCABULARY

	English	Spanish	Pronunciation
Basics			
	Yes/no	Sí/no	see/no
	OK	De acuerdo	de a-**kwer**-doe
	Please	Por favor	pore fah-**vore**
	May I?	¿Me permite?	may pair-**mee**-tay
	Thank you (very much)	(Muchas) gracias	(**moo**-chas) **grah**-see-as
	You're welcome	De nada	day **nah**-da
	Excuse me	Con permiso	con pair-**mee**-so
	Pardon me	¿Perdón?	pair-**dohn**
	Could you tell me?	¿Podría decirme?	po-dree-ah deh-**seer**-meh
	I'm sorry	Disculpe	Dee-**skool**-peh
	Good morning!	¡Buenos días!	**bway**-nohs **dee**-ahs
	Good afternoon!	¡Buenas tardes!	**bway**-nahs **tar**-dess
	Good evening!	¡Buenas noches!	**bway**-nahs **no**-chess
	Goodbye!	¡Adiós!/¡Hasta luego!	ah-dee-**ohss**/**ah**-stah-**lwe**-go
	Mr./Mrs.	Señor/Señora	sen-**yor**/sen-**yohr**-ah
	Miss	Señorita	sen-yo-**ree**-tah
	Pleased to meet you	Mucho gusto	**moo**-cho **goose**-toe
	How are you?	¿Cómo está usted?	**ko**-mo es-**tah** oo-**sted**
	Very well, thank you.	Muy bien, gracias.	**moo**-ee bee-**en**, **grah**-see-as
	And you?	¿Y usted?	ee oos-**ted**
Days of the Week			
	Sunday	domingo	doe-**meen**-goh
	Monday	lunes	**loo**-ness
	Tuesday	martes	**mahr**-tess
	Wednesday	miércoles	me-**air**-koh-less
	Thursday	jueves	hoo-**ev**-ess
	Friday	viernes	vee-**air**-ness
	Saturday	sábado	**sah**-bah-doh

Months

January	enero	eh-**neh**-roh
February	febrero	feh-**breh**-roh
March	marzo	**mahr**-soh
April	abril	ah-**breel**
May	mayo	**my**-oh
June	junio	**hoo**-nee-oh
July	julio	**hoo**-lee-yoh
August	agosto	ah-**ghost**-toh
September	septiembre	sep-tee-**em**-breh
October	octubre	oak-**too**-breh
November	noviembre	no-vee-**em**-breh
December	diciembre	dee-see-**em**-breh

Useful Phrases

Do you speak English?	¿Habla usted inglés?	**ah**-blah oos-**ted** in-**glehs**
I don't speak Spanish	No hablo español	no **ah**-bloh es-pahn-**yol**
I don't understand (you)	No entiendo	no en-tee-**en**-doh
I understand (you)	Entiendo	en-tee-**en**-doh
I don't know	No sé	no seh
I am American/British	Soy americano (americana)/ inglés(a)	soy ah-meh-ree-**kah**-no (ah-meh-ree-**kah**-nah)/ in-**glehs (ah)**
What's your name?	¿Cómo se llama usted?	koh-mo seh **yah**-mah oos-**ted**
My name is . . .	Me llamo . . .	may **yah**-moh
What time is it?	¿Qué hora es?	keh **o**-rah es
It is one, two, three . . . o'clock.	Es la una. . . . Son las dos, tres	es la **oo**-nah/sohn lahs dohs, tress
How?	¿Cómo?	**koh**-mo
When?	¿Cuándo?	**kwahn**-doh
This/Next week	Esta semana/ la semana que entra	**es**-teh seh-**mah**-nah/lah seh-**mah**-nah keh **en**-trah
This/Next month	Este mes/el próximo mes	**es**-teh mehs/el **proke**-see-mo mehs
This/Next year	Este año/el año que viene	**es**-teh **ahn**-yo/el **ahn**-yo keh vee-**yen**-ay

Yesterday/today/ tomorrow	Ayer/hoy/mañana	ah-**yehr**/oy/mahn-**yah**-nah
This morning/ afternoon	Esta mañana/ tarde	es-tah mahn-**yah**-nah/**tar**-deh
Tonight	Esta noche	es-tah **no**-cheh
What?	¿Qué?	keh
What is it?	¿Qué es esto?	keh es **es**-toh
Why?	¿Por qué?	pore **keh**
Who?	¿Quién?	kee-**yen**
Where is . . . ?	¿Dónde está . . . ?	**dohn**-deh es-**tah**
the bus stop?	la parada del autobus?	la pah-**rah**-dah del oh-toh-**boos**
the post office?	la oficina de correos?	la oh-fee-**see**-nah deh koh-**reh**-os
the museum?	el museo?	el moo-**seh**-oh
the hospital?	el hospital?	el ohss-pee-**tal**
the bathroom?	el baño?	el **bahn**-yoh
Here/there	Aquí/allá	ah-**key**/ah-**yah**
Open/closed	Abierto/cerrado	ah-bee-**er**-toh/ ser-**ah**-doh
Left/right	Izquierda/derecha	iss-key-**er**-dah/ dare-**eh**-chah
Straight ahead	Derecho	dare-**eh**-choh
Is it near/far?	¿Está cerca/lejos?	es-**tah sehr**-kah/ **leh**-hoss
I'd like . . . a room	Quisiera . . . un cuarto/una habitación	kee-see-ehr-ah oon **kwahr**-toh/ **oo**-nah ah-bee-tah-see-**on**
the key	la llave	lah **yah**-veh
a newspaper	un periódico	oon pehr-ee-**oh**-dee-koh
a stamp	la estampilla	lah es-stahm-**pee**-yah
I'd like to buy . . .	Quisiera comprar . . .	kee-see-**ehr**-ah kohm-**prahr**
a dictionary	un diccionario	oon deek-see-oh-**nah**-ree-oh
soap	jabón	hah-**bohn**
suntan lotion	loción bronceadora	loh-see-**ohn** brohn-seh-ah-**do**-rah
a map	un mapa	oon **mah**-pah
a magazine	una revista	**oon**-ah reh-**veess**-tah
a postcard	una tarjeta postal	**oon**-ah tar-**het**-ah post-**ahl**

How much is it?	¿Cuánto cuesta?	**kwahn**-toh **kwes**-tah
Telephone	Teléfono	tel-**ef**-oh-no
Help!	¡Auxilio! ¡Ayuda! ¡Socorro!	owk-**see**-lee-oh/ ah-**yoo**-dah/ soh-**kohr**-roh
Fire!	¡Incendio!	en-**sen**-dee-oo
Caution!/Look out!	¡Cuidado!	kwee-**dah**-doh

Salud (Health)

I am ill	Estoy enfermo(a)	es-**toy** en-**fehr**-moh(mah)
Please call a doctor	Por favor llame a un médico	pohr fah-**vor ya**-meh ah oon **med**-ee-koh
acetaminophen	acetaminofen	a-say-ta-**mee**-no-fen
ambulance	ambulancia	ahm-boo-**lahn**-see-a
antibiotic	antibiótico	ahn-tee-bee-**oh**-tee-co
aspirin	aspirina	ah-spi-**ree**-na
capsule	cápsula	**cahp**-soo-la
clinic	clínica	**clee**-nee-ca
cold	resfriado	rays-free-**ah**-do
cough	tos	toess
diarrhea	diarrea	dee-ah-**ray**-a
fever	fiebre	fee-**ay**-bray
flu	Gripe	**gree**-pay
headache	dolor de cabeza	doh-**lor** day cah-**bay**-sa
hospital	hospital	oh-spee-**tahl**
medication	medicamento	meh-dee-cah-**men**-to
pain	dolor	doh-**lor**
pharmacy	farmacia	fahr-**mah**-see-a
physician	médico	**meh**-dee-co
prescription	receta	ray-**say**-ta
stomach ache	dolor de estómago	doh-**lor** day eh-**sto**-mah-go

INDEX

NOTES

NOTES

NOTES

NOTES

NOTES

NOTES

ABOUT OUR WRITER

Central America–based freelance writer and pharmacist Jeffrey Van Fleet has spent the last 15 years enjoying the isthmus' long rainy seasons and Wisconsin's cold winters. (Most people would try to do it the other way around.) No matter what the time of year, he never passes up any chance to partake of the incredible variety that is Guatemala. Jeff is a regular contributor to Costa Rica's English-language newspaper *the Tico Times* and has written about Central America for United Airlines' inflight magazine *Hemispheres*. He has contributed to Fodor's guides to Costa Rica, Peru, Chile, Argentina, and Central and South America.